A KID
TO THE CORPS

A MIDWESTERN BOY'S LIFE
WITH
MOVIES AND THE MARINES.

BY WILLIAM J. K. BEAUDOT

© 2015

II GEMINI RISING

A kid to the Corps: A Midwestern boy's life with movies and the Marines/ William J. K. Beaudot

Published 2015 by Gemini Rising

Milwaukee (Wis.) — 20th Century – History — Fiction

Wisconsin – History – 20th Century – Fiction

Marines — United States — Fiction

United States Marine Corps – Fiction

Marine Corps Recruit Depot (Calif.) – Fiction

Boys – Wisconsin – Milwaukee — Fiction

City and Town Life – Wisconsin – Milwaukee – Fiction

Bildungsromans

ISBN 978-0-9844290-9-7

813.54

Also by William J. K. Beaudot

The 24th Wisconsin Infantry in the Civil War (Stackpole Books, 2003)

In the Bloody Railroad Cut at Gettysburg (Savas Beatie, 2015)

An Irishman in the Iron Brigade, co-author (Fordham University Press, 1993)

Four for the Corps: The Education of a Peace Time Marine (in progress)

Dedication

To the next generation:

Mary and Kayla Schroeder

Collin, Jarett and Camden Krause

Lauren and Katherine Beaudot

Fonsi and Xavi Crespo-Beaudot

Acknowledgement

Without Rod Holloway, the incomparable camera artist, this manuscript would never have been transformed from mere typewritten pages to book.

My bosom pard and former Marine, Ron Schiessl, waded through the reams of copy, and provided invaluable counsel.

The manuscript would not have gone anywhere without the good offices of Renee Crespo-Beaudot, my youngest daughter and "in-house editor."

I thank my other children – Chellie, Corinne and Andre – who read all or parts of the manuscript, as well as Dina Merz, Kathy Bergeron, Dean Sarnowski for their contributions.

There were many, old friends from days of yore, whose stories are incorporated in this fictional memory. The old Marines Ron Blackburn and Rich Prossen; and Chuck Smallish, the tireless spinner of stories; Art Tyszka, my old muzzle-loading bunkie now on heaven's firing line, and many more who contributed recollections willingly and unknowingly, and provided guidance and encouragement. I name Gerald Duane Coleman among them.

To others I have inadvertently failed to mention, thank you, too.

While she did not live in that time or place, my wife, Bev, contributed several of her family tales that were transmuted from her life into this narrative. She's a captivating story teller in her own right. I am grateful for her patience when I spent too many hours on the keyboard.

Table of Contents

Also by William J. K. Beaudot .... *iii*
Dedication .... *iv*
Acknowledgement .... *v*

PREPARATORY COMMAND .... *viii*

CHAPTER 1 1
    GUNG HO!

CHAPTER 2 47
    GUTTIG

CHAPTER 3 83
    LOCK AND LOAD

CHAPTER 4 125
    CLÉMENCE

CHAPTER 5 176
    JARHEADS

CHAPTER 6 227
    RELATIVES AND KIN

CHAPTER 7 301
    SEMPER FI

CHAPTER 8 342
    VILLARD AVENUE GANG

COMMAND OF EXECUTION 407

In Marine Corps parlance, a Preparatory Command is the preliminary order for an imminent movement or maneuver e.g. "Forward" or "Right."

The Command of Execution is the order to execute the Preparatory Command viz. "March!" or "Face!"

Preparatory Command

G arson just knew he was going to die.

"A month past my seventeenth birthday, I feared I'd never see Ma again," he remembered.

Those lines were prelude to a story Garson reiterated to family, friends, acquaintances or anyone who cared to listen; he embellished and embroidered it, and finally set it down on paper as part of a memoir of his early life. This is how he fashioned it:

Some 70 young men, teenagers mostly, were wedged into a quonset hut at MCRD, the Marine Corps Recruit Depot in San Diego. It was late October, almost a year after Dwight D. Eisenhower had been elected, the first Republican president in a generation. The U. S. Supreme Court was considering a case brought by Oliver Brown against the Topeka, Kansas Board of Education. The Korean War truce had been in effect since July of that year, 1953, the same month that a scruffy 26-year-old revolutionary named Castro attacked the Moncada Barracks in Santiago de Cuba. Joe McCarthy, Wisconsin's scowling and sweaty United States senator, was hunting supposed Communists in the army. Marlon Brando portrayed Marc Antony in the movie "Julius Caesar," and Garson fell in love with Audrey Hepburn, Princess Anne who called herself "Smitty" in "Roman Holiday."

A true Marine stood in the midst of these teenagers lately arrived from Milwaukee, Detroit and a few other locales. Heads shorn to the skin, they wore rumpled gray sweatshirts over civilian trousers and shoes. The staff sergeant contrasted sharply with their disheveled appearance: Standing more than six-feet tall and weighing a compact 180 pounds, he wore his uniform with absolute authority – razor-creased dark-green wool trousers cinched by a canvas webbed belt and gleaming brass buckle; the starched khaki shirt tailored like a glove to his torso was set off on each sleeve with four green chevrons edged in red on each sleeve, and a matching tie held in place by a polished bar.

A tan campaign hat perched on his head, its brim spare inches above his straight nose; brown hair was cropped at the sides nearly to his skull in what recruits came to know as "white side walls." A dark eagle, globe and anchor emblem the size of a half dollar seemed to glare menacingly at the timorous assembly. His head had the roundness of a pumpkin, his face burnished by the California sun. Garson studied details of the Marine's appearance and other aspects in due course over the coming months — blue eyes, wide mouth with a thin upper and full lower lip as well as a smile never more than tentative, and a ramrod demeanor that personified the Corps.

"My name's Staff Sergeant Maddox," he began, "I'm your senior drill instructor." Garson expected a basso profundo delivery, even orotund. But the sergeant's words were measured and nicely modulated. "To you maggots, I will be addressed only as 'sir.'" There was emphasis on the final word. Here was a real Sergeant Stryker, the John Wayne character from the movie "The Sands of Iwo Jima" who had been influential in Garson's presence here.

Maddox was perhaps ten years older than Garson. By the campaign ribbons above his shirt pocket, he had likely seen combat in Korea and service in Japan. Maddox slowly swung his head, eyes shadowed by the hat brim. As Garson recalled those moments, he and his fellow recruits nearly cowered as they listened to the sergeant's introduction.

"You are Platoon 023. You are the lowest form of existence on earth right now, so low a snake can crawl over you. We will be together for the next three months, and during that time I will begin the very long process of transforming you from amorphous civilian crap into proud defenders of our nation. I can see already that many, no, most of you, won't make it through this training. Only the best will survive to become members of the finest fighting force on the face of the planet – the United States Marines." He again surveyed the young men before him, almost sucking oxygen from the atmosphere as he gathered his final words.

"So from now on, I will be your mother and your father, your sister and your brother, your uncle and your aunt. I'll even be your sweetheart." Tendons twitched at the hinge of his jaw, and his light eyes bored directly and particularly into Garson.

"And I'll be your *JESUS...CHRIST!*"

Those last words hung there, palpable, nearly visible. Breath caught in Garson's throat; he had difficulty exhaling. He wanted to glance at his teenage pals, Preston and Rusty, but feared removing his gaze from the drill instructor.

Was this possible – such utter blasphemy? Garson wondered. Despite the fact that his connection to life-long Catholicism had frayed in recent years, he had never heard the name of the Redeemer used in that manner. He had never suspected it could be. Was this Marine, a man after all, who controlled his existence so all powerful that he could aver such a thing calmly, dispassionately and with impunity? Might he be struck down from the heavens at this moment?

In that instant Garson concluded queasily that he would not long survive in Boot Camp. He would surely be dead in a week, his body stuffed into a bag and found in a dumpster, later to be shipped home to his grieving mother. Ma, for he called her that, had been right: He had made a bad decision.

Regardless of Garson's fate, Staff Sergeant Maddox would become one of the most influential men in his life.

That vignette was well known to my older sisters and me. We heard it in one version or another that we could recite some of the details. It was part of a substantial manuscript several inches thick that my Pop, the protagonist called Garson, had created — a memoir of his early life in Milwaukee at mid-Twentieth Century that led up to his enlistment in the Marines. He tinkered with the narrative between the publication of three minor books of Civil War history, and for years after – something like the great gray poet, Walt Whitman who the Jesuits told us worked and reworked *Leaves of Grass* for almost a lifetime.

As an aside, let me say here that he hated to be called Pop, just as his mother, my grandmother, hated to be called Ma. "Makes me sound old," she reputedly told him; "I like mom or mother." Maybe, he felt that Pop was too flippant; he preferred dad. Still, since it's given to me to cap his narrative, I'll use Pop.

In addition to the typescript, my Pop had a myriad snippets from legitimate historical sources, newspapers and magazine clips, additional drafted scenes and scenarios, character sketches, impressions and observations, some jottings made in the dead of night from fragments of dreams; nearly all were hand-written on five-by-seven inch lined, yellow sheets. That habit of note-taking, he said, started while he studied under an old Marquette University history professor who required such research notes instead of traditional file cards. If all of these oddments were added, the manuscript would double in size at least.

He worked fitfully on the opus for years. Memories tumbled from him so steadily that an old pal asked if he'd maintained a journal of those times. He hadn't.

"There're just too many good books to read and re-read, too many good movies, drama and ballet to see, children, grandkids, friends and other life matters that are more important," he answered when friends prodded him to complete the memoir. "Just so I get it done in life's good time."

In all of this, I was reminded of an article published after the death of Ralph Ellison in 1994 that described hundreds of files – episodes, drafts and other details, more than 2000 pages of a novel the author never completed.

My Pop's effort ran the gamut from memoir to history to genealogy, at times slipping into confession and nostalgia. Then there was the film "Starting Out in the Evening" that he insisted I see, about the writer Leonard Schiller, who worked on completing his latest book for nearly a decade. Thing of it is, I often called my Pop's narrative the book that'd never be finished.

So, you might quip of my Pop's creation, that "some assembly was required." It was left to me to add some scenes and episodes he'd not yet incorporated into the manuscript, to clarify several points and downright challenge things that I knew or suspected to be untrue.

This recollection bears kinship to critic Richard Schickel's 2003 memoir *Good Morning, Mr. Zip, Zip, Zip.* He was fitfully crafting his memoir about the same time as the newspaper critic. I read parts of *Good Morning,* and I doubt my Pop intended to duplicate Schickel's book. But both authors grew up only a few miles apart in Milwaukee and about the same time. A few years older than my Pop, Schickel's circumstances were affluent and professional.

Both men, of course, were of a movie-centric generation, deriving much of their outlooks, values and more from the filmic frame of reference. But Schickel brought to bear decades as a professional cineaste in his memoir, producing more cogent analysis. Pop's views sprung mostly from the simple fact of seeing thousands of movies by the time he was a teenager – not in screening rooms or on television, but in actual theaters, sometimes as many as six in a week; virtually every showing was a double feature, after all. My Pop calculated he'd seen about 3000 movies before enlisting.

It had all began when he accompanied his mother to the neighborhood movie theater on Milwaukee's north side to screenings for predominantly female audiences. Pop nodded through tear jerkers and melodramas, but was captivated by classic show biz musicals.

"Reason I wanted to be a writer," he told us, "was because of movies I saw as a kid — movies about the world of newspapers and reporters — fast-talking, cracker-jack news guys with press cards stuck in their fedoras clacking away on city room typewriters, shouts of 'Copy boy!' and 'Stop the presses!' Of giant webs of news print rolling off presses, street corner newsies barking 'Read all about it!' There were many such films like that when I was a kid, when newspapers and journalism meant something important and vital."

As an only child, he was introspective, left largely, as he was, to his own devices by two working parents during the late Depression and war years. He exhibited better skills as a questioner and listener than a talker, complaining frequently that a proper riposte always popped into his brain after it was needed. Perhaps that's why he wanted to be a writer. There was also this:

"Since my days in the reporting lab at Marquette's journalism school," he said, "thoughts and arguments flowed better through a keyboard."

My Pop and I often disagreed politically. He subscribed to the observation of political satirist Stephen Colbert that "reality has a liberal bias." I don't. He also railed against self-centered Cry Baby Boomers, as he called them, a generation that turned its back on the great social promise of the Sixties to become Randian reactionaries 30 years later, building sterile suburbs and malling green spaces, reducing everything, even life itself, to the cash nexus. He concurred with D. H. Lawrence's condemnation: "I hate the impudence of money, and I hate the impudence of class."

While I'm not the voracious reader that he is, I judge my Pop's writing as competent. I confess to never reading his Civil War books, but I found his memoir interesting for the most part. While writing in a formal style and eschewing contractions, he disdained lean prose, as the reader will see. Put it this way: He found it difficult to set down a naked, unmodified noun or verb, and worked to decorate his memoir with literary frills and flourishes. His penchant for alliteration was occasionally overdone.

"The great coming-of-age novel of mid-America at mid-century, the Twentieth, hasn't yet been written," he proposed. "It's clear that the artsy West Coasters and effete East Coasters don't understand the great center of the country." As witness, he recalled the gushing critical sentiment over the wedding scenes in "The Deer Hunter," saying he found nothing unique about them.

"We went to weddings like that several times a year."

His generation, wedged between the Greatest Generation, tested in cataclysm, and the soft and spoiled Boomers was called the Fortunate Few because many Depression parents deferred or curtailed child-bearing, creating more educational and employment opportunities decades later.

As a memoirist, my Pop wrote to understand himself and his time, I presume, to discover what shaped him, at least during his early years, particularly how movies, that grand formative influence, had stamped and shaped him.

It was British novelist John Fowles who wrote: "You do not think your own past as quite real; you dress it up, you gild it or blacken it, censor it, tinker with it, fictionalize it, in a word, and put it away on the shelf – your book, your romanced autobiography." My Pop, I think, wanted more than to just put his recollections on a shelf; he hoped for a work of some significance not merely a bagatelle or farrago. But, I really don't know how many outside of our family could be interested. Perhaps my older sisters might find amusement in its pages, but I can tell you that my youngest sibling will make the "Time Out" gesture with her hands when she encounters some of the seamier scenes, declaring that's too much information. She never knew my Pop as a fulltime father, after all, and likely never spotted his feet of clay.

Although each of us knew my Pop differently, my sisters and I agreed he was a man of routine, of regular habits and organization;

thus, it may be understandable why he was attracted to the Marines at so early an age. More comfortable with predictability than serendipity, he abhorred inefficiency and ineptitude. Patience was not a virtue he had in abundance; sadly, all of us share that trait. Thing of it is, he wore his status as a high school dropout like a badge of distinction, and regularly proclaimed himself common and without connections.

Of modest stature, my Pop was fairly well maintained for his age. While he appeared younger than his years, he was fond of paraphrasing Henry Fonda's character in "On Golden Pond" who proclaimed: I'm almost 80 years old, and I don't know how I got here so fast. In a few recent photos, you notice weary depth about the eyes, a bit of geezerliness, if you like. He drew his looks equally from my grandparents – slightly olive skin that tanned readily, oval face, mid-brown hair and eyes, and a nose that seemed more prominent as he aged. His voice was undistinguished, and in all but a few times, he held his temper in check. My Pop exhibited a confident martial stride: Head up, eyes front, shoulders back and chest out. Some said they knew him from a distance by his walk. He thanked the Corps for that posture and gait.

He had no affinity for mechanisms and only warily embraced binary technology. He possessed an almost unerring inner clock, and once boasted a similarly unerring memory. He hid insecurities well save for certain circumstances when his educated veneer might be chipped.

As readers will see, my Pop's life didn't have the stuff of Dumas or Melville, but it has small doses of Dickens and Eliot. His experiences were common and prosaic. There was no overarching tragedy, great awakening or catharsis; no tales of sin and redemption, revenge or retribution. There were no stories of addiction or abuse, deprivation, murder or mayhem, long lost siblings or warm-hearted prostitutes who taught him passion.

He didn't, nor do I, claim his youthful world was better than today. But it was decidedly different. For one thing, black shirts, white ties and five o'clock shadows meant villains; for another, only Marines, sailors and the fat lady in a freak show flourished tattoos.

The age was more innocent, less cynical and concussive, when humor didn't devolve into ridicule; when there was an abundance of wonder and awe; when the deluge of distraction and diversion didn't drown out contemplation and meditation, and when sociability was as valuable as singularity. It irritated me when he said that the popular music of his youth was more than the ephemeral noise that it is today – a cacophony that, he sneered, has overwhelmed more substantial forms — classical and jazz and the Great American Songbook.

As I warned before, he took literary license in an effort to flesh out his recollections, and I'm sure, pulled factual punches, changing chronologies, introducing people he knew from later times, and merging several personalities into one character. He was occasionally redundant. I'll do my best to smooth some of the edges and narrative stumbles, to clarify what he might have wanted to say. I'll try to keep these intrusions to a minimum; they'll be set off in italics. Call me, if you will, something like a movie voice-over.

You know what they say in the movies: "Based upon a true story." Or: "Inspired by real events." Better (from a more recent movie): "Some of these things actually happened." Too, my Pop insisted upon citing Dickens's caveat from *Bleak House*: "[Everything set forth in these pages is substantially true, [or] within the truth."

One final note: My Pop thought long about the name he'd use in this narrative; like Dickens he toyed with it the same way he did with other character names. He finally selected Garson as his *nom du jeune*. Many who read what follows will, like me, suspect that the name is a turn on the French *garçon*, a boy, a kid. They might be correct.

So here's my Pop's story – set down over six decades after the events occurred.

***

Chapter 1

GUNG HO!

"Las Vegas! Next stop Las Vegas!" announced the conductor. Garson's head jerked up from his chest, roused from light slumber opposite his two pals. The black-suited conductor gripped each seat back to steady his progress along the swaying railcar.

"City of lost wages!" the conductor shouted as he slid the end doorway aside to repeat his announcement for the next car.

Garson, along with two dozen or more from the Milwaukee recruiting office had been traveling for two days and a night – 2000 miles — since departing on that uncommonly hot October afternoon en route to the Marine Corps Recruit Depot in San Diego. In retrospect, the past several weeks, indeed almost the entire summer, had passed in the proverbial blur since Garson dropped out of summer school and convinced his parents that enlisting in the Marines was a proper prelude to his future.

Facing him on the adjoining seat were his pals, Preston and Rusty. Back home, they were called the three musketeers of Villard Avenue because they had associated for much of their youth. Lackluster students all, the trio had forgone their final year in high school to enlist, but still appeared as little more than unripe boys.

Garson remembered Preston from second grade as the kid whose laced, high-top boots he envied. They had become reacquainted a few years back. He was tall and angular with an underdeveloped chest and shoulders which the Corps would square up manfully. His voice bore a nasal character. Many found his regular features, dark eyes and impeccable pompadour handsome, despite an occasional haughty manner.

Rusty, whose name was apt, was the other pal who threw in his lot with Garson and Preston that summer, turning his back on high school and taking the oath to defend the Constitution. Standing just at the minimum height for enlistment, he was shorter than Garson. A parchment complexion was sprinkled with freckles, and his ears flared wider than most. Garson long thought his pal's ferret face and sharp nose denoted a particularly prickly demeanor used to compensate for an underwhelming stature. Garson sometimes thought of Rusty as a sneering imp with a smart mouth and derisive laugh, but they got on well as part of the trio. The pals were perfect grist for the Marine Corps military mill.

Garson's life before this day lacked real drama or tumult. The death of his grandfather, Guttig, had been the only true tragedy he had experienced. Garson grew from common immigrant roots, sometimes proclaiming himself a "second generation D.P." – displaced person. He was the product of an upper Midwestern city of some remark, a gray and gritty industrial eminence on Lake Michigan leavened by a score of breweries and tanneries, all bearing German names. Milwaukee, of course, was overshadowed by Chicago 90 miles to the south.

More, Garson had lived nearly all of his years against the background of war – in newspapers, on radio, newsreels and movies. He was born during the war in Spain between Loyalists and Republicans; his recollection of the pall in his household when Japan bombed Pearl Harbor remained clear; he was in second grade when the Marines landed on Guadalcanal and in fourth when the Allies stormed Normandy beaches; he graduated from ninth grade when United States troops were sent to Korea, and had decided to drop out of high school to enlist even though that conflict seemed to lack the drama and heroism of the world war. Still, he was dispirited that a truce was signed in two months before his parents permitted him to enlist.

For youth of his generation, unlike the pampered Boomers who followed, the expected rite of passage to adulthood included three or more years of military service. Garson rationalized that he and his pals were merely embarking a year early. He supposed that inchoate patriotism and idealism may have played some part in joining the Marines at age 17, but the larger purpose was to leave the prosaic and mundane behind, to leave Milwaukee and find adventure – to see the mountains and the Pacific Coast.

Garson, in fact, had done so poorly in his junior year that he was forced to attend summer classes at the public high school. He bore up only a week, during which the city officially recorded some of the hottest days ever: Nearly 100-degree temperatures in late June created stifling classrooms, making it impossible for him to concentrate on boring geometry lessons.

"The Marines?" His mother's voice was filled with exasperation. For as long as he remembered, from boyhood on, she had preached the same message: Do well and finish school. Go to college.

"Your dad and I don't want you to work as hard like we did." Certainly, Garson found no future following his father's occupational footsteps, and had agreed that college was in his future. He had become interested in the newspaper business since he was a boy, sitting in the show house, the tiny Ritz Theater, with his mother, fascinated with quick witted and fast-talking screen reporters like Cary Grant and Rosalind Russell in "His Girl Friday," and Jimmy Stewart in "Call Northside 777." He had also developed an interest in creative writing, taught himself to type on a used portable his mother purchased, and attempted to create little fictions. He knew college was necessary to attain such goals. But that could wait.

"MA-aa," he mewled. It was a tone he, an only son, had perfected for years to break down his mother's resistance. She rebuked him yet another time for calling her "Ma," preferring Mom or Mother.

"I can get my GED in the Marines, get the G. I. Bill after, go to Marquette. Study journalism." The line was well rehearsed.

"Why not the Navy or Air Force?" she offered in compromise,

aware from recent history that the Marines were always ordered into the fiercest battles – the Pacific Islands and now Korea. They were strong, resolute – the first to fight, the first to die. The Corps claimed strong public support, and raised a clamor when President Truman threatened to merge it into the army? No, no other service would do for Garson.

Only a few years before, Garson sat through "The Sands of Iwo Jima" at least three times at the neighborhood theater, convinced by John Wayne's portrayal of Sergeant Stryker, the hard-bitten combat leader with a streak of empathy. Garson had also read a newspaper account of John Bradley, the Wisconsin Marine who helped raise the flag on Iwo's Mount Suribachi. He and two other flag raisers had stopped in Milwaukee to sell war bonds late in the war.

Then, there was Mellish, another of Garson's boyhood friends. A small scrape with the juvenile justice system had resulted in his enlistment before he finished high school. He had returned from Boot Camp at Lackland Air Force Base that summer and regaled Garson, Preston and Rusty with tales of military life. Certainly, Mellish was an evocative story teller — he always had been — adept at embellishing and dramatizing experiences to a fine, entertaining edge.

He told of early risings and physical exertions, of crisp uniforms, polished leather and brass, of the thrill of being part of a unit that marched with precision, of learning to shoot the famous M-1 Garand rifle, earning a medal and a stripe.

Finally, for Garson, enlistment meant seeing far more of America than he had heretofore. Like his parents, he had ventured no farther from Milwaukee than Green Bay and Chicago, had not, in fact, even ridden on a railroad train before, discounting the 90-minute trips to Chicago aboard the North Shore interurban line, the rocking, "Vomit Comet." He wanted to see the West, the grand vistas of Monument Valley used in John Ford pictures. Now, here he was, aboard the Atchison, Topeka & Santa Fe Railroad's El Capitan, almost like the movie, "The Harvey Girls."

Two of Garson's other youthful pals had made this very trek months before. Toby and Rowdy climbed into the resuscitated 1936

Buick Roadmaster and spent weeks driving to California and back, over the fabled Route 66. Their stories about the Pacific Ocean, Los Angeles, San Diego and Tijuana, Mexico sounded like finding the Seven Cities of Cibola, like Tyrone Power, Pedro De Vargas, and Cesar Romero, Hernando Cortez, conquering the Incas in "Captain from Castille," of Jean Peters, the beautiful Catana Perez, lover and wife of Pedro. Toby and Rowdy had brought back evidence of their adventures – a painting of a bullfight rendered on black velvet and Mexican cigarettes of acrid black tobacco.

There was another town that gripped Garson's fancy. Toby and Rowdy had regaled him and others about their time in the storied gambling mecca. The Santa Fe slowed to a halt.

"Las Vegas!" called the conductor as he opened the railcar door and dropped the steel step. "Fifteen minutes for Las Vegas!"

The two dozen enlistees aboard elbowed from the railcar onto the Union Depot platform. Straight ahead lay Fremont Street, and a block east beckoned the tall neon cowboy Toby and Rowdy had talked about – Vegas Vic, he was called. In twilight, thousands of lights glowed fantastically. The Golden Nugget sign towered on its rickety frame, ribbons of neon pulsing against the pink-gray eastern sky. Garson was uncertain if it was his memory or Toby's description of a sign that proclaimed "NO GIMMICKS."

Several of the Milwaukee volunteers raced headlong toward Glitter Gulch. Garson was too overwhelmed with the gaudy neon glitter to see where Preston and Rusty trotted. Red, yellow, orange and blue blinked – Lucky Strike, Las Vegas and Boulder Clubs, Payless Drugs. He followed a half dozen toward the nearest casino on the right, its sign winking Salsagev. Ahead of the little pack, Springer, the burly older recruit with thick eyebrows that nearly bridged his brow, pushed open the glass door. Garson followed, but was immediately confronted by a barrel-chested man wearing a string tie who spread his large hand forward like a traffic cop.

"You 21? Gotta be 21 to get in here."

"But he..." Garson pointed to Springer who was already inside. Garson knew the tall youth was no more than a year older; but because of his size and cheeks shaded with light whiskers, he looked like a man. Deterred, Garson turned on his heel, dodged two cars on Fremont, and dashed across to the Las Vegas Club on the opposite corner. Another man wearing a huge jade ring on his pinkie glowered from inside the door. Garson pulled up short.

Through the glass door he spotted rows of slot machines, one-armed bandits, they were called — cast metal torsos of cowboys in black Stetsons, pointing six gun handles. Lights flashed as a stout gray-haired woman who overwhelmed the tall spindly chair watched the whirling display. That brought to mind the less ostentatious machines at Fosland's Restaurant on the Illinois side of the state line. Once, when he was a small boy, his Uncle Hervé handed him a half dozen nickels, and on the third pull of the handle, 20 coins clattered into the hopper. His body thrilled and hands shook as he scooped out those shiny new coins; he had kept them for months, meting them out slowly.

The casino coursed with activity. Deeper inside, he spied a comely girl, blonde hair piled high, wearing a skimpy Gay Nineties outfit and net stockings; she spun the roulette wheel. Beyond her were situated blackjack and crap tables crowded with players. Suddenly, a handful of his fellow recruits dashed past toward Union Station. The train was soon to depart, and he raced back to Main Street and the depot, leaping aboard the El Capitan. The train lurched forward, couplings cracking. Preston, Rusty and others were already onboard. But inside the slowly moving coach, a clamor arose.

"Come on!" voices shouted. "Come on, Springer!" Through the window, Garson saw the tall youth sprinting alongside. The Milwaukeean had boasted of playing football; his legs churned like a running back. All watched in amazement as a conductor stretched his arm toward the runner, and almost at the last moment pulled Springer aboard. It was a scene out of the movies.

Springer was winded by his sprint, but his large-featured face was alight with pleasure. From his trouser pockets he pulled two fistfuls of half dollars, and danced about like Walter Huston, the grizzled old timer, Howard, who found gold in "The Treasure of the Sierra Madre."

"Man, I plugged a couple of half dollars in a machine. Lights flashed and bells rang. Then clack, clack all of the coins jumped out." Several voices asked how much Springer had won, but he did not know for certain. It must have been plenty, perhaps – 25 or 30 bucks. Before long, all would learn that was more than a recruit's monthly pay.

Garson was content aboard the streamliner, cosseted since Chicago by smiling Negro porters, and surfeited by fawning waiters in long white aprons. Food was served on crisp table linen, and place settings were crowded with more utensils than he had ever seen before; ice water was poured into frosty stemmed goblets. Railroad china was adorned with California poppies.

Less than a day passed before the Santa Fe veered south at Barstow, a town Toby and Rowdy had mentioned, then toward the Pacific coast. They passed Oceanside, California where one of the recruits whose brother was in the Marines said Camp Pendleton was situated. Garson had heard that "The Sands of Iwo Jima" and "The Halls of Montezuma" had been filmed there.

"San Diego," the conductor announced not long after. "Next stop, San Diego, and the United States Marine Corps Recruit Depot. Semper Fidelis!" He pronounced the second word "*Fi*-delis." Garson's throat knotted as he settled his gripsack on his lap.

"Well, here we go for four years," he said to his pals. When he and his father had discussed enlistment options with the handsome Marine recruit sergeant in Milwaukee, Garson needed to decide on three, four or six years. Rusty's words played in his mind.

"You know, if we enlist for 20 right away, we'll get a good deal, man," his pal had reasoned. The musketeers had agreed that sounded like the thing to do.

"I'll take four," Garson had said to the recruit sergeant. Garson's father cleared his throat, and the knot on the Marine's tie jumped as he swallowed.

"Well, here's what I'd recommend," replied the sergeant. "Enlist for three years now. If you find it's what you like and it's the life for you, ship over, reenlist, for more." Garson's father nodded in agreement. But he would not be deterred, and signed for four years.

"What do you mean, four years, man?" was Preston's reply when the train slowed before the handsome depot. He and Rusty looked at one another. "We enlisted for three!" Garson's spine tingled and he felt his ears redden. Since their birthdays were separated by several weeks, each had visited recruiters independently. He assumed the initial agreement between them would be honored. He had no more than a few minutes to collect himself when the passenger train halted at the handsome station with spires that evoked a California mission. As the Wisconsin enlistees trooped into the vaulted station, they were met by three Marines in dress green uniforms, each wearing a red armband and carrying a holstered pistol. In a nearby passageway that led to the street, the corporal in charge halted the group.

"If any of you people got aftershave, hair tonic or any other pussy shit, get it out right now." Garson rummaged through his gripsack and withdrew bottles of Vitalis and Aqua-Velva after shave.

"Smash them right here!" the hard-eyed corporal barked. Hesitant, Garson and Rusty looked at one another: Right here, against this ornate tile? Suddenly, the sound of smashing glass echoed from either side. Garson threw his bottles, and soon the orange and blue wall motifs ran with liquid; glass shards sparkled from the concrete floor.

"And if you got any rubbers, get rid of them, too," the corporal smirked, "'cause you ain't dippin' your little dicks anytime soon!" The Marine recruiter in Milwaukee never mentioned anything about any of this, Garson thought.

"Now get aboard that cattle car," the Marine in charge pointed. Towed by an idling diesel truck stood an articulated olive drab trailer featuring horizontally-barred windows. To Garson, it looked like some prison conveyance, right out of the movie "Brute Force." The ride through San Diego's commercial district took no more than 10 or 15 minutes. There was a sense among a few that they traveled south toward San Diego Bay until the cattle-car turned from the thoroughfare. In minutes, civilian life was left completely behind as the vehicle was waved through an imposing double portal by guards wearing white helmets and side arms.

Garson's eyes widened as the vehicle passed under an impressive double archway; at the apex, a large terra cotta eagle, globe and anchor proclaimed the entrance to the Marine Corps Recruit Depot. Inside, he was immediately awed by the largest expanse of concrete he had ever seen. It seemed to sprawl for miles, certainly several football fields in both directions. The bright gray surface reflected sunlight, causing Garson to squint. Small green rectangles of Marines marched under the clear California blue sky. Only drooping palm trees along the periphery of the expanse softened the starkness, but only a little.

Garson and others came to know this central rectangle, the beating heart of MCRD, as the "Grinder," a virtual Marine millstone where soft civilian individualities were scoured away to be replaced by finely polished components of a fighting military machine. Looking back from more than seven decades of subsequent life, Garson remembered the countless hours of drilling and marching during his transformation into a faceless component, a cog in a vaunted fighting machine. MCRD would be the nexus of Garson's existence, with little interruption, for months. While struggling to fall asleep over the next night or two, he found it difficult to conceive of life during the coming months. Almost like a movie flash-forward, his mind reeled.

On the south side of the sprawling drill field were arrayed numerous rows of quonset huts, perhaps 200, Preston thought. Just then, the cattle-car jerked to a stop on the north side of the parade ground adjacent to a series of two-story buildings, all of handsome Mission style with red tiled roofs connected by arched colonnades. There, the timorous band of new recruits disembarked.

The Wisconsin recruits remained at the receiving barracks for one day during which the process of disabusing them of civilian ways and sensibilities began – at the top of their heads.

"Just trim the top and sides a bit, if you please," cracked Rusty to the barber, his lip curling in a typical sneer. Garson, next in line, stifled a guffaw at his pal, ever the streetwise wit. The barber, who had likely heard such comments before, exhibited no reaction. He knew that the Marine Corps offered no mere trim and may have taken pleasure in virtually shearing the like of which no sheep would have been contented. Garson and others concluded afterward that MCRD barbers needed no particular tonsorial skills.

With an angry buzz, the electric trimmer cut a two-inch swath down the middle of Rusty's hennaed locks, a reverse Mohawk. In no more than a dozen swipes within a handful of minutes, Rusty's cranium virtually glowed. As he left the chair, he glanced into the mirror and ran a hand over his scalp.

In minutes, Garson was similarly denuded. He, too, was shocked by the dramatic new appearance. His generation of teens, of course, took great pride in its leonine coiffures, the glossy sweep back from the temples and rakish duck's ass part down the back. With the hirsute abundance removed, skulls, misshapen at birth and scars and dents remaining from childhood injuries, were revealed, often risibly. Garson fingered the tiny white pucker on the right side of his head caused during childhood when he accidentally tripped and fell headlong into a radiator.

The absence of hair also caused dramatic changes in facial appearances. Ears that once seemed normal now flared widely. His mother told him she had taped his ears to his head as an infant, lest he develop what she called "open car door ears." Many noses now grew to nearly proboscidean proportions. More, some eyebrows took on prominences undreamed – thick and brushy, several bridging brows, caterpillars creeping above noses. In aggregate, the newly glabrous seemed feast for phrenologists.

Next, the assembly of freshly shorn lined up at a window on the first floor, where bedding was distributed – pillow cover, sheets and mattress covers now known as "fart sacks" and a green woolen blankets with "U.S.M.C." stitched in black. In a galvanized bucket Garson surveyed a scrub brush, bar of Fels Naptha soap, a dozen wooden clothes pins, olive drab towel and wash cloth, tube of Barbasol shave cream, shaving brush, a double-edged safety razor and other oddments. Garson did not know what he might do with the razor as none had ever touched his childlike cheeks.

When ordered, Garson donned the gray sweatshirt that was

issued and plopped a green dungaree cap – he quickly learned it was called a "cover" – on his head. It drooped over his ears and down to his eyebrows like movie boob. He felt that he, like all of the others, appeared clownish – diminished and degraded. More indignities followed.

That first night, Garson was sleepless after final notes of "Taps" sounded. Apprehensive, pulse beat into his pillow, his mind whirled with scenarios and regrets. Fitful slumber finally took him into troubled scenes of his mother scolding him for not going to college.

"Daylight in the swamp," she had often awakened him for school, unceremoniously rolling up the bedroom shade. Half awake, his mother's voice gave way to jolting bugle notes of "Reveille!" Windows revealed no daylight.

"Drop your cocks and grab your socks!" a corporal shouted at one end of the squad bay, rattling a broom handle around the inside of a metal trash can. Rude awakening.

"Fall out on the Grinder. On the double!" Within spare minutes, Garson and his fellow Wisconsin recruits augmented with other newcomers stampeded down from the second floor and onto the parade ground, knotting together in a pitiful assembly. There had been little time to relieve himself, brush his teeth or even splash cold water on his face. In the darkness outside, a corporal of surly mien pushed and pulled the three dozen recruits into a semblance of formation. After calling the roll, Garson heard foreign words of command.

"For'ard. Harch!" He assumed they meant "Forward march." The collection of nascent Marines strode off, shambled and stumbled, no more than a few striding in cadence.

"Detail, halt! Dress ranks!" The corporal's voice was like a bellowing bull. "Come on, come on! Fuckin' dress it up." Somewhat re-ordered, they set off again, and within several steps, the same result. Another halt was ordered.

"Jee'zus, fuckin' Christ! I never seen such a collection of fuckin' skin-headed fucks in my life." Every word exploded from the Marine's mouth. Had there been sufficient light, Garson was certain that spittle sprayed visibly.

"Listen to the goddamned cadence, people! Left, right, left. Left, right, left. Jeezus fuckin' Christ, you only got two fuckin' feet!" Trouble for Garson was that the bulky recruit marching in front of him did not know his left foot from his right. He lumbered side to side rather than strutted. The recruit behind seemed to lope, barking Garson's heels at every footfall. The corporal was utterly frustrated.

"Close ranks. I want you fuckin' Boots to march asshole to belly button now." Garson mused that they were now regarded no higher than footwear. He was also uncomfortable with his torso molded with recruits to his front and rear, and wedged shoulder to shoulder with those on either side. They marched off yet again, a comic collection of individuals. Garson felt his fine suede shoes, carefully tended back home, being scuffed and abused in the dreadful mélange. They maneuvered – it could not be called marching — south across the Grinder toward the mess hall that squatted midway between the compact quonset ranks. Here, the Marine dismissed the recruits – he seemed relieved — and with a glance at his watch, ordered them to reappear on the opposite side within 15 minutes.

In the steamy mess hall, amid the clatter of metal trays and cups, they shuffled down the cafeteria line. Onto Garson's tray, mess men dolloped fruit cocktail, two pieces of toast over which was ladled ground beef swimming in a viscous white sauce. Garson soon learned it was called "S.O.S. — shit on a shingle;" despite its name, he would grow fond of the morning gruel.

During the hurried consumption of the breakfast, hundreds of other recruit Marines wearing green dungarees eyed the newcomers in rumpled gray sweatshirts and gleaming white heads. Here were fresh fish, as Civil War soldiers derided newcomers in the preceding century, so low snakes and vermin might crawl over them. Most ignored Garson and the newcomers, but he was certain faces wore smirks of disdain and superiority; these Boots, salty MCRD "veterans" were farther along in training. In two months, Garson would similarly sneer imperiously at new rivals from his lofty station as a "salty" Marine.

After wolfing down the breakfast gruel and gulping acrid coffee, Garson and about 20 others, returning to the receiving barracks, and gathered their gear. Clutching bedding to their chests and carrying gripsacks and buckets of Marine oddments, they were herded to the south side of the Grinder – nearly two football fields across. During the height of the Korean War, Garson later learned, MCRD had erected hundreds of quonsets. Now arrayed before them were uncounted arched corrugated billets, arrayed in rows of five along the length of the Grinder.

Such quarters were to be the locus of Garson's existence, before and after being billeted in the rifle range's tent city north of MCRD. Months of intensive and taxing training lay ahead during which each recruit was divested of useless remnants of civilian life, and inculcated in vital ways of the Corps. Quonsets were set on 20-by-48 foot concrete slabs, arching corrugated roofs were pierced by four high windows on the long side and two at each end that provided paltry daylight. Along the walls inside stood a dozen double bunks, sleeping accommodations for 24 recruits. A rarely fired oil stove was situated midway in the hut. Bare bulbs hung from the vaulted ceiling, providing insubstantial illumination. Garson and his apprehensive Boots were dispersed to three huts, each separated by about ten feet of sandy, anemic soil.

It was in this environment that the Boots first encountered their senior drill instructor, starched and memorable Staff Sergeant Maddox, who would become for Garson the personification of the United States Marine Corps. They were also confronted by the platoon's junior drill instructor, Corporal Reid, a bandy rooster whose coloration, temperament and demeanor resembled Garson's feisty pal Rusty. But while Rusty was a benign rascal, Reid was sardonically cruel. The diminutive NCO would play the role of bad cop to his superior's .

"You're the sorriest load of fuckin' shit I've ever seen," Reid pronounced at an early interval. "Most of you fuckin' skinheads just ain't gonna make it in this man's Marine Corps. And I'm the one to fuckin' make sure of that." Garson had heard similar sentiments in war movies. "So, right now, you can give your fuckin' souls to God because your fuckin' asses're mine."

One of the paramount initial instructions was the method of making a proper Marine bunk. Garson, who in 17 years never once made his own bed, observed the DI's demonstration closely, determined to follow the precise military prescription: Bed linens were to be pulled as taut as a drum head, corners crisply folded, black stitched "U.S.M.C." letters on green wool aligned precisely. No Boot dare lay nor sit on his rack, as the bunks came to be called, between "Reveille" and "Taps." In time, Garson became adept at folding his body into his bedding like a letter into an envelope; each morning, he extricated himself carefully so that only a few tucks and tightenings returned his rack to order.

"Man, you must sleep at attention," one buddy later observed.

Soon, nights were short and days long. That first night with Platoon 023 was restless for Garson. Diffuse thoughts paraded through his mind, thoughts of his mother, "Ma." He now admitted he had taken her for granted, ignoring advice and counsel, even at times exhibiting impatience and hostility. His head throbbed in remorse. A recruit in the rack nearby cleared his nose, and across the way, another whimpered. Garson contemplated the enormity of what lay ahead. For a 17-year-old, 90 days stretched endlessly; four years was inconceivable. He did not even have Preston and Rusty for support since they had been assigned to a different platoon quonset. He was utterly alone, defenseless against the implacable forces that now controlled him. It came to him that this was Halloween.

"Taps" sounded at ten and blaring notes of "Reveille" startled Garson awake in the darkness of 4:30.

"You'll address me and everyone but another Boot as 'Sir,' and answer 'Aye, aye, sir' loud and clear." Corporal Reid unleashed more lessons. "Floors are decks, walls, bulkheads; doors were hatches. The shitter's the Head," the cocky junior DI growled. Nautical lingo prevailed because the Corps was part of the Navy Department. More commands came with bewildering rapidity. Smoking was only permitted when a drill instructor "lit the smoking lamp."

"Camels're the cigarette of Marine Corps drill instructors. Don't fuckin' forget it. When you hear, 'One fuckin' Camel to the Duty Hut!' someone better move at the double with a Camel in hand." In time, Garson and others muttered among themselves that DIs seemed never to purchase their own smokes.

Garson slept on a top bunk above a Boot from Detroit named Liska whose face was pock-marked with acne scars; his pale blue eyes were almost startling. When he wrote about Liska, Garson brought to mind the Charles Dickens description of Joe Gargery in *Great Expectations*: He had "eyes of such a very undecided blue that they seemed to have somehow got mixed with their own whites." He and Liska would become well acquainted over the course of months ahead. Even as he enjoyed his buddy's experiences, Garson was invariably uncomfortable gazing at length into those pallid eyes. Had he possessed any poetic bent, he might have used the word refulgent to describe them.

"Whenever a DI enters a billet," continued Reid's orientation, "the first Boot who sees him will sound off 'Attention!' You all will drop every fuckin' thing you're doin', and snap to attention. Not one word, not one sound, not one fuckin' move until the Marine departs. Do you understand?"

"Yes, sir!'

"Can't fuckin' hear you!"

"Yes, sir!" Decibels bounced from the quonset bulkheads.

Garson was now a trifling component of Platoon 023 – Zero-Two-Three – Charlie Company, Second Recruit Training Battalion. Two other platoons comprised the battalion, and these would, during the months ahead, constitute competition for an important distinction.

"I led many platoons through recruit training before you," Sergeant Maddox crowed early on, "and never failed to win Honor Platoon. You people will not fail me in this new quest. Do you understand?"

"Yes, sir!"

"Can't fuckin' hear you!"

One of the three platoon quonsets, designated as the Duty Hut, was partitioned, its front half serving as administrative and living quarters for the drill instructors. Meek and mild Boots need not enter here; fear and trembling lay beyond its grey portal. Strict protocol was prescribed for admittance to this hallowed sanctum. Almost in his sleep decades later, Garson could recall the procedure. He stood at attention before the door, and sharply rapped three times, followed by these words:

"Private Garson, Platoon Zero-Two-Three, sir!" The supplicant waited.

"Get the fuck in here, shithead!" Garson smartly opened the door, ripped the dungaree cap from his head, closed the door behind him, took two steps in, faced to the left, one step forward, and stood at attention before the desk, eyes riveted on the wall. Here, he was ordered to state his business. Should he fail in any one of those movements, a torrent of invective and at times the flat of a hand was the result. Often, an offender was made to repeat the entire process numerous times until every movement was carried out as prescribed.

Garson and his north side Milwaukee peers were, of course, more than conversant with scatology, blasphemy and curses of all kinds; out of his mother's earshot, he laced conversations with offensive words and phrases. The four-letter word, however, was a thing apart, reserved only for times of extreme tension. To use it liberally, to draw that verbal sword frequently, would rob it of its power. "Friggin" had been a suitable substitute in the past. But, at MCRD, the actual utterance was common, almost mandatory.

In those first days at MCRD, Garson felt assaulted by the once-potent four-letter word. But in no more than days, he came to regard it as an essential part of Marine Corps vocabulary. The shock of its prolific use soon wore off, and Garson embraced it with abandon. "Fuck" served not simply a noun, verb or adjective, but as an adverb, conjunction and virtually any part of speech. Only rarely was it meant literally, and was often used risibly.

"Jesus, fuckin', Christ. What fuckin' time is it?" And the reply: "Four fuckin' o'clock." At times, there was a rush to imbed it in every phrase or sentence; it was ubiquitous, inescapable. MCRD recruits were "fuckin' Boots", "fuckin' clowns", or "fuckin' people." They could be "fuckin' shit heads," "fuckin' cruds," even "fuckin' pussies," the latter an indicator of particularly low caste implying weakness and temerity. "You're so fuckin' low a snake could fuckin' crawl over you." They would hear that description endlessly. In the mess hall, a standard request went like this:

"Pass the fuckin' juice down here" — juice identified as anything other than coffee or milk. When he wrote of those days decades later, Garson recalled an incident while he was home on leave. Sitting at dinner with his parents, he blurted out the usual request. His mother's face drained of color, and he almost read her mind, wondering what the Marine Corps had done to her only son.

Perhaps, Garson later concluded, Jack London may have described many Marine Corps drill instructors when he characterized Wolf Larsen, the demonic captain in *The Sea Wolf*.

"Oaths rolled from his lips in a continuous stream. And they were not namby-pamby oaths, or mere expressions of indecency. Each word was a blasphemy, and there were many words. They crisped and crackled like electric sparks."

What was more, aspersions were often cast on ethnicity; Corporal Reid was heard to say "Polack" or smirk over surnames, calling a recruit "Stosh" or "Ski." Derogatory comments about "dumb Texans" or "Okies" were common. But in the Marine Corps of Garson's era, the phrase "son of a bitch" was rarely used. Mothers and country, after all, were high on the list of loyalties, ranking just below the Corps itself.

Despite Sergeant Maddox's blasphemous remark that first day, he defamed the deity only in rare instances. The junior drill instructor, on the other hand, often spewed "God dammit!" yet he rarely uttered "God damn you!" These Marines, Garson conjectured, did not want to push that envelope too far. A man's beliefs were a thing apart, something not to be trifled with. If either NCO was a believer or atheist, there was no indication. In only one incident directly involving Garson was Sergeant Maddox given pause. He may have been omniscient over his recruits, but his power had limits.

Clothing and equipment were stored in foot lockers stowed under the lower rack.

Another early prescription was to padlock the wooden trunk at all times when not in use. Failure to do so would have consequences, the sergeant warned. The platoon returned to its billet after a day of classes, Garson found his locker upended and its contents scattered about — deliberately, it appeared. His heart sank; he had failed to snap shut the padlock. He began to gather the contents and repack the locker, picking up a small plastic statue of the Christ child his mother had given him just before he boarded the train in Milwaukee.

"He'll watch over you," she said. While religion had not been a pressing concern in Garson's life for several years, he regarded the little artifact as a talisman, a good luck charm, a memento of his mother. Adorned in a red cloak, the boy figure's arms were outspread in supplication.

"Ten-shun!" Garson quickly dropped the item and stood rigidly. Sergeant Maddox strode imperiously through the hut. He passed between the bunks slowly, then stopped in front of Garson, studying the scatter of clothing and belongings. It was obvious to Garson that he had dumped the contents during an inspection earlier; now, it seemed, he came to gloat. He spotted the plastic Christ Child lying there, and picked it up. His lips curled haughtily.

"What you got here, clown, a doll?" he said slowly and deliberately, scrutinizing the figurine. Garson said nothing, muscles quivering. Maddox lifted the two-inch haloed statuette toward his face to get a better look. In seconds, he recognized what it was, then handed it to Garson.

"As you were," he said almost quietly, turning on his heel and striding toward the doorway.

"Now, turn too, and get this fuckin' area A. J. squared away," Maddox shouted over his shoulder. That night, before falling asleep, Garson replayed the incident, concluding with a smile that he had bested the most powerful man he had ever known. The little icon would also play a part in another encounter with the senior drill instructor.

The previous year, Garson had noticed a copy of John Steinbeck's new novel, *East of Eden*, laying on a table in the neighborhood public library. It was a thick book, over 600 pages, something he would not contemplate reading. But he riffled through the tome, stopping at a passage that partially came to mind in the early days of Boot Camp.

"They'll first strip you of your clothes," the Trask family patriarch said of the military, "but they'll go deeper than that. They'll shuck off any little dignity you have – you'll lose what you think of as your decent right to live and be let alone to live." This was a lesson Garson's father could not impart because he was too young for the Great War and too old for the World War. Grandfather Guttig had served in the Austro-Hungarian military, but he never shared those experiences with his young grandson.

"They'll make you live and eat and sleep and shit close to other men," Cyrus Trask said. "And when they dress you up again you'll not be able to tell yourself from others." Indeed, one of the initial activities was shucking off the civilian clothing and sending it home.

As suggested by the Milwaukee Marine recruiter, Garson wore the same clothing for the entire journey from Milwaukee, changing only his underwear and socks. A PFC at the supply warehouse where uniforms, undergarments and footgear were issued asked if Garson cared to sell his suede shoes. Although somewhat intimidated, he demurred and boxed them with the other items. When he posted the package, it felt like the last vestige of the civilian umbilical cord had been severed.

Marine clothing, too, took on nautical taxonomy. Undershorts became skivvies, and head gear was called "covers" as: "Get that fuckin' cover on, you fuckin' idiot!" Covers were to be worn outdoors but never inside.

"What the fuck did you call them, shit head?" was the instantaneous retort to civilian verbiage.

"Pants, sir," Garson replied.

"Pants! Pants? Only fuckin' pussies wear pants, you fuckin' clown. Marines wear trousers, not pants. And don't you forget it." Another lesson ingrained.

"This is your bible," Sergeant Maddox held aloft the red *Guidebook for Marines.* Garson had no more than a few minutes in the swirl of events and activity to inspect the 500-page soft-cover volume.

"You will keep it on your person at all times. Fold it in half like this, and carry it in your right rear pocket. It's the Corps's bible, its Ten Commandments in 35 chapters. This is vital information you'll need to become a Marine – which many of you won't. Your noses better be in this bible every spare minute. You will eat, sleep and shit with this *Guidebook.* It's the only book you'll ever need." The *Guidebook* was one of the most important printed documents of recruit training.

To describe the 60-some recruits of Platoon 023 as a cross-section of American male youth in the early 1950's would be to misstate. The majority was composed of 17- and 18-year-olds, many, like Garson, high school dropouts. Even among the 19 and older component, several did not carry diplomas. Only one or two, like the right guide, Barker had attended college. The majority of the platoon consisted of city youths, and most of these called Milwaukee and Detroit home. A handful hailed from small town or rural environs; a few Texans were sprinkled in.

In the main, the unit represented a generally blue-collar socio-economic stratum. Garson correctly surmised that most, like him, were sons or grandsons of immigrants – Germans from Milwaukee, Poles from Detroit along with Irish and others from several places. Zero-Two-Three was white with a only few Mexicans and Puerto Ricans dotting the platoon ranks; one Indian, a swarthy, taciturn youth named Felton whose expression was nearly always sour, marched with the unit. A half dozen Negroes were scattered in the battalion's two other platoons.

Generally unintellectual, largely inarticulate and under-informed, the unit was malleable raw material for Marine Corps indoctrination and inculcation. Whatever values existed in the recruit baggage would be challenged and eradicated. Boots would digest the proscriptions and prescriptions of Mother Corps.

"You from Wisconsin, right?" The questioner was a tall, rangy Detroiter who introduced himself as Jensen. Except for his long neck and prominent Adam's apple, he was handsome, his face perfectly proportioned; he had one of the widest, whitest smiles Garson could ever remember seeing outside of the movies. He was one of the more articulate recruits.

"I can tell," he said, "Milwaukee guys pronounce 'th's' as 'd's' most of the time." He also observed that most did not pronounce the "l" in their city's name. "Sounds like 'Ma-waukee,'" he said.

"Name's French, right?" Jensen queried. "Lots of French names around Detroit, places named after the explorers, voyagers and such. Detroit, you know, should be pronounced 'DEE- tra'" he rolled the "r." It meant the "straits," *le detroit*, he said, identified in the 1600's by Antoine de la Mothe Cadillac. "Cadillac should be 'Ca-DEE-ya.'" Garson was captivated by the loquacity and erudition. Jensen was one of the high school graduates.

"We have this main street we call 'Gra-shut' which is really Gratiot – 'Gra-TEE-o'," he said. Over time, Garson learned that Jensen had studied French at St. Clair Shores High. The community was a leafy suburb north of the city with wide lots and splendid brick and stone homes; he lived on Jefferson Avenue with its expansive view of Lake St. Clair. His grandparents once lived in Hamtramck, the Polish community smack in the middle of the city where his dad opened a tool and dye business; when the business flourished, the Jensen family moved out of the city into more verdant environs.

"Actually, the family name's Jezierski, but when my grandparents arrived at Ellis Island, they had trouble spelling it. So they changed it to Jensen right there and then." While composing his memoir, Garson learned that such anecdotes about Ellis Island name changes were usually family legends. Immigrants themselves often modified their names, trying to establish themselves as Americans. Garson knew that his mother embraced Americanization, preferring Marie to Mary, her christened name, even as her sisters clung to the European Eva and Terez.

Garson liked Jensen immediately. The affable young man often flashed a magnetic smile, and like Garson's boyhood pal, Mellish, was a natural raconteur, ever ready with some family fable. Jensen was also something of a prankster who could relieve Boot Camp tensions with a swoop of a poncho in front of his face on a dark night, miming Bella Lugosi's Dracula.

Over six-foot, Jensen had played high school basketball and as a senior was selected second team all-metro by the *Detroit News*. Garson had never participated in organized sports in his two years at Messmer High. The closest he had come was a few brief stints on the impromptu neighborhood football team, the North Side Tigers; his occasional success as an undersized linebacker came when he knifed through the offensive line to bring down ball carriers; he also recalled fleetly running back kick-offs and punts.

After drill instructors, the most important man in Platoon 023 was the burly and athletic Right Guide Barker. He would have been handsome with a full head of hair; his eyes were steel blue, and his jaw was square. He had spent a year at a college in Detroit, one of the recruits told Garson. At nearly 21, he exhibited a kindly, almost fatherly demeanor. When ordered to do so by a drill instructor, he could come down hard on some miscreant Boot. Garson knew, however, that he often clandestinely talked to the offender afterward, trying to ease frayed feelings. Barker was roundly liked and respected.

Garson also gravitated to a kindly-faced recruit named Hupner, who slept in the bunk across the aisle. Chesty and well-proportioned, he spoke with a soft Texas lilt. A farm lad who lived in Blanco County. The left side of his barren head bore a puckered scar of over three inches, the result of a farm accident, Hupner explained; it had the look of a natural part on his skull. Hupner had an incredible secret: He was unable to read or write, and could only sign his name.

"My daddy said I knew enough after a couple'a grades. He said it was time to go to work." The story evoked something from Garson's past – both his parents had attended school only through the sixth grade; they, too, were needed on the farm.

Hupner explained that he had simply guessed on the military's multiple choice entrance exams; his scores had been sufficient for enlistment. He followed that practice during Boot Camp testing. As far as Garson knew, his debility was never discovered beyond a small circle in the platoon.

A few weeks later, Liska talked to Barker, and told him in confidence about Hupner's disability. Neither Barker, Liska, Jensen nor Garson, the only four who knew the secret, betrayed the confidence. Barker, in a twist of irony, designated the Texan as platoon mail clerk.

Garson and a few others shared the task of reading Hupner's letters to him and drafting replies; in the course of those events, Garson learned much about the gentle big fellow. His ancestors had lived in West Texas for decades.

"My daddy said our kin came to Texas even before it was a state during the time the Mexicans had it." He explained that German was spoken widely in his community; he knew some words himself. "*Ich spreche ein wenig Deutsch,*" he boasted. Garson suspected Hupner's family name was originally spelled with an umlaut as *Hüpner* and pronounced "Heepner."

"We have Oktoberfest and German celebrations all the time," Hupner explained. "I miss mamma's sauerbraten and ham hocks. Her *küchen* and *schnecken* are really good too. My daddy said that Texans took after our kin during the Great War. They said we was loyal to the Kaiser, and said we should go back to Germany." Hupner had two older cousins who fought in World War II; one had been killed on Tarawa Island beach. That was reason he had joined the Marines, to pay respect to that relative.

The other recruit from Texas was named McCracken. A bulky-bodied kid who seemed far removed from anything remotely handsome: His nostrils gaped porcine, and enormous ears sprouted from his head. The absence of hair amplified these outsized facial features. In the classroom, Garson noticed, McCracken wobbled his legs incessantly, rocking his upper body like a metronome, like a *Quar-onic* student in a madrassah. He proved to be a classic fuck-up, and was often caught smoking when the "lamp" was not lit.

On several occasions his actions resulted in penalty being meted out to the entire platoon — "mass punishment." Even reasonable Right Guide Baker developed antipathy toward the Texan. In time, Garson and others would deliver retribution.

During the second week of recruit training, McCracken, obviously fed up with training and treatment, reported to Sergeant Maddox that he was only 16 – a fraudulent enlistment, it was called. That information, of course, was transmitted from platoon to company to battalion and up the chain of command. Days passed, then weeks and still McCracken continued to train and march with the platoon.

"They're gonna cut your discharge next week, McCracken," announced Sergeant Maddox every Monday. Corporal Reid ordered the underage recruit to change the procedure when requesting admission to the Duty Hut.

"Private *Going-Home-Next-Week* McCracken, Platoon Zero-Two-Three, sir."

Despite the fraudulence of his enlistment and his reluctance to continue, "next week" stretched into a month and McCracken remained with the platoon until it departed for the rifle range at Camp Mathews in November. But before he was separated from the unit, McCracken caused his fellow Boots more difficulty, and sustained retribution.

"'Ten'shun to the roll. When your name's called, sound off!" As with any question, the response was to be loud and resonant.

"Krupa?" Corporal Reid called out

"Here, sir!" He was one of the youths who had traveled with Garson, Preston and Rusty from Milwaukee. Garson had had some conversation with Krupa on the train, discovering that he had attended South Division High for three years before dropping out. Of average height, before the Boot Camp shearing, he had sprouted a shock of sandy hair; his full lips appeared as though augmented with pink lip rouge. He and Garson, cherub-faced boys, came to be known as "Baby Marines."

"Krupa? The drummer?" the corporal queried as he scrutinized the recruit in the front rank.

"No, sir, that's Gene, sir."

"Gene who?" Reid smirked.

"Gene Krupa, sir."

"*You're* Gene Krupa?"

"No, sir, the recruit is Stanley Krupa." A Boot always referred to himself in the third person. Reid peered at the clipboard roster he held.

"Think I'll call you Stosh then."

"Name's...the private's name is Stanley, sir." His widely set eyes bulged and his voice quavered.

"Stanley Kowalski?" was the response.

"Sir, no sir!" A few in the ranks sniggered until Reid's gaze shifted to them.

"Think I'll call you Gene, then," the corporal continued. "Gene Krupa."

"Sir, no sir." Confused, the recruit's face and ears clearly reddened. "The private's name is Stanley Krupa, sir."

"The drummer?" Reid asked forcefully. The flushed boot was stunned into silence. Garson and others quickly learned that such verbal encounters were always losing propositions. On occasion, Sergeant Maddox joined the act. When a drill instructor passed between the ranks, all eyes were to remain riveted forward. Not one eyeball dare waver. In one formation, Garson furtively shifted his eyes as the senior DI passed.

"What the fuck're you looking at?" Maddox had turned on his heel and stood before Garson, jutting his face to within inches of Garson's nose.

"Nothin', sir!" In his Milwaukeese, the word sounded like "Nuttin."

"Nuttin'? Am I nuttin'?"

"Sir, no, sir!" Garson swallowed audibly.

"Think I'm pretty?"

"Sir, no, sir!" Garson's mouth went desert dry.

"You don't think I'm pretty, then?"

"Sir, no...yes, sir."

"Oh, you *are* queer for me, then?"

"Sir, no, sir."

"But you think I'm pretty?"

"Sir..." Garson sputtered, thoroughly deflated and defeated.

"Or are you a queer boy, a faggot?"

"Sir, no, sir!"

"Well, you look like a pussy to me." Maddox stared unblinking into Garson's eyes for a moment more.

"And what the fuck is this?" the sergeant demanded, grabbing the top metal button of Garson's dungaree jacket in thumb and forefinger. "Think you're some kind of salty Hollywood Marine? This is to be buttoned at all times. Do the rest of you people fuckin' hear me?" Maddox was not often given to the four-letter verbal assault.

"Sir, yes, sir!" Garson blinked and exhaled as Maddox strode away. In retrospect, Garson concluded that such encounters were not intended as mere exercises of abuse. They were demeaning, of course, but the purpose was to eradicate civilian assumptions and attitudes. Independent thought and action were of scant merit here. Like a California tremblor, the Boots were being shifted from their former foundations.

Garson learned that his name was less important than his number – a number that was ingrained so deeply that it would never be forgotten. 1427801. That identity was stamped onto the dog tags along with name and blood type that hung around his neck from the first day at MCRD.

"Whatever you thought you knew before you came here, forget it," Sergeant Maddox pronounced. "There's only one way to do things – the Marine Corps way. Your loyalty will be to your fellow Marines. A few of you – very few, I add — will be transformed from soft, useless civilians to proud members of the foremost fighting force on the planet. You'll not fight for mom, country or apple pie.

You will fight for the glory of the United States Marine Corps. *My Marine Corps.*" His jaw was taut.

Other lessons came quickly. Some sounded petty and risible.

"Who the fuck injured one of my plants?" It was Corporal Reid's nasal gusto. Each morning's routine included sweeping the company street, and grooming the ground in front and between each quonset. Buckets of water were splashed onto the parched dirt, and the dampened soil raked with neat lines, taking great care not to harm the tiny tubular plants that clung to life in the nutrient-poor plots.

"You fuckin' Boots better take special care of my little plants," Reid warned. "If I see one broken or injured and find the fuckin' skinhead who broke it, there'll be two of us going to sick bay – me and one who's got my boondocker up his fuckin' ass. Treat these ice plants like your girlfriend's hot little titties." The fragile vegetation was religiously watered and nurtured with great care. The pale green vesicles, resembling smooth, thornless cacti, grew not at all.

Much of those early days, Garson remembered, was taken up with physical and dental inspections, and psychological and intelligence testing. Once again, indignities were heaped upon recruits as they paraded past Navy corpsmen, medical personnel assigned to duty in the Marine Corps, to be thumped, made to cough and peer at eye charts. The Boots shuffled between the gauntlet of Navy corpsmen that seemed to throw, like darts, hypodermics at biceps and buttocks.

"Drop your drawers, bend over and spread 'em wide!" a corpsman commanded as the ranks ignominiously bent forward while he flashed his light. Garson harked back to his mother's constant admonition to avoid sitting on concrete because it might lead to bleeding piles. More indignity followed.

"Milk it back and skin it forward," an examiner barked. In what was called a "short arm inspection," another corpsman scrutinized genitals, looking for discharge and disease. During the dental exam, it was discovered that Garson's rear teeth were diseased. In childhood, he had not been given to proper dental care; his mother's constant chiding went unheeded, and now he would pay the price.

"These gotta come out," he heard the dentist conclude. "We'll need to cut out the wisdoms and fit the mouth for prosthesis." Many in the platoon were dentally deficient, several displaying decayed, broken or missing teeth. Springer and a few others, Garson learned, would have every tooth extracted and complete upper and lower dentures created. After extractions, Garson and the others would spend nearly the remainder of Boot Camp without complete dentition. When he smiled, Springer's mouth was a dark maw and he spoke, tongue against palate, with an old man's slur.

"I don't want to hear a sound out of you," the corpsman ordered as he plunged in the novocain needle, "you're supposed to be a Marine." While the anesthetic masked much of the pain, the sound of dental tools slicing open gums, breaking through enamel, the pressure of extraction, the metallic taste of blood all made his heart lurch. He tried to distract himself during the painful childhood procedure, thinking of the time his father had taken him to the Marquette Dental School downtown to have a recalcitrant baby tooth extracted. He remembered the odor of the rubber mask and gas anesthetic, the blood on his shirt and the woozy feeling on the drive home. It had been such a dreadful experience that he had refused to visit any other dentist. At MCRD, there was no choice.

After a brief recovery, Garson was sent back to his unit. When he arrived, however, the platoon was at class. He pounded three times on the Duty Hut door but was unable to speak because his mouth was clamped down on blood-saturated cotton. There was no response. He pounded a second time, and with trepidation, swung open the door. Corporal Reid's eyes bulged, and he reached across the desk, preparing to grab the offensive Boot who had the temerity to enter without permission. But he quickly noticed the blood, and ordered Garson to his rack. It was the only time he dared laying on a bunk before "Taps."

Garson said he felt confident about exams to determined fitness for various military occupations the Corps offered. He found the Army General Classification Test fairly easy. When it came time for him to choose possible occupations from the MOS — Military Occupation

System — he selected air traffic control and public information. The latter suited his intention to become a newspaperman one day. After all, he and Jackie Adams, his second grade classmate, had created a few editions of an uncirculated newspaper, emulating the actions that he remembered from "His Girl Friday," the movie about the Cracker Jack profession.

But he scored poorly on the AGCT, ending in Grade IV. That coupled with his school dropout status resulted in a 0300 MOS — basic infantryman, rifleman, cannon fodder. When he later learned that his pals Preston and Rusty had somehow been assigned to Marine air wings as mechanics, he was doubly chagrinned.

That week, too, Garson and the other Boots filed into a studio for recruit photos — images that were later printed in a commemorative volume. Garson called it the high school drop-out yearbook. They were posed in Marine dress blue blouses and brass buttons, and a white-covered barracks hats. But like attire for funeral corpses, the uniforms were mere facades, slipped on like a strait jacket and fastened at back with hooks and eyes. Garson mused about the portent.

Garson looked no more than 14, 15 at best, in that black and white image, trepidation obvious behind a feigned smile. Long after, he wondered anew how he had presumed to become a Marine.

"Zero-Two-Three to the Grinder! I wanna see nothin' but fuckin' assholes and elbows out here," growled the senior DI. No more than a few minutes must pass before the platoon was smartly arrayed on the parade ground. Should the unit not be formed in the rapidity that Maddox or Reid demanded, it was dismissed to the huts and recalled repeatedly, until it assembled to their satisfaction.

Recruits were arrayed lengthwise in four ranks of about 16. Each rank was headed by a squad leader whose right bicep displayed a green band; Right Guide Barker, the foremost recruit, wore a yellow arm band denoting his position as interlocutor to the drill instructors.

"Now, when I command 'Raaht haace' – he meant "Right face," of course — "you will swivel on the ball of your left foot and heel of your right, like this." Maddox demonstrated. The recruits practiced that basic maneuver and its opposite — "Lauff haace" – literally thousands of times. It was evident early on that the senior drill instructor, like most others, was a martinet. He drew his lips tightly beneath the brim of his campaign hat that perched two inches above his nose.

"He's gotta look up to see the deck," some joked about Maddox's rakish, low-riding hat brim. With his non-commissioned officer's sword tucked in the crook of shoulder and torso, he was a commanding presence.

"You will step off on the march with your left foot." Even late in his life, Garson always began his stride in that manner, harking back to another basic lesson of close order drill.

"Those of you who don't know your left foot, it's this one," Sergeant Maddox said patting his thigh.

"*THIS* is your left foot." From Fletcher Pratt's little history of the Civil War that a high school teacher had him read, Garson remembered the practice of attaching hay and straw to new soldiers' shoes. Instead of calling "Left, right," the command was "Hay foot, straw foot."

Both drill instructors commands to "Forward, march" sounded like "Forr-err, harr," the "r's" like growls. Consonants were almost always guttural and vowels stretched with diphthongs. "'Toon, hoa" was "Platoon, halt." Boots quickly learned that "Rid o-bleek, harr," designated "right oblique, march;" and "To a'right flaa, harr" was "To the right flank, march."

They practiced the basic movements and maneuvers for several hours that day and nearly every day during those initial weeks. Only a few in the ranks had had experience in drill, but in time, nearly all gained confidence; close order drill became as natural as breathing. A recruit platoon moved continually on foot, and at every step, drill instructors exhorted, harangued, admonished and threatened until Platoon 023 trod the Grinder in perfect unison and alignment — almost.

Each drill instructor exhibited a distinctive voice and rhythm of calling cadence, as unique as a finger- or voice-print. Commands arose from deep in the throat, resonating in belly and chest, some words bursting forth like cannon shots. Other voices were gravelly and guttural, some sing-songed. A few sounded lupine, like baying wolves. Neck tendons strained, mouths pursed, lips contorted in all manner of shapes to project the words. Much later, Garson mused that like pups for their mother, recruits could identify their own drill instructor by his commands. Sergeant Maddox exhibited a nicely modulated voice; he did not need basso profundo bellows.

"Lauff, ri-dle, lauff" – "Left, right, left."

Garson recalled the actor James Whitmore's cadence in the movie "Battleground," a film that impressed him in his youth.

"Hreep, hup, a-ree, 'our," platoon leader Kinnie called, waddling in those rag-wrapped frozen feet. Bob Leckie, the World War II Marine whose memoir *Helmet for my Pillow* in part depicted life in Boot Camp at Parris Island, described the cadence call as "Thrip-faw-ya-leahft, thrip-faw-ya-leahft."

"It's like an incantation," he wrote, "but it is merely the traditional 'three-four-your-left' elongated…made sprightly by being sung."

There was always a pause between what was called the preparatory command and the command of execution. No movement, not a muscle or tendon twitch before the second command was given. But many recruits leaned forward slightly after the preparatory "Forward," anticipating. Occasionally, a few lost their balance.

"Fall on your faces, you clowns," Maddox grimaced. "I've told you hundreds of times not to move a hair or a muscle until the command of execution is given. Now listen up. For-arr." They stood stock still until Maddox sung out "Haar'," then strode forward, left foot first. It was another lesson for which Maddox had to give too many reminders, and he often grew more impatient with the platoon's lack of progress in such elementary instructions. More perceptive recruits thought they sensed his anxiety over 023's ability to compete for Honor Platoon.

"Lauff, ri-del, lauff! Lauff, ri-del, lauff. Wan, two, wan, two." One always sounded like "wan."

"Swing those arms six to the front and three to the rear," the sergeant harangued continually. "One heel. One heel. Shoulders back. Lean back and strut. One heel. Heels, heels, heels."

A proficient marching platoon exhibited, Garson discovered, splendid fluidity. The recruits marched with a slight rearward lean. Heels struck the ground as one at every footfall. "Dig 'em in! One heel! One heel!" Maddox would remind constantly, "one" always pronounced as "wan." Every head rose and fell in unison. "The DI shouldn't even need to call cadence." Garson's chest swelled manfully when the DI remained silent on the march. The platoon maintained the proper pace without words.

The unit, of course, was organized by height, taller in the front and shorter in the rear. Garson, one of the "feather merchants" or "short rounds," found himself the third last recruit in the fourth squad. In standing array, he was near the far left of the back rank, but in marching formation, after facing to the right, he strode in a flank squad.

In front of him marched a recruit named Fletcher who bunked in the same quonset. An almost immediate antipathy developed when they first met. Corporal Reid pejoratively called Fletcher "Goggles." Three others in the platoon who wore spectacles were likewise nicknamed. Fletcher's black-rimmed glasses were thick, enlarging his black eyes owlishly; without glasses, his left pupil shifted, misaligning with the right.

"Can't see eye-to-eye with him," Garson once quipped. Fletcher overhead the remark and never forgot it. There were other aspects that grated on Garson. Fletcher's mouth was crowded with stumpy, widely spaced teeth with virtually no gradation in size. More, he had no discernable lips at all, and at chow, his mouth reminded Garson of an ungulate chewing its cud. He knew little about Fletcher save that he was one of the Detroiters; the two never shared more than passing conversation.

The characteristic that most inflamed Garson was that Fletcher could not march; he loped, he ambled, he bounced. His head was large, outsized for his potato body and stumpy legs. A finely-honed marching platoon flows, all heads rising and falling in unison with every step like sea swells. From his vantage near the rear, Garson could appreciate the precision. But Fletcher's head popped up at every footfall; he was always a bit out of step.

"Dammit, Fletcher," Garson murmured in the Boot's ear. "Get the fuck in step, man!" Taking a page from the junior DI's playbook, Garson rode Fletcher unremittingly.

"Fuck you!" Fletcher muttered. "Fuck you!" In time, much more would come of this.

Platoon 023's younger drill instructor's faint eyelashes and brows connoted the same Gaelic ancestry as Garson's pal, Rusty. His face was also dusted with freckles. Even in the formal portrait that was printed in the commemorative book, he exhibited a crooked, cocksure smile.

"Fall out for wash call!" Wash call, when recruits marched to the open air clothes scrub racks, was voluntary. That day, recruits speculated, Reid wanted simply to relieve the monotony of his weekend duty. Only about 30 formed on the platoon street. The junior DI was livid.

"Zero-Two-Three, fall out for fuckin' wash call, every last swingin' dick!" The meaning was clear: Everyone was required to clean clothes this day, needed or not. Ranks formed, each recruit hugging the scrub bucket to his chest.

"Now, you fuckin' people will duck walk to the wash racks," Reid commanded. Every recruit squatted on his haunches. Duck walking became one of the most excruciating exercises devised by drill instructors. At the command to march, Garson and others dragged one leg in front of the other like a flock of fowl, not permitted to rise even a bit to relieve cramped muscles and strained tendons. Within ten to 20 yards, Garson's thighs, calves, knees were ablaze in agony. His lungs audibly sucked in air. Reid counted cadence, but it was impossible to mind the step.

"Now because you look like fuckin' ducks, I want you to sound like fuckin' ducks. Quack! Let's hear it!" Garson knew the others felt as foolish as he did.

The corporal halted the platoon two or three times with a

voracious harangue to mind the cadence. The distance to the wash racks was hundred yards – Garson felt it may have been a mile; several times, he thought he could not make the distance. He was in agony. Some one dropped his bucket, and Reid glared. When they were halted, the combined gasping for breath and gulping air sounded like a chuffing steam engine.

"I hate Reid," Garson said to nodded agreement.

They dutifully scrubbed clothing with brush and bar soap at the long line of slanted racks, each with a cold water spigot. There was no way to extract all soap residue in cold water rinsing, even when a pair of recruits twisted dungarees between them. The lack of proper rinsing coupled with clothes drying in the hot California sun caused light green dye to take on a faded hue after several weeks. But the so-called "salty" appearance became a badge of pride for recruits, an overt sign that they were gaining Boot Camp longevity.

The more acclimated some Boots grew, the more they became conduits for scuttlebutt that invariably permeated the platoon. Most of the rumor was without source or veracity.

"You know they put saltpeter in the chow," offered Buchman a few weeks later. He was another of the Milwaukee recruits who had traveled to MCRD with Garson and the others. Perhaps 18, he seemed more worldly than many in Platoon 023. One of the taller platoon members, he was a dropout from West Division High. Garson recalled that prior to MCRD shearing, his hair was the color of corn, and wiry eyebrows were diffuse. All of his teeth had been extracted the second week at MCRD. Like Springer, some of Buchman's words were slurred like an old man's.

"When I was a kid, they called me 'lemon head.' I fuckin' hated it. But my old lady said I was special 'cause my hair was like the sun." He was usually given to more titillating information.

"They put saltpeter in the food here, you know. Yeah, that's how they keep you from getting a hard on." While Garson and other recruits were somewhat skeptical about that information, they were fascinated when Buchman described a drink additive called Spanish Fly, said to make girls pliant and frisky. Garson had heard of the substance before, putatively a kind of aphrodisiac; yet, despite Buchman's emphatic testimonial, he doubted such a potion existed outside of novels and movies.

Buchman was one of several recruits who had a girlfriend. His sweetheart wrote frequently, and until told otherwise, printed "S.W.A.K." – Sealed With A Kiss — on the envelope flap. Corporal Reid enjoyed seeing these letters at mail call. Boots like Garson without girlfriends took secret pleasure in the exercise.

"What's this, some fuckin' pussy mail, shitbird? Any fuck pictures in here?" The envelope was opened on the spot, and Reid riffled the sheet to insure no snapshots were included. DIs seemed puritanical and censorious. Chaste, formal portraits were tolerated, but provocative poses and nudes were absolutely prohibited.

"Now eat that SWAK shit!" Buchman blanched, his Adam's apple bounced.

"Eat it, sir?"

"I want you to put it in your mouth, and chew it 20 times like you mommy told you. Then fuckin' swallow it. Right here! Right now!" Mail call was halted and the entire platoon waited.

Buchman's eyes bulged as he gingerly placed the envelope in his mouth. He chewed, hoping to rend the paper into small pieces with his bare gums. Finally, he forced down the wad with an audible swallow. Reid ordered him back to the ranks. Should an envelope be adorned with an actual lipstick kiss, it provided similar fodder. That ordeal was repeated many times until every girlfriend was informed to eschew such markings.

Garson waited for several weeks to hear from Betsy, in fact waited in vain, knowing their relationship was tenuous. He was confident that Lana, his childhood "sister," would not add such envelope adornment. When her letters arrived, they were filled with news of their Villard Avenue friends, and reports of extra-curricular activities at Custer High, including her hope that she would be featured in a school musical review.

There was another matter that came quickly to the fore at MCRD. Some of the more gastronomically robust, like Hupner, avoided any difficulty, but most, like Garson, suffered distress adjusting to the new diet. Intestinal concerns became the subject of conversation.

"Man, I got the shits," was a common complaint; others called the malady the "trots," "Tennessee quickstep," or "thin and dirtys." Relatedly, the lack of privacy for bodily functions took some getting used to: The atmosphere in the Head was noisome, almost noxious. Garson long prided himself on developing an efficient inner clock, and he learned to anticipate reveille by many minutes, time enough to trot to the Head ahead of the morning rush to gain some privacy.

Garson had never been a true smoker as a youth. He puffed cigarettes as a teen out of affectation not addiction. In Boot Camp, it became a habit. It was a release even though smoking was only permitted at times designated by a DI.

Normally, the platoon was informed before entering the mess hall that the smoking lamp was lighted after chow. Those who were hooked on the sot weed raced through the meal to gain time to smoke two cigarettes before the platoon was marched off. They assembled in a sandy field behind the mess hall in sight of Lindbergh Field, the commercial airport adjacent to MCRD.

"Field strip your butts," was another smoking related directive. When the cigarette was finished, procedure demanded a strict routine.

"You will extinguish the butt, then tear the paper down the seam." Corporal Reid held up a cigarette, demonstrating in words of mock solemnity. "You will then scatter the tobacco to the four winds, roll the paper into a tight, tiny ball and discard it." Reid further explained the rationale: In combat, Marines must not reveal the location of bivouacs with discarded butts. The tiny balls were less visible to the enemy. Garson was skeptical, as the sandy assembly area was salted with thousands of miniscule paper wads.

"The smoking lamp is lit for one cigarette" could mean either of two things – each Boot was permitted to smoke one cigarette, or, when a DI meted out punishment for some shortcoming, it meant one cigarette for the entire platoon. As Reid or Maddox watched, the lone cigarette was ceremoniously handed to the Right Guide

Barker positioned at the far right of the unit. He did not smoke, but simply got it alight from a drill instructor's match, then handed the cigarette to the Boot on his left.

Each smoker, in turn, took a single, shallow puff and passed it on. Waiting for the cigarette, Garson remembered a similar routine in boys' high school lavatory: He had been suspended for that infraction twice during his junior year. Since Garson, one of the "feather merchants," formed near the end of the fourth squad, the communal platoon cigarette was a veritable torch when it arrived. Carefully pinching the stub and inhaling quickly, Garson lungs rebelled against the searing heat.

The Texan, McCracken, claimed he had smoked steadily since he was 12. He was addicted to nicotine. He clandestinely smoked despite threats and punishments. On several occasions he was discovered, once even caught puffing inside the steel waste dumpster. He was given extra duties, made to stand at attention while others were at ease, and more. After several incidents, cigarettes from the entire platoon were confiscated.

"If one a you fucks up," Reid explained, "everybody suffers. Everybody's gotta learn that one fuck-up can undermine an entire unit. One fuck-up in combat can jeopardize an entire platoon, even a battalion. One fuck-up can lose a battle. It's up to all of you to straighten him out."

Garson reluctantly took part in the blanket party planned for McCracken. It was not that he hated the big-headed, porcine Texan, albeit he was repulsed by the Boot's utter ugliness. Garson was a member of a unit that needed to take disciplinary matters into its own hands. Some hours after "Taps" one night, every recruit in McCracken's hut rendezvoused near his bunk. Four men held him in place and muffled his mouth. With soap bars inside pillow covers, 15 recruits flailed at the miscreant. The next morning, he stumbled from his bunk, with a reddened cheek; some who saw him in the shower said his bulky body was covered in bruises. A day later, when the drill instructors learned of the blanket party, all but McCracken's cigarettes were returned.

"Goggles." Reid pointed to another of the Platoon 023 Boots

who wore spectacles. His name was Priech, pronounced "Pree-ch." Garson sniggered at an early roll call when he heard it. He surmised that the ungainly recruit had, as a child, been the target of teasing and harassment over that family name.

"Name's what? Preek?" Like many, Reid had difficulty pronouncing the German "ch" sound; it sounded like "k."

"Sir, no, sir. Priech," the recruit said gutturally. Garson was unable to see the Boot's expression, but he *knew* that his eyes were nervous.

"Says here its spelled P-R-I-E-C-H, " Reid looked down at the roster.

"Priech." The recruit stressed the "e."

"Could it be Prick? Like your short arm, your little dick?"

"Sir, no, sir!"

"You got a prick, Prick?"

"Sir, yes, sir."

"You a virgin, Prick?" The young man stood stonily, uncertain how to respond. Behind those thick lenses, his eyes fluttered.

For days, until the corporal tired of it, Priech was verbally assaulted. Of about Garson's height but with a doughy body, he carried his head in a sagging position, probably from the incessant browbeating, Garson thought. His cheeks and chin were always florid. Heavy footed, he was like Fletcher, another of those unsuited for the martial stride, of squaring shoulders, of digging heels into the concrete. He stomped rather that strutted; his arms sometimes swung the wrong way.

"Prick, get the fuck in step, goddammit! Lean back. Dig 'em in! Dig 'em in!"

"Why's he always grinding on me?" Priech later asked of no one in particular. With his right hand, he resettled the large glasses on his nose. One of the Detroiters said Reid's oral jabbing was something akin to a verbal game called "The Dozens" that colored guys played.

"They throw dirty insults at each another, even about mothers, like 'your mama wears combat boots and bays at the moon,' until one of 'em loses his cool." Garson and others agreed that the DIs' penchant for assaulting physical deficiencies, ethnic backgrounds and more was a test of a recruit's self-control.

Garson and Priech would be bunked in the same tent at the rifle range, and they got to know one another.

One of the regular duties required of all recruits was Fire Watch, to many a Marine in retrospect, a rather pointless and onerous Boot Camp activity. Its putative purpose was to be on alert for fire, and to sound the alarm when flames are spotted. From "Taps" to reveille, recruits patrolled the perimeter of the platoon's huts. Being awakened from deep slumber at midnight or two in the morning to stumble almost somnambulantly for two hours was an unforgettable experience.

More, every Boot was to commit 11 General Orders to memory, and to recite any and all upon command from a superior.

"Your General Orders are more important than the Ten Commandments" was another Boot Camp maxim.

Fifty years later, Garson could still, like a Catholic Mass server's Latin responses, rattle off many of them: "Number One. To take charge of this post and all government property in view. Two: To walk my post in a military manner, keeping always on the alert, and observing everything that takes place within sight or hearing."

Garson was anxious since he long had difficulty memorizing school subjects. He read the general orders incessantly, fearful lest he be challenged on fire watch. "General Order 11: To be especially watchful at night, and during the time for challenging, to challenge all persons on or near my post, and to allow no one to pass without proper authority." This last order would create a potentially serious offense for Garson in the months ahead.

Fire watch, particularly during the dark, quiet hours, was lonely. Garson's thoughts often turned to home. Civilian aircraft arrived and departed Lindbergh Field only a few hundred yards distant from the platoon's huts, and Garson for a time fantasized about vaulting the tall chain link fence, scampering across the runway to sneak aboard some east bound plane.

In addition to the swirl of physicals, exams and other matters that occupied those early weeks, the new recruits attended classes on numerous military matters. One of the first was a description of the UCMJ – the Uniform Code of Military Justice. Not that any of the platoon, Garson recalled, had more than passing experience with the civilian justice system. But having taken the oath to serve and defend the Constitution of the United States, an instructor emphasized, they were now under military jurisdiction. There would be no jury of peers to weigh evidence and decide guilt or innocence. Only Marine and Navy officers would sit in judgment for offenses. A captain's mast, the lowest level of judgment, to Special and General Court's Martial were described. It reminded Garson, he recollected, of something he had seen in the movies.

As important were lectures about the history, traditions and lore of the Corps, distinct from other armed services, instructors boasted. "*Semper Fidelis*" — Always Faithful. Slow and steady indoctrination was a regular classroom feature; much was not found in text books, however, but was the stuff of the oral tradition, myth and legend. Most Boots knew the first verse of the Marine Hymn; some, like Garson, had memorized it before enlisting. But the song had several verses that were soon committed to memory.

'If the Army and the Navy, ever look on heaven's scenes,' the last one intoned; 'they will find the streets are guarded by United States Marines.'"

From its pre-Revolutionary founding at Philadelphia's Tun Tavern in 1775, the Corps had fought in every war and military action of the nation, recruits were informed. They had served as ship boarding parties against the Barbary pirates, gaining the name "Leather Necks" for their protective collars; in the Mexican War, tradition had it, the red stripe on dress blue trousers was earned with blood at the Battle of Chapultepec; Marines fought during China's Boxer Rebellion, in the Spanish-American and First World War, where Germans identified them as *Teufel Hunden,* "Devil Dogs. Marines were most valorous in the World War II Pacific and Korea. They became Gyrenes and to disparaging sailors, Jarheads and sea-going bellhops because shipboard Marines were disliked for their duties as hard-case shipboard sentinels and brig guards.

MCRD lectures highlighted incidents and tales of legendary Marines, especially enlisted men — heroes like Sergeant Dan Daly who rallied his men at Belleau Wood in France against attacking Germans during the Great War with the famed lines: "Come on, you sons of bitches. Do you want to live forever?" He won two Medals of Honor.

The most decorated Marine in history was Colonel Lewis "Chesty" Puller who had led units in such harrowing actions as Guadalcanal, the Solomons, Pelilu, Tarawa and Iwo Jima, and later in Korea. Profane to the last, he once balked when underage Marines were denied liquor.

"Give my boys booze and broads," he demanded. He earned medals at Korea's Chosin Resevoir, where the Corps, surrounded by invading Chinese, battled their way to safety, carrying with them every dead and wounded Marine and piece of equipment. They were not retreating, the story had it, they were advancing in another direction. The only heroes Garson regarded before Boot Camp were screen idols – Wayne, Flynn, Power, Lancaster and others.

In 1953, the Marine Corps November 10th birthday was the Tuesday of the third week at MCRD. The day was appropriately sunny and mid 70s. It was the 178th anniversary of the Corps's founding in Philadelphia – a year before the Revolution itself, the instructor boasted. It was the *only* day on the Marine calendar. Christmas, New Year, Independence, Decoration and Labor Days all paled in comparison to that anniversary. Special chow was prepared, and recruits feasted on a repast of Thanksgiving proportions. Corporal Reid was somewhat less onerous that day, and the following morning his sclera were striated red, and the odor of alcohol wafted from him.

When he served a weekend duty earlier, it was whispered that the corporal clandestinely consumed alcohol. Rumor had it that while cleaning the Duty Hut on Monday morning, an empty pint of what someone said was Old Smiley Apple Wine was found in the trash can. During those first four weeks, Reid seemed unrelenting, unmerciful, a hard-bitten disciplinarian who tolerated no deviation or mishap. It may have been some weeks later; it was a Sunday, Garson remembered.

Loyalty to unit also involved personal hygiene. The biblical *Guidebook* stated that showers should be taken at least twice weekly, but Garson showered more frequently lest others buddies accuse him of being a "crud" – after cowardice in the face of the enemy or disloyalty, one of the most heinous offenses among Marines. A blanket party might result. There was good reason.

"If one of you people fails to keep himself clean and develops some kind of rash or creeping crud as a result, you can infect others. You let the Marines of your platoon down." Most of such lessons concerned combat.

"If you're cruddy and get sick, someone'll have to take care of you, reducing unit fighting strength, threatening combat effectiveness" one salty instructor stressed. To Garson, he carried an air of a battle-hardened vet. Even oral hygiene was important since bad teeth could also rob a Marine's fitness.

"If you're not combat ready, you knock out two Marines – the sick one and his buddy who's gotta help him to sick bay." Even DI's frowned on recruits who answered sick call, as Garson would discover. Like athletes, Marines nascent and real were expected to bear up to mere aches and pains.

An unofficial but ludicrous corollary to the necessity for cleanliness was abroad in Boot Camp, a warning to those who showered: "Don't drop the soap!" It required someone else to explain its significance to Garson.

Then there was the unrelenting issue venereal disease. Grainy war vintage films, marred by copious scratches and jarring jump cuts, dramatized scenes to impressionable servicemen who had fallen prey to bar girls and prostitutes. The narrator warned that any woman who made herself available probably bore disease. Garson squirmed in the darkness at the graphic depictions gonorrhea and, worst of all, syphilitic chancres that could lead to madness and death. It reminded him of those unsettling grade school Biblical tales of lepers.

Long decades later, Garson was amazed to discover that the training film, entitled "Sex Hygiene," had been created in 1940 by one of his favorite movie directors, John Ford.

"Keep your little dicks out of trouble. Keep 'em tucked in your skivvies," admonished the instructor, who tried for the most part to maintain stony seriousness. A few recruits thought they detected smirking pauses during his lecture.

"If you gotta dip your tiny dicks – get fucked — use a prophylactic, a rubber. And use only good quality ones like Trojans." Another film demonstrated how to roll a prophylactic on a glass test tube – simulating an erect penis — showing how it should be properly fitted. Garson surmised everyone could have figured that out. A few recruits snickered in the dark.

"If you gotta get fucked with a rubber, make certain to wash your little dick, scrotum and groin thoroughly — any area that touched the whore. Lather it up real good. And, for god's sake, don't eat any of that pussy. You'd be askin' for big trouble." Again the underlying message related to combat.

"If you go down with clap or gonorrhea or syph, you endanger your buddies. With you gone, they'll be one less in the fire team. A battle might be lost because one rifle was missing." The tone was ominous. To Garson, that message and the documentary film scenes of afflicted men kept him, all but once, from patronizing what he referred to as "business women." Insinuated, but unrecognized in all of this was the propagation of a warrior ethos that, coupled with Old Testament chauvinism, viewed women as temptresses, willing or unwilling vessels, no better than pliant helpmates. During these months at MCRD Garson and others were severed from the world they knew, and purged of civilian purposes and values. In place, the Marine Corps inculcated its potent philosophy, attitudes and outlook.

It was mid-November that Platoon 023 was marched to the base armory, and there issued M-1 rifles, the potent .30 caliber Garand that had served so dependably in World War II and Korea.

Garson immediately memorized the weapon's serial number. He was somewhat chagrinned, noting that the manufacturer was International Harvester, the farm implement maker. He had hoped for something classic and steady like a Springfield.

Also issued that day was what was identified as 782 gear – webbed ammunition belt, bayonet and scabbard, canvas back pack, canteen, poncho and other combat equipment. All this was in preparation for the second phase of recruit training – rifle training at the Camp Matthews range that was miles to the north of San Diego. The platoon was scheduled to depart on the Sunday before Thanksgiving.

San Diego featured the country's most even-tempered climate. Most days were beautifully balmy, unlike Milwaukee whose temperatures at that time of year were depressing into the 40s with dreary gray skies. Daytime MCRD temperatures averaged in high 60s with a few days rising into the 80s. There was only a trace of precipitation until mid November when it rained on two days. Garson could appreciate the conditions, for back home, he knew, diminished daylight heralded freezing nights and winter on the near horizon.

Pay days for Marines was the first and 15th of every month. That meant Garson received about the same amount of money he had earned on his paper route when he was a kid. Paid in cash, money could be spent at Marine Exchange to purchase cigarettes, toiletries and sundries, but not used for such prohibited food stuffs as candy bars, temptingly displayed on shelves. Called "Pogey Bait," a corruption of the Chinese word for whore, candy became an obsession to some recruits who calculated means to obtain the forbidden fruit. Coin operated machines were situated at several sites in MCRD's quonset city, available only to DIs and permanent staff. The nickel dispensers were as shimmering oases to thirsty Bedouins, but always out of reach, chimeras, mirages almost. Some Boots would pay a dollar for a coin in an effort to garner sweet morsels. They joined peanut butter and jelly sandwiches as treats worth the price of gold.

"Who's this fuckin' fat boy?" It was Corporal Reid again, focused on another target, a recruit who stood out in Platoon 023 because of his uncommon rotundity in the platoon's collection of slenderness, Garson and others especially.

"Sir, the recruit's name is Brtek, sir." He used the Americanized pronunciation, "Bartek." His high-pitched voice was almost comic.

"Brtek, huh? Polish?"

"Sir, no, sir." He knew Reid's routine, and did not want to reveal too much.

"Don't you even know what the fuck you are, fuckin' shit for brains? *Jee-zus!*" Reid bored in, his eyes ablaze, enjoying the confrontation. "Think I'll call you Polish sausage, or maybe lard ass. That OK with you, fat boy?"

"Sir, yes, sir."

"You lard-assed fuck, get those double chins tucked in." While he felt guilt, Garson and several of the smaller recruits took their cue from the junior DI to bait Brtek. He stood an inch or so taller than Garson, but his girth, at the outset of Boot Camp, deprived him of agility to counter the teasing feints and darts of his harriers; he quickly flagged in a chase. Garson could not recall seeing anyone that round among his friends and acquaintances back home. Dimples were visible where fingers met his palms, and he had a Kirk Douglas cleft at the point of his chin.

"You might be the weak link in the chain, Polish sausage" Reid proclaimed. "Being fat is a weakness. You gotta keep up. You can't fall out because you're fuckin' fat." Brtek bore up surprisingly.

"Looks like a beach ball with legs," Rusty whispered behind the shield of his hand. But the portly recruit, another Detroiter, came to reveal uncommon intelligence and amiability. He was not of Polish heritage at all, but Bohemian, those smoky-eyed, swarthy minions of dubious lineage that Garson's father called "Bo-hunks."

An integral part of recruit training, of course, involved a steady physical regimen, but Garson found little pleasure in hours of physical conditioning. While he had no difficulty running and jogging, his slender, unmuscular frame and attenuated limbs struggled at jumping jacks, chin ups and push ups. He strained vaulting barriers, climbing ropes and nets; they caused aches and strains, at least for a time. But he was confident that after these first weeks at MCRD, he was gaining some tone and definition to his body.

"Hey, you, muscles," sniped Corporal Reid at a tall and broad recruit during an exercise session in the sandy expanse between the quonsets and Lindberg Field.

"Sir?" Garson knew the recruit as Collins, another Milwaukee Boot, who tried to maintain a low profile in the unit.

"How'd you get so fuckin' big?" Henna-headed Reid was a small man, perhaps the size of Garson's friend Rusty with a narrow physique. Collins dwarfed him.

"Big, sir?"

"You know, shit for brains, fuckin' *big* – all those muscles?"

"Layin' bricks, I guess, sir. With my dad."

"Why, you're a real fuckin' Charles-At-Last, ain't you! A real John Wayne Jones."

"S'pose so, sir." Reid was what was later called an equal opportunity tormenter, but this was the last confrontation Garson recalled. The recruit platoon would soon be out of his clutches. The night before the unit was slated to uproot and depart for rifle training at Camp Matthews, Garson's mind played a jumble of disparate scenes, like a poorly-edited movie. He wondered when Betsy would write, even worried that somehow his mother had not gotten his address to her. He had received two letters from his mother, pencil written sheets with news of work and relatives; his father had added a few labored lines. He had a dream of his mother that night, in her white uniform, washing dishes at Shorty's Restaurant on Villard Avenue where he had worked as a busboy – so long ago now, it seemed.

Chapter 2

GUTTIG

Guttig, Garson's grandfather, was a bastard.

As remembered from childhood, he was a kindly, laconic man, a gentle caregiver and protector. That was the reason Garson gave him the name Guttig, derived from the German word for good – *gut* — and pronounced "Goo-tich." He considered naming him Fleischer for a time, but that meant flesh or meat, and for a man of average stature and not overly generous girth, that connoted too much.

More, Garson toyed with Germanic sounding names for others in the narrative such as Frische (fresh), Spieler (player), Essig (vinegar) and the like to provide character clues. He favored such a Dickensian device.

Garson was not yet eight when his grandfather died during the Second World War, so only disparate, indistinct impressions of the man remain. When writing about it as an elder of Guttig's age himself, Garson found it difficult to sufficiently lift memory's shroud more than a few inches on those early childhood years. Further, he struggled to separate his recollections from those of his mother and aunts who virtually reverenced their father.

What is certain, among all the missing facts and amid embroidered family history and selective memories is that Guttig lived the first half of his life in Europe and the latter half in Wisconsin – many years in rural Dodge County and almost two decades in Milwaukee. He sired three daughters, the youngest of whom was Garson's mother, before coming to America where three sons were born.

One clear image remained — a cabinet card of Guttig, rigid in a high-necked Hungarian army uniform that revealed little beyond youthful physical appearance: A square head, pale eyes, taut thin lips, mustache, jutting chin and hair closely cropped in the military manner.

There were several other candid photos from later in his grandfather's life that Garson recalled, many out of focus or of Guttig out of frame; in some of these, he even exhibited reticence before the camera. But the cabinet card and other images were all incinerated in a house fire. Garson was able to assemble only a few duplicates and photocopies to augment his meager memory.

Not a tall man, Guttig's body was square; during Garson's infancy, his grandfather carried a few extra pounds after a dreadful accident that disabled him into a sedentary life. A widower then, he became his grandson's caregiver and early mentor.

As recorded at Ellis Island, Guttig's complexion was florid. His narrow eyes were blue, unlike his two older daughters who took their earthy coloration from their mother, Garson's grandmother. Guttig's mouth was wide and his nose generous – the latter feature passed to most of his children and grandson. He always cultivated a mustache, sometimes brushy and other times wispy and trim. Save for occasional moments when a bit of sweet red wine loosened his inhibitions, he was taciturn, a man of serious mien and formality. Garson unsuccessfully scoured his memory to recall the tone or timber of Guttig's voice, but it must have contained some vestiges of a Germanic or Magyar accent.

To Garson, his mother invariably contrasted her father with her husband, reminding the boy that Guttig always maintained a cleaned, pressed suit and shined shoes for Sunday mass. Guttig shared a bedroom with his grandson, and Garson seemed to recall those clothes carefully hung and shoes neatly arrayed in the closet. From duplicate images Garson cadged from cousins and aunts after the house fire had destroyed family photos, Guttig was usually depicted wearing a suit and tie, certainly no less than a vest. In winter, he wore a long, dark overcoat and a mannerly Hamburg hat.

The writer, Louise Erdrich observed in one of her novels that "if there is embellishment [in family history], it only had to do with facts." I thought my Pop sometimes laid on facts more than necessary as you'll see. I think sections sound like dull, dry genealogy, even high school history. Facts stalled the narrative. Now, I wasn't a good student of history and haven't read much about Milwaukee, so let that judgment pass.

Guttig traced his distant ancestry to southwestern Germany. During the 18th and 19th centuries, his forebears answered enticements from the Habsburg rulers to immigrate to lands in Hungary ravaged by over 150 years of warfare with the Ottomans. Tens of thousands came, and the Magyars called the new settlers "Swabians," from the region of their origin.

The German émigrés usually lived side by side with other ethnic groups. Garson long ruminated about his mother's antipathy, downright suspicion of Bohemians, Slovenes and Czechs – all of whom, in her mind, exhibited shadowy countenances and shady habits. She created a clear European caste system with Slavs and frightful gypsies near the bottom of civilization with Germans and Austrians perched at the pinnacle.

Teutonic émigrés were reputed to be better farmers, and most master craftsmen were German – millers, tailors, shoemakers, masons and others. Many Swabians had assimilated to such a degree that some modified their family names to Magyar versions; a similar practice played out in America. Thus, Guttig was baptized Janos and not Johan; and his wife and second daughter bore the name Terez not Theresa.

When Guttig immigrated to America three decades later, his birth year was recorded as 1872. This created a documentary discrepancy because his Wisconsin gravestone cited August 18, 1871 as the date. Such were the inconsistencies of his history.

The village of Kisdorog in Hungary is situated some 75 miles southwest of the twin cities of Buda and Peste. Garson's cousin, Jean, keeper of family genealogy, traveled to the town, conversed with distant Guttig relatives and paged through old church records to find facts to support or rebut family legend. What she learned was unsettling to Guttig's daughters. Jean recalled whispered conversations she had with one aunt, Terez, about her father's paternity. Garson's mother, the youngest daughter, never revealed any of this to her son, fearful perhaps that it would tarnish the revered reputation of her father. Guttig's mother, documents revealed, was unwed when she bore him.

It might be concluded that a single woman with a child in that era would have suffered ostracism. But to Jean's amazement, she discovered that one-third of all births in those years were illegitimate. In one family story, Guttig was given his mother's surname and not that of his sire. Other relatives were said to know more details, but they died before Garson showed any interest in such matters. So it is left to meager facts augmented with surmise and speculation to complete his grandfather's story. Was Guttig's progenitor a Swabian or a Hungarian? In a flight of dramatic fancy, Garson mused that perhaps some passing Magyar royal might have tussled with his great-grandmother in a rude bed or pile of stable straw.

When he was five, as attested by official records, Guttig's mother married the town tailor, Herr Gith; he was not the father of the bastard boy and refused to give the child his name. The new couple soon had a daughter, Margaret, and moved to another town; Guttig remained to work as a youthful hired field hand near the village of his birth. The tailor was understandably repelled by another man's leavings.

It was dark, affable and gregarious Aunt Terez who provided Cousin Jean with a different twist to the family saga. She said that Guttig's real father had indeed married the boy's mother before the birth. But that man, she claimed, Herr Guttig, died after being badly burned in a kiln fire. Here, of course, was a story that removed taint from Guttig's origin.

"Our grandfather loved his mother very much, and he trudged many miles to visit her each Sunday," Terez explained. In truth, however, Garson's cousin discovered from records in Kisdorog, that Guttig's mother never married her son's sire. The only marriage recorded was to the tailor Gith. When Garson's cousin confronted her aunt with these facts, she expressed disbelief.

"She refused to accept that documentation," Garson's cousin related; "I felt she didn't want to accept the story of her father's illegitimacy, and I didn't push it."

"I think that the true story began to fray our grandfather's tether to the country of his birth," Garson's cousin surmised. His attachment to his mother and her new family was fraught with difficulty, and his prospects as a common laborer were limited.

When Guttig came of age, compulsory military service in the Dual Monarchy of Austria and Hungary required every man to serve three years of active service. At this point, family legend again intrudes. Grandpa, his daughters always insisted, acted as a servant or valet for none other than the emperor, old Franz Josef, who turned 66 about this time. White hair everywhere but on the top of his head and fearsome mutton chop whiskers lining his craggy face, the ancient ruler was given to military uniforms bedecked with a score of gaudy medallions. As Emperor of Austria, King of Bohemia and Apostolic King of Hungary since 1848, he resided in the opulent yellow baroque palace of Schönbrunn in Vienna, hundreds of miles from Kisdorog, Hungary.

That a landless, bastard son of an unknown sire might have gained a position at the right hand of the emperor is unlikely. But some evidence supported the tale. There was, first, that cabinet card image, destroyed in the house fire, of trim Guttig in military uniform that Garson clearly remembered. As a boy, Garson also played with his grandfather's sword, a weapon that featured a simple steel blade, an unadorned brass handle and hilt designed for a non-commissioned officer, In the basement where it was stored, Garson parried and thrust with the weapon, aping his boyhood idol, Errol Flynn. Some years later, he lamented selling that sword for a few dollars during his early teen years, feeling he had somehow betrayed his grandfather. While Guttig's military service seems a certainty, Garson discounted the tale of a body servant to an emperor.

Sometime before the new century, Guttig fulfilled his military service. Living in a village east of Kisdorog, he met a comely maid named Terez Schwarz. She, Garson's grandmother, died two years before his birth so he had only photos and the recollections of others to guide him. Terez had tawny complexion, high cheekbones and dark, deep-set eyes that were passed to a grandson she did not live to see. Her surname was decidedly Germanic, but her features bespoke of something more exotic, more Mittel than Western Europe — at least in Garson's vision.

"Did you ever hear any stories about how grandpa met grandma?" Garson asked his Cousin Jean. She did not know, and he lamented that question was not posed to his aunts and mother before they died. He may have constructed a romantic episode from such facts.

So Garson was free to speculate at a distant remove about when Guttig eyed a slender, dark-haired girl four years his junior as she strolled about the town in her fetching dirndl and carrying a market basket. She, a tailor's daughter, must have been a striking woman in her youth. How long they courted is unknown. How he characterized himself to Terez and her family is only conjecture. Did he reveal the truth of his paternity? Did it matter? It is probable that her father offered no dowry or prospects for a marriage. But in only a decade after the union, Guttig would acquire sufficient funds to book passage to America for himself, and, only a year later, for his family as well.

Janos and Terez married sometime prior to the arrival of the new century. He was about 26 or 27. Their first daughter was born in 1900. A second girl, christened with her mother's given name, arrived two years later; the youngest daughter, Garson's mother, was born in 1904. It was perplexing to Garson that his mother, Maria, eschewed her given name as an adult because it was insufficiently American. Interesting, too, was this: As a child, she was anxious to disguise her immigrant roots yet failed to naturalize as a United States citizen until she was 40.

Two of the Guttig's girls, the oldest, Eva, and last born, took favor from their fair father – light skin, hair and eyes — while the middle daughter clearly carried the darker features of her mother. She, Terez, of the dusky skin, flashing, nut brown eyes, high cheekbones and ready smile, had an infectious laugh; her speech was tinged with slight Old World inflections. As a boy, Garson was always drawn to this aunt for reasons he could not articulate. Perhaps it was because she bore that "taint" of Magyar. His own mother demurred when he suggested it, insisting that the family was purely Austrian, even listing that nationality on her marriage certificate.

What provided the ultimate impetus for Guttig to immigrate to America was lost to Garson's generation. But late in the old century, government reaction to worker unrest caused legislation banning unionism and strikes. A laborer like Guttig earned a miserly 134 florints annually – precious little for a family. A financial depression created more hardships. Guttig likely was acquainted with people who had uprooted from Hungary for America. A departure rate to the new nation grew from thousands annually when Guttig was born to a floodtide of four times that when he began the odyssey to America. In all, about 600,000 Catholic Hungarians reached America before the second quarter of the new century.

With $30 or $40 for a steerage ticket, Guttig made his way 250 miles southwest to the Austrian port of Fiume on the Adriatic coast. There he booked passage aboard Cunard's White Star Line steamship, "Carpathia." The handsome vessel, only four years in service, featured a single funnel and four masts. At over 550-feet, its three decks provided accommodations for 100 first and 200 second passengers. Guttig settled among 2250 steerage travelers. Likely in a dark suit, high top shoes, hat and carrying a battered valise, he fitted himself into a lower deck birth amid tiers of bunks and common sanitary facilities. Garson visualized such crowded, cramped and noisome quarters from the movies of his childhood.

At the end of the three-week Atlantic passage, Guttig disembarked, and with thousands of others, was herded onto one of the waiting ferry boats that shuttled new arrivals across to Ellis Island. There is no record or recollection of Guttig's initial impression of the colossal copper-clad Statue of Lady Liberty that arose above a spit of land nearby. What impressions came to his mind at his first glimpse of teeming New York City with its scores of docks, expansive bridges and dramatic collection of soaring buildings, edifices and church spires? Certainly, he had never before seen such a metropolis. At age 35, did he feel that he was on the threshold of realizing a dream?

Valises and grip sacks firmly in hand, passengers entered the steel-framed red brick immigration center, four 100-foot copper-covered towers rose at each corner; massive arches with molded eagles and shields capped many windows. Inside, the arrivals traipsed up a wide stairway to the registry room, a massive space with a soaring ceiling. Guttig shuffled along narrow aisles divided by iron railings, the miasma of thousands of unwashed bodies permeating the premises. A large portrait of a robust American president, Theodore Roosevelt, hung on one wall. Was Guttig's heart hammering, his breath shallow?

An official verified Guttig's name against the steamship's manifest. He was listed at just under five-feet-six, and recorded his weight of 147 pounds. Another man in a blue uniform squeezed the muscles of Guttig's arms, and pounded his chest with the flat of his hand; he also painfully lifted the newcomer's eyelids with a button hook, checking for disease, particularly trachoma that would bar any immigrant from entering the United States. Further, the middle-aged German-Hungarian was asked several questions in his native tongue; his answers evinced no sign of feeble-mindedness.

According to a history of Ellis Island, Guttig arrived during an ongoing debate about immigration. Influential forces demanded stricter rules for admission, fearing the deluge of immigrants would depress wages; many native Americans were concerned that some immigrants could not earn a living and would become "public charges;" others demanded that those with physical and mental impairments be denied entry; still others argued for intelligence testing, even English fluency. The average immigrant of this era carried about $9, but there was discussion about raising the requirement to $25 plus a rail ticket to the ultimate destination.

Between 1903 and 1907, three and a half million immigrants entered the United States, most passing through Ellis Island; Guttig was among the million who shuffled through the gateway the year he arrived. Spring and fall were the peak months of arrival, nearly three thousand passing the reception center daily.

Guttig, family history averred, held a rail ticket to Wisconsin where he had made contact with a family of German-Hungarians living there; they may have been sponsors who promised work. The state bore a clear stamp of Germanism on its map. Readily identified were towns and communities with names such as Fussville, Freistadt, Hustisford, Germania, New Holstein, Rhinelander, not to mention Germantown, Berlin, Hamburg, Bavaria and Wirtenberg.

Milwaukee, where Guttig likely found language comfort, was once known as *Deutsch-Athen,* the German Athens, on Lake Michigan. While Garson still had many uncertainties about Guttig's early years in the state, family legend revealed that he initially worked in back-breaking circumstances with hundreds of immigrants – Poles, Czechs, Slovaks, Italians, Hungarians and others. As a common laborer, he mucked out a river bottom preparing footings for expansion of Gimbel Brothers department store in the central business district.

The gleaming building stood on the west bank of the Milwaukee River, facing the main thoroughfare of the city, Grand Avenue. Guttig and other workers constructed a coffer dam in the water before deeper pilings could be imbedded below the surface. When the refurbished Gimbel Store was completed, white stone cladding covered the full five stories, and featured *trompe l'oeil* Corinthian columns that contrasted sharply with its garish commercial neighbors.

During months of wielding pick, shovel and carrying buckets of river muck and shoring lumber, Guttig could not help but notice that the iron swing bridge over the Milwaukee River. He must have noticed that the streets between east and west sides of the city did not align; every downtown bridge stood catty wampus to the other shore. Some of workers may have heard the history of two separate and competing towns of the last century that refused to align their streets with the rival.

When Guttig lived in the city, Milwaukee retained a distinct stamp of Germanism despite the fact that in recent decades it had become a polyglot Lake Michigan metropolis of almost 375,000. Half of the residents were either German immigrants or their sons and daughters.

Everywhere Germanism was evident: Pabst, Schlitz, Blatz and Miller were the large brewers of the day; Pfister, Vogel, Tröstle were prospering tanners while machinery works such as Harnischfeger were growing. The Pabst Building, soaring to its German baroque peak, stood across the river from Gimbel Brothers; a few blocks to the north, the goddess of liberty, Germania, raised her arm from the upper reaches of a building bearing her name; and the solid Pfister Hotel on Wisconsin Street east of the river was the desired destination for visitors. Streets such as Teutonia, Volkman, Fiebrantz and others ranged on city maps. German beer gardens and saloons and Turnverein gymnastic societies all proclaimed Teutonism in the city's fabric. An opulent mansion blocks west of the river on Grand Avenue, once owned by a Milwaukee railroad and banking magnate, now boasted the name *Deutscher* Club.

In less than a year, Guttig sailed back to Europe, gathering wife and three daughters, now ages eight, six and nearly four. By the same route he took before, he led his family to the Dalmatian coast, and again aboard the *Carpathia*.

"Our grandmother was very uneasy about the voyage," Garson's Cousin Jean knew. "The presence of our grandpa apparently steadied her nerve enough during the weeks-long passage through the Mediterranean and across the cold, roiling Atlantic Ocean. "She had been very worried about the voyage," having never dreamed about such an expanse of troubling waves. But Guttig, already having experienced such a voyage, knew the rhythm and roll of the ship, and eased his wife's anxieties.

For whatever it's worth, my Pop found it without note to mention that three years after his grandparent's voyage, the White Star line vessel on which they sailed became famous when it was dispatched to rescue passengers from its sinking sister ship, Titanic.

It was documented that the family arrived in New York on March 26, 1908.

Likely, since Guttig had already passed through the immigration procedure, he eased the family's angst amid the Ellis Island cacophony. The three daughters were not mature enough to display more than impatience at the long lines, and none remembered the poking and prodding of medical teams. As adults, they never mentioned the cruel button hooks used to peel back eyelids. Neither Terez nor the girls exhibited any signs of mental instability or feeblemindedness, and were permitted to enter the United States.

There existed a formal portrait of Guttig and his daughters taken at this time, a photocopy obtained from one of his relatives of a cabinet card image personified the new immigrant experience. Guttig sat in a chair, a broad, bushy mustache accenting a satisfied expression. Wearing a dark suit and collarless shirt, a dark fedora perched on the back of his head – as though the photographer wanted to avoid shading his face. The girls, standing in pretty, knee-length dresses with puffy sleeves and high, button shoes, wore large bows in their hair. It is obvious that Garson's mother's hair was golden. Her left hand rested on her father's knee.

Guttig's name appeared in Milwaukee's city directory for 1909. The family resided in one of the German wards west of the Milwaukee River, a waterway that cut through the 65-year-old city, separating one half of the town from the other. He was listed as a laborer.

Garson once thought it may have been heartening had his grandfather achieved great things as a farmer or entrepreneur, or attained high political office or notoriety. But such was not the case, for Guttig was, as millions of his brethren, no more than a man of common means and attainment. With his wife, he did raise what in time became six children, leaving many memories of a kind, caring father and grandfather.

After an unspecified time living in Milwaukee, the family boarded a Chicago, Milwaukee & St. Paul railcar for the trip to the Dodge County hamlet of Rubicon where other Germanic acquaintances waited. Everywhere in the township family names such as Hauser, Moser, Gehring, Pieper, Neu, Schmitt, Weiss, Roethle and Kling were evident. His oldest daughters, in fact, would marry into two of those rural clans.

The landscape of gentle, undulating hills, small creeks and streams, and patchwork of farmsteads and fields, may have reminded Guttig of Hungary. Wheat, oats, barley, rye, corn and hay were dominant crops; dairying was gaining favor in the state.

Since plat maps of the era evinced no Guttig name, the family must have rented acreage. It might be surmised that Guttig regained the rhythms of farming since that had been his occupation as a young man in Hungary. Milking cows, slopping hogs, tending to livestock were regular farm routines while seeding, tilling, harvesting, thrashing, shucking and more were seasonal demands. It is clear from informal oral history that the Guttig girls spent considerable time at such farm chores. While Garson's aunts talked about it without rancor, his mother grimaced at the memory of those demands.

There must have been something in the air or water of America, Garson mused, that caused his grandfather to sire three sons in the new country. The oldest boy, named after his father, was born in 1910. The second followed three years later, and the final child born in 1915. The girls were German-Hungarians, and the boys Americans. Guttig was 44 when his last son was born; his wife was 40.

About the time the Guttig family put down roots in Rubicon, St. John's Church listed 70 families with 32 students attending its school. Sisters of St. Francis with names such as Euphrosina, Tharcissia and Annuntiata taught the six grades while the pastor, Father Maas, provided religious instruction.

Garson's mother, four years old when the family arrived in America, had no clear memory of Hungary, save, perhaps, recollections repeated from parents or sisters. She among the girls had no trace of accent, and wanted to be considered an American. When she left the house for school, she removed earrings her mother insisted she wear.

"Pierced ears were a sure sign you were from the old country. I didn't want kids in school to know," she told Garson at the remove of many years. "I didn't want to be an immigrant." On her way home from school, she replaced the earrings so her mother would not know. Garson would years after be reminded of that story when he saw the movie "Hester Street," in which the Russian Jewish immigrant Jacob became Jake, the Yankee.

Mary had completed six grades of school when her youngest brother was born; her father ordered her to stop formal studies.

"That's enough. We need you for chores around here now," she remembered her father saying, nonplussed because she had enjoyed formal learning. For the remainder of her life, she lamented not having had more education and a chance to better her life.

"You're going to college," she proclaimed to her son even before he understood that notion. She would often hold up her gnarled fingers to underscore the message. That refrain was uttered endlessly until Garson entered Marquette University in Milwaukee after his discharge from the Marines. When he enlisted after dropping out of high school, his mother was disconsolate, believing he had sidetracked himself from the path to a good career.

They called her "*Schimmel*" — white horse. Her thick, fly-away hair was the color of flax, and her narrow eyes were hazel-gray albeit when anger overcame her, they darkened. Eyelashes were undiscernible at a distance. She had a small, blunt nose, rosy cheeks, narrow lips and a demure smile. Garson's mother always claimed to be five-foot-four, but that was an exaggeration by an inch at least. She shied from candid photos taken when she was not properly groomed or attired. Before pregnancy plumped up her weight and she became what was called *softig*, she was small breasted but shapely.

Rail tracks of the Chicago, Milwaukee & St. Paul cut through the heart of Rubicon, at Main and Fuller Streets. St. John's Church was situated on a gentle prominence to the east, and a collection of commercial buildings and residences scattered on both sides of streets. Rubicon boasted an opera house, a modest building that was commonly known as Fireman's Hall, a facility for dances, roller skating and movies. Mary was immediately captivated with movies – she called them the picture shows – from her first screening. She was charmed by the gigantic images projected on the screen, huge faces and galloping scenes. A town teacher played an upright piano to accompany the silents.

"That's where I used to dance," Garson's mother pointed every time they passed through the crossroad village on trips to visit her sisters and their families. "I was a good dancer, and always hoped to marry a man who liked to dance." She would peer at the man behind the wheel with an expression that even a little boy could interpret — that his father was not that man. Garson often watched his mother waltzing or fox-trotting across the kitchen linoleum, her "partner," a dish towel stretched between two hands; she was light afoot, a smile always turning up her mouth.

How the eruption of the Great War affected Guttig is not known. Did he recall any old soldier friends with whom he had served in the Hungarian army? Was there any concern about the effect of the conflict upon European relatives and friends? Anti-German sentiment swept across most of Wisconsin during four years of war, many people appalled by news reports of atrocities visited upon Belgian civilians when that neutral country was invaded in the first months of the conflict. The "Huns," depicted as gorillas in spiked helmets, and the Kaiser with his despotic mustache were responsible.

In Milwaukee, despite its Germanic stamp, sauerkraut became "Liberty Cabbage." The bronze Goddess Germania was pulled down from her pedestal, and the building bearing her name changed to something less offensive. Even the respected Deutscher Club neutralized itself, becoming the Wisconsin Club. An evocative photo existed, indicating overt support in rural Dodge County for the nation's war effort. Guttig posed with a group of neighbors and his two youngest sons preparing to participate in the Third Liberty Loan drive that commenced in early 1918. In his Sunday best suit and fedora, he wore an expression of satisfaction after a dozen years in his adopted country.

In war's aftermath, the fractious Austro-Hungarian Empire was no more, sundered into various independent parts by the controversial peace accord. This may be another reason Garson's mother later unequivocally declared she was of Austrian origin, even though the land of her birth was clearly Hungary. It was another opportunity for her to eradicate any taint of Magyar background.

Around this time, Guttig gained employment at the Kissel Motor Car Company in Hartford. He must have acquired some industrial skills before or since he immigrated to America. The manufacturer produced automobiles, fire engines, hearses; during the war, military trucks had rolled from its assembly line. In time, Kissel Kars, as they were called, earned the mark of excellence.

At some point in the 1920s, Guttig's wife Terez was diagnosed with diabetes, a predisposition she passed on to her youngest daughter. It is possible that there was an imperative for the family to relocate to Milwaukee where more sophisticated medical care was available.

Guttig turned 55 in August, 1926 when the family moved back to the city, living in an expansive frame house in a west side ward. He would again become a common laborer. His two older girls were both married to Dodge County farmers, and settled into rural life. The Guttig house in Milwaukee was situated in a neighborhood established by German immigrants a generation before. It was an area of massive residences, most two-family duplexes, or "flats" as Milwaukee called them. They featured large, high-ceilinged rooms, copious windows and side bays, many with leaded glass uppers, expansive porches and large yards.

The house on Garfield Street was about three miles west of the Milwaukee River.

In all probability, Guttig rented the lower flat. When Garson visited that neighborhood over 80 years later, the house was gone, demolished, as were so many in that area when fears of racial change caused owners to abandon the west side.

At 24, Garson's mother was elated to be back in the big city, removed from farm drudgery and tedium. She wanted to meet new people, to socialize and dance. She soon discovered west side picture show houses, some ornate and commodious, others utilitarian and unassuming, and all within easy walking distance or streetcar line. She adored movies, the way in which they opened her world, especially now that sound had been introduced. It was a pleasure she would impart to her son. She took to calling herself Marie instead of Mary, hoping to slaw off any Old World vestiges; her mother likely disapproved. She was no longer the girlish *Schimmel*. In photos Garson later studied, her once white, untamed hair had darkened, and was bobbed and permed in the mar-celled style of the day. Her smile revealed a happy, determined young woman.

Guttig found Milwaukee had much changed since he had departed years before. Its population now surpassed half a million. City Hall on Water Street and the Pabst Building on the river across from Gimbels, where Guttig briefly labored, remained the tallest edifices north of Chicago. Radio stations now broadcast music and programs. In recent years, grand and opulent movie palaces, some seating more than a thousand, had been erected downtown, much to Marie's delight.

Dan Hoan, a Socialist, was still the Milwaukee mayor; he had been elected ten years before, and would serve more than two decades in office. But he, like his fellows, was not an ideologue. Known as "Sewer Socialists," he and his party were pragmatic politicians, stressing public works coupled with graft-free and efficient government oriented toward working people.

The Germanic character of the city, while still outwardly apparent, had been leavened. Bilingualism had ebbed although German was still widely spoken. Other ethnic groups now asserted political, cultural and artistic influence, particularly the Poles of the south side. Modeled after St. Peter's in Rome, the community's St. Josephat's Church would shortly be designated a basilica.

Living in the Garfield Street's lower unit were Guttig and his ailing wife, their three sons and youngest daughter. Many things fell to Marie because of her mother's illness; she was likely occupied with household chores in addition to various employments outside the home. But, it could be supposed, she occasionally joined friends at the movies or at one of the downtown dance venues such as George Devine's on Wisconsin Avenue.

"Oh, I drove the tractor on the farm," she said, but never learned to drive a car, perhaps intimidated by urban traffic. Thus, she grew accustomed to the city's extensive transit network – gas buses, new trackless trolleys and the rattling old orange streetcars. On one of the lines, she gained the acquaintance of a young motorman who displayed a ready smile and amicable manner. Of average height, he had olive complexion that darkened quickly in the summer sun; his hair, parted down the middle, was pitch black; bold coffee eyes seemed to penetrate hers. When Garson grew to notice such things, he thought his father, as a young man, resembled the actor Tyrone Power. There once existed a handsome formal street railway photo of Garson's father in his natty uniform and motorman's cap; he stared confidently at the camera, his slightly parted lips turned up in an incipient smile. It was easy to see why Garson's mother found him handsome.

"We had a streetcar romance," she said, smiling in the memory of those romantic days. "He was handsome back then, charming even." She may have been indifferent to his flirtations at first; he was a stranger after all. But in time, conversations lengthened and stories shared; laughs and flirtations eroded her resistance. Each time they encountered one another, he likely wheedled and cajoled. The streetcar swayed and the troller arced sparks from overhead electric wires. He was from Green Bay, he told her, and had come down to the big city with his brothers a few years earlier. They began courting. But she worried.

She recalled only one distressing incident during those days of courtship: One of the electric company's interurban lines ran to an amusement park called Muskego Beach southwest of the city. On a summer outing, she donned a modest bathing suit and waded into the chilly lake. Water lapped at her ankles, then her calves and knees, and finally her waist. She would go no deeper, shading her eyes against the reflected sunlight. Suddenly, a shadow under the water seized her. She was upended, gulping a mouthful of the pea-green water. Garson's father emerged, laughing raucously. Sputtering and pulling seaweed from her fair hair, she glared at him and marched from the water.

"I took off that bathing suit, and never put it on again for the rest of my life," Garson's mother stated emphatically, a deep crease forming between her eyes.

The worrying impediment between them remained. When he first introduced himself, she stiffened. He was French or Belgian, she concluded, and that would not sit well with her mother.

"*Er ist ein Franzose*" – "He's a Frenchman." That might have been the first reaction, delivered sotto *voce* perhaps, from Terez when her daughter told the family about the new acquaintance. Old World antipathies remained, and Terez could not mask prejudices. While not a large woman, she could assume a bristling, intimidating mien.

"Your dad did everything he could to please her," Garson's mother explained at a later remove. "He shopped for her and took her to stores and ran errands for her. Why, he even learned a little German so they could talk. But she never warmed to him." In contrast, his mother's reception among potential in-laws up North was warm and welcoming; ethnic difference presented no problem. The Fermiers were a generally gregarious lot. The two younger brothers were even mildly flirtatious toward the pretty young Hungarian woman with a winsome smile and trim figure. When romance blossomed fully, a proposal was made and accepted. Three months after the celebrated Long Eagle, Charles Lindbergh, completed his solo flight across the Atlantic, the couple was married on a cool but sunny October day. She was 24, and he, four years older.

From cousins, Garson obtained copies of wedding photos to replace those lost in the tragic house fire. The reception was held in the yard beside the Garfield house. His mother's lace calf-length wedding dress featured a drop waist and long sleeves; she complimented the ensemble with white hose, slipper shoes and a gauzy train; a tulle headpiece featuring a fan-like crown three inches tall was striking. Guttig, slender and serious in a dark, three-piece suit, retained the broad mustache. He and Terez flanked the bride. Wearing a long, shapeless, matron's dress, she appeared fleshy, probably caused by illness, but her hair was still dark. Her expression was no warmer than resignation. This was the only image of his grandmother Garson remembered.

At one point that afternoon, the camera caught Marie's long, gauzy veil billowing in the fall breeze, nearly caught on some shrubbery. Her sister, Terez, the maid of honor, prevented a potential disaster, one of the guests remembered.

Garson never saw his father so resplendent as in the formal wedding portrait. A dark suit was accented with a rose boutonnière, crisp white shirt and bowtie; his shoes gleamed. His hair was neatly trimmed and, as usual, parted down the middle and slicked back. While neither he nor his bride smiled in the pose, they appeared content and happy as newlyweds should. Garson knew the glow from the image would soon fade. The newlyweds took a brief honeymoon in Chicago, visiting a new brother-in-law, Hervé, and his wife on the north side of the great city. They returned to almost immediately pack their bags for a move to the Fermier farm near Green Bay.

"I hated it up there, really hated it," Garson's mother often recalled. "They spoke Belgian all the time, and I didn't understand anything they said. I never wanted to be like my sisters, you know – farmers' wives with lots of kids, milking cows, the stink of manure. I liked Milwaukee and missed my family."

Garson never heard his father's side of the story; he could only imagine it. Perhaps his parents left the city because of employment concerns. His father might have lost his job as a motorman because electric company cutbacks; TMER&L, as it was called, introduced single operator streetcars and one-man trolleys and gas buses.

On the Sugar Bush farm, Marie used her wiles; she was good at getting her way, a trait she later transferred to her son: She caviled and complained, nagging ceaselessly, according to his father's version of things. In perhaps less than a year, the couple returned to Milwaukee. They were welcomed back to the city by Black Thursday, the catastrophic stock market collapse.

Milwaukee was hit hard in the early Depression years because of its reliance on manufacturing. Metal and machining manufacturing suffered heavily for a few years before flirting with recovery, only to slip back again. Typical was the premature proclamation by a Milwaukee newspaperman that the city's industry and commerce had discarded their "crutches and walked out of the depression sick room." The writer lacked prescience, of course, and another downturn occurred three years later.

The community shouldered a great load of relief for its residents. Subsistence payments to a thousand families rose to staggering 140,000 – one in five living on the public dole. Food kitchens and soup lines grew longer. Two years after Wall Street collapsed, Milwaukee certified that over ten thousand men worked one ten-hour day weekly at a salary of 60-cents an hour. Pick and shovel brigades toiled to improve the city's parks and playgrounds and other projects.

When the Roosevelt administration's Federal programs commenced, more construction projects – water purification, streets and roads, renovation and repair of municipal buildings — were undertaken. At one point during these trying years, the city printed its own script to pay its workers; such notes were used to pay property taxes and purchase goods from local merchants. Grandpa Guttig, a municipal laborer, was likely paid with Milwaukee money.

For the next several years the documented employment history of Garson's father was sketchy. Garson's parents briefly lived with Guttig at Garfield Avenue flat before moving to a confining apartment above a noisome neighborhood tavern on the north side. Marie fortuitously secured employment at Geuder, Paeschke & Frey, a sprawling manufactory in the city's sooty, odiferous industrial valley. She earned piece-work wages during the mandatory 48-hour week.

"I was good," Garson's mother many times boasted, "quick with my hands, and got steady wages." But she hated gimlet-eyed floor walkers and time study men who spied on workers; the latter increased production quotas every few months. What was more, her pay envelopes contained half of what male workers received. And she detested the clamoring, foul-smelling atmosphere in that long, gloomy factory. Meanwhile, Garson's father gained employment at the same company as an apprentice welder. But he soon joined other workers agitating for better pay and conditions as well as union recognition.

"Got my head popped once," Garson's father once told his son. "We talked about the auto workers in Michigan who organized a sit-down strike at General Motors and after weeks, won recognition, better pay and shop conditions." But when workers began a job action at Geuder, Paeschke & Frey, police, seemingly unsympathetic to unions, were called to quell a melee between workers and replacements.

"Scabs! Damn scabs!" Garson's father scowled. He described the surge and jostling amid the maelstrom of workers, of being shoved into a policeman on horseback. The animal, eyes white with fright, snorted and reared. The rider flailed his baton, catching Garson's father with a glancing blow. Scant blood was drawn, but he carried a knot on his head for several days. The memory of that incident was long-lasting, and it seemed to symbolize the union movement for father and son.

"Because of unions," Garson's father repeatedly proclaimed, "we got the eight-hour day and 40-hour week and many other good things for workers." Garson's mother was focused on other important concerns.

"I missed only a couple of weeks work when you were born," she proudly told her son. Indeed, Garson recalled no time when she did not work — almost to the day of her death.

"No self-respecting husband makes his wife work," was one of the initial life lessons imparted by mother to son. "He should support his wife and family." A quarter of the nation's workers were without jobs at this time, but that was insufficient reason to the contrary, she asserted. Before Garson was born, the national economy collapsed anew, into the Depression's deepest drowning depths. Garson's father had a difficult time finding steady employment. For a time, city directories listed Garson's parents' employment at Geuder, Paeschke & Frey, the metals assembly plant. But his father may have lost that job because of union organizing. Documentary records were vague in the best of circumstances,

The 1932 city directory listed Garson's mother as Maria not Marie or Mary, still toiling in a clattering, grimy metals manufactory in the foul-smelling Menomonee River valley. She would be steadily employed there, her wages based solely on the number of pieces she stamped out on dangerous punch presses. Quick and accurate, she was later promoted to bench handler, annealing "ears" to galvanized buckets. Garson often envisioned her hands, blurred as they flew across the oily work bench.

At that time, Guttig worked as a common laborer before gaining stable employment as a municipal worker. The 60-year-old man joined a city crew that collected coal and wood ashes and other debris from homes, loading it into horse-drawn steel dump wagons. Those crews regularly featured a polyglot of workers characteristic of Milwaukee as a whole – gangs comprised of immigrant and second generation Germanics, Poles and Central Europeans, Italians, even a Negro or two.

Meanwhile, the diabetes that sucked away Terez's vitality worsened. She required insulin injections, but detested needles; she resisted syringes. Her youngest son, Anton, remembered walking to the neighborhood grocery before school to buy foods with low sugar content. As a youth, he likely helped inject medication. Finally, the withering disease felled her. Not yet 60, she died on a cold February day in 1934. Her body was transported to Rubicon where it was interred in the St. John's Church cemetery. She was the second grandparent Garson would never know.

Not long after, Guttig sustained a devastating injury on the job. While shoveling ashes in an alley, an immense draft horse spooked – by something as simple as a boy on a bicycle. It lurched, crushing Guttig between the heavy steel wagon and a concrete block garage. He was hospitalized and county doctors removed a lung. At age 63, his work life was over. Within a year, the Garfield flat was left behind, and Guttig came to live with his youngest daughter and son-in-law.

At the outset of 1936, Garson's mother became pregnant. Garson often wondered why his parents waited nine years to have a child – their only one. Had there been earlier pregnancies? Miscarriages? Perhaps the dreadful economic conditions of the Depression gave them pause. But if that was the reason, how was pregnancy prevented? Garson's mother was secretive and evasive about such matters.

Some years earlier, when they believed they would be steadily employed, Garson's parents secured a loan to purchase a house in the former village of North Milwaukee, a community recently annexed by the city, centered on the major intersection of 35th and Villard Avenue on the far northwest side. Much of the area lay undeveloped, but the Milwaukee Lumber Company was constructing numerous houses. The firm erected three of its signature bungalows on the corner of 41st and Sheridan Streets just a block south of the town of Granville. Each cost $3000.00. For working people, loans were available if a down payment was in hand.

Another recollection intrudes. Garson's memory was distinct about driving to Milwaukee's east side near Lake Michigan where his parents visited a gray, childless couple living in one of the numerous stone apartment buildings that crowded above the lake's bluff. On each visit, an envelope passed between his parents and the Stuveys – that name remained clear. After years, he surmised that it was cash repayment for down payment money borrowed to secure the home loan. Somehow, he suspected his Uncle Vin, a gregarious valet and bartender who long resided in that part of town and knew wealthy people, had been instrumental in arranging the transaction. The Stuvey's apartment was immaculate, each living room chair adorned with starched antimacassars. A pendulum clock perched on a table. Ornate China crowded in cabinets and dust-free bric-a-brac rested on most surfaces. Oval wall frames bordered dour portraits.

"He's so cute, such a cherub." The dowdy woman wearing a bun doted on the bored little boy. Garson's mother invariably bade him to recite some lines from a book of ABCs that he had memorized at an early age. He did not recall how frequently they visited or how long it took to repay the borrowed money – he was always uncomfortable in the antiseptic atmosphere. Surely the loan included above market interest.

Garson's parents and widowed grandfather moved into the new home on 41st Street a few months before his birth. The first winter in the new bungalow was one of the coldest on record in Milwaukee. What portent that had is left to speculation.

"I had a hard time with you because I was small," his mother said, usually reticent about such matters. "After hours and hours, the doctor asked your dad what he should do. He didn't ask me at all. But your father said to cut me open – Cesarean." Here was another of those many traumas in her life whose blame lay at the feet of her husband.

"They ruined my insides, and that's why you don't have a sister or brother," she went on. Indeed, when Garson accompanied his mother to a physical exam 40 years later, the doctor explained that she had never properly healed from the birth incision. "Doctoring" was never a part of either parent's vocabulary.

Garson cited a curious array of markers for the year of his birth. He noted, of course, that Franklin D. Roosevelt was running for re-election, and would be victorious about six weeks after his birth. The year before, the president and Congress enacted legislation establishing two of the most seminal programs in the nation's history — Social Security and unemployment insurance. Garson also observed that *Life* magazine started that year, and the two halves of the new Golden Gate Bridge were finally joined.

After these events, movies were prominent birth indicators: "Follow the Fleet" and "Swing Time," the sixth and seventh Astaire and Rogers movies, Greta Garbo's "Camille," "My Man Godfrey" with William Powell and Carole Lombard, all were box office favorites. The MGM studio released two Jean Harlow movies that year – "Libeled Lady" with Powell, and "Suzy" with Franchot Tone; the voluptuous, platinum blond was a sensation. She died less than a year later.

That year, too, Milwaukee Mayor Hoan, the socialist, was featured on the cover of *Time* magazine; Milwaukee was touted as the best governed city in America. Within a year of Garson's birth, his two favorite composers, Maurice Ravel and George Gershwin died, and Benny Goodman and his band played Carnegie Hall. Margaret Mitchell's romantic opus to the old Confederacy, *Gone With the Wind* was a best seller in 1936 along with James Cain's *Double Indemnity*, Walter Edmunds's *Drums Along the Mohawk;* Carnegie's *How to Win Friends and Influence People* sold thousands.

Don Hutson of the Green Bay Packers caught a three-yard touchdown pass from Arnie Herber to beat the Boston Redskins and win the professional football championship. Three weeks before

Garson's birth, the minor league Milwaukee Brewers clinched the American Association championship with a double victory over Minneapolis at city's Borchert Field. A month after Garson's birth, Jesse Owens shocked the Nazi Olympics at Munich, winning four gold medals and setting three sprint records.

Garson's childhood milieu was quite ordinary, a neighborhood of modest houses with common features. Of a practical floor plan, the Milwaukee bungalow in which Garson lived boasted little more than a thousand square feet of space; it was situated on the west side of a shaded street on a typical city lot measuring 120-by-40 feet. Morning light shone into four living room windows, passing through colored prisms of leaded glass uppers. Garson often daydreamed, watching dust motes dance in sunny streams. Living and dining rooms featured built-in book cases and China cabinets augmented with handsome hardwood floors and maple woodwork; walls swirled in light Spanish plaster. Below the living room mantle, a faux stone fireplace occasionally glowed with a red light bulb. The low-rise residence featured two bedrooms – Garson and Guttig shared the one overlooking the backyard and garage. Rope wash lines laden with drying clothes swayed above his mother's cherished rhubarb plants, their leaves fanning like palm fronds. His parents slept in the larger bedroom. A kitchen and dining room completed the living space. An unfinished basement and barren attic completed the bungalow.

Garson's parents furnished the living room with a chocolate mohair couch and chairs. As a child, Garson often gazed languidly at the painting his mother hung above the couch: Sunlight streamed through soaring trees and thick foliage into a glade, tiny patches of light spotting the forest floor. When he stared at the ornately-framed art work, Garson sometimes imagined a dappled cow looking at him, its body tilted unnaturally to one side. He was equally fascinated with a copper-lined tobacco humidor of dark wood; instead of cigars or cigarettes – neither of his parents smoked — it contained playing cards and chips, coasters and other occasionally used items. When company played cards, a solid wood folding table, whose tin surface displayed four poker hands, was brought down from the attic.

Steam heat emanated in each room from three-foot tall radiators. At an early age when Garson dashed about the living room among visiting relatives, he tripped over Uncle Hervé's outstretched legs, and pitched headlong into the cast iron radiator. Garson staggered to his feet not wanting to act like a baby. He felt no pain, only a little trickle of wet oozing down his forehead. He shook his head, whipping a spray of blood.

"God damn!" his uncle blurted. Other relatives shouted for Garson's mother. The commotion frightened Garson, and he loosed a wail.

"Oh, I can still hear the sound of that crack," his mother reminded him. "Your head split open. I ran into the living room with a bath towel, and covered the gash." She scooped up her son, ran out the front door and to the corner house. Viv, a nurse, lived there. "She stitched you up right there in her kitchen."

"Hold him still," Viv demanded as Garson wiggled on a kitchen chair. "And, you," she said sternly to her patient, "stop crying, this instant!" Her command caused Garson to quiet himself, at least a bit. She retrieved a medical bag from the bathroom, and withdrew an assortment of medical implements, jars and ointments. Slowly, she removed the towel and daubed at the wound.

"Oh, he'll be fine," she comforted. Pain grew more intense. She shaved away hair with a razor. Pinching the flesh, she began suturing, plying needle and catgut back and forth just like his mother did when she darned socks over a light bulb. Garson bit his lower lip. Viv swathed half of Garson's head in a bandage, and bade his mother give him aspirin. Garson displaced his father that night, cuddling with his mother in his parents' big bed. Save for the time his head was shaved in Marine Corps Boot Camp, the inch-long scar was invisible until his hairline receded in later years.

In summers, night creatures serenaded Garson's neighborhood from a nearby bog, chirring, thrumming in sensual symphony. In season, Garson's mother shuddered when tobacco brown June bugs snapped at screen doors and windows, scaly legs clinging to the mesh. Cicadas whirred shrilly, the sound only occasionally overpowered by the comforting wail of the railway freight train.

For many years, the bungalow's exterior was well groomed. A sentinel line of low hedges guarded the front yard with a small arbor vitae tree rising from the middle of the lawn. Growing beneath three living room windows and flanking the small front porch were hollyhocks, snowball and peony bushes, punctuated by tall Tiger lilies.

Along the walkway to the rear of the house were planted a dozen or more hostas that served as a barrier to the property of a family named Hexe. Theirs was an old house, one of the first on the block — a tall, frame, two-story dwelling that reminded Garson of his Uncle Essig's farm house in rural Dodge County. Sometime after Garson's parents took possession of the house, Roland Hexe died, leaving widow and son. Almost from that moment, a dispute over a property line began that rippled through the years, creating antipathy between neighbors.

An alley ran past the two-car garage in the rear, separated by a tiny expanse of lawn and a garden. Garson's mother's beloved rhubarb plants inhabited that cultivated rectangle. He recalled several happy summer snapshots taken with his father seated on a slatted white bench in the middle of the yard.

It's hard to visualize my Pop as a child, but I saw a large portrait of him among the few images recovered from my grandmother's house fire: The tinted studio photograph shows a roly-poly boy wearing a yellow romper, white shoes and socks; his hair was fair and curled atop a round head. Like my grandma's, his eyes were narrow but dark.

"Your dad was chubby til he started walking," she told me when we looked at that photo together; the fire had charred the edges. "But as soon as he was on his feet, pounds dropped off."

When Garson was home on leave from the Marines, his mother informed him that as a newborn, his ears protruded the same way as her brothers' did. "I taped them to the side of your head so they wouldn't look like open car doors." Garson often wanted to ask how long she did this, and whether it caused him discomfort as an infant. He sometimes worried about the effects of such minor traumas upon his character.

While not the *lingua franca* of the house, German was often spoken. Never fluent – even after studying the language in school – Garson was minimally conversant.

"*Mein kleiner Schatze*" or "*Liebschen*" — "My little sweetheart" or "Lover" — a doting mother called her boy. Guttig referred to Garson as *Hanswurst* or *kleine Schnickelfritz* when he was obstinate. When Garson learned to converse in his grandfather's tongue, he, too, would often respond with, "*Ach, ja!*" – "Oh, yes." His mother often serenaded Garson with "*Du, du, du legist mir im Hertzen*" – "You, you reside in my heart" – and similar ditties.

While Garson's father was sometimes given to ribaldry, his mother had but one, oft-repeated joke in her repertoire. As the yarn went, Sofia's husband, Heinrich was late coming home from work, and dinner grew cold on the kitchen table. She wrapped a babushka about her head, and visited the local tavern.

"Vash my Heinie here?" she asked, always in unpolished English.

"No, ma'am," replied the saloon keeper. She entered two or three other taverns, posing the same question, and receiving the same response at each stop. Exasperated, she ducked into the barber shop. Now frantic, her voice was a scream.

"Vash my Heinie here? Vash my Heinie here?" Calmly, the barber replied:

"No, ma'am, we only cut hair here." Garson's mother invariably chuckled at her little yarn. And for those who did not understand, she explained that *Heinie* meant hinder, one's behind. The joke did not always play well, but her harrowing tale of nearly losing her son to a kidnapper did. She recounted that episode to anyone who would listen.

The Lindbergh's infant son was kidnapped in 1932, and found dead ten weeks later. The story raged in newspaper headlines for months. Then, two years later, Bruno Richard Hauptmann was arrested, tried and convicted of the heinous killing. He was executed the year Garson was born.

As Garson's mother recollected, she was visiting the city zoo the summer following his birth. Even in later years, Garson recalled one or two photos taken that day, of him seated in a stroller — it was of yellow metal, he was sure of that — eyes squinted in the sun, an animal cage in the background. They later stopped to watch polar bears lounging on faux rocks – she was always clear about where the incident occurred.

"A woman walked up to me and smiled at you in the stroller. 'He's such a cute little boy,' the stranger said. 'Can I take him for a walk?'" His mother said she was shocked. "I held onto the handle til my knuckles were white. I told the strange woman, 'Absolutely not!' Can you imagine someone asking that?" She always concluded the experience with this statement:

"Who knows what would have become of you or who you might be now if I hadn't saved you from that stranger." When he was old enough to understand the import of that possibility, Garson threw his arms around his mother's waist, hugging her tightly for minutes. He sometimes shuddered in her embrace. Other photos provided Garson with fragmentary evidence of his childhood.

At one time, thousands of family photos were stored in shoeboxes, loosely and without organization. His mother sometimes said she planned to put them all in an album someday when she had time. In his boyhood, Garson occasionally rifled through them, studying his parents as younger people or scouring his memory to vivify an event of childhood that was depicted.

One series, Garson surmised, had been taken at the Garfield duplex in early 1936: Guttig stood with his six grown children. Despite the fact that the older daughters had already borne several children, they remained slender. His fair-haired mother, by comparison, exhibited thickness about her waist; she was apparently in the middle stage of pregnancy. Sadly, the lifetime pictorial cache was destroyed.

A repairman rummaging through the charred interior of his parents' fire-gutted house around 1980 found, along with the tinted studio portrait of infant Garson, a small packet of black and white negatives that had somehow escaped the flames. Garson developed them, hoping to fill more blanks in his history. But nearly every image was out of focus. Still, they depicted events around the time of his birth. One series was shot on a warm October day in front of the house during Garson's baptism. Relatives in short sleeves posed with infant Garson on the front lawn; his paternal uncle and aunt were godparents.

Other candids depicted a chubby, toothless infant laughing on the chocolate brown mohair sofa, and Garson in an obligatory nude bassinette pose, both blurred by movement. In another, taken during Christmas, a three-month old sat in that yellow stroller next to the family holiday tree; at his side perched a stuffed Mickey Mouse. From these poor images and copies of others he later obtained from relatives, Garson reconstructed a few family events.

Even from the remove of decades, one photo of his mother holding her infant son evoked a distinct sensory memory, of a clingy brown crepe dress she wore with two lines of pink rick-rack along the hem and cap sleeves; even as an adult, Garson clearly recalled the pleasant feel of the fabric. His narrow-shouldered mother had not shed pregnancy weight at this time. Several other images were taken while he was in infancy at family gatherings in Rubicon, usually at the farm house of his mother's oldest sister. Most of Garson's cousins were older than he at that time. He was a toe-headed little lad in corduroy pants and striped shirt in that series of candids. In one or two, Guttig held Garson.

"He liked you best of all," Garson's mother said when browsing wistfully through those photos. "The other grandkids, 'specially my sister's boys, were rowdy farm kids. Your grandfather liked children to be quiet." When Garson studied those images, he concurred that Guttig revealed a sunnier expression around him.

The roll of film had apparently remained in the camera for several years, for there were photos of Garson from infancy until he was about two. Despite poor print quality, from these was gleaned a considerable number of facts. There were half a dozen snapshots of Garson with his grandfather taken at the 41st Street house, Guttig usually hovering protectively near his grandson.

The alley behind the house was a wonderful playground. Several of the blurred photos showed Garson and his grandfather there on a spring day, likely 1937. Both wore sweaters and caps against the spring chill – Guttig's of a style Garson called a "robber" cap because most movie villains of the era wore them.

At one point in that alley, Garson recalled his grandfather tensing; he reached down to grab his grandson's hand. A short figure in virtual tatters shambled along, a babushka wrapped about her head and cheeks. At first, it was impossible to determine the creature's gender, but when Guttig muttered *"Ziguener"*, gypsy, Garson knew it was a woman. She carried some sort of a dirty duffel bag over her left shoulder. Here was the person some in the neighborhood called harridan. Her only known name was "Deaffy" because she never uttered even one word. She might have been a character in a Dickens novel.

Over many years, Garson developed a portrait of the woman, but at a late remove, it was impossible to separate the real from the fancied, the truth from the exaggeration. Dark leathery skin was deeply wrinkled, like a prune; low scraggly eyebrows obscured eyes of an indescribable color; a deep vertical crease divided them. When she parted her lips from time to time, only a few discolored teeth were visible. She sometimes was known to chew tobacco, spitting like a stevedore, Garson's father said.

Deaffy lurched into the center of the alley away from Garson and his protective grandfather; Guttig slowly turned his head to follow her progress. As Garson watched, the wraith-like women stopped at intervals, lifting trash can lids, obviously searching for edible foodstuffs and discarded items she might use.

In the months and years to come, Garson encountered Deaffy numerous times but never close. He would hear disparate details, true and not, facts and fiction, about the sorry life she led. She resided on the corner diagonally across from Garson's house. The residence may have been torn from a page in *The House of Seven Gables* save that it was not a mansion at all, only a miniscule shack no larger than a garage.

The insubstantial abode clung precariously to the alley side of a property that was dominated by an overgrowth of struggling saplings, shrubs, vines and creepers inside a chicken wire fence. Amid this verdant tangle were indifferently strewn an incredible jumble of detritus, objects large, small and diverse, that Deaffy had gathered over the years. Like the Collyer Brothers of Harlem, Homer and Langly, almost in the same era, she collected a mélange of objects, including wheels, a rusty wagon missing a handle, what looked like a three-legged carousel horse whose paint had peeled away, a huge glass globe covered in soot and perched on a ceramic base, bedsprings, bones from some large animal and numerous indescribable oddments. When foliage fell away in fall and winter, like a curtain parting to reveal a stage play, it revealed Deaffy's sad treasures. Some neighbors swore she had been a nurse in the First World War, and suffered shell shock. After that, she had become a recluse. There were other, more rambunctious rumors about the old crone.

"A kid I know said her real name's Deaf and Dumb Tilly," his childhood pal, Larry said. Garson's first childhood pal, he lived next door, in a bungalow next to Nurse Viv; it was similar to his house save for a doghouse dormer. Despite being months younger than Garson, the neighbor was taller, rangy like his parents. Garson recalled several photos of the childhood pals taken on a sunny day. Garson's cheeks were still chubby and his belly protruded under the waist band of his shorts; his mother, as was her wont but to his dislike, propped a little cap on his head.

Garson found it amusing that while he was unable to recall most details, a sense of color remained. He recalled Larry's brown shoes, a cream and chocolate two-tone shirt that coordinated with dark short pants. Garson found those colors unusual as his mother always dressed him in light shades – striped shirt, blue shorts and white shoes. Both boys detested wearing short pants, and at about age four asked when they might wear long ones like big kids. After their next birthdays, they were told, as though their mothers colluded in a unified response. Another summer passed before the pals were permitted to don long pants.

Larry's dad was a burly, trumpet-voiced sheriff's deputy who rode a motorcycle with a sidecar. He often delivered summons and subpoenas, but he was also known to chase speeders on local streets. In winter, he wore a uniform of leather, head to toe; when wind howled piling snow into deep drifts, he threw a leather blanket across his legs to ward off the brutal blasts.

"You Polish?" Garson asked Larry when he began to understand the significance of such things. Larry's family name sounded Polish to a usually unattuned ear; his mother said it was probably Bohemian or Slavic.

"Pa said we came from a place called Silesia," Larry insisted, meaning his forebears, "where there was lots of coal, and I think my grandpa was a miner, and he came here after the old world war, and worked up in the mines in Minnesota, and he came to Milwaukee after my dad was born, and...."

As always, Garson had to interrupt Larry because his friend prattled on and on, stringing thoughts together in lengthy, breathless sentences until he lost the sequence or exhausted himself. Despite their proximity to one another, the two were close friends only in early youth. For reasons Garson could not remember, they drifted apart about the time of first grade when Garson left public school for Holy Redeemer. Although Garson was an unenthusiastic student, he was never held back like Larry. About that time, Garson shifted loyalties to Toby across the street, a brash, confident months older boy who became a mentor of sorts. While Larry's hair was fair like Garson's, Toby's was dark; the former pal was reticent while the other was mischievous and daring. Garson soon became an acolyte of Toby's adventurous ways. But it was Larry with whom Garson had one of his most memorable childhood adventures.

Again, there was another recollection of color during his childhood years. Summer sun was welcomed into the bungalow living room, blue and red leaded glass panels creating a pattern that crawled across the carpet. Shades adorned the two kitchen windows, suffusing the room with a tan-yellow light when the days were long.

It was at the kitchen table that Guttig and an old friend sat, filling pipes with aromatic tobacco and sipped sweet red wine. Garson knew the man as "Mister Socks," a funny-sounding name. He was Austrian, his mother said.

A small man about the height of Garson's mother, he had close-set eyes the color of tea, a bushy mustache and a fringe of white hair that curled above his ears. Like Guttig on Sundays, he was nearly always attired in a three-piece suit, tie and Hamburg hat. If memory was accurate, he visited on Sunday afternoons following Mass at Holy Redeemer. Mister Socks exhibited a courtly manner, removing his hat when he entered the house, and bowing slightly to Garson's mother. Garson found it odd that he manipulated his fork with left hand and knife in the other. It was Continental style his mother said. She loved the deferential demeanor he displayed toward her.

He could not say why, but Garson assumed Mister Socks to be Viennese, perhaps once a professor of literature. It was nothing that his mother ever mentioned or Guttig explained. It was merely a feeling. Perhaps he taught at the German-American Academy downtown.

Garson long retained memories of Grandpa Guttig and Mister Socks sitting at the kitchen table in that yellow-brown afternoon light, chatting and laughing in a restrained manner. Sitting at the drop-leaf table with its flannel-backed tablecloth of green and white gingham, they conversed in German much of the time, but also in what was called *"Plat-Deutsch,"* an amalgam of German and English. Garson's mother, whose fluency had faded, interjected such adulterated vocabulary when she was unable to summon the proper verbiage.

Garson understood many of the words that passed between the wizened old men albeit he may not have understood the topics they discussed. He thought he recalled names such as Schiller and Goethe, Bismarck, Kaiser Wilhelm and Maria Theresa passing between them.

Garson stood at the edge of the table many times, watching the friends stoke their pipes and fill the room with pleasant-smelling smoke. As Hitler and the Nazis gained more power and menace, the two friends talked about the Sudetenland, *Landsman*, friends and acquaintances in Europe. The Austro-Hungarian Empire they knew was no more, having been sundered more than two decades before.

Its component parts were in the cauldron of new conflict.

Garson's mother often poured small glasses of red wine for the friends from a cut-glass decanter stored high on a pantry shelf. She seemed only to add an observation or two before busying herself with household chores, delayed because of her daily job at Geuder, Paeschke & Frey. The visitor and Guttig continued conversation. Mister Socks frequently carried letters, multi-paged missives filled with tiny script.

"*Sie möchten nach Amerika kommen,*" Mister Socks said as he turned the final sheet. "*Aber sie haben nicht genügend Geld. Sie baten. Möglicherweise schicke ich ihnen einiges.*" "They would like to come to America. But they have not enough money. I may send them some to help out."

As a child, Garson did not fully comprehend the gravity of those affairs across the Atlantic, of course. Occasionally he heard the word *Juden* in those conversations, about *Kristalnacht* years before when mobs burned and destroyed shops and synagogues. Conversational tones grew more somber as political and military events gathered momentum. The German army invaded Poland when Garson was about three, and in 1940, the goose-stepping millions attacked France the same way they had 26 years earlier – through Belgium. Guttig and his friend often read newspapers, as Mister Socks regularly shared copies of Milwaukee's German language weekly, *Die Abend-Post*, that offered a slant on the news often different from city dailies.

Local affairs usually took a secondary focus to the events occurring in the Old Country. But in the fall of 1940, Milwaukee's long-time Socialist mayor, Dan Hoan, who had served for more than a quarter century, was defeated by an upstart, Carl Zeidler, a political newcomer. Garson long suspected that if his mother had been a citizen at that time, she would have voted for the younger man because of his handsome blond mien, and a singing voice that thrilled thousands during the campaign. Zeidler would generate great sorrow in Milwaukee, however, when he resigned his mayoralty two years later to enlist in the navy. A photo of him perched in the back seat of a yellow Packard convertible was printed below a huge headline in afternoon news. Twenty thousand citizens cheered his final appearance riding down Wisconsin Avenue. An officer, he was lost at sea that year, 1942, and declared dead before the war ended.

Mister Socks lived proximate to Garson's house, and always walked for his Sunday visits. He occasionally carried a memento for Garson's mother – a small box of candies or a nosegay which bloomed in a tiny vase for several days. She received such favors with radiant gratitude. This was how men should behave toward women, she felt.

It was the first Sunday in December 1941 that Mister Socks did not appear as expected. Before Mass that morning, radio news reports proclaimed that the Japanese had bombed Pearl Harbor in Hawaii. The United States was at war.

To learn more about the courtly Viennese man my Pop wrote about, I checked city directories and discovered that his facts were suspect. Yes, there were entries for a man named Sachse who lived in the neighborhood about that time. But he wasn't the educated and cultured classicist of my Pop's narrative, a teacher at the German-American Academy. The actual man, whose wife was Clarissa, wasn't an educator at all, but a salesman for the Usinger Sausage factory in downtown Milwaukee. Does this invalidate the colorful story my Pop constructed? Readers must judge.

***

Chapter 3

LOCK AND LOAD

"Route step. *Haar!*" Staff Sergeant Maddox's barked. Garson and the others relaxed. Instead of leaning back and strutting in unison as they had at the march's outset, the recruits were permitted to stride loosely without cadence. The narrow unpaved lane was flanked by towering arbor vitae trees that swayed in the breeze. The rifle sling dug into Garson's bony shoulder as he tramped north with Platoon 023 through the Pacific coastal "boonies." MCRD and the San Diego's urban environs were behind them.

An hour earlier, on the Sunday before Thanksgiving, the unit had departed MCRD aboard articulated "cattle cars." From the barred window, Garson had observed with sadness the passing scenes of normal life – houses and buildings, streets and traffic, civilians moving freely, purposefully. He felt like a prisoner. Out of the city, the Marine green vehicles convoyed up the Coast Highway a short distance, then rumbled to the northwest before stopping to disembark the recruits.

It was uncommon, seeing the senior drill instructor in mufti, "out of uniform." He was a spit and polish Marine, the personification of recruiting posters – normally adorned in sharply creased green trousers, crisp khaki shirt and perfectly knotted tie, brasses and shoes gleaming, campaign hat cocked low. This day he was in the same uniform as recruits save that his dungarees were starched and creaseless, his boots polished. Instead of red wool chevrons, four stripes — three and a rocker below — were stenciled on his sleeves.

It was a slog of perhaps ten miles, Garson calculated decades later, studying topographical maps of the terrain. The four files skirted west of Mission Bay. As Garson treaded, dust billowing from thousands of footfalls caused him and others to cough, hack and spit. He worried that the dust was coating his weapon, clogging its recesses. Resettling the rifle sling on his shoulder, he briefly recalled the time when his M-1 had been issued at the Depot.

"What'd you call this weapon, maggot – a *gun*?" Sergeant Maddox erupted when Garson uttered that forbidden word.

"This is a rifle, an M-1 Garand rifle. Don't you ever fuckin' forget it." His face contorted in anger, and he ordered Garson to hold the weapon aloft with one hand, and clasp his crotch with the other, the while shouting a demeaning ditty known to every Marine.

"This is my rifle," Garson uttered, pumping the Garand with one hand above his head, "and this is my gun." He squeezed the front of his trousers. "This one's for shooting, and this one's for fun." When Maddox was unsatisfied with the fortissimo and pantomime, the performance was repeated several times, much to the amusement of the recruit audience, even his Milwaukee pals, Preston and Rusty.

On the march that Sunday, Garson assumed he, like the others, was taking on a cadaverous pallor in the billowing dust. The platoon might have been an animated terra cotta legion that guarded an ancient Chinese emperor's tomb. The morning was cool, late fall temperature having dipped below 50 as November waned. Still, sweat crept down his spine, and the leather rifle sling dug into his bony shoulder. The route was terra incognita to Garson, but a voice from behind him supposed that they must be near the ocean; that recruit detected the smell of salt air, but Garson could not. To the left rose Soledad Mountain, soaring over 800 feet, and the route rose and fell away, often squeezed between steep bluffs.

"Think I saw a sign — Torrey Pines Road," Fletcher muttered over his shoulder. Someone in an adjoining rank thought they might be somewhere above the coastal town of La Jolla, pronouncing it as a "J" and not the Spanish "La Hoya." The Scripps Institute of Oceanography was somewhere over there, too. Garson noticed portly Brtek a rank over withdraw his canteen from the canvas carrier at his waist, and take a swallow of water. Garson cringed.

"You go out with a full canteen," ordered Sergeant Maddox that morning, "and you better return with a full canteen." Brtek would suffer more verbal abuse when the platoon, under the gimleted eyes of the drill instructor, later poured out the canteen's contents at journey's end. The two or three with empty canteens were made to stand at attention for a long period. Thirsty as he and others were, most did not even dare touch their canteens.

"Instead of sucking water, put a smooth stone in your mouth," went another Corps dictum. "Keep working up saliva to slake your thirst." Garson scoured the ground beneath his feet for a small rock, but was fearful of bending over to snatch one.

Platoon 023 had a new junior drill instructor now, a private first class named Duff. Corporal Reid, some whispered, had remained at MCRD to face disciplinary action because of his penchant for imbibing; only a few believed that scuttlebutt, however. Physically, Duff contrasted with his florid predecessor: About Maddox's height, he was dark and willowy with narrow cheeks and a jutting nose. More, Garson saw something in Duff's mien that said he did not find pleasure in harassment that Reid did. Certainly, the PFC expounded all the requisite demeaning language, but Garson did not detect the same underlying malice that characterized his predecessor. While Maddox set the platoon's pace on the march, Duff roistered from the rear, threatening laggards.

After uncounted hours, the flagging platoon arrived at the gate of the Camp Matthews rifle range, its home for the next month. Named after a famed Marine marksman of the 1930s, the facility sprawled over hundreds of acres amid the coastal highlands, measuring a mile and a half west to east, and about a mile north to south. It was a landscape of scrubby vegetation – unenthusiastic grasses, pitiful brush and pitiful copses of trees that struggled for footing in the gray sandy soil.

The terrain undulated in plateaus and hummocks, some rising precipitously with foot trodden defiles dipping between rises. The largest promontory, Garson and others soon learned, was ominously named Big Agony. The daunting summit was attained by a torturous path that climbed for dozens of muscle and tendon inflaming, lung-bursting minutes. A companion bluff, called Little Agony, rose nearby; it jutted up perhaps two-thirds the height of its companion.

Camp Matthews featured several firing ranges — great swaths of flat, barren ground over 500 yards long interrupted at intervals by terraced firing lines. The target areas were located below ground. Garson and his fellow Boots would spend three days in these butts, preparing and scoring for other units. On this and smaller ranges, Platoon 023 would practice and qualify with the M-1 rifle and became familiar with other weapons in the Marine arsenal.

Nearly 600 recruits – about ten platoons — were billeted in a tent city laid out in a dozen rectangles, each containing 48 canvas enclosures. Platoon 023 occupied a dozen of these. Two cots were situated on three sides of each enclosure. The musty olive drab shelters immediately reminded Garson of "The Sands of Iwo Jima" where John Wayne and his Marines were housed. The peaked canvas was held aloft by a central pole from which dangled one naked bulb; Garson never accustomed himself to the gloomy interior. Every morning before Garson and his bunkmates departed, waist-high canvas sides were rolled up to admit light and much dust.

Low-slung cots, providing as much support as the MCRD racks, sat on wood planked flooring; instead of the creaking metal stays, the canvas groaned when Garson rolled over at night. An extra blanket was tucked over the pillow during the day to prevent dust from invading the bed linen. Only woolen blankets and collective heat of the tent's occupants kept most of the outside chill at bay. One night, Garson recalled his father's boast of sleeping with his brothers in the unheated family farmhouse attic near Green Bay, awakening in the winter morning with snow on their pillows.

"Know Sheepshead?" asked Hal, one of Garson's tentmates. He spoke of a card game, similar to whist, peculiar to Wisconsin.

Garson nodded, having played that game regularly in Silver Spring Park during summers; he recalled Preston, Rusty and others playing five-handed games on picnic benches. What was more, his Grandpa Guttig, father and maternal uncles played during family gatherings, calling the game by its German name, *Schaffskopf.*

"We could play three-handed. Too bad we don't have any cards," Hal added wryly. He and Heissen had enlisted together after graduating from high school in the central Wisconsin village of Berlin. When they spoke of their hometown, they accented the first syllable and not the second as in the German city of the same name. Hall, tall and broad shouldered with a large jaw and small mouth from which winked a tiny silver filling in his right incisor; dark fuzz atop his head attested to a month's worth of growth since the Boot Camp shearing. His nasally voice resonated from a large nose. To regard him as voluble was an understatement as he would become the platoon gadfly and raconteur, and discourse tirelessly about gambling and Las Vegas.

Heissen, his doughy, fair-skinned companion, had narrow eyes the color of concrete. Steady and earnest, Garson soon learned that his knowledge of baseball was keen. He recalled attending games at Milwaukee's new County Stadium when the Braves moved from Boston the preceding spring.

"Couldn't wait for the team to start playing. My dad, uncles and I came down from Berlin to see games. The Braves set a big league attendance record in Milwaukee, you know. The town was starved for major league baseball." Heissen was also, like Garson, an avid movie-goer; but his analyses were incisive and informed – far beyond Garson's pedestrian observations.

My Pop's portraits of these guys grew quite vivid, as readers will see. But I've long suspected something was amiss, that they didn't belong in this context. I believe he didn't meet Heissen until after Marines when he was at Marquette University. I'm not sure about Hal, but later in the narrative as you'll see he calls Hal "PFC Faltschaft." It may be an overreach, but think about it: Faltschaft – Sir John Falstaff, the rollicking, boisterous pal to Prince Hal in Shakespeare's Henry plays? Maybe my Pop's memory was hazy about names so many years later, but more likely, as was his wont, he took literary license, changing names and adding their stories to his own Boot Camp experiences. Remember what Mark Twain said when asked if his autobiographical writings were true:

"Yes," he replied, "literally they are true, that is to say they are a product of my impressions – recollections. As sworn testimony they are not worth anything; they are merely literature."

The others in the tent included laconic and awkward Priech, pale-eyed Liska from Detroit and the burly illiterate Texan, Hupner. Garson and others recalled that the platoon's other Texan, jug-eared, going-home-next-week McCracken, the fraudulent enlistee, had been marched across the Grinder with his seabag the day they departed for the rifle range, never to be seen again.

Preston and Rusty were somewhere down the dirt "street" near where Right Guide Barker and the squad leaders shared a tent. Drill instructors were housed in permanent quarters some distance from the tent city. However, Sergeant Maddox would be rarely seen in the coming weeks, likely taking most duty back at MCRD. More responsibility fell to Right Guide Barker and the platoon's squad leaders.

While rifle training was the primary focus of life at Camp Matthews during the ensuing month, the first week entailed mess duty for the platoon – a mandatory period when recruits helped prepare and clean up after meals. Furthermore, all privates and PFCs in the Corps were obliged to serve a week of mess duty annually. But to Garson's misfortune, he would be assigned that onerous duty three times in the first year of his enlistment.

"Drop your cocks and grab your socks!" a squad leader shouted, poking his head into the dark canvas interior. Reveille for mess duty was at 3:30, earlier than the other Boots aboard. In darkness of late November mornings, Garson and others trooped to the sprawling frame building whose lights poked into the darkness; in the morning chill, windows were often fogged by heat from stoves and ovens.

The complaint about the lack of skills by Marine cooks was universal.

"They turn the best meat, produce and foodstuffs into inedible garbage" or similar assessments were articulated by Boots and regulars alike. Garson, who had never done so in his previous life, began salting chow liberally – "in self-defense." Unlike most Marines, cooks tended toward stoutness. More, they were, like grimy men working in the motor pool, a disheveled and unkempt lot. On duty, cooks wore baggy white trousers, generally soiled aprons and barracks caps. While recruits addressed them as "sir," they applied less stringent discipline, primarily focused on getting chow to the troops.

When Garson first learned about mess duty, he had movie-inspired visions of peeling huge mounds of potatoes. But he was assigned to pots and pans, one of the unenvied wallopers with the tedious task of scrubbing and scouring large cooking containers, vessels and utensils. It was particularly onerous, as often scrambled eggs, chocolate pudding and similar burnt offerings were crusted onto the huge pots; it was like chipping paint from a barnacle ship's hull, someone surmised. Garson and others also cleaned the massive mixers in which potatoes and dough were prepared.

During those days, Preston and Garson joked about their experiences the summer before when they and Mellish were hired as grease jockeys at A & P Bakery in Milwaukee. Then, too, they cleaned large dough and icing mixers and other bakery equipment, and greased hundreds of cake and muffin tins, and bread pans for the bakers.

"Remember Hans?" Preston asked. One of the bakers, a quirky Austrian immigrant, was able to squirt liquid from his eye at unsuspecting human targets several feet away. The boys made wide berths around him.

"*Diese Tisch ist besser als meine Frau*" — This table is better than my wife, the baker proclaimed with a smirk, implying that the waist-high table on which he kneaded great slabs of dough was more pleasurable than his spouse. Garson and his pals larked constantly, once trapping on an open freight elevator an apprentice baker, a young German immigrant whose command of English was limited. They bombarded him unmercifully with cream filling from the floor above. He complained and the boys were summarily fired. Mellish enlisted in the Air Force later that summer.

Despite his months working at a restaurant busboy back home, Garson was amazed at the speed of military food preparation and service in such immense quantities — scores of steam trays mounded with meat, potatoes and vegetables, mountains of scrambled eggs, tall stacks of toast and bread, gallons of coffee, milk and juice, rows of cakes and pies.

"We're having 'queer toast' this morning," announced one cook. This was another of those Marine Corps pejoratives, this equating breakfast toast to the weak military prowess of the modern day France army, as well as to sissy boy behavior. At the conclusion of another breakfast, a jocular cook, disposing of leftover dough, poured out a pancake the size of a continent. Laughing, two cooks turned the immense cake, and when baked, it was dropped onto the floor as an ersatz mat.

Mess hall decks and bulkheads were scrubbed constantly, and every surface cleaned. Preston and Rusty shared in this duty, but were usually assigned to the chow line for each meal. The three Milwaukee pals sometimes joshed and chamfered just as they had before enlisting. Preston boasted of the power to dole out smaller portions to recruits he found as arrogant as himself. Rusty was reprimanded after cleanup of the drill instructors dining area located in a segregated section of the mess hall. Unlike recruit tin trays and cups, DIs ate from ceramic plates and drank coffee from mugs; even napkins were provided. Rusty, unfortunately, broke a plate when clearing the table one day, and was thereafter reassigned to the recruit chow line with Preston — but not before Rusty had poked his finger into several peanut butter jars that served DIs. Garson and others could only yearn for that delicacy of their former lives — peanut butter and jelly sandwiches.

As the week of mess duty proceeded, Garson grew uneasy with some of the larking, considering the Boot Camp experience as serious business intended to prepare recruits for hard service ahead. Yes, he realized that most of Platoon 023 was largely composed unwashed teens like himself, but he considered that they might one day not measure up in the crucible of battle.

Almost as soon as the chow hall was cleaned after one meal, preparation for the next commenced. In all, Platoon 023 worked on 21 meals, including the large Thanksgiving Day repast that included the expected fare – turkey and dressing, potatoes, cranberry sauce, pumpkin pie. To Garson, the meal tasted not at all like his mother's, especially the turkey stuffing which she always made with ground-up liver and gizzard. His recruit palate, however, was becoming accustomed to the Marine Corps menu.

"Hunger ist der beste Koch," — Hunger is the best cook was his mother's favorite proverb. After almost a month in recruit training, Garson had added a few pounds to his slender frame. While his muscles were not pronounced, he sensed a bit of definition.

The Monday after Thanksgiving, rifle training began in earnest.

"You'll get to know your rifle better than your girlfriend. You'll handle your M-1 better than your girlfriend's little titties. You'll know every angle and curve, every screw, characteristic and movement. Someday this Garand rifle'll save your life."

The Marine sergeant with a jutting chin stood before them in an open-air classroom. He was one of the permanent staff of about 150 or more who called Camp Matthews their permanent duty station. The Preliminary Marksmanship Instructor, or PMI, wore dungarees lightened from a myriad launderings – "salty" as the saying went; but the uniform was invariably starched and pressed. Unlike Sergeant Maddox, most PMIs wore their campaign hat brims curled jauntily at the front.

Many of the PMIs were swaggering Korean War combat veterans; others had served on Okinawa or Japan. Some were draftees waiting for discharges. Garson overheard conversations about Seoul and good liberty in Japan. He learned scores of new terms, part of a bastardized Asian taxonomy: The enemy was no longer a Jap or Nip, but a Gook – North Korean or Chinese. Of Japanese derivations were such words as *Ichi bon* – Number One. A *ghee-dunk* or slop-chute was a bar, and a pogue meant a sandbagger, a malingerer. Candy and sweets were pogey bait, delicacies Garson had not tasted since departing Milwaukee.

"The M-1 rifle is a gas-operated, clip-fed, air-cooled, semi-automatic shoulder weapon." Like a General Order, it was another of the rote factoids Garson could recite six decades later. The *Guidebook for Marines* reinforced the verbal lessons: Rifle weight, 9.5 pounds; average rate of fire, 30 rounds per minute; chamber pressure, 50,000 pounds; muzzle velocity, 2600 to 2800 feet per second; maximum range, 3500 yards. In open air classrooms amid spindly trees, PMIs used outsized cutaway models of the M-1 and other shoulder arms, many times life size, to display the inner workings of the weapons. They drilled recruits on the nomenclature, the importance of each part and how to disassemble – called field stripping – and reassemble the weapon.

"You may have to do this in the dark in combat situations, so you'd better know how every part feels," the PMI said. Often tested with blindfolds, Garson and most others became adept at the procedure. The M-1 Garand was an excellent and dependable weapon, and millions were used in World War II and Korea. Numerous companies manufactured Garands; Garson's, for example, bore the stamp of International-Harvester, the farm implement maker.

Recruits cleaned and dusted their pieces incessantly, nearly every waking moment, Garson seemed to recall. Now the shaving brush that had been part of the receiving barracks bucket issue came to use — its sole purpose had nothing to do with shaving but employed to rid rifle recesses of every untoward mote or particle in the bore, receiver, trigger mechanism or elsewhere.

"The tiniest piece of dust or dirt can cause a malfunction. If your rifle fails in combat, you're useless to your unit, to your fellow Marines." Several PMIs repeated that mantra. Rifles were inspected repeatedly, and severe repercussions resulted when wayward dust, grime or corrosion was discovered. Worst of all, any hint of blemish or rust was tantamount to treason.

Bayonets were likewise cleaned and dusted incessantly. Once, PFC Duff scrutinized Garson's bayonet and found an untoward particle in the recess that fitted onto the M-1's lug. Garson was ordered to hold the bayonet tip in his thumb and forefinger, and extend his arm at full length.

"Now, hold it there til I tell you to stop," Duff demanded. Garson locked his wrist and elbow, but in scant minutes, his arm began to tremble. Muscles soon rebelled and tendons protested; fingers cramped. It was impossible to maintain the position, and his arm dropped below horizontal.

"Get it up there, clown, and keep it up." Garson raised his quivering arm. His eyes watered. His mind reeled. He could not continue much longer. At any moment now, he might drop the bayonet with more dire consequences. Somehow he held. When he was finally relieved of the task, his arm tingled from pit to fingers.

Finding the even miniscule metal discoloration anywhere on a rifle resulted in similar repercussion. While Garson avoided such punishment, an offending recruit was made to hold out his arms, and the nine-and-a-half pound rifle laid across his wrists. He was ordered to hold the weapon for an interminable time during which, Garson surmised, minutes seemed like hours. He became discomfited by the punishment as Duff observed with narrow eyes, threatening grievous bodily harm if the rifle dropped.

There seemed to be little rancor in my Pop's recollections of such treatments. Thing of it is, I suspect, it's as though he felt he and other Boots needed such corrective actions to expiate the egregious shortcomings of civilian former life. I don't understand it, but, in the telling, his words seemed to convey gratitude. Maddox, Duff and others, I think he was saying, introduced discipline that had never been there before; they were steeling his backbone for the expected vicissitudes of military life, of warfare perhaps.

The weeks-long Camp Matthews weapons training proceeded from familiarization of the M-1 to final qualification day on the rifle range — long, tedious instruction hours and arduous practice. Posted prominently in many open-air classrooms was the "Rifleman's Creed," a sacred screed to the M-1 Garand that the Corps had codified after the last world war. Garson carefully studied the bold-faced words.

This is my rifle. There are many like it, but this one is mine. It is my life. I must master it as I must master my life. Without me, my rifle is useless. Without my rifle, I am useless.

I must fire my rifle true. I must shoot straighter than the enemy who is trying to kill me. I must shoot him before he shoots me. I will. My rifle and I know that what counts in war is not the rounds we fire, the noise of our burst, or the smoke we make. We know that it is the hits that count. We will hit.

My rifle is human, even as I am human, because it is my life. Thus, I will learn it as a brother. I will learn its weaknesses, its strengths, its parts, its accessories, its sights and its barrel. I will keep my rifle clean and ready, even as I am clean and ready.

We will become part of each other.

Before God I swear this creed. My rifle and I are the defenders of my country. We are the masters of our enemy. We are the saviors of my life.

So be it, until victory is America's and there is no enemy.

In quiet moments, Garson mused about the earlier "combat at arms" in his hometown. Many Milwaukee residential thoroughfares were adorned with graceful lighting fixtures called harp streetlights — beehive glass domes cradled in curved cast iron housings with finial tops. The black fixtures perched atop concrete poles and were suspended over intersections. On summer nights, the illumination amid soaring elms on city residential blocks created characteristic chiaroscuro effects, long memorable to Garson.

As an early teen, Garson's pal Toby acquired a .22 rifle. But when Garson broached the topic with his mother, he knew she would demur; she had never permitted him even a BB gun. But against his mother's wishes, he gained his father's support and acquired a used .22. Under his pal Toby's tutelage, Garson lavished great care of the weapon, re-staining the stock and burnishing it with polish. For long months, it was little more than a show piece.

The rifle featured a peep sight, and during a visit to Uncle Essig's farm, he learned to adjust the aperture, and quickly became adept at hitting targets. But his memory of killing a *Spatze*, a sparrow, in his uncle's barn remained painful even years later, of holding the limp body in his hand, gazing into the dead, milky eyes. He was washed with the same guilt as had overcame him when the snapping turtle died in his garage.

One evening in fall while both parents were working, he uncased the rifle and pushed a shell into the chamber. Opening the front door, he took careful aim at the harp streetlight hanging over the intersection about 30 yards distant. He squeezed the trigger, and the beautiful beehive globe shattered. He quickly replaced the rifle in the hall closet. While quite satisfied with his marksmanship, he felt guilty for days until city repairman replaced the glass.

At Camp Matthews, Garson and the platoon were issued what was called Ten-X shooting jackets with reinforced leather elbow pads and shoulder protectors.

"If you begin rifle training wearing a sweatshirt underneath the Ten-X, you damn-well better end with it," PFC Duff commanded. This meant that a recruit must choose to wear either a thick sweatshirt or only a skivvy shirt under the jacket. Once marksmanship training began, no change would be tolerated. Several doubted the theory that even a slight difference in thickness between rifle and shoulder would affect the strike of the bullet on target.

"Is he gonna make a list of who's wearing what," Hal, ever the iconoclast, pitched in.

The southern California sun camped low on the horizon each morning during those weeks leading toward winter solstice. It was nearly midday before dewy December shadows were chased from the deep defiles that led to the ranges. Garson often saw his breath before his face on the march. Overnight thermometers sank into the 40's, and several hours were required to burn through the chill lingering in rugged ravines and gullies. Afternoon temperatures hovered in the high 60s and low 70s. Garson was one of those who held the morning chill at bay by wearing a sweat shirt under his Ten-X, but the price was profuse sweating during the dull afternoon dry firing drills on the terraced snapping-in range.

For Garson, the most tedious activity at Camp Matthews was dry-firing. A series of terraces had been bulldozed on two sides of a plateau, and simulated firing positions marked off. With rifle slings tight on biceps, the nascent shooters simulated the four marksmanship positions – off-hand or standing, sitting, kneeling and prone. They lay under the punishing sun for hours, opening and closing rifle bolts in pretense of loading, aiming and firing. PMI's patrolled the curved dirt tiers, correcting posture, adjusting grips and imparting advice. Sometimes, such drills required that one recruit slam back the bolt after his partner clicked the trigger to affect recoil.

Despite his modest stature, Garson was not particularly supple. He found it difficult to coil his body tightly, especially in the sitting position, his left elbow beneath the rifle and the other clamped by the right knee. On a few occasions, a PMI leaned his weight onto Garson's back, forcing him almost into an ovate shape. The tight rifle sling often caused numbness. His mind wondered back to that date with Leora at the Warner Theater.

"Get your fuckin' head down on the stock,' the PMI growled. "Cheek caresses the wood like feeling your girlfriend's titties. Keep your elbow under the piece," meaning that the left elbow must be forced into unnatural alignment beneath and perpendicular to the rifle, acting as a supporting fulcrum.

"Man, we're in the thick of thin things," Hal whispered during a tedious afternoon drill under a typical cloudless sky. Garson was learning that the Berlin recruit was ready with such arch observations and peculiar aphorisms, many of which Garson did not understand.

"I'm bored out of my gourd," Hal muttered. The hours of snapping in were indeed monotonous and taxing. Sighting a rifle into open space for hours deadened the mind. Garson reminded himself of the sighting mantra.

"Each click'll change the strike of the bullet one inch at 100 yards." The function of front and rear sights were given particular attention, the latter, a peep sight, was easily adjusted by windage and elevation knobs. Other details were many: Rifle butt tight to the shoulder. Take a six o'clock sight picture — balance the bulls-eye like a ball atop the tip of the front sight. Take a full breath. Let out half and hold the rest. Take up the trigger slack. Then squeeze.

"Squeeze it gently, like feeling your girl's little titties," the PMI reminded. There it was again, that penchant to view every Boot's girlfriend as sadly underdeveloped. Was that written in every Marine instructor's script?

"Geez, when we're in combat, we ain't gonna shoot our weapons like this. Who's gonna put that sling on when Gooks're comin' at us?" caviled one of the platoon's rural youths who was conversant with shooting and hunting, complaining about the hackneyed prescriptions of rifle training. Garson saw the merits of the argument, but failed to comment. He was driven only to qualify.

As indicated, discipline was somewhat loosened at Camp Matthews. The rigors of close order drill on the Grinder were missing since the paramount focus was weaponry and qualifying with the M-1 rifle, an annual requirement for every Marine. Spit, polish and close order drill were secondary concerns. Then, one evening, Garson was thrilled with a welcome punctuation in routine.

"Gonna see a 'Shit-Kicker' tonight, a Western picture," announced PFC Duff after chow. It was an uncharacteristic gesture of diversion. Until two months ago, Garson was habituated to movie theaters, sometimes seeing three or more double features each week. He surmised he had viewed thousands of movies in his lifetime.

The movie "Shane" played at the Ritz after Garson had departed for California that fall. The Camp Matthews movie venue was not a theater at all: Films were projected on a large sheet hung between trees; at times details were distorted in the screen's vertical folds and draped creases. The audience sat on two-by-four planks nailed to upturned logs. Despite the Spartan venue, Garson was thrilled.

"Don't take seats until I tell you!" Duff yelled as the platoon filed between the rows. As they stood at attention, other units waiting for the movie to begin watched with audible amusement.

"Ready! Seats!" Duff commanded, the word "seats" pronounced as "heats." As usual, the order was not carried out with sufficient dispatch.

"On your feet, you fuckin' clowns," the corporal ordered. "I want you to get it fuckin' together."

"Ready! Heats!"

"On your feet! Now, when I give you the order again, I want to hear only one asshole — one fuckin' asshole. Ready! Heats!"

From the other platoon, sniggers and chortles burbled. Their DI had already absented himself. After two more attempts, Platoon 023 slammed onto the boards to Duff's satisfaction. "At ease." As soon as the studio logo appeared, the DI departed.

Watching Alan Ladd in such surroundings was a pleasant respite from the rigors of the rifle range. Garson enjoyed seeing one of his favorite heroes, this time in a Western epic. Despite his underwhelming stature, Garson had enjoyed the actor in earlier hard boiled roles: "This Gun for Hire" and "The Blue Dahlia." He liked the timbre of Ladd's confident voice, staccato delivery, even the manner in which he styled his fair hair. He liked the Jean Arthur character, even though her role of an unadorned prairie wife in the Western contrasted with earlier gritty performances in Capra comedies opposite Jimmy Stewart and Clark Gable.

As "Shane" neared its climax, a fine evening mist began that gave way to light rain. Garson donned his poncho. As minutes passed, the precipitation became more insistent, distorting some scenes. Garson huddled, disgusted that movie images were blurring and washing out. In ones and twos, recruits began filtering from the open air theater. Garson and a hardy few bore the discomfort, determined to see it through. But the rain became a torrent, obliterating the moving images; it was unwatchable. Even Heissen, the avid movie-goer, gave up.

When Garson arose, disappointed and dispirited, he was the last recruit to depart. It would be many months before Garson witnessed the climactic draw-down between fair-haired buckskinned Shane and dark and demonic Jack Wilson, a signature role for Walter Jack Palance, whose jutting cheekbones, boxer's nose and angular presence became synonymous with villainy.

The movie triggered intermittent discussions among many recruits in days ahead, particularly among the urban youths whose lives had been filled with motion pictures. Even when he added little to the conversation, Garson was keenly interested in others' observations and analyses about his favorite entertainment.

"We lived across the street from a show house, the New World on 6th Street," Heissen said during one conversation. That was near National Avenue in Milwaukee, across the Menomonee River Valley from the downtown, Garson knew. The noisy cross town streetcar lines from South Milwaukee to the northern suburbs, and the interurban to Chicago that ran past the show house sometimes intruded upon movie soundtracks. He had watched movies in that small theater after the war when his father rented a nearby commercial front for his business. Like the Ritz on Villard, the New World booked features many weeks after they were screened in first-run houses downtown – opulently-appointed theaters such as the Palace, Warner and Riverside. Like Garson, Heissen rode streetcars to those luxury venues on Wisconsin Avenue.

"My folks let me go quite a bit," Heissen said. Movies for Garson, Heissen and others were their generation's *lingua franca*. Most grew to adulthood bathed by the silvery images, washed with their artistic, cultural and social values. There was something about a hunkering down in a darkened movie theater, Garson agreed, being absorbed into a movie milieu, soaking up lessons about manhood, morality, honor, loyalty and more. Coming late in his life, television never rooted so deeply.

"You know, I even got excited when those movie studio symbols appeared on screen: the Paramount torch lady, the Paramount mountain peak, Warner Brothers shield, the RKO tower and cheesy lightning bolts, Leo the lion for MGM, "*ars gratia artis.*"

"Means 'art for art's sake'," Heissen put in.

The love of movies had been introduced early in Garson's life, starting with popular Dish Nights at the unassuming Ritz Theater in his neighborhood. Garson several times explained to buddies that his mother, two years old when her family immigrated to America, became enamored with moving pictures early in her life when she lived in the crossroad Wisconsin village of Rubicon, northwest of Milwaukee. Some nights each week, the old clapboard dance hall gave way to a temporary movie theater; she and her older sisters were permitted to pay the nickel admission.

She enjoyed the flickering silent images at first, but quickly became addicted to talkies. By the time her family relocated to Milwaukee, she was in her early 20s. Several of the city's numerous neighborhood show houses were a convenient streetcar ride away. She doted on domestic dramas and farces, on "weepy" romances and sparkling musicals starring Fred Astaire, Ginger Rogers, Dick Powell, Ruby Keeler and others.

She carried that fascination into marriage, but her husband did not share in such celluloid ephemera. In the developing town of North Milwaukee, a small commercial strip anchored by an unassuming theater, the Ritz, was within walking distance from her new house; here she found diversionary sustenance. While her husband bowled, she escaped the drudgery of Depression factory work in black and white fantasy. When her son was about five, she shared that fascination.

Each season, theater management introduced a new pattern of ceramic serving ware, a piece given with each admission — plates, cups and saucers, creamers, sugar bowls and more. Extra pieces were available for purchase. Audiences on those weekly "Dish Nights" were almost exclusively female, Garson clearly remembered, and the showings catered to them. He recalled distinctly that during a few features, a piece of dinnerware slipped from a lap, shattering on the theater's concrete floor. He found it curious that such incidents were usually greeted with generous applause, as though perverse delight greeted misfortune.

While usually attentive to the first feature of the double-bill evenings, Garson often became bored or tired during the second, leaning on her arm to slumber. He distinctly recalled falling asleep near the end of "Wuthering Heights" even though he was captivated by dark and alluring Merle Oberon; Garson felt his mother's sobs with the war deaths of "The Fighting Sullivans" and the tragic wartime romance of the "The Clock," and was roused by her laughter at Cary Grant and Katharine Hepburn hijinks in "The Philadelphia Story."

Garson's memory was distinct enough to develop antipathy for some screen stars even in those early days. While Hollywood churned out numerous new titles, it also began the practice of re-releasing older 1930s features to second and third-run houses like the Ritz, exposing Garson to stars of an earlier era. Too young to know why, he never developed empathy for the histrionic Bette Davis with her heavily-lidded eyes, or found favor for with such potent females as Norma Shearer, Joan Crawford or Barbara Stanwyck.

Despite his mother's fondness for the parade of cookie-cutter films, Garson was bored with treacle Shirley Temple, warbling Deanna Durbin and skater Sonja Heinne. He was impatient with performances of Greer Garson. In contrast, unlike his mother, boyhood Garson was attracted to voluptuous Jean Harlow and crackling Carole Lombard as well as the powerful dancing of leggy Eleanor Powell. Had he seen any of Greta Garbo's sultry roles, he might have been enamored, too. He enjoyed the debonair and comedic Cary Grant, gangly Stewart and confident Clark Gable.

Like Garson and his mother, Heissen had little interest in publicity lives of movie stars, eschewing ubiquitous magazine and news features about them. Instead, he simply preferred actors' screen portrayals, particularly when they seemed to lose themselves in disparate characters. Garson envied his buddy's incredible command of details – actors, directors, scripts, scenes and themes. It was from Heissen that Garson learned that one of his favorite films, "His Girl Friday," was based upon a Ben Hecht drama, and the Rosalind Russell character, Hildy, had been a man in the Broadway production. Hal was certain to provide some humorous anecdote.

"When we lived in Berlin, we always thought the owner of the Rex Theater on Main Street cheated us. Guy named Sharkey. We got movies months behind Milwaukee. And he sold us stale popcorn." The owner operated a two-tier ticket price – one admission for adults and another for kids under 12. The latter was limited to seats in the first four rows.

"Hackbart looked older than the rest of us, and once, tried to be a smart-ass. He and his girl sat down in the adult seats even though he paid for kids' tickets." The uniformed usherettes, high school girls, patrolled the show, and spotted Hackbart. They ordered him and his date to move up front with the rest of us kids. Hal's silver flecked incisor caused a touch of sibilance. "He didn't move at first, but we all laughed when he and the dame finally got up and left."

Television had come late in the lives of many of Garson's generation and had not influenced it as much as movies. Garson was in his teens when his mother purchased the large walnut console that dominated the living room for a few years. Until the novelty wore thin, Garson watched a few nightly programs, particularly the inventive Sid Caesar's comedy; he was mildly diverted by frenetic Milton Berle's antics.

If there were regularly television programs that captivated him it was sports, particularly Pabst Blue Ribbon boxing on Wednesday nights, and Gillette's Friday Night Fights. Munching baloney clamped between peanut butter slavered pieces of white bread, he watched classic contests with slick Sugar Ray Robinson, powerful Rocky Marciano, Carmen Basilio, lumbering "Two Ton" Tony Galento, persistent Jersey Joe Walcott and even the old champ, Joe Louis, whose heyday had long since passed.

Garson had also been taken with such disreputable sports as roller derby, admiring dynamic women skaters, Ann Calvello and Joanie Weston and others, dueling furiously at Chicago Stadium or Los Angeles Coliseum. Much to his mother's dismay, he was also occasionally diverted by wrestling programs featuring Milwaukee grapplers Crusher Lisowki and Dick "The Bruiser" Affils, Polish villains until their television rehabilitations.

"Why you want to watch that junk for?" She thought better for her son.

"I saw those guys on TV, too," said Springer, the dark, toothless Milwaukeean. Such were the shared recollections that aired during unstructured times at Camp Matthews. Of course, recruits constantly tended to their M-1's and other gear often sitting on foot lockers that were dragged into walkways in the tent city. During such scutwork, they also compared backgrounds and experiences. As in his former life, Garson was an attentive audience for the graphic story tellers who illuminated their tales with anecdotes.

Not only were recruits deprived of movies, but newspapers and magazines as well. For all intents and purposes, there was no world outside of Camp Matthews or MCRD. Perhaps the only facts known for certain were that Dwight Eisenhower remained president and General Lemuel C. Shepherd was commandant of the Marine Corps. Movies and life before the Corps were prime topics of diversion.

"My folks were immigrants, too," Heissen offered when Garson spoke of his parents. "When they asked my grandpa's name at Ellis Island, he answered 'Herr von Eisen' – Mister Von Eisen. But when they wrote it down, it became Heissen. That's been the family name since. That's what my grandma told me."

Garson tried to draw out Priech, the awkward and diffident tentmate, about his background.

"*Sprichts du Deutsch*, Prick, er Priech?" Garson asked, using the familiar form *du* instead of *Sie*. He still remembered considerable German from his childhood when it was spoken in his household.

"*Ja, ein kleines bischen*," Priech replied. His forebears had come to Wisconsin about the time early in the century that Garson's Grandpa Guttig immigrated from the Austro-Hungarian Empire.

"My kin came to Dodge County, too, and they raised diary cows. Some governor back then was trying to expand dairying in the state."

"William Hoard," Heissen put in. His knowledge was apparent.

"My grandpa worked for the Kissel Kar Company in Hartford," Garson said, "before he moved to Milwaukee, my Ma told me. She hated the farm, and was happy when they moved. Called her *Schimmel* because she was like a white horse. Met my dad on a streetcar; he was a motorman before the Depression. Born in old century."

Like Heissen and Hal, Priech had graduated from high school. But he was discouraged from following his father into dairying, knowing older brothers would split the acreage when they came of age. Thus, his prospects were uncertain. He related that he had spotted a poster in downtown Hartford of a Marine in dress blues. Drawn to the heroic image, he decided to join, thinking three years in the military might improve possibilities. Even while he could not ameliorate the continual harassment of Priech by DIs, Garson felt protective of his florid-faced buddy even as he was relieved the Prick deflected attention from himself.

"My pa came over with my grandparents when he was about 13, I guess," said Liska, another of those voluble recruits to whom Garson was attracted. "Claimed to be a tried and true Yankee, but said he was always proud of what the Poles did, especially in America." Liska's voice was moderated and measured.

"Don't know if it's true or not, but pa said two Polish explorers named Sanduski mapped much of Ohio Country way back when. But when the maps were made, they changed the spelling to Sandusky so it wouldn't sound Polish." He added that the Polish general, Koscuisko, who fought in the Revolution, selected the site for West Point, but was not given credit for it. Garson listened to Liska's family stories with rapt attention. The Detroiter spoke of a cousin in Florida called Ben whose real name was Benkovic. He was nicknamed "Bruiser Bear" because he wrestled in the south Florida circuit.

"He wasn't too tall, not much more than me, but weighed a ton. Ate all the time to stay big. Once, in an eating contest, he consumed a 12-pound turkey with all of the trimmings in an hour. My dad told me Ben ate a dozen lobster tails in an all-you-can eat restaurant once."

"Milwaukee had a couple of Polack wrestlers from the south side who were on TV," Garson interrupted.

"When I was a kid and we visited Ben," Liska continued, "he'd lift me up and pretend to give me a bear hug, grunting with his arms around my body. He once wrestled the famous Yukon Erik to a draw," Liska said.

"*The* Yukon Erik?" Garson asked, "from TV?"

"Yup." He explained that his uncle also had a magnificent tenor voice and on Saturday nights he sang operatic arias at the town band shell. A heating and ventilating worker by trade, Ben still lived with his mother at age 30. But he finally met the girl of his dreams,

Stella by name; they planned to marry. He expanded the house that he and his bride planned to call home, and constructed a back cottage for his mother. But one day, Ben went missing. Mother and prospective spouse were frantic. After a protracted search they found him dead in the crawlspace beneath the house.

"They said he had an underdeveloped heart, and he died putting in the ductwork."

Liska almost proudly boasted that a distant cousin had run booze around town for Al Capone during Prohibition. Once, he was driving from Chicago to Detroit on Highway 12 with a load of Canadian liquor when the cops chased him near Kalamazoo.

"He ditched the car and booze in Kazoo, and hitchhiked home. Never said what happened to the car or liquor" There was another relative who carried bootleg whiskey across the river from Windsor, Canada. As a kid, Liska said he admired photos of sleek and fast cabin cruisers used in the trade.

"Times were tough back then, especially for immigrants. They did what they had to, to survive. "Had another uncle who knocked up a girl, Eva was her name, but claimed he wasn't the father and wouldn't marry the girl. His mother went to the hospital to visit the baby. Took one look at that baby and said: 'That's a Liska kid, and you're gonna marry Eva no matter what.' They did, too," Liska concluded, "and they're still together after all these years."

"Joined the Corps 'cause a favorite uncle of mine was in the Marines. Wounded at Guadalcanal and fought on Okinawa." Liska said the uncle had terrible dreams when he came home from the Pacific, and slept apart from his wife because he flailed about at night and once choked her almost insensible.

"His arms and chest were covered in tattoos," Liska noted, and he always wore long sleeved shirts to hide them. "Said that he and his Marine buddies never thought they'd survive to return home anyway." The skin decorations included a helmeted Devil Dog with drooling fangs, a Chinese dragon, two perky pinups, one nearly naked, a dagger with the words "Death Before Dishonor" on its blood-dripping blade and more.

I hope you'll indulge another intrusion here in my Pop's account. As is obvious by the paragraphs just past, he was given to long digressions and tangents. Of course, they're calculated to flesh out characters and enhance situations, but I think they sometimes slow the narrative. I think this kitchen-table memoir is sometimes diffuse, haphazard, repetitious and lacking in proper transitions. It needs a real editor, not merely a subjective son, so I didn't change much, letting readers to decide if I'm right or not.

Baker, the largest of the Camp Matthews firing ranges, was designated as the site for Platoon 023's marksmanship qualification. Before actually firing live ammunition, however, the recruits spent three days in the rifle butts, those deep, shadowed trenches below the target line. Recruits pasted bulls-eye and silhouettes onto backers, and practiced lifting and lowering counter-weighted frame stanchions in unison. The Baker Range butts were run by a rotund gunnery sergeant whose name Garson could not pull from memory. Some claimed he was a "lifer," a career Marine. A Southerner with graying temples, ready laugh and easy manner, he permitted a decided slackness from rigorous discipline; recruits were permitted to open the top button of their dungarees and untuck jackets from waists while they engaged in sweaty work. But the Gunney was intolerant of ineptitude and inefficiency during qualification matches.

Baker Range featured 50 firing positions. It was imperative during rapid fire sequences that frames be hoisted in unison and withdrawn with dispatch when time expired. The Gunney brooked nothing less.

"Now, my chillun, let's get ready for a string of *ree*-pid fire," The sergeant sang out in a distinctive basso profundo voice. Heissen said he sounded like Wallace Beery in "Salute to the Marines."

"Stand-by-eee. Aaa-uuuup!" the Gunney roared, his mouth cocked to one side.

"Not good enough," he complained. "Let's do it again, chillun." And for a half an hour or more, recruits practiced like automatons until the tech sergeant was satisfied that target frames were raised and lowered in perfect accord.

It was also essential during slow fire that shot holes be located quickly, round cardboard markers poked into holes and shot values indicated for shooters. Values were identified by round metal discs held aloft on long poles – white upon the black bulls-eye and black on the surrounding white. Should the shot be a miss, the target crew waved a red flag, the dreaded "Maggie's Drawers," meaning no points. A ready rebuke awaited any two-man target team that needed a reminder to pull and score. The radio call, "Mark on target 33" meant the shooter was waiting for his score to be displayed.

After three days in the butts, the anticipated day to fire the M-1 with "live" ammunition for the first time arrived. Even after weeks of instruction and routine, of dull dry firing, Garson was nervous and fitful. Every step in the process of loading and firing seemed rote but he was still given pause as he sat on the edge of an upturned ammunition canister, waiting behind the firing line. He tried to mask his apprehension, mentally reviewing every step in the firing process yet uncertain how hard the rifle would recoil against his bony shoulder. Shooting a .22 rifle the week before provided no preparation at all. A .30 caliber round propelled by 50,000 pounds of chamber pressure was another matter. When Garson was summoned to the firing line that morning, and ordered into the prone position, he thought the PMI might hear his palpitating heart. He was handed one .30 caliber round, a brass jacketed lead bullet.

"Lock and load!" The command echoed from range speakers along the firing line. Garson fumbled the bullet, nearly dropping it. He noticed the instructor shake his head. Trembling fingers finally fitted the round into the chamber. He racked the bolt closed.

"Ready on the right? Ready on the left? All ready on the firing line. This'll be a string of slow fire. *Commence fire!*"

Garson screwed the rifle butt into his shoulder and propped himself on his elbows — as he had practiced thousands of times at the snapping-in range. He clicked off the safety, and peered through the sight aperture. The PMI gently reviewed the salient points:

"Now, take a full breath. Leave half of it out. Hold the rest. Take up trigger slack. Squeeze. Don't jerk. You don't want to know exactly when the round goes off, else you'll flinch or buck the rifle off target.

Feel the trigger the way you tickle your girlfriend's little titties." Certainly that exhortation was also printed in every PMI's notebook, Garson mused fleetingly. But he had never felt any girl's titties, had actually seen real ones only twice — indistinctly in the dim backseat of Toby's old Buick, and more recently in the murky light of a Mexican brothel. He brushed away those fleeting recollections.

Heart throbbing in his ears, Garson applied slow pressure on the trigger with the pad of his finger. Before he realized, the powder exploded in the chamber, and drove the lead bullet down range. Recoil jammed the right thumb knuckle into his cheek, and the muzzle jerked up and settled back. Two hundred yards down range, the target frame disappeared.

"Call your shot," the PMI said. He meant that Garson should recall his sight picture at the instant of discharge. Garson had not flinched, but could not recall exactly. He guessed low. The target frame reappeared from the butts, and the black marker outside the bulls-eye.

"See there? You're low and right," the instructor observed. "Gimme three clicks elevation and three windage." Garson made the correction, and was handed another round. After the second shot, the Marine demanded one more corrective click. On the third and final shot, he hit the black nearly center.

"That's the dope for your rifle then," the instructor said. "Good luck tomorrow." Garson was dismissed from the firing line, and returned to an upturned ammo box in the ready area, trying to settle himself after the ordeal. A thick-set Marine with a craggy face and deep coppery complexion strode along the ready area. He was neither recruit nor PMI, but carried an M-1.

"See that Indian there?" a nearby instructor tipped the brim of his hat toward the shooter. "One of the best off-hand shots in the Corps. Scores perfect 50s one after another." Heavily-lidded, expressionless eyes gave him a nonchalant, almost somnambulant appearance; cheekbones were so sharp that they threatened to pierce his skin. Look at that barrel chest, Garson thought; no wonder he could hold the rifle so steady: He just propped the weapon on that generous expanse.

The week before Christmas, the long-anticipated final test began – Qualification Day. Fifty shots comprised the course of fire, five ten-shot strings. There were three distances – 200, 300 and 500 yards, and four positions – standing, sitting, kneeling and prone — slow and rapid fire, the former on standard bulls-eye targets and the latter on silhouettes, the so-called "head and shoulders of an enemy." Rapid fire events required the shooter to position an empty clip inside the receiver, and wedge two loose rounds into position. The closing bolt rammed one shell into the chamber. After the second shot fired, the empty clip ejected with a distinctive sound. Even in the distant memory of a septuagenarian, Garson could "hear" the metallic "*twang*" of the clip as it kicked out high and right.

To qualify, a recruit needed to score at least 200 points of a possible 250 to earn a Marksman's badge. A score from 210 to 219 was accorded a Sharpshooter medal while 220 and above gained the top award, Expert. Garson had long dreamed of that decoration.

Since his arms still remained underdeveloped, he was most concerned about off-hand and kneeling positions at 200 and 300 yards. The day before, Pre-Qual it was called, he had proved proficient at two rapid fire positions – standing to sitting and standing to prone, scoring a "possible," 50 points, at the latter. He had earned the same points at prone 500-yard slow fire. Still, he was unsatisfied with that 217 tally, and tossed largely sleepless that night, the vision of a handsome Expert medal, the coveted chimera, dangling above his head. As the platoon marched to Baker Range that Friday morning, Garson felt leaden.

High wooly clouds blanketed the sky. Gauzy fog clung to the gullies between hillocks. As the platoon trudged from its tents, the rim of rosy pink appeared at the shifting cloud edge. On the range, Garson sat impatiently in the ready area, waiting for the sky to brighten. He was a bit chilled in air that had not yet reached 50 degrees. Minutes before 6:30, the sun appeared, burning through the haze. Wind was light, and the day was promising. He breathed easier.

"Helps reduce the glare," advised Hupner, sitting next to Garson in the ready area. From a smoking smudge pot used to blacken and reduce sight glare, the Texan had smeared carbon above his cheek bones to prevent sun reflection. Garson followed his lead, and also wedged cleaning patches into his ears to dampen the sound — an almost useless gesture since his ears rang the entire day after shooting. As he waited, he once more snugged the rifle sling above his left bicep, ignoring tingling numbness.

After weeks of absence, Sergeant Maddox appeared to witness his platoon's performance. He would pace behind the firing line, often scrutinizing scores chalked on a large black board. Part of the drive to achieve the designation of honor platoon would be based upon the unit's rifle scores.

Finally, shooting commenced. At 200 yards, Garson scored a sorry 37 in the opening slow-fire string – off-hand standing. His left arm could not steady the rifle, the front sight dancing and rolling around the bulls-eye. Similarly, after moving back to the 300-yard line, he was unable to stabilize the right elbow on his knee in the second slow fire string; he managed another pitiful 37 points. His head hung. He had lost too many points already; an Expert medal was virtually impossible now. But, then, to his surprise, he surged in rapid fire standing to sitting.

"With a clip and two rounds, lock and load!" range speakers barked. He loaded with ease.

"Ready on the right? Ready on the left? All ready on the firing line." Garson glued his eyes downrange. "Commence firing!" He drove his behind into the ground, snapped the rifle butt into his shoulder and squinted through the sight. He rocked back with recoils, the rifle steadying back again after the shots. The empty clip twanged free, and without fumbling he jammed in a full clip. Garson's right cheek ached, but he was determined to maintain a steady hold, accepting the battering as the price. The second empty clip clanged free of the receiver.

"Cease fire! Cease fire!" Garson exhaled, dropped the rifle from his shoulder and squinted at the butts. When the frame popped back into view, the group of ten shots was tight but three had leaked low out of the silhouette — a score of 44. He was on course to qualify with an average total, only a Marksman.

While he sat dejectedly on the upturned ammo box waiting for his next relay — the second rapid fire sequence — he briefly fingered the little Christ child statuette his mother had pressed upon him, the talisman Sergeant Maddox had discovered at MCRD. Garson's heart sank when he discovered one of the out-stretched hands had broken in his pocket during earlier firing. Bring me luck anyway, he thought. He adjusted the sight elevation screw several clicks.

"Man, your cheek's all red." Hal sat on the ammo box next to him. Garson swiped at his face in acknowledgement. The soreness meant he had placing his cheek on stock consistently. He would trade the pain for a good score.

"How you doin'?"

"Shit so far," Hal responded with a frown. "Gotta get my fuckin' shit together, man, or I won't qualify."

Later, Garson stood on the firing line for the second rapid fire match. At the command, he loaded the two rounds and narrow-eyed the silhouette target. When frames jumped into view, he dropped into the prone position, pulling the rifle into his shoulder. The black head and shoulders perched above his front sight. He squeezed off two shots, and reloaded rapidly. Deep breath. Exhale half. Hold. Six o'clock sight picture. Take up trigger slack. Squeeze. Crack. Recoil. Rock forward. Deep breath. Exhale. Hold. Six o'clock. The M-1 felt good, almost a part of his body. The empty clip clanged and arced out before time had elapsed. Fuck! He had shot too fast. The rifle sling had cut the webbing between his left thumb and forefinger.

He waited interminably for his frame to reappear. When it was raised, his heart leapt. All of the white shot hole pins were clustered tightly. The white and black metal disk was spun. It was a possible – 50 points. He was thrilled. As he marched back two hundred yards with the platoon, he calculated that he might still attain Sharpshooter.

Garson had scored well in the slow fire prone match the day before. But the targets were tiny at this extreme distance, no larger than a pinpoint it seemed. He sucked at the trickle of blood on his left hand, and tightened the rifle sling once more. Confidence welled in him. Still, there were details to consider. Traveling at 2700 feet a second, the bullet would reach the target in half a second, less time than an eye blink. The M-1 had a maximum range of 3500 yards, and this final string of fire was only one-seventh that distance. The late morning temperature had risen to the mid-60s. The bright sun caused heat rises at this distance which created an occasional distorting shimmer. Was his sight dope from yesterday still valid?

Methodically, rhythmically Garson loaded and fired every round. Each time the target frame reappeared after scoring, it displayed a white disk in the black center – five points. Ten shots. Ten bulls. He scored another 50. Arising satisfied, he dusted off his dungarees for the final time and removed the rifle sling. He strode to the center of the line to verify his score. Indeed, a 218 – one better than the day before and only two less than Expert. He glowed inside. He would wear a Sharpshooter medal! When Sergeant Maddox made note of the score, he strode to where Garson rested on an ammo box.

"Still carrying that?" the drill instructor said. Garson was absently fingering the little religious icon.

"Yes, sir!" Garson replied, almost defiantly. "Brings me luck. Fired a 217 in Pre-Qual yesterday. Got 218 today." He paused a beat before adding "sir." Maddox said nothing more, only studying Garson briefly before inhaling deeply and striding away, beaten once more, Garson liked to suppose, certain the DI would remember his name.

Heissen and Hal each qualified as Marksmen. Liska, who told Garson about his shooting prowess as a teen, gained an Expert medal as did a few others, including portly Brtek. To Garson's chagrin he later learned that goggle-eyed Fletcher had also fired Sharpshooter. Preston and Rusty were Marksmen.

For the remainder of days at Camp Matthews, Boots who did not qualify were made to wear their dungaree jackets and caps backwards, and march at the rear of the platoon. Like Hester Prynne, they were marked as unworthy — shitbirds, fuckups who would endanger any unit to which they were assigned. Priech, who almost everyone had taken to calling "Prick" now, was predictably among these. Even later, when Garson scrutinized the platoon's formal photograph, the absence of rifle badges on dress uniforms stood out glaringly.

While the platoon cleaned rifles that Friday afternoon, Garson told tentmates the anecdote about Springer winning all of those half dollars at Las Vegas when they traveled from Milwaukee.

"Springer? Guy with no teeth?" Indeed, the tall Milwaukee youth with the black hair, Dracula widow's peak and prominent nose had been one of those, like Garson, who suffered extractions at MCRD. But where once Springer exhibited a noticeable overbite there was now only a dark maw with gums and tongue. Many words slurped like an old man's. Hal, the inveterate anecdotist, segued from Springer's good fortune to a story of hitchhiking alone from Berlin when he was 16.

Hal had a grab bag of wagering tales picked up in Vegas, Reno, Carson City, Elko, in prosperous casinos and dingy betting parlors. A few of the shaggy dog tales stuck in Garson's memory, including one about a Midwesterner who had lost all but a few dollars. He was driving back east, across the desert, cursing malevolent gods and the fates when an arrow of light daggered onto his forehead, seeming to pierce his skull. The Camp Matthews audience closed around Hal, and he reeled it in.

"Go back! Go back!' whispered an ethereal voice." At first the gambler ignored the words, thinking too much Lucky Lager beer had addled him; but after several miles of insistent heavenly entreaties, he made a U-turn. The voice guided him back to town, along Las Vegas Boulevard and to a specific roulette wheel at the Golden Nugget.

"Bet on 20 red," the voice advised. With his last dollar he followed the celestial admonition. The huge wheel spun. It whirled and slowed, the ball clattering into 20 red. He doubled his money.

"Bet on 20 red," the voice reiterated. And on it went, the gambler accumulating chips, thousands of dollars worth, in successive spins. Those tokens piled exponentially. A crowd gathered to watch, pushing tightly toward the table. The comely girl who operated the wheel smiled broadly. After several more winning spins, the bettor reached toward the stacks, intent on quitting the game. But the seraphic voice insisted he let the money ride on 20 red. Reluctantly, the man pulled back his hands, and watched the black ball whirl about the groove. After long seconds, inertia overtook it, and it clattered loudly into a slot. Observers gasped and in unison. It was 31 black!

"Well, whadaya know!" whispered the ethereal voice. Hal's silver filling winked as he smiled at his audience. Garson and other Marines groaned, several shuffling away.

Hal was also free about small town events that captivated the population in Berlin.

"There was the night the Baptist Church burned," he recounted. As the firemen fought the intense blaze, Revered Beasley, the minister, observed calmly. Most townsfolk who gathered to witness one of the most well-known events of the year were not of Beasley's flock.

"It's a good 'un!" someone said, commenting on the intensity of the blaze and the actions of the volunteer firemen. The fact that the building was a house of worship was of no consequence. "They just wanted see the spectacle, a big show," Hal concluded.

That story joined in Garson's memory with the fire that had burned a tiny neighborhood church in his neighborhood back home. Rumor had that the Holy Roller congregation, a strange Pentecostal sect, engaged in riotous and bizarre rituals and behaviors. Garson's "sister," Lana, told him she had slipped unobserved into one of those Friday evening gatherings; she claimed the people pranced about wildly, shouting gibberish — glossolalia. When her widowed mother heard of it, she chided her daughter for taking such a foolish chance. The congregants came from other parts of the city, so gossip and supposition about weird goings-on went unchecked on Garson's block. The fire's origins were said to be suspicious; in time the frame structure was demolished to make way for a commercial building.

Hal also served as a conduit for the scuttlebutt that circulated through Boot Camp, sometimes like wildfires. If the rumor was traced back to its origin, Garson suspected, the real story might be quite different. His Wisconsin buddy was adept at polishing presentations. Garson liked the hearsay Hal offered about that ominous Camp Matthews eminence called Big Agony that rose perhaps 40 or 50 feet above the flat scrubby landscape. Platoon 023 had several times been marched over it, and Garson recalled his labored breath, protesting muscles and stretched tendons. His rifle weighed a ton.

"Ya know, one guy told me about a DI who made his platoon duck walk up Big Agony, calling cadence from below." Before any skepticism was expressed, Hal launched into another story he heard about another platoon that was forced to hold mail call on that prominence. "Those fuckin' bastards were assembled down below, and the DI sounded off the names of those who had letters. Pity the poor son of a bitch who got more than one, 'cause he had to make that climb for each one." His fierce dark eyebrows yo-yoed at the telling and the silver filling flashed. Hal segued without transition, simply piling one yarn atop another.

"Hear about the dumb fuck who lost his rifle?" Garson was in disbelief because a recruit would sooner lose an arm than his rifle.

"Yeah," Hal said, "fell asleep on a two to four fire watch. When the Right Guide woke him, the M-1 was gone."

"Fuck! Come on, Hal!"

"No, really, man. Guy in 022 told me. Said he thought a PMI or somebody snatched it and sold it T-Town."

"Can't be. What happened to him?"

"Went to the brig, I guess."

"If it'd been Reid, they'd a found that shitbird dead in a garbage dumpster."

During the early weeks at Camp Matthews, Garson received a few letters — one from his mother who wrote of long hours washing dishes at Shorty's Restaurant and the cold and snow in Milwaukee. His father had appended three labored lines, wishing him well and asking him to take care of himself. Garson still waited for a communication from Betsy, the girl from high school who had evoked uncommon feelings in him.

The Texan, Hupner, still served as platoon mail clerk despite his illiteracy. Garson read a few letters from his parents over the weeks, and wrote as the burly recruit dictated. Garson would learn many things about his tentmate. Some mail calls produced humorous incidents.

"Krupa," Duff shouted at one mail call.

"Here, sir." The recruit sprinted forward to accept an envelope. Back in the ranks, he opened it; enclosed was a small photo. Duff noticed.

"What's that, Krupa, a fuck picture?" Formal studio poses and chaste candid photos were acceptable. But anything too provocative was prohibited and confiscated. Nude photos, called "fuck pictures," were completely outlawed.

"Who's this?"

"Girlfriend, sir,"

"Your tootsie, Krupa? What's her name?"

"Heidi, sir. Heidi Beduzak."

"Heidi Ba..." the PFC blurted, then guffawed. A few recruits snickered.

"Really, now, Heidi Beduzak you say?"

"Sir, yes, sir!" Krupa shifted his weight from one foot to another. The PFC studied the photo for a minute or more, before handing it back to Krupa.

"Well, Heidi Beduzak ain't no Betty Grable, that's for sure. Her titties're too tiny. Cute face though," Duff concluded. After mail call, Krupa turned to Barker, ever sympathetic, asking what was so funny. He had earlier been the butt of Corporal Reid's harassment at MCRD.

"Heidi's a Swiss or German name. Remember those Shirley Temple movies when you were a kid? I suppose the DI just thought Heidi with a Polish last name was incongruous." Krupa did not fully understand.

One of the most traumatic experiences during those weeks at rifle range involved swimming. Garson had never overcome his fear of water, but all Marines were required to pass the swimming proficiency test that included a leap from a two-story tower, simulating an escape from a sinking ship.

Instructors on the tall platform explained the proper feet-first pose when jumping: Body vertical, ankles crossed, one hand cupped under chin and nose while the other protected the "family jewels," the groin. The pose was said to prevent injury when hitting the water from such a height.

While Garson and the non-swimmers were schooled in proper strokes and breathing, Preston, Rusty, Heissen, Hal and the rest climbed the tower and plunged. Then, matters came to a halt, and everyone's attention shifted to the tower where a little drama was unfolding

"Come on, Chief, let's fuckin' do it!" an instructor up there growled. Felton, the platoon's lone Indian, hesitated, unwilling to step off the platform. Try as he might, the instructor was unable to order or coax the Boot to leap. The Marine grabbed Felton, trying to push him off, but the recruit locked arms around a wooden railing, wagging his head. He would not go. Everyone on the tower and pool deck, and in the water was riveted to the confrontation.

"Chief, if you don't fuckin' jump now, I'm gonna grab you by the fuckin' stacking swivel and beat you severely about the head and shoulders," Hal swore he heard those words. "I'm gonna knock the sorry, fuckin' shit outta you, you cowardly fuck." Still, no movement from Felton, his arms viselike about the railing. After many minutes and consultations with other instructors, the tower was vacated and Felton permitted to climb down. He never did make that leap.

After the drama's climax, Garson was ordered to swim two lengths of the pool. He and others had earlier practiced the proper strokes in the chilly water. He plunged feet first into the deep end, and flailed his arms wildly and kicked his feet fitfully. To his surprise, he made modest progress. The pool floor reached up to meet him, and he completed the first length of two required for qualification. His confidence rose, but only a little. He stood, looked back over the final 50 yards and pushed forward. Slowly, the pool floor slipped away under him. His breath was shallow, and his strokes irregular. He gulped the putrid chlorine water. His body felt heavy and he began to founder. He thought it was about halfway back that a long pole poked down to him. He grabbed at it in panic, and was pulled to the concrete. The instructor scowled as he climbed out.

During the final week at the tent camp, recruit platoons became familiar with other small arms in the Marine arsenal – firing the light carbine, a lightweight .30 caliber weapon usually carried by NCOs, and the heavy BAR, blasting 120 to 150 rounds a minute.

"Short rounds, you little guys get assigned as BAR-men or assistants," explained another of the salty PMIs. "Why, you may ask? Because you're smaller targets." Marine combat units were built upon the foundation of four-man fire teams each organized around the Browning Automatic Rifle. Three teams comprised each squad in the platoon. After graduation from MCRD, when Garson was ordered to nearby Camp Pendleton for advanced combat training, he was designated an assistant who often "humped" that 20-pound weapon and its bulky ammo. But unlike the M-1 rifle, Garson never became proficient at field stripping — disassembling or reassembling the cumbersome automatic.

"You got big hands for a little guy, grappling hooks almost," remarked a gruff tech sergeant who coached on the .45 pistol range. He observed carefully as Garson jammed the clip into the pistol's handle. The slide slammed forward, pushing a round into the chamber.

"She's loaded, now, so watch where she's pointed." Garson would become extremely proficient firing the bulky pistol, and boasted that he qualified Expert every year in the Corps. From the Aleutian Islands, that skill would allow him to depart a month early from a year-long deployment, transferred to the month-long Western Division Rifle & Pistol competition. But he was not adept enough to stand out in that competition.

The most harrowing experience occurred on the Camp Matthews

grenade range. The platoon spent an entire morning there, instructed by lecture and grainy films about the nomenclature and various types of grenades. The night before, Garson had perused the *Guidebook for Marines* chapter on those weapons, hoping to get a leg up on the information. After the classroom, instructors handed out heavy dummy fragmentation grenades, demonstrating proper stance and throwing technique. The palm-sized explosive device was to be lofted and arced toward the target, launching it from shoulder height, more like a shot-put than a baseball. Garson was unnerved by muffled explosions in the distance; another platoon was in the pits.

Then, 023 marched forward to several waist-high pits lined with sand bags. Garson strapped on a steel helmet, sweaty from the previous wearer. Fear tingled along his backbone. Preston and Rusty said afterward there was nothing to it. Garson's instructor, a tall corporal with a mustache, seemed bored, apparently having spent much of the day guiding palpitating recruits like him in such dangerous business.

"Now do as I say, and you won't get hurt," the Marine said in a heavy voice. "This is serious, fuckin' shit, and I don't wanna be killed because you don't listen to what I have to say." He handed Garson the serrated steel grenade.

"Don't try to be a John Wayne Jones and throw the thing a mile. Remember, you only need to get it 15 or 20 yards." Did Bob Mathias throw shot-put when he won last year's Olympic decathlon?

"Pull pin!" Garson hooked his left index finger into the ring, his right hand holding the safety lever tightly against the grenade body.

"Prepare to throw!" He leaned back, stiffened his left arm at an upward angle – a kind of aiming aid — and cocked the right fist near his ear. He trembled. Dire scenarios ricocheted around his brain. If this thing exploded right now, fragments would rip the two of them apart. He thought back to the training film: It depicted the devastation caused by such a small hand weapon. He stared ahead, noticing thousands of shrapnel fragments that had savaged the dirt in front.

"Throw!" Garson heaved as hard as he could, but the throw felt anemic. The safety spoon popped loose and the fuse hissed. Immediately he ducked below the sandbag retaining wall. Instantly, the instructor grabbed his jacket and pulled him back into a standing position. His shoulders were above the parapet. What the hell's he doing? He mind reeled. The grenade, he should have remembered from the *Guidebook,* had a four or five second delay. Roughly, the instructor pushed him down below the sandbags, a mere heartbeat before the blast. The grenade exploded, a shower of dirt pelting Garson's helmet. And just like that, he felt immense relief.

Since the focus at Camp Matthews was on weapons training, precious little time was spent on close order drill. The platoon did sometimes mind the cadence as it marched to chow or to classrooms, but Camp Matthews provided no large paved expanse like the Grinder to perfect drill proficiency. Route step, marching without cadence, was *modus operandi.*

Away from the more controlled and scrutinized environment of MCRD, many DIs sounded suggestive cadence calls when platoons moved from place to place; some emanated from recent history. Despite the Marines' fighting withdrawal from the Chinese encirclement at the Chosin Reservoir in Korea three years before – the commanding general called it an advance in another direction – the Corps proudly proclaimed that it had carried out every wounded and dead Marine, and every piece of equipment. At the same time, unofficial Corps history was critical of the army's performance. A marching ditty was often heard at the rifle range.

"Hear the pitter patter of little feet, the whole 5th Army's in full retreat," Duff sang out as the platoon trudged along. "They're movin' on, they're movin' on. See the Chinese Reds comin' through the pass, playin' the burp gun boogie on the doggie's ass. They're movin' on, they're movin' on." Similar little evocations, inappropriate for MCRD where a few women Marines were billeted, were laced with lewd, chauvinistic innuendo and double entendre. At the very least, they mentioned tiny titties and tight twatties.

"Why'd you join the Corps?" asked Liska, Garson's pale-eyed tentmate while they stood smoking after chow in the final days before departing Camp Matthews. He was several inches taller than Garson with a broad Slavic face and badly pocked complexion — acne, Garson guessed. His query was often heard in Boot Camp, recruits wondering what had brought others to such a brutal experience.

"Get outta school, I suppose," was Garson's reply. "Did you finish?"

Liska had graduated from the Salvatorian Brothers high school in Hamtramck and had hoped to go to Wayne University in Detroit. But his father demanded he join the family real estate and insurance agency. Garson empathized because his dad had similar plans for him in the confection business.

Over the course of weeks, they and others compared backgrounds as well as hopes and fears. On one particularly balmy Sunday, Garson and others dragged footlockers into the company street to clean rifles and gear in preparation for departure from the tent city. Liska's grandfather, an immigrant from Krakov, offered a simple philosophy in life when he was an old man in his 90's:

"If you can eat, sleep and shit regularly, that's all that counts." Once again, Hal pitched in with an unconnected anecdote of dubious veracity from unnamed sources. His yarns were wearing thin.

"Guy told me that years back the heads here at Matthews, instead of flush crappers, had troughs with water running under the holes. One smartass lighted a wad of toilet paper and sent it down the sluice. Guys dumping their loads jumped up as their asses got burned." No one in the platoon ever heard that one before.

Like most of Platoon 023, Liska had not yet seen the Pacific Ocean. As a boy, he had spent several summers in Florida and had waded in the Atlantic. Now, he hoped to swim in the Pacific when they graduated from Boot Camp.

"Ocean's right on the other side of the airport at MCRD, you know," Liska said. "Less than a mile, I think." And so they later discovered, that beyond Lindbergh Field rested Harbor Island where San Diego Bay met the immense blue Pacific. In less than two months, Garson and several others who remained at the Depot after graduation would step into those salty waters.

Bayonet drill that had begun at MCRD was reinforced at rifle range. They practiced thrusts and parries, butt strokes and more on straw-filled torsos wearing tiny caps with red stars. Slanted eyes were crudely inked on the burlap. Recruits of Platoon 023 were also sent through a true obstacle course complete with live firing.

"Do they shoot machine guns with real bullets over our heads?" Prick asked while the platoon strapped on helmets. "We could be shot to flinders." Garson was amused at what he took to be another of the recruit's antiquated words.

"Weren't you fuckin' listening this morning, man?" was the reply. Garson was sometimes testy with his buddy's naiveté. During the pre-course classroom instruction, a Marine had described in detail that they would crawl a distance of one hundred yards, the while a stream of bullets firing overhead.

"Keep your noses in the dirt. Don't for any reason whatsoever raise your head. We don't want any casualties out here today." Several Boots commented that this instructor, an older staff sergeant, was not given to the usual salvo of four-letter words; by his verbiage and demeanor, he seemed un-Marinelike — civilized, almost human.

On the obstacle course, belly down, Garson gripped his M-1 sling at the top swivel and dragged it along. When he encountered barbed wire, he rolled onto his back, using the rifle to lift the spiky wire away from his body. Explosives detonated at various intervals, splashing muddy water while the .30 caliber machine gun clattered overhead. Occasional fiery red tracer bullets seemed to pass inches above his nose – just as in movies. He learned afterward, however, that the heavy machine guns were locked down, precluding any untoward traverse or elevation change. It was all pretty safe. Prick hesitated at the start, but once he set his mind to the task, he made it successfully.

"Good job, Prick!" He smiled back through mud-spattered glasses. In the shower afterward, someone remembered that Robert Taylor fired the same heavy machine gun in an old movie.

"Yeah, it was in 'Back to Bataan.' Remember that last scene

where he's blasting away through the ground fog at the fuckin' Japs slinking toward him. He fired that water-jacketed .30 caliber. 'Come on you sons-of-bitches,' he said although you could only see him mouth the last words."

"No, no, man, that wasn't 'Back to Bataan,'" Prick corrected his tentmate, "that was 'Bataan.' 'Back to Bataan' had John Wayne. It came out near the end of the war. 'Bataan' came out during the war, and Taylor played Sergeant Dane." Garson and several others gaped at Prick's knowledge.

The site for Marine weapons training at Camp Matthews would remain for only a few more years after Garson trained there; after 1956, recruits would be shipped up the coast to sprawling Camp Pendleton near Oceanside for marksmanship training. Years later, Heissen told Garson that he visited the old rifle range sometime after it was vacated by the Corps. He felt a certain eeriness walking over empty acres, recalling those weeks in the tent camp.

"Pretty sure I saw the Baker Range target butts," he said. "No buildings were left, so it was hard to know for certain. But you could still see the depressions were probably millions of bullets burrowed into the earth." Big Agony was still there, too, he thought. "My legs'll never forget that hill."

I'll interrupt again to say that I was there myself, maybe 40 years after my Pop and his buddies were there. The University of California at San Diego campus is laid out in the rolling hills of the old camp. The handsome university library is a huge upturned ziggurat; illuminated at night, it seems to hover in the coastal hills. Thing of it is though, like Heissen, I couldn't get a sense of any rifle ranges.

The weeks of Camp Matthews culminated in a cacophonic display of weaponry. A cavernous amphitheater had been gouged out in the desolate terrain, and several platoons gathered to observe most of the fire power the modern Marine Corps could muster. Several squads of rifleman, light and heavy machine guns, bazookas and mortars put on the stunning demonstration while tanks spewed napalm — July Fourth on steroids. Garson felt concussive shock waves as the heavy weapons pounded concrete bunkers and rusted vehicle hulks. Tracer bullets glowed and white phosphorous shells exploded in great mushrooms of blinding light.

The finale included the newest weapon in the Marine arsenal — an ungainly looking self-propelled, tracked vehicle resembling a First World War tank. Called *Ontos*, Greek for the "Thing," the ten-ton weapon was festooned with firepower – six .106 caliber recoilless rifles that could be rotated, raised or depressed and rapidly loaded by a two-man crew; a .50 caliber spotting rifle found range and distance for its heavy shells. While the Korean War seemed to be settled, Garson felt secure that his Corps was prepared for any eventuality while he served.

Garson tossed in troubled sleep that final night in the tent camp, awakening at several intervals. Curiously, an image of Deaffy filtered into his dreams, an uncommon smile playing on her leathery face. She was the neighborhood deaf and dumb "Gypsy" woman back home, collector of refuse and detritus that was piled in her tiny abode and strewn about her junk-clogged yard. Despite her benign nature, she had seemed a harridan to Garson and his childhood pals. In his dream, however, the image shifted slightly, dissolving into the tawny, filigreed face of his grandmother in Green Bay.

It was the week before Christmas 1953 that Platoon 023 returned to MCRD. Garson's recollection was vague: He thought they did not march but were trucked back south to the Depot in those green cattle cars with barred windows. Once again, he was "home" in a familiar quonset next to the Grinder.

***

Chapter 4

CLÉMENCE

Garson's grandmother, Clémence froze to death in a roadside snow bank in northern Wisconsin. More than 90 years earlier, she was saved from incineration in the great Peshtigo Fire of 1871. Ice and fire – her omega and alpha.

As he did with Guttig, Garson long pondered a fitting name for the only grandmother he ever knew. He considered Glacé, Cecite and others but none seemed suitable. Through many drafts, he simply left the name blank. He could not say why he finally fixed on Clémence; perhaps he just liked the sound of it.

The tiny girl of five cried. She shook in fright. She was hot, laying under the porcelain bathtub her parents had tipped over her. Now the fiery tornado raged all around, tall pine trees exploding into flames like Civil War artillery.

It was fortunate that the old claw-footed tub, long ago replaced by a new one, had been transformed into a yard planter that usually sprouted fiery summer flowers. But now, as the inferno grew in intensity, her parents had dumped out the earth and wilted blooms, and screamed above the roar that she should curl up like a ball. Throwing a sodden blanket over her body, they tipped the tub over her and quickly banked dirt around its edges.

It was a scene novelist Jeannette Walls may have created in the next century, using instead the dramatic flash flood episode that opened her novel *Half Broke Horses*. Certainly, she would have written about Clémence's horror with a surer hand. It was Garson's aunt, his father's older sister, who was said to know the story of her mother's ordeal. But she died years before imparting the tale to her nephew. Garson had but a few facts and fallible family legend to guide him.

In five years of life, Clémence could not remember a summer or fall without constant smoke and fire. She was startled a few days before when a deer bolted from the forest, staring at her before darting off in confusion. For several days, too, she had amused herself, watching tiny glowing trails that writhed through the dense matting of pine needles and detritus at the forest edge – like red snakes.

In the era following the Civil War, Wisconsin was a dynamic lumbering state. One historian called it the Empire in Pine. Each winter, swarms of burly men in red plaid shirts and spiked boots, carrying saws and axes assembled in the forests above Green Bay to begin the annual harvest. Millions of board feet of pines and hardwoods were felled and trimmed; logs were skidded along ice roads or down streams and rivers. It was estimated by authorities of the time that almost half of downed trees and trimmings ended up as waste, strewn and scattered on the forest floor amid millions of stumps, to decay and rot.

What was more, circular saws at the mills produced massive mounds of sawdust that piled up alongside other refuse. Much was put to use, of course: Streets in small towns like Peshtigo and Oconto on the west side of the Lake Michigan bay, and Williamsonville and New Franken on the east side, were literally paved with the dust.

Everything was tinder. Roads in and out of the forest were of corduroy; bridges constructed of planks sat upon lumber, and sidewalks were boards; every home and building was constructed of logs and roofed in wood shingles; railroad ties and telegraph poles were numerous. It was a rare saw mill or woodenware manufacturer that did not sustain at least a small fire at one time or another;

serious conflagrations became more common as the new decade approached.

Even before October arrived, the earth and atmosphere had been parched for months because of the absence of normal moisture. Now the wind dried the land even more. It was only a matter of time and condition.

Two days before, a stiff wind whipped up from the southwest and Clémence's parents and neighbors chased small fires that lighted on their property, beating them out and dousing house and outbuildings with water. Choking smoke thickened; eyes reddened. On Sunday night, October 8th, the wind surged even higher, fanning the orange fiend into tornados of fire. Like cannon shots, pine trees literally exploded in flames that quickly soared hundreds of feet into the night air. The heat was intense. It was hard to breathe. A wall of fire bore down.

"Gotta get to the river!" Clémence's father shouted above the swirling inferno.

"She can't run fast enough," her mother replied, hands cupped as a megaphone. "She's too little." There may have been other children to carry.

"Leave her."

And so the five-year old found herself alone in the farm yard beneath an upturned bathtub. At first, the soaked blanket was chilling, but in time it dried as the temperature rose. She grew uncomfortable in her porcelain cocoon and closed her eyes. The sound was deafening, not just crackling, but a vibrating vortex that howled like a banshee. Clémence could not calculate how long she lay there; her mind may have shut down in shock and fear. Or she may have cried herself to sleep in the roar and din.

How long she avoided the horror in slumber, shock or abject fear was unknown. Certainly it was hours. She was awakened by a drumming of heavy rain on her sanctuary. She waited. Then her father's hands overturned the bathtub, and took her up in his arms.

"She's alive!" he proclaimed. He was a cindery wraith, white with ash from head to foot. With a handful of neighbors, Clémence's parents and siblings had taken refuge in the middle of a river, constantly dousing one another with water as the hellish onslaught of wind and flame threatened incineration. Afterward, the only memory Clémence retained was of a moonlike landscape, devoid of anything upright save an occasional charred stump or the skeleton of a building.

Clémence walled off the memory of that horrid day, and was unable to recall more than a few impressions of it for the remainder of her life. What was more, she was known to be uncomfortable in hot, humid weather. And she detested the sound of crackling fire.

Everything her parents owned had been destroyed. Within days, they transported their daughter north of the Wisconsin border, to Menominee, Michigan where she was raised by an aunt. Older children were scattered among other kin.

That same day in 1871, the great Chicago Fire destroyed tens of thousands of buildings, and killed 150 people. That news overshadowed the calamity on both sides of the Lake Michigan bay and up the narrow Door Peninsula, ultimately destroying nearly everything in a 15-by-60 mile swath. The death toll was never accurately calculated, but more than a thousand lost their lives.

Clémence's story during the next 20 years is now known only in vague outline. Garson's aunt, keeper of family genealogy in record and memory, might have answered numerous questions, and explained chronologies to Garson, had she lived long enough. He was devoid of any interest in such matters in those years, even sniffing at folks who traced ancestry while he worked for Milwaukee's local history and genealogy library. Even as he assisted such people, he disdained pedigree seekers and lineage searchers, proclaiming that he was interested in the future not the past.

In her early 90s, Clémence died while Garson was in the Marines. When he set his memories to paper, the circumstance of his grandmother's demise had been made clear to him. During a bitter and snowy winter and in the late stages of senility, she wandered away from her son's farmstead in rural Sugar Bush. Garson's uncle and his family frantically searched the barn and farm outbuildings before alerting the Brown County sheriff. After many hours of careful searching, a deputy happened upon a crumpled body lying in the deep snow drift at the side of the road a mile from her son's home. Dressed only in a wispy coat, apron and dress and shod in house slippers, she had been dead for some time. Garson imagined the tiny woman lying there, curled up and ossified like some movie, like the Native-American corpses at Wounded Knee.

"I think she was trying to walk back to the old homestead," was what they conjectured afterward. She had been addled for many years.

A Belgian woman, Clémence was born on the western shore of Green Bay the year the Civil War ended. But Garson's mother doubted that story of her origin.

"She was part Indian," his mother insisted without any credible evidence to support the assertion. "Look how dark she is, those cheekbones." That area of northern Wisconsin was home to numerous native tribes, notably the Menomonee whose reservation consumed a large swath of a neighboring county, and the relocated Oneida who lived north of Green Bay.

There were secrets hidden in old census records, secrets not part of family legacy, Garson discovered. It is unknown how long Clémence lived with her aunt in Michigan, but she came to maturity about 1885. Somehow, by arrangement or happenstance, she met a man named Fermier. A widower with a son of about 12, he was reputed to have emigrated from France where he had farmed outside of Paris. But, contradicting family assertion, he might just as easily have migrated south from Canada.

The 1895 census conducted by Wisconsin revealed that Fermier was married to a woman with an odd name – Geredinal. But this could have been an error as Garson knew from transcribing many Civil War soldier letters. Census canvassers' handwritten ledgers were often no more than scrawls, and when permanent records were later transcribed from these, mistakes were commonly made. But was Geredinal a first wife or somehow a misspelling of Clémence? Likely not, since eighteen years passed between the birth of Fermier's first child and the second. Were there miscarriages during that long period, offspring who died in childbirth? Again, Garson's aunt never provided clarity on these points.

Garson had no idea where the photograph came from, but when he took up his family story, there was a cabinet card image of his paternal grandparents – it may have even been a wedding photo, for all he knew. Fermier sat in front of a *tromp l'oeil* studio backdrop, expression formal and somber, features regular with light eyes, wispy brows and a thin, almost invisible mustache and high forehead; he wore striped wool trousers of the period, a dark gray coat buttoned at the neck, vest, white shirt and striped cravat. His hands, resting on knees, were large and knobby – farmer's hands. He was a handsome, steady looking man of perhaps 40.

Beside him, one hand on her husband's shoulder and the other akimbo at her waist stood comely Clémence ten years her husband's junior. Utterly striking, she stared confidently at the camera with those eyes the color of chocolate under almost perfect brows; dark hair piled atop her head. Her lower lip was full, and her complexion, even in sepia, appeared flawless. She was formally attired in a dark ankle-length woolen skirt over underpinnings and tight button bodice with satin accents; a broad starched bow adorned her neck. Small of breast, she did not measure five feet in height.

Garson retained less than vivid memories of his only grandmother from visits to the Sugar Bush farm when he was a child. Clémence was widowed many years, Fermier having died before Garson was born. Early in the world war years, she operated a tiny store, no more than a shack on a vacant Green Bay lot, selling chickens and farm goods. Already well into her 70s, wire-rimmed spectacles framed her eyes. Garson recalled her little cackles of amusement and the chipped front tooth of ill-fitting dentures.

When senility began to rob Clémence's mind, Garson recalled a very different woman: Even tinier than he remembered, she was wizened and vacant, her eyes fixed upon some unknown object. Wiry white hair was not completely unkempt, as though someone had tried to tame it; her skin, like parchment, was almost desiccated on her skeletal arms. As a child, he was unsure of this woman, reluctant to get too close.

"Well, sit by your grandma," Garson's father admonished. "Give her a hug and kiss." Garson did as he was bade, but when he sat down, the odor of his grandmother's unwashed body rose to his nostrils, and he was repulsed. Obediently, he reached toward her with one arm, noticing the tiny hairs spouting from her chin. Holding his breath, he kissed her quickly. Tears glinted in his father's eyes as if he knew something his son did not. Clémence gave no reaction, moving not a muscle. While there were later visits, Garson was unable to summon them from memory. He was probably in his teens when he saw her for the final time. News of her death came to him in a letter while in combat training at Camp Pendleton.

For 15 years beginning in 1891, Clémence bore seven children – two girls and five boys. Garson's father arrived before the century turned, and when the last son was born, she was 42 years old. The family had established itself in eastern Brown County, at the foot of the long peninsula that jutted into Lake Michigan. It was near a village named for a grove of maple trees, Sugar Bush, where Belgian and French surnames mingled with Scandinavian and Polish. Villages such as Luxemburg, Bellevue – they pronounced it "Bella-vo" — and New Franken were proximate; a half a day's ride got one to Brussels.

Garson's father was nearly a boy when the 50th anniversary of the Civil War was marked by old veterans, and not yet ten when Mark Twain died. He was in his teen years when Germany invaded Belgium for the first time in 1914. Only one of his brothers served in the Great War, and he was felled by non-fatal malady, likely malaria, in a Georgia camp and sent home. His closest brothers formed a rowdy rural trio, and listening to some of their yeasty youthful antics made Garson's mouth hang open. They slept in a huge attic bed in the farm house. And when one flatulated, he forced a brother's head under the blankets. Garson's father often repeated tales about sleeping in that freezing upstairs room. They kept a window above the bed ajar for ventilation, even in winter.

"Many's the time we woke up in the morning with snow on our pillows," his father noted, often when criticizing his son for being a soft momma's boy. While Garson and his father were not particularly close, especially during Garson's childhood when Guttig provided the majority of care, he did share tales of derring-do on the Sugar Bush farm.

"One Halloween night, we played a prank on the neighbor. We moved his back house off the foundation, and had your Uncle Vin stand in the doorway, hooting and hollering." The angry farmer barged out of his back door. There was just enough light to spot the boy taunting him 20 yards away, so he charged across the yard. With only two feet separating him and his tormenter, he plunged into the noisome soup of waste. Garson cringed, imagining the scene, and his mother chided her husband for telling another of those awful stories.

Worse was the tale of the boys hoisting a neighbor's calf atop a barn with block and tackle. The frightened animal bawled for an hour or more until the farmer and his family woke and maneuvered a ladder to rescue it. Garson thought his father's savage story about lowering another calf into a well was more fanciful than real. He never knew his father to be so cruel.

Garson's father was a handsome youth with intent, dark eyes and a full lower lip like his mother's as evidenced by a studio photo of him and two brothers taken about the time of World War I. His nose was narrow but prominent, and his thick hair was combed back neatly. Curiously, the face of one of the brothers in the photo had been cut out. It is impossible to tell which one, but it was likely Vin, and the defacer, Garson's mother. She had a long antipathy with her brother-in-law for several reasons, and she wanted his image expunged from the photographic record.

As exemplified by his father, Garson thought most of his paternal relatives spoke with odd-sounding Francophonic cadences and inflections. Any word beginning with an "h", for example, was pronounced in a breathy gush. When Garson and his parents visited relatives near Green Bay, his father tended to inflect his words in such a manner, as if to evince that he was among his kind. He told his son of youthful trips to Casco and the shoreline towns of Dyckesville and Bay Settlement for dances and other events. He liked several girls, but was not adept on the dance floor. The youngest brother, Hervé, was the family dandy, and he cut a handsome figure in those dance halls.

The most important event on the annual calendar on the peninsula was Kermisse, celebrated in fall around harvest time. Begun among the Belgian Walloons of Wisconsin during the late-1850s, the event was centered on the town of Rosiere some 20 miles southwest of Sugar Bush. The affairs, copied in other towns, lasted two or three days, and featured traditional Belgian foods such as chicken and beef, special pies and those seasoned cottage cheese balls that Garson detested as a child. A special Catholic mass, games, races, bands and dances added to the festival. Even after Prohibition took hold, homemade beer, wine and liquor was ready at hand. Thousands were attracted to the events. Even after the Fermier boys moved away from Brown and Kewaunee counties, many were drawn back to the event of their youth.

Garson's oldest aunt, a devout Catholic, was long attracted to the mystic visions that occurred in Wisconsin. It was about the time that Kermisse began that a young immigrant girl from Belgium proclaimed she had been visited by the Blessed Virgin who exhorted Adele Brice to dedicate her life to serving others; she became a nun. For four decades Sister Adele collected funds to erect a chapel, school and orphanage on the site where the Virgin appeared in the Brown County village of Premier Belges.

While the brothers never exhibited particular religious fervor, they dutifully followed their older sister to pray at the shrine on occasion. Then, when Garson was 13, another woman, Mary Van Hoof, declared she, too, had seen the Virgin near Necedah on the western side of Wisconsin. Another shrine was subsequently constructed. Despite the Catholic Church's declaration that the apparition had been faked, Garson's aunt made hours-long pilgrimages to the site; she would give her nephew a rosary that was consecrated there, a gift he lost while in the Marines.

Garson was reminded of this when he and his mother, during the war, watched actress Jennifer Jones portray a young French girl to whom the Virgin made an appearance at Lourdes in "The Song of Bernadette." His throat had tightened during scenes of the glowing celestial visitation to the teen.

Garson recalled fingering through shoe boxes chocked full of family photos – thousands of them. Those containers were stored in dining room's breakfront drawers, and as a child, he many times perused images of his father's youthful expeditions to lake and stream, displaying long strings of fish; he also studied photos of deer hunts with hanging carcasses and men with guns.

"You know I worked with Curly Lambeau," Garson's father boasted. He was a handsome man with a broad nose, full lips, and thick neck and chin; the reason for his nickname was easy to discern. Indeed, Garson had seen numerous images of his father's early work years, and recalled with fair certitude several images of a group of men at the Acme Packing Company in Green Bay. They stood in the company yard, wearing white coveralls and high boots. The photo was too small to discern the dark and wavy-haired Lambeau, however. He founded the semi-professional Acme Packers the year Garson's father turned 19, playing football clubs from around the state and Midwest. In 1921, its name now Green Bay Packers, the team joined the professional circuit.

It was apparent to Garson's father and his younger brothers that opportunities in Brown County were limited. An older brother worked the family farm, and it was clear he would inherit the acreage. Thus, in 1925, the three youngest sons boarded a train, traveling south many hours to Milwaukee. They were bound to make their fortunes. The oldest of the trio, Garson's father, was 25, Vin 21 and Hervé 18. They roomed with a family – "a shirt-tail relative," was how Garson's father described it — on the near west side of the city for a few years.

Milwaukee, known as the "Cream City of the Lake" in the past century, boasted a population of nearly a half million then. While Prohibition had taken the wind out of the brewers' sails, and tanning was slowly ebbing, the metropolis had become an industrialized powerhouse. The Menomonee River valley and south side were populated with metals manufacturers, forges, machine and stamping factories. Cutler-Hammer, Harnischfeger, International Harvester, Falk, Harley-Davison Motorcycles were all hiring. Firms such as Geuder, Paeschke & Frey on the lip of the industrial valley that separated north from south sides of Milwaukee churned out millions of pieces of finished goods each year; its byproducts of odor and gritty air were discernable for miles. The Cream City's once bright bricks had grown dingy and stained.

The superficial flavor of Teutonism still clung to the city with many buildings and landmarks, breweries, streets and restaurants bearing Germanic names. But, truth be told, only seven-percent of the residents were now German immigrants albeit second and third generations still bore such surnames. Poles on the city's south side were a significant minority along with pockets of Italians and a growing enclave of Negroes who had escaped the Jim Crow South.

The brothers readily found work with the oldest of the trio gaining employment with the streetcar company, The Milwaukee Electric Railway & Light Company — "TM" it was called. There was another cabinet card image that Garson recalled vividly, an official company photo – his father in formal pose dressed in his motorman's uniform. He wore the prescribed dark blue double-breasted serge suit and hard cap with silver shield. His expression was friendly with dark brown eyes, like strong coffee, and tanned skin; his lips were parted slightly in a tentative smile – a handsome motorman, all in all.

Garson's father occasionally told him about his experiences on the long, articulated streetcars. As a cost-saving measure, "TM" introduced the coupled two-car units on several cross-town city lines, attempting to generate more revenue with reduced labor cost.

"We used what was called a 'Motorman's Friend,'" Garson's father explained. How the subject of this device was raised was a curiosity because his father was not usually given to such topics. What was more, Garson's mother would surely frown at such information.

"Yeah, when we got to the end of the Number 20 line, especially on the late night 'Owl Cars,' way out there in the sticks on the north side, there weren't any car barns or toilets." The heavy green-liveried cars took a couple of hours to trundle their way through the city from Forest Home Avenue, across Wisconsin Avenue and out to the far fringe of the city.

"There was a turnaround track but no place to take a leak." "Leak" was the strongest euphemism he ever used. Like his co-workers, he had purchased a copper container similar to a pint hip flask that was strapped to his calf. A rubber hose ran up the trouser leg and was fitted onto his privates.

"You'd take a leak during a layover with nobody the wiser."

Garson years later claimed that he stumbled onto one of the devices in an antique shop many years later. The hose and attachment were missing, obviously rotted away, but the copper container was as his father had described. Garson did not purchase it; nostalgia went only so far.

"I missed only a few weeks of work when you were born," Garson's mother told him early in his life. She became pregnant around the start of the new year, 1936, but quickly returned to the factory, spare weeks after giving birth.

Garson recalled as a boy accompanying his father to one of several short-term jobs after he left Geuder, Paeschke & Frey, when he worked as a grease monkey in a Wadhams gas station with its Pegasus red horse flying atop a tiled pagoda roof. For some reason, Garson collected cash register receipts, banding them into neat stacks until his mother discarded them one day. She was a saver of money, not such useless things.

"You'll die owing someone," one of Garson's friends would chide him when, as a married man, he verbally worried about debts.

"I knew someone who died owing no one," would be Garson's instant rejoinder — another of his mother's life lessons, imparted by deed as well as word. An ardent saver, she detested bills. Through lean years and better times, she paid every penny owed. Her savings rate was remarkable under the circumstances. In little more than ten years after purchasing the house on 41st Street, the down payment borrowed from the childless, elderly east side couple had been repaid, the mortgage erased and the metal cash box on a high closet shelf stacked with thousands of dollars in government savings bonds.

During the hard-scrabble times, Garson's mother, like millions of other blue collar workers, often sought refuge in the movies. As a girl in Rubicon, she recalled watching celluloid images projected onto a tattered screen at Fireman's Hall. She adored moving pictures. Now, her small son would be her show house companion.

On Villard Avenue, the main street in old North Milwaukee, beckoned the Ritz Theater. The year of the venue's construction, 1926, eight new movie houses opened, joining a list of more than 80 already in existence. Grand movie palaces were arising downtown, several seating audiences of more than a thousand, some even many more; they featured expansive balconies and organs, and flaunted carpeting, brocade drapery and thematic ornamentation.

The Ritz, in contrast, was a venue of few pretensions and extravagances. The marquee was unassuming and the neon name modest. The lobby and concession stand were little more than counters. The house floor declined slightly toward a narrow stage, and seats bore no upholstery; a pair of *faux* balconies flanked the draped screen. That undistinguished theater's offerings would become a significant mentor during Garson's boyhood, nearly as influential as his parents and the school sisters who taught him.

Accompanying his mother, Garson was studious of beguiling movie posters that flanked the box office. Not long after these early years, he often walked to the theater just to view these attractive advertisements. Along the lobby walls were mounted more posters of the "Coming Attractions," each one promising adventure, romance and mystery, comedy, drama and musical. He was invigorated when classic movies produced years before were re-released during the new world war. He watched transfixed as Fred Astaire and Ginger Rogers glided across dance floors, breathless as Errol Flynn thrust and parried swords, and studied newsmen like Cary Grant manage big city dailies.

I don't fully understand what my Pop was driving at when he told me about viewing movies back then, knowing that he'd probably never see them a second time:

"Movies were intimately entwined with our hopes and dreams, and we watched more attentively. Back then, I think we scrutinized those black and white images – as a kid, I was mesmerized by *women's sparkling sequined gowns, the shadow play of film noir. We were ravished by glorious colors when rare Technicolor pictures played. We were bathed in grand movie scores,"* he opined.

"We studied characters, comparing what we saw with our own ordinary lives, emulating heroes. We took our cues about manhood and loyalty, relationships and family from movies. While our lives felt safe and secure, movies helped us understand fear and dread, apprehension and disappointment. We found out what tragedy, heartache and horror might be like."

As did all movie houses in that era, the neighborhood Ritz offered nightly programs of double features in addition to a newsreel, short featurettes and coming attractions. The opening film began around 6:00 weekdays, followed by what was billed as a co-feature, a lesser quality offering, after which the main movie was repeated. The entire program ended after ten.

"This is where I came in," was an announcement that Garson heard regularly. There was no prescription to arrive before the main feature began since it was shown a second time. Late-comers simply sat through the opening of movie scenes they had missed, and then departed. There were many nights when Garson and his mother sat through the second showing until its climax. When "The End" appeared on the screen, the manager raised a light pole to illuminate the theater.

The Ritz was a third-run theater, and weeks passed before movies that played in the grand downtown houses arrived in North Milwaukee. What was more, the Ritz management was sensitive to the dicta of the Catholic Church, the city's largest religious denomination. Legion of Decency films labeled condemned or wholly objectionable were never screened on Villard Avenue. Garson knew that sins accrued from viewing such forbidden titles. Still, he joined pals on bus and streetcar rides to other neighborhoods to see such proscribed films as "It Happened One Night" with its double entendre dialogue that few understood. Garson was curious about unwed pregnancies of Ginger Rogers and Betty Hutton in "Kitty Foyle" and "Miracle of Morgan's Creek." His Protestant pals dismissed the Legion's censorious activity as "baloney."

As might be expected, when Garson accompanied his mother, he was subjected to domestic dramas, Capraesque social comedies and similar movie fare. She preferred stories where everything came right in the end. But when any film played loose with marriage and light with divorce, she bristled. He did not share her captivation with handsome Lew Ayers in the endless "Dr. Kildare" features, or Ann Sothern's treacly portrayal of Maisie Ravier and similar Hollywood floss. He fussed impatiently with saccharine romances starring skater Sonja Henie or songbird Deanna Durbin. It was the true musicals that Garson found fascinating — stage door stories like "42nd Street" and "Gold Diggers" that were made available again during the war. Invariably bored with saccharine plots, he perked up when Astaire and Rogers took to the dance floor, thrilled by their grace and elegance, and dazzled by the swirl of her chiffon dresses. When Astaire danced with leggy Eleanor Powell to "Begin the Beguine," Garson was exhilarated.

There was another musical sequence, a nugget that remained polished in a lifetime's memory. But it was something Garson never shared with his mother or anyone, for that matter. His boyhood pals would find it appalling, he knew. It occurred during another of those childhood movie nights with his mother.

But he could not pry from memory whether it was sequence in a feature or some selected short. Only after assiduous searching when setting down his memoir, did he discover its origin. It was a sensuous serpent dance performed by the specialty duo of Janine Janik and Christian Arnaut. The scene as Garson recalled was this:

Amid an arc of nightclub tables, a turbaned charmer played sensuous fluted notes as a rope descended to the floor. The female partner attired in a skin-tight body suit that revealed every muscle, tendon and sinew. Garson was transfixed as she writhed and wriggled to lonely notes — a reticulated temptress out of the Garden of Eden.

When the fakir, Arnaut, set down his instrument, an unseen orchestra took up the East Indian strains. Slowly, she circled his feet and began to coil about his ankles. Troubled, the man extricated his legs, and stepped aside. But she persisted, writhing and coiling her lithesome body; Garson thought she had no bones. More persistent, she spiraled once more about her partner's legs, a seething, writhing undulation of body and limbs, sinuous and seductive. Her partner's resistance began to ebb. At six or seven, Garson, entranced by the stage drama, felt a tingling in his loins.

With music intensifying, the woman slithered across his shoulders and arms, wriggled between his thighs, and wound about his waist. He struggled to loosen her grip, to free himself, like some jungle explorer fighting hopelessly against a giant Amazon anaconda. Drums were frenzied, incessant as he flung his partner about. Once more she wrapped about his neck and head, her entire body in a tight circle, squeezing, seducing. The dance drama ended with a crescendo of drums and cymbal clash, the couple prostrated on the polished floor. When they arose and bowed, the audience greeted them with abundant applause. She pulled her head loose from the hood, and her thick henna hair exploded. Garson's head swam, and he felt a tingling in his groin. He said nothing to his mother about this.

Virtually any movie involving Catholic characters and Irish-named actors like Pat O'Brien, Dennis Morgan and especially Bing Crosby attracted Garson's mother. If any of these actors portrayed a priest, the movie was irresistible. "The Song of Bernadette" and "Going My Way" won particular approval. Garson remembered his mother's tears when Sister Benedict, Ingrid Bergman, was sent away to a tuberculosis sanitarium in "The Bells of St. Mary's." Garson, however, was skeptical of her portrayal since he had never known a nun to wear lipstick. Mother and son often shared pleasant recollections of movie scenes and episodes.

"Remember when that little kid shot the man's finger with his slingshot?" It was a reminder of a humorous incident in a movie neither of them could name. A snooty couple – she in a shiny dress and beady-eyed mink stole, and he wearing starched white shirt and dark suit — dined at a restaurant. The pretentious man sipped coffee with his nose and little finger jutting imperiously. Their son wore a prissy Little Lord Fauntleroy outfit with hair lacquered in place.

"They all had that uppity air," Garson said. A few tables away sat a family of five, *hoi polloi* obviously. Their son, blonde hair unkempt and wearing faded bib overalls, withdrew a slingshot from his back pocket. With his left eye squinted, he took careful aim at the offensive pinkie, the tip of his tongue peaking from the corner of his mouth.

"Yeah, but that man put his cup down." Garson chuckled in the retelling. "And every time the boy aimed, the man stopped drinking," his mother said, continuing the scene. Finally, after three or four false starts, the boy quickly drew back the sling's band, sending a marble past several tables to the target. The cup shattered in a shower of hot liquid. A waiter smirked in satisfaction. "Well, I never!" the woman sputtered. Without paying the bill, the trio stomped from the restaurant. Mother and son frequently laughed together recalling movie episodes. Garson wondered if his pals had similar experiences with their parents.

Several score children of Garson's age lived on the block during the war years, one of them a strange boy named Johnny, the youngest son of a Widow Klatsch. The two words were always joined – Widow and Klatsch. She and her son lived in the massive two-story flat toward the south end of the block. In front, amid the cathedral of arching elms stood an expansive catalpa tree; Toby, Garson's childhood pal, called it the Indian Cigar tree.

The frame residence was similar to the one owned by Mrs. Hexe, who lived next door to Garson. She was as wraithlike and taciturn as Widow Klatsch was rotund and garrulous. The oldest structures on the block, the houses were the only ones featuring angled storm doors like the Kansas house in "The Wizard of Oz."

With thick hair piled atop her head and held in place by shiny bobby pins, penciled eyebrows fluttered as Widow Klatsch spoke; she was given to billowy print dresses and clashing pinafore aprons.

"She's such a Molly Putz," Garson's mother remarked, the name she always used for those who wore uncoordinated clothing. While she was called "Widow" Klatsch, some whispered that her husband had actually fled. The neighborhood gadfly, she spent many summer evenings ensconced on various porches, revealing the latest gossip about "this one or that one," as Garson's mother put it.

To say Widow Klatsch's boy was unusual would be true. To say he was benign would likewise be true. He had a shock of hair that was yellow, like kernels of field corn. A square torso was topped with a pumpkin head; his eyes were of indeterminate color, and a sallow complexion was set off by gray circles beneath hollow eyes. Johnny walked with a troubled, clumsy gait. Garson was unable to recall any words he had ever spoken. Other kids on the block either avoided or teased him, and he often played alone in the dusty yard. Garson felt guilty.

"Why don't your sonny boy play with my little *Scheisster*?" she asked Garson's mother. Amused, she did not at first think Widow Klatsch literally meant that her son was a shitter; but perhaps she did. Like Garson's mother, the woman spoke *plat-Deutsch*, that amalgam of German and English.

"Oh, Johnny's so weird," his childhood friend, Magdalena proclaimed. "He stinks and picks his nose all the time." She had also reported that the sorry boy even chewed and swallowed the diggings from his blunt nose. But there was something even more peculiar.

Magdalena's mother and the Widow Klatsch were once visiting Garson's mother; the trio of children, bored sitting on the porch steps, went down to the basement. Perhaps Garson wanted to show them his grandfather's sword. A thick gray water pipe descended into the basement, and at the moment Johnny spotted it, he hoisted himself, wrapping his legs and arms tightly. Magdalena ignored the behavior. With tongue worming its way from the corner of his mouth, Johnny energetically worked his pelvis up and down. Eyelids fluttering, he seemed in a trance of some sort, oblivious to everything but that pipe. After minutes, he simply stopped.

Whenever Johnny accompanied Garson to Silver Spring Park, he studied trees as they walked. Suddenly, unannounced, he would stop, selecting one of specific circumference, then clamber up several feet to start his rut, for that was what it was, someone said. For the most part, Garson, Magdalena and those who knew him ignored Johnny's antics; that was his peculiar way. Widow

Klatsch and her strange son moved from the block during the war. Decades later, Garson was reminded of that strange boy when he read Lawrence Ferlinghetti's poem "Johnny Nolan Has a Patch on His Ass," whose first line read: "Kids chase him thru screen door summers[,] thru back streets and all my memories."

To call Buster Johnny's dog, or even Widow Klatsch's, was inaccurate. Buster was his own animal, one of uncertain pedigree who was about the size of an Australian dingo; his dun-colored hair was short, and his tail curled over the back – a handsome pet Garson thought. Whenever he passed that yard, Buster lay there, head resting on his crossed front paws; he never barked or growled but followed Garson with his eyes, studious of every footfall and movement. It was disturbing. But there was a time when the dog came to the Garson's aide.

One afternoon shortly after Garson had learned to balance his ten-inch bicycle – he was one of the last kids his age to graduate from a three-wheeler — overconfidence overcame caution. Trying to turn around in the street, he lost balance and the bike tipped. He fell, skinning his knee badly. Leaving the bike behind, he screeched his way home. His mother ministered to the injury for many days, but it failed to knit. He howled when she suggested visiting Viv, the nurse nearby. He remembered the pain she had caused when mending his head years before. The knee wound scabbed, only to tear open when Garson flexed it. Ugly suppurations continued.

"Buster'll help," Widow Klatsch said on one of her evening visits. Garson's mother looked quizzically.

"*Ja*, his saliva'll heal that."

"Saliva?" Dubiousness was apparent.

"*Ja*, it's got something in it. I'll bring Buster around tomorrow."

"Mom!" Garson whined when told of the arrangement. On the next night, with Garson seated on the porch, the widow and her dog arrived. She pointed to Garson's knee, and Buster nosed at it, then began licking. The sensation was strange, uncomfortable, the animal's tongue tickling the skin. He watched the incessant ministrations, his knee dripping with the dog's saliva. The animal did not stop until the Widow Klatsch commanded.

"*Ja*, that's enough now, Buster. We'll do this till it heals. Trust me."

And so it passed, night after night that summer, Garson presenting his wound to the dog's tongue for ten minutes or more. He occasionally avoided the treatment by staying away until the widow and her dog departed. But, little by little and to the surprise of Garson and his mother, the suppuration stopped. To his amazement, the wound began to knit shut. Garson could not recall how long the canine treatment lasted, but the knee ultimately healed perfectly, and not even a scar remained. His mother several times thanked the widow. And while he was grateful to Buster, Garson still remained wary of the dog. The animal still scrutinized him carefully whenever he walked past the widow's yard.

Deaffy, the neighborhood's *eminence grise*, still scuttled about, collecting discards and refuse. Many decades after these wartime days, Magdalena – she would call herself Lana by then – asked Garson if he remembered the strange woman named Anna who lived on the corner near his house.

"Anna?"

"You know, she lived on the corner by you."

"Oh, you mean Deaffy."

"Deaffy?"

"Yeah, that's what we kids called her. She was deaf and dumb."

"No, she wasn't." Magdalena told him of her encounter in the alley. She saw the woman emerge from the tiny shack in her usual attire of tatters and battered hat, rusty wagon in tow. Lana said she was hesitant at first, and thought of turning back down the alley. But she sucked up courage, and walked forward.

"When we met, I said 'Hi!' She stopped and looked at me for a few seconds, and then said 'Hi'' back." Magdalena said her mother, like Garson's, always set out used clothing and household items for Deaffy. But Garson doubted his friend's story that the odiferous neighborhood denizen spoke. He and his chums, after all, had never heard her utter a sound. Magdalena also repeated a rumor that Deaffy, or Anna as she called her, had been abused as a child, causing her to become addled.

Deaffy was another of those presences who threaded her way through Garson's early life. Her clapboard residence was rumored to be heated only by a pot-bellied stove; indeed, small piles of wood were banked near the door. The corner lot was completely fenced in by chicken wire affixed to metal posts. In summer, it was overrun with a riot of vegetation – trees of several years' growth, unkempt shrubs, a tangle of vines and creepers, thigh-high thistles and grasses, all upon a bed of decaying leaves and matted detritus. News sheets and paper clung to the chicken wire, blown there on windy days, faintly reminding Garson of a partially de-hided animal carcass

In fall and winter, when leafy vegetation disappeared and withered brown tendrils remained, the sprawling mélange of Deaffy's collections became visible. Garson was amazed at the size of some of the items, and wondered how such a tiny woman was able to maneuver them about. There were numerous rusting machinery parts, auto wheels, skeletons of what looked like bicycles, bricks and cinder blocks. Garson thought he spotted a chipped terra cotta head of some Roman deity and a rusty sundial.

One afternoon, Garson carried garbage to the alley for his mother. As he replaced the can lid, Deaffy shambled a few yards away, wearing accustomed attire – heavy men's brogans and a misshapen purple hat with a dropping plume. She stopped short, sweeping him with a gaze. Her foul odor repulsed him. Garson shuddered audibly, and feared she heard him. He had been with his pals on several occasions when they followed the woman down the alley at a safe distance.

"Deaffy! Deaffy! Dumb Deaffy!" Such encounters lasted spare seconds before the poor woman trudged on with her wagon. His mother, who took pity on the recluse, reproached her son when Larry told her what they had done.

"*Ja*, she was once wedded to a Lake Michigan sailing man," Widow Klatsch told Garson's mother on one of her summer evening visits. His mother – he had known her to spread gossip and rumor only rarely – replied with a nod. The story related that Deaffy had met the captain when she was a pretty, young woman, if the truth were told. He skippered a schooner from Milwaukee across the lake to Muskegon, Michigan.

"*Ja*, there was a child, too," the Widow Klatsch said. "Don't know whatever became of it, a little girl by the talk of it." No expression betrayed his mother's reaction. The widow's tale continued that the sailing man failed to return one day after the child was born.

"*Ja*, someone in Grand Rapids said they saw that sailing man. He was married to another woman." She wagged her head, castigating the bigamist sailor. Deaffy was devastated, the widow said, and with the few dollars she had, bought the undeveloped lot on the corner. She became reclusive and addled after several years, shunned by neighbors, and developed strange compulsions. No one knew what became of the child. Deaffy was a curious character in Garson's boyhood.

About the time he turned ten, he had seen, along with numerous other movies, a score or more of those colorful tales of indomitable dogs like Lassie and horses like Flicka, all populated with kid actors Mickey Rooney, Elizabeth Taylor and doe-eyed Roddy McDowall. But unending sequels rolled out of Metro-Goldwyn Mayer and 20th Century Fox studios began to wear thin on Garson and his pals. During the war years, a dozen titles were released, wholesome fare, adults said. Every film appeared at the Ritz. How many ways could a dog come home and a horse win a race? he wondered.

He knew horses, after all, but not thin-legged thoroughbreds. Heavy-bodied draft animals with huge hooves pulled wagons delivering milk and ice, or dragged massive steel conveyances in alleys collecting furnace ashes and garbage. His grandfather, it was remembered, was seriously injured when one of those ponderous horses bolted. Weekly, peddlers plied their wares in the streets in horse-drawn drays, men named Balistreri and Balducci, weighing vegetables and fruit in swaying scales. In a battered and stained fedora, a man made annual rounds, sharpening knives and scissors.

"Aaa-Rakes! Aaa-Rakes!" The familiar call emanated from

a battered rig. A swarthy man in tattered vest and a jacket held together by a large safety pin, head wrapped in a gypsy scarf, trundled slowly, spoked, steel-rimmed wheels grating on the alley pavement. Garson's dad called the man a "Sheeney." In many ways, the man competed with Deaffy for refuse – threadbare clothing and bed clothes, cardboard and discarded wares.

His horse appeared older and sadder than most, its head drooped low, dark eyes rheumy, reflecting Garson's image when he stood close. The animal's mouth foamed around the steel bit, its back was badly swayed, and its hide taut about sharp ribs and pelvis bones. The shroud of leather strings that hung on its body failed to ward off flies. Garson felt sorry for the haggard animal, especially when the driver snapped his reins. He thought movies were unrealistic because he had never seen such horses in them.

"You don't see horse shit in movies either," came a crude comment from Toby. Indeed, the stench on some Milwaukee summer days was repellant.

"Think I look like a cowgirl?" dark-haired Magdalena asked Garson when she thrust a photo in his face. A few days before an itinerant photographer ambled through the neighborhood with a pinto pony in tow. Like many others who plied that trade, he carried his own props. Garson's mother had once posed him in a goat cart for one of those images. He hoped his pals would never see it.

In her photo, Magdalena was adorned in wooly chaps and fringed vest; a fancy Western hat perched on the back of her head. Her broad smile displayed the gap between her front teeth. She posed imperiously, a kid Annie Oakley or Calamity Jane, Garson supposed.

Her father, an immigrant from Stuttgart, met and married Magdalena's mother shortly after coming to America. He was a butcher, and established his business east of the Milwaukee River, serving wealthy clientele who lived in massive stone mansions along Prospect and Farwell Avenues above the lake shore. She was christened Magdelana not after the Biblical woman, it was said, but for a famous German stage actress named Magda. As an only child, Garson found her willful and independent. She was among the best dressed and coiffed girls on the block, attired in crinolines and starched bonnets. She was the only girl Garson ever saw outside of the movies who carried a muff in winter.

"Yeah, my mother always thought we made a cute little couple right from the start," she mewed. When she told Garson about it, he was aware that his mother had no tolerance for such a match. Magdalena was a Lutheran, after all.

Garson could summon only a few scraps of memory about Magdalena at this early age. But as an adult, she would share childhood photos to jog his recollection. In one, she was pictured with page boy hair accented by a curly tress at her forehead. The tinted studio portrait revealed a round head, rosy cheeks and thin lips. Garson did not discover until years later that Magdalena's eyes were startlingly, seductively blue. Also among those photos was a pose of her, Larry and Garson had taken on a snowy March afternoon. The trio was arrayed on the concrete steps in front of her house, she in a pretty hooded coat, Garson wearing a balaclava and Larry in a knit cap. Neither boy presented a smile for the camera.

By school age Garson knew virtually every sidewalk crack on both sides of the block. He counted 30 houses. More than half were older than his parents' bungalow; and several, like Widow Klatsch's and Mrs. Hexe's ancient residences, reminded Garson of the tall farm houses on his uncle's place in Dodge County — high windows, staircases and finished second-story rooms, tongue-and-groove ceilings and creaking wood floors.

He paced off the block when he began crudely mapping his world on a loose-leaf sheet. Forty-first, a north-south street, measured exactly 250 yards. It intersected with Custer, like all east-west thoroughfares, two-thirds as long. Most residential Milwaukee thoroughfares were shaded by mature elms that arched cathedral-like over sidewalks and roadways, creating leafy gothic vaults that provided cooling shade on hot summer days.

Several vacant lots dotted the neighborhood, most, like the one adjacent to Mrs. Hexe, featured a few sickly stunted trees; in summer, these open lots, carpeted in crab grass, thistles and wild thorn patches, were convenient arenas where games were played, battles fought, truces called; after the war, one was the locus for a boyhood secret.

In preparation for his narrative years later, Garson studied city directories that listed names such as Gummerhausen, Keutz, Liebel, Hebein, Volk and Schmidt who shared the block with Thoms, Moran, Szopinski, Rogers, Korinek and Wilson.

As Garson seemed to remember, it was about the time that Magdalena was in the middle grades, that she began insisting on being called Lana after the movie actress Lana Turner; neighborhood boys, however, teased by calling her Maggie. Garson understood the need to change one's name to something more suitable; by the time he was 11, after all, he would assume the daring name, "Blackie."

"Why can't I go to Carleton?" Garson asked when his mother led him to the public school for kindergarten. That tidy building to which he referred was only a block north.

"Carleton's not in Milwaukee; it's in Granville." As a five-year-old he did not understand that Silver Spring was the city's northern boundary. He needed to walk five blocks east and two south to the three-story white brick building adjacent to a city high school named after a hero of the Civil and Indian Wars, George Armstrong Custer.

He clearly remembered his first teacher, Miss Marble, thinking it a funny name. A tall brunette with a kindly demeanor, she dressed smartly in long pleated skirts, and two-tone high heels; many times she wore a glen-plaid or checked jacket whose square shoulders made her appear larger. As evinced by the official kindergarten photo, she also favored shiny white blouses and pearl necklaces.

In that photo one boy's face was blurred. He was long curious about the classmate's identity and was surprised, 50 years later, to learn who he was. Mellish, in time, would become an important pal and confidant, and a friend later in life. From a large family, Mellish regaled his pals with a storehouse of tales and adventures.

"My Ma said I was a nervous kid," Mellish told Garson. "Said I had St. Vitas Dance." Garson recalled that Mellish sat at his school desk, legs and knees wobbling incessantly, arms and upper body twitching. When the class photo was taken, Mellish was in motion.

For some reason, Garson's first real class friend was not in that photo. An incident involving her grew in importance as the years passed since it was the only time Garson witnessed unkindness by his grandfather.

Within the first days of kindergarten, Garson met Sally, a little coffee-colored girl with wiry hair and large, plum lips a shade lighter than her complexion; her eyes were iridescent black marbles. Her name was just above Garson's on the class list, meaning that their hands were often joined for games and in queues; her tiny hands fit comfortably in Garson's larger ones. She stood half a head shorter than Garson even though he was among the smaller students. Their blanket edges touched at nap times. They may have chatted as five-year olds might, and he learned that her name was Salomea, from the Old Testament, but he could call her Sally, she said in a tiny voice. It was the first little girl of color he had even met. He was utterly smitten.

One day that warm fall, he must have asked her to walk home with him. It was only a short way, he said, and they could eat peanut butter and jelly sandwiches at his house. He was anxious for his grandfather to meet this unusual little girl, and was happy at the prospect. Garson and Sally skipped part of the way. They entered the rear door, and began to climb the half dozen steps toward the kitchen door when they encountered his grandfather on the landing, arms folded over his chest, a sentry; the door behind him was closed.

"This is my friend, Sally," Garson smiled. His grandfather offered no response, but only glowered for some seconds. Garson felt a tingle along his spine. He detected nothing untoward in Sally, but grew uneasy. Finally, his grandfather responded, his voice forbidding.

"Not any farther than the back hall," his grandfather growled uncharacteristically. He seemed to grow taller and stouter, towering over Garson and Sally. He said nothing more, then or afterward, or uttered any denigrating comments about the girl. Despite his shock, Garson did not protest. He did not understand his grandfather's proscription; he had many friends visit before.

"Let's just sit here," he told Sally. They paused for a few minutes until Garson ran to his bedroom, retrieving a cigar box with many of his treasures – a few purey marbles, several Milwaukee Brewers baseball cards, streetcar passes and more. Sally gazed at each item handed to her. Meanwhile, Garson's grandfather prepared sandwiches, poured milk and delivered them on a tray. Garson noticed that Sally's milk was not in a glass like his, but in an old jelly jar. The next day, the container was smashed in the trash.

They may not have tarried long after finishing the milk and sandwiches. Sally did not initiate conversation, and Garson could think of nothing more to say. He told her that he would walk her back to school. He did not recall any anxious mother or a car waiting for his little friend, but there must have been someone who met her. He continued to be her mate during games, and his fascination grew. Curiously, however, Sally did not appear in the class photo; she seemed to have left the school before the term ended.

The winter Garson attended kindergarten, the Japanese attacked Pearl Harbor. With his parents, he heard Roosevelt proclaim the "Day of Infamy" when the president addressed Congress. An atmosphere of palpable dread was discernable in the house, even to a five-year-old. After an absence of a Sunday or more, Mister Socks returned. He looked drawn and forlorn. At the kitchen table, he and Guttig talked ominously about Germany's declaration of war and what it would mean. Garson did not understand every detail the old men discussed. But soon those Sunday visits from Guttig's old friend grew less frequent as the early months of the war progressed, and matters in Europe and the Pacific became more ominous.

Before Garson's sixth birthday, he was enrolled at Holy Redeemer Grade School, a 10-minute bus ride or 25-minute walk south of his home. His mother insisted on a Catholic education. The principal suggested his mother wait until the following year for first grade, but his mother was adamant, insisting that her son, small for his age, knew his ABCs and could count to 25.

Why Garson remembered the first day of school at Holy Redeemer is a mystery, but the recollection was distinct, thanks partially to his mother. She packed a paper bag lunch and pulled him to Holy

Redeemer in a coaster wagon. Garson enjoyed his morning with new classmates and the kindly nun. After eating his sandwich, he simply walked back home, content that the day had gone well.

"What're you doing here?" Surprise was obvious in his mother's tone.

"Ate my lunch and came home." He thought that was the routine, just like kindergarten. His mother quickly rolled out the wagon again, and briskly returned him to school. She apologized that her son had not understood.

Teachers were the school Sisters of St. Francis, the same order that taught his mother in Rubicon. She was confident her son was in good hands. This new generation of teachers did not bear those burdensome names of old. To Garson's recollection, those former names had nodded toward Greco-Roman ancients — Cletus, Damian, Domitia and the like. While still unusual, Garson's teachers bore less antiquated names; he studied under Sisters Agatha, Flavia, Bertrum, Isadora and Jude. Tall and slender with long fingers, most teachers wore rimless spectacles. The odor of harsh soap hung about them. Heavily starched wimples fit snuggly to foreheads and cheeks, with stiff collars and wooden crucifixes about their necks. They wore flowing, ankle-length black habits with thick rosary beads snugged about their waists. For a time Garson regarded them as ethereal.

He bore no recollection or psychological scars that he could discern, of domineering nuns or priests. Certainly, one or the other teacher might tug a boy's sideburns for some infraction but little more. Garson's most serious primary grade failure was holding his pencil too tightly; a large callus on his second finger attested to the grip. While practicing penmanship, Sister Flavia circulated silently about the room, slipping pencils free from hands. Invariably, Garson's tight grip caused a problem.

"You must hold it lightly, lightly," Flavia admonished. Garson looked up, mouth open. He knew the consequence.

"Hold it out" his teacher commanded. He set down the pencil, and held his hand palm down. Whack went the wooden ruler. The nun seemed to take pity on him, small boy that he was, rapping his knuckles only once. No complaint was made to his mother as he knew he had done wrong.

Holy Redeemer provided instruction for first through ninth grades, following a Jesuitical model that included as much liberal arts, math and science as religious instruction. He recalled little of Old Testament lessons, and more about ancient Greece and Rome, less of the times and trials of Jesus as of the American and French Revolutions. When he wrote of those days, Garson could still discern the Latin roots of many words, and describe the difference between Ionic, Doric and Corinthian columns. At the end of ninth grade at Holy Redeemer, he had read Hawthorne and Eliot, memorized Marc Antony's eulogy to Caesar, had seen school productions of "The Mikado," and "Arsenic and Old Lace," vividly recalling charging "Teddy Roosevelt" and the hidden bodies. Looking back, he was ever grateful to the good St. Francis sisters for introducing him to history, politics, literature, music and performing arts.

Construction of Holy Redeemer Church was halted by the war, and services were conducted in a roofed-over basement, spare and utilitarian with minimal adornment. School children attended mass every morning. Since the two-story brick school building was inadequate for the crush of students, temporary classrooms were erected on the parish parking lot — wooden, military-style structures that each housed two classrooms. Of clapboard construction, they stood upon concrete block footings. Lower grades studied in these drafty and dreary facilities that reminded Garson of the housing constructed for the Japanese who were rounded up and shipped from the West Coast for internment. Indeed, students called these classrooms "the barracks."

It was during first or second grade that Garson spotted his mother's purse lying open on the kitchen table; several pieces of currency were visible. Hesitantly, he pulled one bill from the sheaf, a ten dollar note. Folding it tightly, he secreted it in his pocket. Perhaps the next day after lunch, he told one or two classmates he would buy them candy. He strolled confidently to the counter that sold snacks and school supplies. The nun – she was older and no longer taught – retrieved the candy Garson had selected. He unfolded the ten dollar bill. Staring at it for a moment, she asked if he had a quarter or a dollar bill. When Garson wagged his head, a feeling of discomfort stabbed in his throat. She bade him wait and walked away. In minutes, the old nun returned with Sister Bertram, the principal.

"Where'd you get this?" she waved the bill. Suspicion was evident in her scowl.

"From my mom," Garson answered with confidence.

"I don't think so, young man." Mortified, Garson saw all of the candy returned to the counter. That afternoon, Sister Bertram called Garson's mother. The money was folded into an envelope that Garson carried home. His mother admonished Garson as sternly as she could – not an easy task for her only son. That was stealing, she said, stealing from your own mother. Garson was contrite, but was most worried about his father's reaction.

"We won't tell your dad about this." His mother's words were balm to his ears.

Garson long retained the class photo from that early grade; it was posed on the steps of the school on a blustery January day. When she first gazed at it, Garson's mother was mortified that her son had chosen a tattered sweater to wear that day.

"You look just like a Molly Putz," she caviled. Because of his small stature, he stood in the front row, and his favorite brown shoes were obviously scuffed; unknown to her, he had wedged cardboard inside to plug holes in the soles.

Among the students in that class photo was a girl who became another object of Garson's attraction. While she bore a dour expression against the cold, Garson thought her lovely. Long-necked with shoulder-length hair, she reminded Garson of the blond movie actress Betty Hutton. Diane smelled of talcum and baby oil, something like the odor of a doll. Another child without siblings, her mother daily dressed her in pretty party frocks. On photo day, she wore a hooded faux leopard coat – daring and dramatic, Garson thought, right out of the movies. But the dream of holding her hand in line was unrequited since she was among the taller kids in his class; the largest boy always had her hand – Paul Lenominstons; Garson would never forget that mouth-filling name. To his chagrin, Garson was invariably paired with a gnomish girl whose pinched face featured a threatening overbite; knee socks invariably drooped about her ankles.

In that same photo a tall boy held the class pennant. His mien was always haughty and self-assured; Garson disliked him immediately. Attired in dark corduroy knickers, he wore tall boots that covered his calves, high tops they were called, with laces threaded in metal eyelets. Garson envied those boots, but unsuccessfully begged his mother for a pair.

The boy's name was Preston. But he did not attend Holy Redeemer for many years, transferring to a public school. In less than a decade, however, Preston, a boy named Rusty and Garson would become close friends who dreamed of becoming Marines. Mellish, the boy who was a blur in the kindergarten photo the year before also stood in the first grade photo. While his knees still wobbled in class, he stood still for the photographer.

"That Emily Bogard stinks," Garson overheard Mellish report. Emily and her siblings seemed to sit in every grade, and all were shunned by classmates. Mellish said there were about ten in the family, and they lived in a forlorn old farm house in the countryside north of Silver Spring Drive. Mellish reported that the house had no electricity, and an old kerosene stove provided heat while smoky lamps emitted yellow illumination. Every Bogard smelled of fuel oil.

As expected, the children were typically attired in tattered and mismatched clothes and wore shoes whose uppers appeared like raw leather. Garson disallowed a story from Mellish that one bitter winter day two Bogard boys wore boxing gloves to school.

"Don't you remember that Holy Redeemer held clothing drives for the family?" Mellish further claimed that when he and his brother visited the Bogards, all of the donated clothing the family had acquired was heaped in the middle of the living room. The siblings rummaged through to find items that fit.

Because he was uncommonly small, Garson early on was the target of two playground bullies. Try as he might to avoid them, the rowdies invariably located him in the crowd, setting upon him nearly every day. They shoved and humiliated him, calling him "sissy" and "mama's boy." One grabbed him from behind, pinning his arms to his side, but Garson backward kicked his heel into the boy's shin; the assailant yelped and released his grip. Garson fled. But during one recess the hostile students cornered him; Garson expected renewed harassment, even pummeling.

"Leave him alone," a deep voice behind him demanded, as Garson attempted to avoid a shove. His tormentors immediately backed away, cowering. When Garson turned to face his protector, it was Charles Hill, the only colored student in the entire school. Tall for his age, he glowered at the antagonists, menacing. Garson never knew for certain why Hill, who was a grade ahead of Garson, came to his defense. He was bright and well-spoken, and earned good grades; he was a favorite of the nuns.

Garson and Hill never met outside of school, but they regularly acknowledged one another for the remaining years at Holy Redeemer. Occasionally, the bullies hurled maledictions, but they never again physically confronted him. It was a welcome relief, and provided freedom on the playground. More than 25 years later, Garson would happen upon Hill, who had by then earned a prominent position in state government. Garson recognized him immediately.

"What's your name?" Garson asked, thrusting his hand forward.

"I'm Chuck Hill," he said with a direct but curious look.

"Well, you don't remember me, but you were my playground protector at Holy Redeemer against school bullies." A broad smile brightened his face, and he accepted Garson's hand. They shook and exchanged a few pleasantries before parting; it was the only time they met.

Garson enjoyed some school subjects, particularly American history, literature and writing, but was unable to generate more than a modicum of interest in religious instruction — catechism and dogma, the Bible, saints, martyrs and popes. He dutifully memorized the Ten Commandments, but sometimes stumbled over one or two when asked to recite. He soon forgot most of the Eight Beatitudes. Heaven, Hell, Purgatory were understandable places, but Limbo, where souls of dead, unbaptized children basked in complete happiness, lacking only the sight of God enjoyed by those in Heaven, was a confusing concept. He recalled the seven sacraments with some ease, but never could grasp the event called transubstantiation when a simple unleavened wafer of bread was transformed into the actual body of Christ.

Further, Garson found amusing the reaction of some boys to lessons on Baptism.

"If someone's dying, you can baptize him yourself. You don't need a priest," pronounced Sister Agatha. Water was preferred, she said, but any liquid would be acceptable. A boy raised his hand from the back row. The nun nodded in his direction.

"Can you use soda water, S'ter?" Many boys compressed the word "Sister" like that, but girls never did.

"Yes." Another hand rose.

"Beer, S'ter?" Agatha nodded.

"Whiskey, S'ter?" More hands, always from those of boys seated at the back of the classroom, waved with insistence.

"S'ter, what about urine?" blurted the tall, robust boy who was new to the class. Particularly brazen, he would go on to become a star player for the ninth grade football team. Several boys near him snickered.

"Enough!" the nun brought the "discussion" to an end.

Garson unsuccessfully tried to discern why such a small event as his first confession, like the taste of castor oil, remained distinct in memory for six decades after it occurred. He satisfied himself only in describing the weeks of preparation and practice.

"Now, boys and girls, lower your heads on your desks, and make an examination of conscience," instructed Sister Agatha, the second grade teacher. Dutifully, Garson rested his head on his forearms and closed his eyes. In church, he often watched penitents enter the tiny, curtained booths and heard murmured dialogue inside. It seemed simple enough. But now his thoughts were diffuse as he attempted to collect a list of appropriate misdeeds. He mentally perused the usual ones.

Disobeyed father and mother. Ate meat on Friday once. Used the Lord's name in vain. He was uncertain about something called impure thoughts. His memory rummaged through movies he had seen, and concluded several were on the Legion of Decency list. But none were condemned, he was sure. Among those Seven Deadly Sins, he needed to confess anger and sloth; he had lusted for some of Toby's treasures. Fearful he might forget or seem insufficiently sinful to the confessor, he clandestinely scribbled transgressions on a tiny piece of paper. Patrolling Sister Agatha was at the back of the room.

In church the next day, Garson waited in the pew with classmates. Ponderous Father Dolan and parish assistant, Father Kelly, were hearing confessions; to Garson, they had prepared ambushes in those gloomy booths. He fretted particularly, fearful that he would interact with the florid, large-featured pastor; he was intimidated by the man's grating baritone voice. For several moments, it appeared that he might confess to the lesser of two evils, the usually gregarious Kelly, a priest who reminded him of Bing Crosby's screen portrayals. But then, Eunice, the pinch-faced girl he detested, took a long time in one booth, disrupting the cadence. What sins did that goody two shoes need to confess? Sister Ignacia waved Garson toward Dolan's bailiwick. He parted the curtain aside and knelt with fear and trembling.

"Bless me, father, for I have sinned. This is my first confession," he whispered rapidly. Then, his mind went blank. Unable to recall any of the sins, he pulled the paper scrap from his pocket; but it was too dim to see what was scribbled. He stammered.

"Speak up, my child," Dolan's sonorous tones reverberated. Classmates surely must have heard. Somehow, he muttered a few inconsequential transgressions. The pastor asked if that was all before granting him absolution. Garson smelled coffee on the pastor's breath.

"Say three 'Our Fathers' and three 'Hail Marys'," Dolan grunted. "Now go in peace, my child." Instant relief and gratitude washed over Garson as he passed from the penitential darkness into sinless light. He virtually bounded back to the pew to say the prayers, smiling behind his folded hands. First communion two days later was a breeze; he even avoided touching the tasteless host with his teeth; it melted harmlessly like a candy lozenge. Kenny, the cousin with the Jesus hair, and his pretty little sister accompanied their parents at the house to celebrate. A photo of everyone gathered on the front porch that day was among those incinerated in the house fire long after.

The grand adventure on which Garson and Larry embarked in those years lacked the drama described in Don Robertson's novel, *The Greatest Thing Since Sliced Bread*. Unlike the protagonist Morris Bird III, the boys experienced no explosive climax or the deadly tragedy. Garson and Larry, as second graders, only traveled to visit the cousin with long Jesus hair.

It was the summer after second grade at Holy Redeemer. The church, as did most Milwaukee parishes, conducted a summer festival to raise money for building and other purposes. The soaring stone parish church remained only an architectural rendering displayed on an easel in the basement vestibule. The festival featured food and beverage stands, game booths, and carnival rides arrayed on the black topped playground and parking lot. An advertisement promoted a polka band Friday and Saturday nights. If he remembered aright, Garson's mother gave him a two-dollar bill. He was delighted by the festive atmosphere, strolling about to watch people hurl baseballs at pyramids of concrete milk bottles, throw darts at a board full of balloons, and men hammering a lever to ring a high bell – all hoping to win fuzzy prizes. Elsewhere, he was discomfited for reasons he could not cite when men hurled baseballs at a metal trigger to plunge a pretty girl into a water tank; soaked, she shivered on the tiny seat as boys leered. He purchased a cotton candy, popcorn and a soda but resisted spending more; he returned home with over a dollar in his pocket.

"My cousin's got hair longer than a girl's," Garson told his friend the Monday after the festival. "like Jesus." Larry's response was a look of disbelief.

"Yeah, it was never cut since he was a baby." Garson's cousin Kenny, the first born child of his mother's brother, was three or four years younger than he. His doting mother, one of Garson's favorite aunts, could not bring herself to cut the wavy tresses that flowed down his neck and onto his shoulder like a golden waterfall. Relatives, friends and strangers universally adored the cute little boy with long girlish tresses. Garson just found it strange.

"Want to go see him?" When Garson explained that they would need to ride a bus and streetcar to visit, Larry said he had no money. Garson offered to pay the fare with money remaining from the church festival.

"Gotta ask my mom," Larry said, "'cause she'll be worried about me, and if I'm gone too long, she'll get mad when she can't find me, and I might miss lunch, and my mom said I'm a growing boy and need to eat, and how do we get there, and…"

Garson waved a hand, cutting off his garrulous friend, whose mouth hung open as Garson replied.

"Just let's go – now. I know how to get there."

Indeed, Garson had long been an observant rider, and on trips accompanying his mother, he noted which buses and streetcars to board and where they made connections. Despite Garson's confidence, Larry was reluctant even as he stood a half a head taller than his pal. Larry always seemed to lack any spirit of adventure. It was Garson who invariably took the lead, the opposite of Garson's relationship with Toby across the street. But coax Garson did, and the two pals began their odyssey. Garson told his grandfather they were going to Silver Spring Park.

They walked the two blocks west to Hopkins Street where the bus stopped. The driver, a regular assigned to the daytime route, was named Corrigan; he had a slightly uneven smile like the movie actor Dennis Morgan, and cocked his hat jauntily. Gregarious, he greeted every passenger and kept up a constant banter while he drove, calling out the stops and intersecting transit lines. He seemed happy in his work. Garson's mother found him handsome.

"Hey, boys!" Corrigan greeted when Garson and Larry boarded. "How're ya doin'?" Garson smiled, remembering his mother liked Corrigan and Morgan, both handsome Irishers.

"Now get a transfer," Garson instructed as he dropped two dimes into the glass fare box. They sat in the first seat across from Corrigan to watch him shift and steer, greet riders and call out the stops.

"There's my school," Garson pointed out when they passed Hampton Avenue. Larry, who had been silent thus far, turned to look. He gripped the thin paper transfer firmly in his fingers. His brow was furrowed in worry.

The bus traveled south to Capitol Drive, then jogged on the busy boulevard that bordered the storage yard of the A.O. Smith plant. On an expanse of concrete inside a chain link fence were stacked thousands of bomb casings for the war – most the size of fire extinguishers but some nearly as large as bicycles. Larry silently gaped at the sight.

"They don't have any powder in them. Don't worry," Garson assured his pal.

The ride terminated at the trolley barn where the bus line and two major north-south streetcar lines converged. The cavernous masonry structure was impressive with its three-story, arching clerestory roof and open ends. Larry followed Garson to one end like a lost puppy, awed to silence.

"See," Garson pointed down the street. "There's the Zenith," he said, hoping to impress his pal. A block south stood one of the newer movie theaters set in a handsome stone and brick building with Spanish ornamentation. The horizontal marquee displayed the movie offerings, and the admission price – 15-cents. Garson had been in the splendid theater for a Saturday matinee; he remembered the movie, a crazy quilt comedy and musical review called "Hellzapoppin'."

Suddenly, the screech of steel wheels and a clanging bell announced the arrival of the car in the barn under a shower of orange electric sparks from wires overhead. It was a typical Milwaukee streetcar in orange livery, the framed number 27 sign atop its roof. Garson long fretted that his city did not use the handsome, streamlined streetcars seen in Chicago — sleek and modern-looking conveyances that connoted speed and efficiency instead of the boxy cars that rattled and swayed on his city's thoroughfares.

"Now show your transfer," Garson directed his pal as the pair labored up the high entry steps. They again took the sideways seat across from the motorman to observe the man's actions. Apprehension played on Larry's face as the orange car lurched into life on the outside track and curled south. The lower halves of windows were barred to prevent careless riders from reaching out. On most lines, streetcars passed within inches of one another, Garson thought.

He was soon lulled by the rhythm of the heavy vehicle, listening to the grinding of flanged wheels, the clatter of the trolley pole across intersecting electric wires, the clanging bell and "ta-pokka" sound of the idling traction engine. He watched carefully as the motorman ratcheted the speed controller with his left hand, and applied the air brake with his right.

"There's the Savoy," Garson soon announced, pointing to another movie theater he knew. Larry listened but he was wide-eyed, having already traveled farther without his parents than ever before. Garson later pointed out the Rainbow Theater on Lisbon Avenue. Then the streetcar trundled down a long grade to Walnut Street, then Vliet Street where the Liberty Theater's new art deco marquee came into view. In not many years, Garson would frequent these west side theaters, including the vest pocket Violet and the faded glory of the Colonial.

Finally, Garson stood to pull the cord above his head. The car stopped at State Street, and the boys stepped onto the concrete safety island. When the streetcar roared past, Garson pointed to yet another movie theater, the State, just to the east. And several blocks south, the impressive marquee of the Tower Theater was visible at Wells Street. He felt worldly imparting such knowledge to his insulated pal.

When the street light changed, Garson and Larry walked under the thick canopy of towering mature trees. Garson directed his friend up the steps of a massive stone, two story duplex with a broad stone porch. He motioned to Larry to ring the bell. The day had warmed comfortably, and the inner door stood open. In minutes, Garson's aunt appeared, a toddler perched on her hip. With obvious surprise, she looked on either side of the boys, expecting to see an adult, Garson surmised.

"Where's your mother?" she inquired of her nephew.

"Home." Larry, nervous, shifted his weight from side to side.

"How'd you get here?" Her voice evinced a slight nasal quality. One of his younger aunts, she was an object of Garson's childhood infatuation. Tall and slender, unlike his rotund mother, she had dark hair and movie-star features, always adorned in dresses and sparkling earrings.

"Took the streetcar."

"My gosh! Just the two of you?" Her eyes widened, and a chuckle ushered from her upturned lips. Garson long remembered her easy sense of humor and generous laugh. Then, Garson's little cousin Kenny rushed to the doorway, buttery tresses cascading onto his shoulders.

"Tol'ja!" Garson pointed.

Garson's aunt swung open the screen door, and waved the boys inside. While they played with the cousin with the Jesus hair, Garson's aunt assembled sandwiches of peanut butter and jelly, cutting them in half for the boys and offering glasses of orange Kool-Ade.

"She's nice," Larry said of Garson's aunt. "I liked the ride, too, and the streetcar was fun, and the motorman clanging that bell all the time, and punching transfers, and the sparks and people getting on and off, and...," he trailed off. Garson was chagrined that his pal failed to mention even one of the movie theaters he had pointed out. While the boys later played with the cousin and his sister in the dining room, he overheard his aunt telephone his mother.

"Your dad'll pick you up after work," his aunt informed them.

It was probably an hour or so until his father arrived, and with the boys in the back seat of the dingy Pontiac, they rode home. Larry bolted from the car when they arrived. Garson's father offered not one critical word to his son; he may have been proud of his adventurous spirit. His mother admonished, but it must have been so mild that no memory of it remained.

In another of the early grades, Garson befriended a full moon-faced boy whose parents named him after the second United States president from whom they claimed their family descended. His ears flared from his round head, and owlish spectacles invariably slid onto the tip of his nose. Not among the popular or accomplished students, the pair gravitated to one another because of their fascination with newspapering.

"Gonna be a journalist," Garson boldly proclaimed.

"Me, too!" his new pal replied. He told Jackie about the Cary Grant and Rosalind Russell movie he had seen at the Ritz, about fast-talking reporters who bombarded people with barrages of questions, telephones ever at their ears. Jackie said he had seen the movie, too, and liked the bustling city room, scurrying copy boys, rolling webs of newsprint, and shouts of "Stop the presses!"

"My dad gets the *Chicago Tribune* every day," Jackie said. "He used to live there." The friendly classmate lived a few blocks south of the school, and after class one day, Garson was invited to visit. He knew the boy was, like him, an only child because his doting mother called him "Jackie," not John. In the house, Garson's was astonished: Atop a dining room table squatted a heavy, gray Underwood typewriter, a virtual Rosetta Stone. After the boys shuffled through several issues of the Chicago daily, Jack rolled a sheet of paper into the machine, and urged Garson to type something. Garson was nearly intoxicated as his fingers circled above the keyboard trying to locate letters he wanted. He laboriously typed his name. Jackie instructed him how to shift into capital letters.

After a few visits, the putative reporters decided to create their own newspaper. For several hours one or two times each week, the newsies cribbed paragraphs from the regular afternoon daily, pecking out stories in two-inch columns. They also created original reports about school and playground events, cut out these columns and pasted them onto a standard-sized sheet. Garson hand lettered a masthead and banner. *The North Side Gazette* was born.

Garson could not recall when the novelty of creating *The Gazette* gave way to the drudgery of onerous typing and pasting. Only a few editions were produced, each with a "print run" of one. No impatient newsboys waited in the streets to shout "Extra! Extra! Read all about it!" In time, Garson told Jackie that his grandpa wanted him home after school. Still, in the upper grades, they shared impressions of the new Jimmy Stewart movie, "Call Northside 777," in which the gangly actor portrayed a determined reporter scouring for the truth amid Slavic denizens of Chicago's immigrant south side.

The boys remained pals through the ninth grade, and joined the same Cub Scout pack where they fabricated yule logs and clunky race cars from wood blocks; neither car survived the initial race heats. For another project, Garson's dad helped him create an Indian head band that he proudly wore for the pack photo. Jackie lasted longer in Scouts than Garson, whose parental pleadings for perseverance went unheeded.

With each passing day after Pearl Harbor, headlines in *The Milwaukee Journal* grew larger and darker. Maps of events and military movements, photos of battles on land and sea were regular front-page features. While Garson was not attentive to the detail of such stories, the war permeated virtually every nook and cranny of his life. The pulse of daily life changed.

His father was past 40 when the war began – too old for actual service. But he volunteered as an Air Raid Warden, and was issued a steel helmet, the flat kind used in the previous war. In 1942, the city practiced total blackouts, and Garson's father trudged about in neighborhood darkness, a canvas khaki musette bag slung over his shoulder with whistle and flashlight at the ready. When he noticed even a sliver of light visible at the edges of curtains or drapes, he blasted his whistle, warning the neighbor of the infraction.

While his father was on neighborhood patrol, Garson and his mother peered into the blackness outside. Dogs howled nervously in the inky environment, and searchlights swept the sky to the east, perhaps at the lakefront. What if the Japs attacked Milwaukee? Times were ominous.

"Let's call ourselves 'Victory Garden Raiders.'"

It was probably Toby who gave the small aggregation of boys the name. He was the adventurous one, a leader with the best ideas, the boy who always received coveted birthday and Christmas gifts. Like Larry, he had a sibling at least ten years older, but, for all intents and purposes, he was, like Garson, an only child.

"I saw the picture in the paper," Toby said, "of those kids called the 'Victory Kidines,' like the Marines. They're the Goody-Goodies who help plant Victory Gardens." Garson remembered ubiquitous government posters encouraging families to cultivate produce for home use. One depicted a kindly grandpa with white van dyke, unconvincingly garbed in new bib overalls and a straw hat; he proudly held up a bunch of carrots for an admiring girl. A cornucopia of harvested vegetables rested at their feet while a United States flag waved in the background. "Keep 'em Growing!" the headline charged. Indeed, his mother managed a small vegetable plot adjacent to her robust rhubarb patch.

Garson liked the idea of the Victory Garden Raiders, but Larry evinced expected reluctance. Slowly during the war years, Garson shifted allegiance from Larry to Toby. But the trio made a pact to form the secret society. In late summer and fall, Toby reconnoitered backyard garden targets from the alley. He mapped out the mission, and plotted tactics. After supper, the young raiders followed Toby's daring lead. Only their parents' plots were off limits.

Like the Japs sneaking up on Robert Taylor and his squad in the movie, "Bataan," the Raiders pulled plunder from Pacific island plots of snap bean, carrots, kohlrabies and tomatoes. Only a squeaky gate betrayed their presence, causing an occasional retreat. Toby carried a salt shaker like an army .45 pistol, so their spoils could be consumed before the Raiders were captured.

It occurred to Garson that in some small way he and his pals were subverting the war effort by their thievery. He did not want to ignore the national admonition that scolded "Don't you know there's a war on?" But he lacked the moral force to suggest this to Toby.

His parents, after all, were doing their part, collecting newsprint, tin cans, string and other items. His mother reused cooking grease, and tried to paint stockings on her legs with some tan cosmetic. Tokens were issued for many goods, and Garson recalled ration books for sugar, meat and other consumables. Occasional poultry and beef were cadged from his mother's rural relations when Garson's father rode streetcars to work, husbanding paltry gas available to common "A" sticker holders — four gallons a week – enough for one trip to Dodge County.

"Watch out now," Garson's father shouted after honing a large butchering knife. A crate with two clucking chickens carried back from the oldest aunt's farm sat on the basement floor. Holding a croaking fowl between his knees, Garson's father deftly sliced its neck, then let it loose. While it danced about headless, another fowl was dispatched and the animals flapped about in a bloody *pas de deux* until they dropped. Garson's dreams were filled with sanguine horrors that night, of chickens pecking at his eyes. His parents also ground beef to make sausages. But when Garson's father attempted to introduce rabbits and squirrels to the dinner table, his mother balked. She imparted her detestation of wild meat to her son. Garson's allergy to fresh water fish also frustrated his father.

"He fought Germans and Japs in our front room," Garson's mother told relatives. Indeed, the boyhood Garson conducted campaigns on the mountains of the chocolate sofa and islands of overstuffed chairs. He jumped from an armrest, parachuting into Kraut-held territory, strangling the enemy with antimacassars and pummeling jack-booted Nazis with fireplace andirons.

"Ve haff vays to make you talk," he parroted movie accents, resisting threats of torture. "You haff friends in the Old Country, *nicht var*?" his captors sneered. Garson paused because Guttig might still have relations in Hungary. On all fours, he brushed aside leaves as he crept amid Pacific Island foliage, having been put ashore by Cary Grant's "Destination Tokyo" submarine. Silently he searched for slant-eyed Japs like the actor Richard Loo, who portrayed the despicable enemy in several movies.

"I studied at the University of California before the war, you know," Loo purred to an American airman through a cloud of cigarette smoke. That was how the enemy had learned English.

"Actually, I liked your country." Then he nosed a Nambu pistol to the captive's temple, trying to extract information about the pilot's squadron and mission. Loo and others like him always tortured American prisoners along with gentle, usually pacific Chinese and Filipinos.

There was something Garson enjoyed more than all of this – American war planes. From some source, he obtained a deck of playing cards that displayed, instead of kings, queens, jacks and pips, spotter profiles of aircraft both Allied and Axis. He was especially fond of the twin-boomed P-38 Lightening and magnificent P-51 Mustang of late war vintage. He was also drawn to the rakish art work that adorned Claire Chennault's P-40 Flying Tigers — snarling teeth painted below the propellers. Better, he was attracted to the nose art on bombers and other aircraft, illustrations of curvaceous women, baring substantial thigh and daring décolleté.

Garson endlessly drew dogfights in Holy Redeemer art classes, streams of red dashes for tracer bullets. The aircraft were crudely rendered, as Garson exhibited no particular artistic aptitude. He just liked the action. In time, the nuns complained to his mother during several report card periods, and he was encouraged to choose new subjects for his pitiful creations.

Much to Garson's delight, the youngest of his paternal uncles actually was a flyer in the war. Oh, he did not pilot those furious fighter planes, but he was a crew member on the B-17 Flying Fortress bomber. Garson was given one of his uncle's soft flying helmets, and wore it on several freezing winter walks to school. But Garson's illusions were dashed when the war ended and he discovered that, unlike flyers in the movie "Thirty Seconds Over Tokyo" or "Twelve O'Clock High," his Army Air Corps uncle had not dropped bombs on the hated Jap or Nazi heartland. He had, in reality, spent most of his service years in the United States, and only belatedly flew to Hawaii.

Only a few of Garson's relatives actually served during the war, and none, to his knowledge, was wounded or killed. There were two or three photos taken in front of Garson's house, of his father's cousin, a laconic army PFC with an enormous Adam's apple, home on leave. Boyish Garson was proud of the sailor suit his mother had purchased, even though he had begged for an army uniform – a little boy's show of solidarity with fighting men. It was a chilly spring late war day when the relative visited, so his mother insisted he wear a coat and cap, obscuring his outfit; Garson fussed and frowned for the camera until his father vetoed his wife, permitting his son to discard the offensive coat. A toothy smile played on his lips in subsequent images.

My Pop related that while setting down his recollections of those war years, he had vivid dreams about life back then, of experiences and incidents he hoped to incorporate into the narrative. Too often, such events slipped away because he failed to rouse himself in the middle of the night to jot them down. Thing of it is, he included too much minutia anyway, encumbering his yarn, slowing the flow. The memoir often deteriorates into little more than a pastiche of incidents and sketches. The reader may agree that there are just too many unsynchronized moving parts. But, thing of it is, they say book and movie characters are the sum of living details.

Garson's grandfather was often rapt next to the small kitchen radio, his attention riveted upon war reports. Garson listened, too, yet rarely understood the full import of what was broadcast until later in the war. As a boy, Garson was impatient to change the station from war news to favored radio programs. Listening to "Captain Midnight" was among his daily rituals. He once taped three nickels to a cardboard, sending away for a decoder ring. Away from prying parents and grandfather, lest there be spies lurking, he deciphered secret messages the Captain broadcast to thwart enemy threats. On Saturday, he laughed at the "Smilin' Ed McConnell Show" and the antics of the rapscallion Froggy the Gremlin who only appeared when Ed demanded, "Plunk your magic twanger, Froggy!" Garson begged his mother to purchase Buster Brown shoes for him because

Ed told him to. He liked Tom Mix, too, but detested gritty Ralston cereal. "Take a tip from Tom, go and tell your mom: Instant Ralston can't be beat!" the cowboy sang.

"Let's Pretend" also aired Saturday mornings while "Luxe Radio Playhouse" and "The Little Theatre off Times Square" provided nightly dramas that he did not always understand; but he enjoyed the voice characterizations and sound effects. Garson also lacked knowledge to understand the humor and ironies of "Fibber McGee and Molly" or "Amos 'n Andy," but listened, nonetheless, wondering what those folks really looked like.

War movies evoked newsreels, depicting memorable battles with fictional screen characters a year or more after actual events. While his mother frowned upon violence and rarely attended war movies, Garson and his pals reveled in them, although he fussed at the use of actual combat footage, thinking it was a gyp. He measured great movements of war with such Hollywood-rendered imagery.

"Bataan" was the first all-combat movie Garson recalled with no scenes of home front or women — extraneous matters as far as he was concerned. Sergeant Bill Dane, darkly handsome Robert Taylor, and his squad protected the last bridge from the advancing enemy. The Japs, Garson and his friends were convinced, refused to fight in the full light of day like men. Instead, they slithered beneath billows of mist and ground fog, and fired from unseen palm trees.

"Hey, Sarge, the trees and bushes are moving," noted one of his men as the enemy closed in on the American defensive position. In the climactic scene, Dane was the last man alive. As shadows and phantoms flitted, he pulled the trigger of a .30 caliber machine gun, firing directly into the camera lens that focused on Taylor's grimacing face above the clattering weapon.

"Come on, you sons of bitches!" he snarled. The final three words were drowned out by gun fire and a crescendo of music. Garson and his pals were thrilled that the epithet was clearly mouthed. He replayed that scene in his mind and dreams dozens of times, and the action echoed in boyhood combat on the empty lots of his block.

That and other war-time movies were decidedly inauthentic by the standards of 70 years later, but they created a template and tone. American squads were always composites of the country's races, classes and creeds — a meme that became fixture in later war movies. Actors like Robert Walker, Anthony Quinn, Van Johnson, Ricardo Montalban were regulars along with an occasional Negro character. Garson did not know that America's fighting forces were only integrated in Hollywood. The combat movies, whether on land or sea or air, in Europe or the Pacific, informed impressionable youth and convinced them of the rightness of the Great Crusade.

The early-war movies, like "Bataan," left the deepest impression upon Garson. Another of those with a polyglot cast starred Humphrey Bogart, an actor who usually portrayed flawed characters or gangsters. In "Sahara," he was Sergeant Gunn, a valorous American tank commander retreating after the fall of Tobruk. Non-commissioned officers, it seemed, made the best heroes. He and his M-3 tank named "Lulubelle" hunkered down at a played-out desert well where a disparate band of Americans and British soldiers held a parched German unit at bay. One by one, the defenders were killed. Garson especially remembered the Sudanese soldier, Rex Ingram, the genie from "The Thief of Bagdad."

Later in the war, one of the most vivid documentaries Garson remembered was shown at the Ritz as a co-feature. Directed by the famed John Ford, "With the Marines at Tarawa" depicted one of the Corps's bloodiest battles that came to symbolize all the savage fighting for Pacific islands. Within an area the size of the Pentagon, thousands of lives were lost. That color combat film left a seminal impression upon Garson that may have played a part in his decision to become a Marine less than a decade after. He would see that film with a different perspective during recruit training at MCRD.

War publicity was omnipresent on billboards, and in newspaper and magazine advertising. Little boys in sailor suits were ubiquitous. Four of the 33 boys in Garson's kindergarten photo posed in such military attire. Sweater girl Betty Grable and Royal Crown Cola ads promoted the war effort. Garson recalled that Whitman's chocolates featured a soldier and his sweetheart; a handsome army corporal drank Coca-Cola.

When Garson's mother finally left the metals manufactory to earn better pay, he was proud of her traveling to Schlitz Brewing Company downtown. While her somewhat doughy body did not compare with "Rosie the Riveter," he admired the brown slacks and tan blouse emblazoned with the company logo. It was a uniform. She worked second shift, replacing men who had marched off to war.

Because it was required for brewery employment, she finally filed to become a naturalized citizen in 1944. It is doubtful that she waited all these years because of lack of allegiance to America; she was an American in all but birth. Interestingly, she eschewed declaring her nationality as Austrian as she did on the marriage license. Austria, after all, was now part of the German Reich, and the horrific depredations that the country visited upon its own citizens were appalling. It was safer for his mother to declare herself a Hungarian, something she had often denied before.

To Garson, an eight-year-old third grader, other events seemed to stream past at a breakneck pace. The Allies splashed ashore in Italy and in a few months took Rome; Americans landed in the Solomon Islands; the German army ended its siege of Leningrad and Army Air Corp bombers pounded Berlin. Hopes for an invasion of France were percolating in the public mind.

Through all of this, there were ominous signs, portents in Garson's household for one of the greatest traumas of his early life. His grandfather's visits to County Hospital became more frequent. The lone lung that remained in his body labored, and the 73-year-old heart did not function with sufficiency. Guttig slept a lot those days. Worry was constantly written on his mother's face.

Since he was under the minimum age for visitors, Garson remained outside the County Hospital on Wisconsin Avenue when his parents visited Guttig. They handed him a sack of bread to feed ducks that paddled about the pond in front of the building.
It was his mother's memory, of course, that imprinted in his brain, about the final time his grandfather departed for the hospital. She recalled the scene for him numerous times.

"Before he got into the ambulance, he looked back," she said, tears welling in her eyes even months after. "It was as though he knew he would never see our house again." Garson had known no time when this man had not been with him, except perhaps for an occasional week now and again that his grandfather visited his Dodge County daughters.

"Remember, you were his favorite," his mother reminded.

Guttig died in the hospital on a Wednesday in May, 1944 as tree leaves plumped and flowers bloomed in his parents' yard. When Garson's mother returned home that day, she clutched at her son.

"Your grandpa's never coming back." Her cheeks were awash with tears. She led Garson into her bedroom where they slumped together on the bed face down. She wrapped an arm about his waist. Wailing loudly, her body convulsed. Garson cried, as much for his mother as for his grandfather, for he did not understand the idea of death. After a time, he fell asleep, awakened when spring sunlight had faded. This was another memory that persisted for decades.

Garson never saw the certificate, but it likely listed thrombosis and congestive heart failure as causes of death. Garson did not remember attending the funeral in Rubicon, but it was probable that he did. After mass at St. John's Church, the large crowd of uncles, aunts, cousins and friends he did not know, walked down the gentle slope to the cemetery. The gray metal coffin was lowered into the fresh earth next to the grandmother he had never known.

For what seemed like months afterward, his mother would stop suddenly as tears flowed. She embraced Garson at such times, perhaps thinking to reanimate her father in him somehow. She always held up this man, this quiet, kind and neat man, as a paragon for her son. How would he live without his grandpa?

Guttig's death almost seemed to overshadow the remainder of the war. Events tumbled past in the final year. The D-Day landing at Normandy commanded attention, and people predicted the end of the war was near. When he turned eight, he remembered the newsreel of MacArthur, the general who they said grew up in Milwaukee, splash ashore in the Philippines to fulfill his promise of return. Garson studied other images with care: Mussolini hanging upside down with splayed arms that was printed in *The Milwaukee Journal*. A later headline proclaimed that General Patton's valiant army crossed the Rhine into Germany.

While much attention in news and conversation centered upon the events in Europe, Garson seemed particularly focused upon the actions of the United States Marines. He liked the camouflage helmet coverings and the black eagle, globe and anchor emblem. He studied the handsome dress uniform of blue blouse and mid-blue trousers and red stripe, white hat and the gleaming brass fixings depicted in numerous recruiting posters and in national appeals to buy bonds. The dramatic flag raising atop Iwo Jima's Mount Suribachi in early 1945 was, for Garson, the capstone of the Marines' triumph. He cut out that grand color photo obtained from some source, and tacked up in his bedroom.

Sadness returned shortly after the president was inaugurated for his fourth term, Roosevelt dying in Georgia in April. Garson's parents adored the president. He had, after all, lifted the country from the dreadful Depression, and now had all but ended the war. His mother cried again, not as profusely as when Guttig died, for certain, but a gloomy pall settled in for some days.

Roosevelt was familiar to Garson, he was omnipresent in newsreels and newspapers, on radio with his weekly chats; his portrait hung in classrooms. He cheered for Roosevelt's victories over the prissy, mustachioed Dewey with that dogged overbite Garson detested. The stentorian voice with its patrician inflections, the round head and close-set eyes behind the pince-nez – these had always been there. As an eight year old, FDR was the only president Garson had ever known.

Car horns blared and church bells chimed at the news the next month when Germany surrendered, and the guns were silenced in Europe. Knots of people on the block gathered outside and visited each other, talking excitedly about the magnificent event and peace. That celebration was overshadowed in late summer, however, when Japan capitulated. Sirens screamed anew in the city and bells pealed for hours.

Garson ached to see the grand gathering that the radio described taking place in downtown on Wisconsin Avenue. He was sad that his mother did not permit him to ride the streetcar to join the throng of soldiers and sailors and pretty girls who congregated, packing the street so tightly that not even policemen on horseback could muscle through. He poured over newspaper photos the next day. They were almost like the iconic photo from Times Square, the image of a sailor bending over a girl, arm cradling her head while he kissed her long and hard.

***

Chapter 5

JARHEADS

"Hey, babe, I'd like a double order of you to go!"

That was what Ridley had told a comely blonde co-ed. He was the athletic recruit who had transferred into Platoon 023 upon its return to MCRD from Camp Matthews.

As observed earlier, Garson was given to obscure allusions, and, emulating his favorite, Dickens, experimented with character names. He chose Ridley for this fellow recruit after a noted fable of a generation ago, the novel *Riddley Walker* by Russell Hoban, set in a devastated, post-apocalyptic future; and because one of his favorite movie directors was Ridley Scott. More, Garson's Ridley often discoursed about science fiction in movies and books.

A college boy like Barker, Ridley, whose eyes, the gray of slate, were set in a square, sun-burnished face; thin brows arched below a jutting forehead. A small, sad mouth contrasted with his gregarious and confident demeanor.

"The chick was sitting in the campus malt shop, and I swiveled my stool to face her. She was built like a brick shit house." His large hands cupped in front of his chest to demonstrate. Ridley had been reminded, he said, of the scene in "Stalag 17" when American POW Stosh, who they called "Animal," and Harry Shapiro clandestinely stole up to female Russian prisoners at the delousing station; one in particular, a sturdy, buxom blonde, attracted Animal's attention.

"She's built like a brick Kremlin," leered Robert Strauss who played the role of the goggled-eyed airman.

Ridley had injured his knee on the Camp Matthews obstacle course, and had been held back from an earlier platoon to recuperate. He was reassigned to Platoon 023 to complete the final month of Boot Camp. With two more weeks of hair growth, he stood out from his new buddies. Ridley, who enjoyed an audience as much as Hal, dispensed insights about movies, music and his experiences at Southern California University.

Much to his parents' chagrin, Ridley had dropped out of college after nearly two years, bored and uncertain of what to do with his life. Over 21, he was among the platoon's older recruits. Garson envied Ridley's life, filled as it was with fascinating campus adventures, hoping one day to have similar experiences. Thus far what he knew had been derived from movie varsities exemplified by "Dreamboat," the musical "Good News" and even the Marx Brothers zany "Horse Feathers." He suspected that these were only fanciful depictions. But failing to finish high school would be a deterrent for him in the real world.

He was doubly envious, for Ridley had read widely and his vocabulary was larded with such words as *per se* and *ergo* and *au courant*. The Golden Stater described the Southern California campus situated in south Los Angeles, its largely red-brick Romanesque buildings distinctive and handsome. Palms and other trees along with flower gardens provided reflective punctuations. Garson could almost hear the strains of "Varsity" wafting over the setting. Ridley's fraternity, Phi Beta Epsilon, was located just off campus in a privately-owned mansion.

"My frat brothers and I went to T-Town many times to watch bullfights," Ridley related, describing adventures in Tijuana, Mexico – "just a 99-cent streetcar ride from downtown San Diego."

"Look, we'd sit on the sunny side of the *corrida de toros*, the bull ring, in the cheap seats, and slather on suntan lotion. The bulls came out at three in the afternoon. Expensive seats were on the shady side.

"We cheered for *toro*," he chuckled; locals narrow eyed us and muttered." Garson could visualize the scene, recalling Tyrone Power, Rita Hayworth and Linda Darnell in the Technicolor opus "Blood and Sand." He was fascinated with Ridley's descriptions of the *picadors* and *banderillores*, the gore when a strutting *torero* drove his sword between the bull's shoulders into its heart, dropping the maddened animal like a stone. Movies never showed the bull's *coup de grace*, but Garson's imagination was acute enough to conclude he was too squeamish to witness the real thing.

But there was more to Ridley's experiences about Tijuana that Garson and other virginal recruits found fascinating, yarns of comely, compliant senoritas ready to share a drink and more for the right price. Garson's Milwaukee pals, Toby and Rowdy, had boasted of such adventures after they returned from travels to California the previous summer. Garson's fantasies ran wild with visions of dark, alluring Mexican girls like Carmen Espinosa, skin-darkened Darnell, or similarly-shaded Jennifer Jones as the tawny temptress Pearl Chavez in "Duel in the Sun."

"You'll all get your ashes hauled after graduation," Ridley proclaimed. "You'll dip your wicks and get it on for the Corps and Old Glory!" As December turned toward January, Garson's heart frequently raced in anticipation of the lecherous prospect.

When Platoon 023 returned to MCRD from Camp Matthews the Sunday before Christmas, Garson and the others threw out their chests, displaying a salty swagger. They had seen a little of the "elephant." Their dungarees, scrubbed numerous times, were several shades lighter than most others at the Depot, caps were squarely blocked like the veteran rifle instructors; brogans were worn and comfortable, evincing miles of marching. During the course of the next month, Sergeant Maddox and PFC Duff would attempt, with incomplete success, to sharpen the unit's prowess on the Grinder, further harden young bodies and hone minds while other instructors continued indoctrination and inculcation in the skills necessary for fighting Marines. This included sharpened bayonet drills, heightened physical training and more.

Further, in these final weeks Garson would once more trigger the senior DI's wrath, such that that he suffered through several nights worrying that he might not graduate. To be made to repeat all or part of earlier training was a dismal prospect, to be released from the Corps as unfit would be even more devastating.

Garson could not recall when dress uniforms were issued – before marching to Camp Matthews or after. While no one had ever promised, Garson expected that the issue would include the archetypal dashing dress blues – dark blouse with high collar, jaunty piping, mid-blue trousers with red stripes, barracks hat with white cover – all set off with gleaming brass buttons and ornaments.

The standard issue, contrastingly, was more prosaic — green wool winter wear and cotton and worsted khaki for the warm months and climes. Garson was fitted with a long blouse and a waist-length battle jacket with two pair of trousers. Save for a brass belt buckle and tie bar, all emblems were dark metal.

While not allergic to wool, Garson had long been uncomfortable wearing the material against his legs. For school (jeans were not permitted at public or private schools), he always pulled on pajama bottoms beneath slacks. Now, that was impossible — pajamas were for pussies, of course. Somehow, he toughed it out in Boot Camp, learning to distract himself from the discomfort while he yearned for the khaki season. In time, after much wear and dry cleaning, rough uniform nap was smoothed a bit.

Dress issue also included four shirts – two cotton and two worsted – along with ties, dark brown dress socks, a green raincoat and two hats – the more formal barracks dress hat with its leather bill and metal skeleton on which was fitted a green cover. When the platoon departed from the cavernous quonset where clothing was issued, Garson felt foolish. As the platoon marched, the coverless metal grommets of the hats fluttered like wriggly halos, like a flight of errant earthbound angels, Garson grumbled.

The second piece of headgear was known as a garrison cap, a compressible wool head covering similar to what Scots wore. Sometimes called a "piss cutter," the cap also bore another name because its folds supposedly bore a passing resemblance to women's labia.

"How come they call this a *cunt* cap?" Krupa, the Baby Marine, asked rhetorically. "Marines ain't pussies, I thought." No one had an answer for a conundrum only he discerned. The gadfly Hal concluded that Krupa and his girlfriend Heidi must be virgins.

While Garson and his fellow recruits carefully minded dress uniform components, the cordovan dress shoes needed particular attention – hours of meticulous work was required to create an acceptable shine. Shoe dye was first applied liberally, and then lighted to burn it into the leather. From that point, spit shining was the order of the day –daubing a soft cloth into polish (as Camel was the DIs' preferred cigarette brand, Kiwi was the Corps's prescribed label) applying saliva, and rubbing in small, circular motions — the classic spit shine.

"If you just shine the toes," PFC Duff charged, "it's like taking a crap without wiping your ass." Garson remembered sitting on his foot locker for hours, on several Sundays when no classes or activities were scheduled, swirling polish and saliva, impregnating the leather's pores, working up the shine to a mirror gloss. The robotic work provided time for exchanges about movies, music, girls and families.

"My old man traced his ancestry back to royalty in Poland," Liska claimed. Jensen, another Detroiter, rolled his eyes. The family crest that Liska described featured two curved swords under a slivered moon, denoting that his forebears helped beat back Muslim invaders. It was clear early on that Liska took exception to jokes that ridiculed his heritage. Because much of Milwaukee's south side was populated by Poles, Garson was conversant with Polack jokes, those humorous but demeaning anecdotes involving "Stosh," babushkas and *babkas*, *charnina* and more.

Liska's father had dark hair and eyes combined with swarthy features and prominent cheekbones, he said; one old aunt thought he carried traits from central Asia or somewhere. Liska's father and his wife settled in the Detroit neighborhood around Chene, Ferry and Piquette Streets where Poles congregated. Later, the ethnic community shifted north into Hamtramck where, the story continued, earlier residents who became angry with neighbors threatened to fix up their houses and "sell to a Polack."

Summer evenings in Hamtramck were filled with music, as Liska's father relayed to his son; virtually in the shadows of the Dodge assembly plant and Chrysler headquarters, neighbors sat on porches and stoops, visiting and conversing, playing accordions and singing old country songs. The elder Liska, just learning English, began work life at Murphy Oil Company, and one of his co-workers taught him to say "Kiss my ass!" telling him to repeat the phrase to the foreman; the supervisor was wise to the joke, and did not fire the new worker. Like Jake in the movie "Hester Street," Liska's father rapidly adapted to the new culture.

"They called him a 'shooter' because he was ambitious," Liska said. That coupled with dark good looks attracted a tiny blonde who was assertive and self-assured. To the shock of the family, Liska divorced his immigrant wife by whom he had sired two daughters and married the vivacious American woman. He opened an insurance and real estate agency, selling Hamtramck houses and policies to new immigrants, sired two sons and became a success.

As was his wont, Hal invariably interjected a shaggy yarn that drew groans.

"Yeah, my great grandpop came to America from Europe with only a bindlestiff over his shoulder. In six years, he had a million bucks!" Several of his listeners asked about the bindlestiff.

"Why, that's the thing that bums carry at the end of a pole when they're on the move. Everything they own is inside the rag tied at the end."

"So you say that your great grandfather made all of that money in a half dozen years after coming to America? You kidding me, man?"

"Nope. Inside that bindlestiff was about six hundred thousand dollars in negotiable securities." Hal walked away before someone threatened to kick his ass.

Though Jensen, whose forebear came to America as Jezierski, spoke of a similar immigrant background, he exhibited no more interest in his heritage than did Garson. After only a short time,

Jensen's family had moved out of Hamtramck to the affluent Grosse Pointe community, leaving behind ancestral trappings. Garson's heritage, of course, was multi-hued – an amalgam of western and eastern European strains characterized in America as a "Heinz 57 variety" after the famous soup, and he came to pride himself on being unhyphenated — just plain American.

"My dad worked at Chrysler," Krupa put in. "Before the United Auto Workers sit-down strike at Flint, my dad said bosses called him 'dumb Polack.' After the union got the 40-hour week and eight-hour day and overtime pay, dad said, they called him 'Brother.'"

Over the course of Boot Camp, Garson learned that Liska had been a "sickly kid," as he described himself, who had contracted rheumatic fever and impetigo, the latter accounting for his deeply pocked cheeks. Doctors advised his parents to take him somewhere sunny and warm as often as possible. There was an aunt who lived in Florida, and here the five-year-old learned that things were different in the sunny South, that race and religion had significance.

"It'll be our secret," his father said. At his mother's insistence, Liska and his older brother grew up with Catholicism despite their father's secularism. On the train trip from Detroit, the father cautioned his son not to reveal his religion. There was more.

"Saw some colored guys on the train as we traveled south down the coast, and at one point the conductor walked down the aisle, announcing 'Mason-Dixon Line.' At that, every Negro moved to the last car of the train and were not seen again." In Florida, Liska readily saw signs proclaiming "White only" and "colored only" on toilets, water fountains and restaurants. The word "colored" was always lower case, he remembered, while "White" was capitalized.

"As a kid, I was curious if the water tasted different, and I took a drink from a colored fountain. It was warm." Suddenly, someone grabbed him from behind and lifted him off the ground. A burly man glowered at Liska.

"Boy, don't you know better than to do something like that?" he drawled with a scowl. Liska looked into a red face dominated by a pushed-in boxer's nose. He remembered the man's breath smelled of cigars. Liska's father made things right with the man, and later explained the matter to his son.

"They had a war down here a long time ago, son, a Civil War that caused them to hate colored people. They keep them separate from whites." Liska did not make the connection to religion at that point, but later understood why he had to keep his Catholicism a secret.

The family stayed at the magnificent Hotel Ormond in Daytona; it had been built by the Florida entrepreneur, Henry Flagler, who also constructed the famed Florida East Coast Railroad all the way to Key West. About the time of Liska's birth, the line was destroyed by a horrific hurricane that toppled a train and killed 500 people.

Another of Liska's Florida stories evoked a similar experience in Garson's life – his infatuation with the Negro girl, Sally, in a kindergarten class who he brought home for lunch; Grandfather Guttig had exhibited shocking asperity to Garson's pretty classmate.

No Baptist kids were allowed to play with Liska, the Yankee boy. And their parents were disparaging about the North and Papists. He met the little daughter of a hotel charwoman and was attracted. The other children called her a pickaninny, and warned Liska not to play with her. They had a brief clandestine relationship.

"I can remember clear as day, one sign I saw on the highway near Daytona. I think it was professionally painted, and it said: 'Nigger! Be Outta Town by Sun Down.'

"Another time my dad and I were driving – a very hot and sweaty day — when he pulled over to pick up a hitchhiker. He was a light-skinned colored guy. 'You must be from up North,' the man said, and thanked my dad for the offer. 'Better for me and you, Mister, if you just drive on.' We did." Liska had read somewhere that during Jim Crow years, more Negroes were lynched in Florida than any other Southern state. Over time, he and other Boots revealed much about their lives.

Garson had become accustomed to the balmy California weather around winter solstice, so unlike the piles of snow and numbing cold of Milwaukee in December and January. He daydreamed about the barren trees back home, the frozen park lagoons and resident ducks skating on ice. The city of San Diego, of course, boasted the most perfect weather in the nation – moderate temperatures and abundant sunshine virtually the year round, even when the sun was at its winter angle. During the afternoon of New Year's Day, 1954, the daytime thermometer hovered in the 60s. A week before, Christmas Day was even warmer with puffy clouds drifting across the bright sky. The idyllic southern California climate and holidays provided respite from drilling, training and indoctrination at MCRD.

Since the initial weeks of Boot Camp, a favored few received so-called "Care" packages from home. Occasionally, boxes contained such articles as fancy soaps, shampoos, deodorants, clothing and the like sent by well-meaning relatives or sweethearts; these were promptly confiscated by DIs. Most often, the folks back home sent homemade foodstuffs such as cookies. Under PFC Duff's gaze, Garson opened a box of his favorites – peanut butter cookies with cross-hatched tops that somehow enhanced their taste. The junior DI claimed the few unbroken ones that had survived the journey, leaving Garson to eat and share shards and crumbs – much appreciated nonetheless.

As Christmas approached, shipments increased, and at least a dozen Boots received tinned fruit cakes, those dense and dark confections laden with jellied fruits and flavored with rum. Like nearly every recruit, even DIs turned up their noses at these sodden torts; the cakes were so rich, it was virtually impossible to consume so much in a short time. One recipient foisted pieces on other Boots in an effort to rid himself of the dreadful desert.

"Aw, com'on, man, take a piece. Just one," he pleaded. It grew so difficult, that Garson accepted a proffered slice. After biting off one or two tiny morsels, he strolled outside and then to the Head, flushing the remainder down a crapper.

Then there was Springer, the dark recruit with the long oval head who, along with Buchman remained dentally deficient after these many weeks. As Springer's hair grew, the widow's peak gave him the look of Bela Lugosi's Dracula, Garson thought, even though he lacked blood sucking incisors. He laughed easily when something struck him, and his mouth gaped cave-like, exposing barren pink gums in a black maw.

"It was rough at first," he said, "but after a while, your gums toughen up." He chewed meat and other foods during those months as easily as a wolf. Garson could empathize as he also awaited the issue of the partial prosthesis to fill the space that his immature lower molars had once occupied.

"Now, Springer, I want you to sit right here and eat this fuckin' candy – every last piece of it – until it's all gone," PFC Duff ordered. Another frequent Christmas mailing was candy, the holiday variety – hard sugary pillows and buttons of iridescent purple, red, pink and white meant to be savored for minutes on end. And of all people, toothless Springer received a five pound box. When it was opened at mail call a few days before Christmas, PFC Duff smirked.

The Milwaukee recruit blanched as he gazed at hundreds of pieces. Though tough, his gums could not crack them. He sat for more than an hour, cross-legged like an oversized child, sucking as best as he could, cramming his mouth with as many pieces as could fit. Duff checked back several times. A few daring recruits clandestinely assisted Springer in his chore. In time, the toothless Milwaukeean consumed most of the candy before racing to the Head with his stomach erupting.

"Springer, you have an infectious smile – trench mouth." Hal tried to introduce a bit of levity, but the toothless recruit was not amused.

Wearing dress winter greens, Garson and several other Catholics answered church call on Christmas mass that Friday morning. One of the squad leaders marched the small detail to the interdenominational chapel on the northwest corner of the Grinder. While he was a product of a Catholic upbringing and education, Garson, in retrospect, never regarded himself as devout. Like his father, he followed the rituals and rubrics out of habit and out of deference to his mother's wishes.

Garson attended Sunday mass at MCRD not motivated by newfound piety but because it was a way to briefly avoid the grind each week. He was not the only church-goer, Catholic or other, who regarded weekly worship in that manner. The Marine Corps exhibited an indifferent attitude toward such practices; it ranked religious faith somewhere below fidelity to Corps, and love of country and mothers. Ultimately in life, Garson became totally secular, nearly approaching intolerance for any ritualistic religion.

Still, he found Christmas dinner an uncommon pleasure, even while the fare failed to match the memory of mother's cooking and baking. Still, he had no recollection of formal holiday dinners back home, at least since his mother's steady employment at Shorty's restaurant began four of five years before. She worked at one of the most popular dining spots in North Milwaukee, its tables filled virtually from opening to late at night, particularly on holidays; diners often waited in long lines outside. By the time her dish washing chores were completed on those days, his mother was too tired to prepare regular meals at home. Garson and his dad were usually left to their own dining devices, only occasionally joining the crowds at Shorty's.

In her fiftieth year, his mother was not only worn down by virtually endless work since her teen years, but depressed because of the growing financial precariousness of the household. Not six years before, the beloved family bungalow had no mortgage, and thousands of dollars in war bonds were tucked away. Now, because his father purchased a commercial property for the new enterprise, bonds had been cashed and a new mortgage secured; it hung over the house like a Damoclean Sword. His mother was critical of the financial sacrifice, of course. While industrious, his father, sharing traits with Arthur Miller's Willy Loman, was simply not an efficient small businessman.

"He sells a two-peck bag of popcorn to a tavern for a buck and a quarter, and makes a few pennies profit, then buys everyone a beer." Garson heard that complaint from his mother for years. "That's no way to run a business." More dire circumstances lay on the near horizon.

Still, Garson had pleasant memories of traveling with his father on out-of-town delivery routes each summer. After restocking customers, father and son sometimes rented a boat to fish. They took rooms at quaint village hotels, and ate in dining rooms on such fare as squab, goulash and pork hocks. Garson's father paid him a dollar and a quarter a day on those trips.

At MCRD, Marine cooks turned out a palatable holiday repast for recruits – turkey and ham, potatoes and yams, an array of vegetables augmented with apple and peach pies. Garson, detesting the syrupy institutional fillings that were so unlike the fresh ingredients of his mother's pies; he eagerly traded mess hall canned compote for a buddy's crust. Certainly, it did not rival his mother's light and flaky creation, but it was the best to be had so far from home.

Platoon 023 wore its dress uniforms to Christmas day chow. For many, it was the first time a tie was worn. A cartoon was printed in *Leatherneck* magazine of a Boot Camp Marine who wrote home to his parents, telling them about a meal. With pencil in hand, he inspected his khaki tie, then jotted that he had eaten spaghetti and meat sauce.

"It was Christmas Eve, and they were all feeling Mary," Hal quipped when they returned after chow that day. "And when Mary left, they all jumped for Joy." Garson's raised his eyebrows in quandary.

'Don't you get it? 'Mary,' a girl. 'Joy,' another girl?" Garson popped his forehead with the palm of his hand. This is what passed for holiday cheer.

"Heard McCracken got a BCD." That was Hal with another of those bits of scuttlebutt picked up from some unnamed source. McCracken, of course, was the fraudulent 16-year-old enlistee who admitted his offense before the platoon marched to Camp Matthews. The homely Texan had been responsible for the loss of the platoon's cigarettes when he was caught smoking, and sustained retribution. For many, a bad conduct discharge from the Corps was justified. Still, Hal's incessant rumor mongering was now frequently met with shaking heads and doubtful expressions.

"Think Maddox's married?" Hal queried Christmas afternoon. Expectantly, the senior DI was not on duty that day, PFC Duff fulfilling the assignment.

"Fuck, he can't have a wife. He's married to the Corps."

"Naw, I bet he goes home to his little missus and a couple of kids."

"Kids! You fuckin' kidding me? Why they'd be in a living hell. Reveille and close order drill every day. He'd tell 'em bedtime stories about the Barbary pirates, the blood at Chepultepec, Chesty Puller and the fight at frozen Chosin." Garson would recall those speculations about Maddox many years later while reading Pat Conroy's novel *The Great Santini* and seeing Robert Duvall portray the hard-bitten Marine pilot, Lieutenant-Colonel Wilbur "Bull" Meacham, whose relationship with his oldest son was fraught with tensions.

New Year's Eve 1953 passed almost unnoticed. TAPS sounded hours before the new year arrived, and when they awoke Friday, it was just another day at Boot Camp.

Colloquially known as "Junk on the Bunk," the inspection of clothing was one of the most important events during the latter weeks at MCRD. Like performance on the Grinder, at the rifle range, appearance and comportment, this and other inspections comprised components of the score to determine the battalion's honor platoon. Sergeant Maddox regularly reminded recruits that his previous units had earned the signal honor, and he would not permit 023 to mar his record.

The recruits had taken all evening before the inspection to carefully lay out more than 50 pieces of clothing – everything save for what they wore – onto their bunks, using the *Guidebook* photo template. So as not to disturb the display, they were ordered to sleep on the quonset's deck with but one blanket. It was an uncomfortable and sleepless night for Garson, bony hips protesting against the cold concrete.

"What the fuck's a matter with you, you stupid clown?" Maddox barked as the entire quonset of recruits cowered. During his preliminary walk-through in advance of the battalion commander's inspection, he had spotted Garson's error. The sergeant's hand gripped Garson's collar, throttling him violently. Garson's head wagged like a rag doll, and tongue nearly lolled. He was unable to speak.

Each recruit had been issued two ink stamps to mark clothing – a half-inch and quarter-inch – the latter for smaller items like socks, ties, belts and the like, and the former for larger garments. Before precise instructions were given, Garson, hoping to impress the drill instructor with his diligence, had inked the improper size on three pair of skivvies. Discovering his mistake, he prayed it would not be noticed.

"This is the wrong fuckin' stamp! I suppose you're the ten percent that never gets the word." Waving the garment with his free hand, the DI's face churned with rage, his usually full lips thinned like a taut rubber band. So this is what the sergeant meant when he warned miscreants that he would grab them by the stacking swivel and beat them severely about the head and shoulders. Finally, he shoved, and Garson crumpled onto the deck. Maddox strode away. This was worse than the first confrontation Garson had with his senior DI; he feared repercussions.

When the battalion commander later made the official inspection, Garson held his breath. To him, the incorrect stampings seemed as large as a billboard. But Captain Mundt cast only a casual eye over Garson's bunk, seeming not to notice the error. Garson exhaled relief.

Two weeks later, Garson was much more careful during an inspection on the Grinder during which all of the combat equipment was laid out on a poncho – rifle, bayonet and scabbard, pack, cartridge belt, canteen and cover, entrenching tool, mess kit, first aid kit and other items. He helped the nervous Prick array the 782 gear, and fold away so-called Irish Pennants, the unsightly ends of canvas straps. Garson's heart sputtered when Sergeant Maddox scanned his display, but to his relief, the DI found nothing untoward. The battalion captain's inspection was a cakewalk. Of late, Garson cultivated a neutral facial expression at inspections and formations, to maintain level eyebrows, to dissemble and avoid undue scrutiny. He practiced staring into an indeterminate distance.

"You shave this morning?" At another impromptu inspection,

PFC Duff's eyes bored in on Buchman, the Milwaukee recruit with the light, fuzzy eyebrows whose every tooth, like those of Springer, had been extracted weeks before. New upper and lower prostheses, "Marine choppers," had not yet been fabricated for either recruit. Buchman was another Boot whose girlfriend persisted in scrawling "S.W.A.K." on her envelopes, providing him with a steady mail call diet of envelopes and letters to chew and consume.

"Sir, yes, sir!" Duff confronted Buchman at a morning formation. The junior DI leaned his face closer, studying peachy sproutings. The recruit claimed he had shaved the night before.

"Naw, you didn't. There's fuzz right here. Now go get your razor and we'll fuckin' clean it up." The platoon remained at attention for several minutes until Buchman raced back to the ranks with the instrument in hand.

"Now shave!" Duff commanded, "dry!" Buchman dragged the razor across his cheek without benefit of water or lather. Garson could almost feel the recruit's skin protest even though he himself had not needed to shave in his life, never having cultivated a single whisker. In time, he would need to seek guidance from his father on the proper method of shaving.

"In place... For-ard. Haar!" Duff commanded. Buchman began to march on the spot, 120 steps per minute while pulling the razor under his chin. Later, another recruit who stood nearby said he saw blood run.

"Stationary double time. Haar!" The pace increased by 50-percent to 180-steps a minute. Duff shouted for Buchman to continue shaving. The offending recruit's ordeal went on for many minutes, and Garson surmised others in the formation winced as he did. He was much relieved not to be in Buchman's shoes, to have such attention focused on him. Days later, the recruit's face still bore red divots and scratches from the ordeal, but he was never again seen without a smooth face.

Not long after returning to MCRD, Garson and a few others sensed once more that Maddox was unhappy with the platoon's development in close order drill. Garson thought that he and the other recruits had done well at Camp Matthews. Only a handful had failed to qualify with the M-1. There were only one or two Experts, but almost two dozen had earned Sharpshooter medals, Garson among them, of course. This all augured well for Maddox's quest. Clothing and equipment inspections, physical fitness, test scores and other training had also gone successfully. It was the lack of perfect close order drill proficiency that proved a shortcoming.

"T' rear! Haar!" – To the rear. March! Recruits wheeled 180 degrees, pivoting on the balls of their right feet. Even after hours of instruction, many flailed about, a few turning to the left. Other maneuvers also lacked cohesion.

"By the right flank. Haar!" "By the left flank. Haar!" Dare not anticipate the command of execution, "Haar!" or fail to take the one extra step before beginning the movement.

"Move the rifle around your heads, not the other way round!" Here was another constant harangue. Marching while doing rifle movements – right to left shoulder and back, shoulder to port arms and more – complicated drill. Many in Platoon 023 appeared to lose concentration, ranks wavering and misaligning for several steps while changing rifle positions. There was more.

"What is this – some kinda mass grabass out here? You clowns look like a fuckin' Chinese fire drill," shouted Sergeant Maddox during an afternoon on the Grinder. It was uncharacteristic for the senior DI to use the Corps's favorite explicative; only in the most exasperating circumstances did he inject the four-letter word.

"Maybe I'll hold the entire lot of you back!" The hinge of Maddox's jaw rippled. The platoon had once again veered badly when marching at the oblique. This was a maneuver in which 023 never excelled. The command for the 45-degree change in direction from the former line of march was "to the oblique," pronounced "obleek" by every drill instructor. Within not many strides, the ranks drifted and became unsettled as the tendency, like water seeking its own level, was to align at right angles.

"'Toon. Halt!" Maddox shouted. "Now look around at yourselves, you bunch of clowns." Garson gazed to his right and left, observing the disarray. The sergeant then commanded every recruit to realign himself properly.

"Now this is how you should look on the march. Mark it in your pea brains, dammit! For-aar! Haar!" But in less than a dozen steps, alignment drifted again. There was another halt and realignment. Garson and others grew weary at the incessant badgering, and angry that they were unable to master the maneuver. The senior DI was obviously frustrated. Thus far, he had been unable to shape 023 to his demands. Garson and others, too, were envious when other platoons marched past; they appeared to be perfection, every footfall in unison, every heel striking the concrete at the same instant. As the days to graduation diminished, Sergeant Maddox and PFC Duff were relentless in their hectoring.

Garson and most recruits knew the concepts but unanimity and uniformity of movement were as difficult as mastering the simple dance steps Lana had taught him in her living room in preparation for a school "sock hop." What was more, there were always a few, flies in the ointment, who were unable to mind the step with others. Among them were Prick and, of course, the bandy-legged, spraddle-footed Fletcher, Garson's enduring nemesis.

"Dammit, Fletcher, get in fuckin' step," Garson muttered as the platoon strode along, hoping the DIs would not hear his whisperings. Garson was unremitting in his carping at the goggled-eyed recruit.

"Thirty-inch strides," the DI barked. "Swing those arms. Six to the front, three to the rear. Heels! Heels! Heels!" But Fletcher was unable to feel the military cadence, to catch the rhythm with his stumpy legs and doughy body; he could not maintain a steady 30-inch stride. The Detroiter seemed to lift on the balls of his feet before he took steps, creating a tiny hitch. "Mind the step, dammit! Stop bouncing. You're gonna lose Honor Platoon for us."

"Shut the fuck up!" Fletcher shot back loudly one day. Maddox heard the comment, and halted the platoon. He strode menacingly to Fletcher, demanding to know what he had said.

"His fault, sir," Fletcher inclined his head back toward Garson. When the sergeant asked what he meant, the Detroiter explained that Garson was harassing him constantly about his marching.

"Well, if you two pussies have a beef, we'll get it settled. Report to the Duty Hut after formation," he commanded.

Garson's heart raced like Bill Vukovich's engine at the Indianapolis 500 when he and Fletcher were admitted to the Duty Hut. Their versions of the outburst seemed to be held to no account. The staff sergeant and PFC stared impassively from behind the desk on which laid two pair of scuffed boxing gloves. The antagonists were told to lace them on. Right Guide Barker and several others who were billeted in the hut crowded a doorway – spectators for the contest. Garson said that when he began hanging out with other teens on the Burg, the commercial strip in North Milwaukee, he had a reputation among a few acquaintances as being pugnacious.

The summer before, Garson had overheard comments among his Villard Avenue pals. "Yeah, he's small," he recalled one saying, "but don't mess with him because I heard he's a tough little bugger." Garson had been dumbfounded at the assessment, and curious about the origin of such a rumor. He took it as an undeserved compliment, but if there was truth, it was that he avoided confrontations and hung on the periphery of scrapes.

He had had only one true fight in his life, years before when he spent summers at his father's business building on the west side among a somewhat rough and tumble crowd. With bravado, he had called himself "Blackie" then, donning a hard but manufactured shell. The scuffle had started almost playfully with friendly pawing against a younger boy. But mock blows led to cuffing as Garson gained confidence and aggression, his competitor backing away. Gaining the upper hand, Garson could see his opponent was losing heart. But as triumph neared, the boy's older and stronger brother intervened, and knocked Garson to the ground.

So here he was, 17 years old, wearing a pair of boxing gloves for the first time in his life, and facing a daunting opponent. Fletcher had removed his thick glasses, eyes now uncommonly small; the right one drifted outward, like a wall-eyed Pug dog. As Charles Dickens might have written: Fletcher was decidedly "ill-favored." He stepped toward Garson, some pugilistic experience obvious:

A southpaw, his left fist protected his chin and cheek while his right pawed menacingly. Garson mirrored the stance, and began to circle. He heard a growl from Duff to get at it.

Garson tried to remember the techniques he had watched in the movies — John Garfield as Charlie Davis, the lightweight boxer in "Body and Soul," Robert Ryan as Stoker Thompson in the gritty "The Set-up." When television entered his house a few years past, Garson became a devotee of Friday Night Fights. His mother always worked fish fry nights at the restaurant, and Garson had the set to himself. He watched some of the great ones, Louis, Robinson, Charles, Walcott, LaMotta, Kid Gavilan and others lesser known.

Fletcher thrust his right fist forward, but Garson ducked and weaved, avoiding jabs. He bobbed his head like the professionals, and, wearing his best menacing expression, shuffled about the antagonist. Perhaps I can do this after all, he thought, protecting his face with one bulky glove. As he congratulated himself, Fletcher's curving left hand suddenly smashed into Garson's temple. Fireworks exploded before his eyes. He stumbled but righted himself quickly.

"Come on, you little pussy," Maddox demanded.

Unsteadily, Garson circled to his left again, shaking his head, repositioning the bulky gloves. He wobbled a quarter circle while thrusting one or two weak defensive punches. His rival ducked and danced. He hated that bastard with un-centered eyes and peg-like teeth, and was determined to get him somehow. Again, Fletcher launched another jab, but Garson parried once more.

The instant his mind shouted satisfaction, his antagonist stepped forward, launching a blow like a fast surfacing submarine – a classic uppercut. Garson felt his neck snap and his head jolt. Teeth cut into his gums. Light before his eyes was blinding, almost like that flare of white phosphorous he had seen at Camp Matthews. Garson lost his balance, stumbled backward, finally landing on the seat of his dungarees.

"Fuck!" one observer spat. Garson heard sniggers and guffaws. His head whirled and he tasted blood. Fletcher pranced, an ugly triumphant grin lighting his round face. It had been no contest at all, really; only a few minutes had passed. He was just a pussy, after all, a mama's boy. What kind of Marine would he make?

His chin throbbed. He tried to gather his legs under him, but slumped back down. After a few moments, he raised a glove, waving it in submission. That ratty-faced fuck, Fletcher, had bested him with little exertion. Barker, the right guide, helped Garson to his feet, and pulled the gloves free, then led Garson to the door. It was mortifying, like watching old Joe Louis pummeled by Rocky Marciano.

For the remaining weeks at MCRD, Fletcher and Garson maintained an unfriendly truce. Fletcher never attempted to intimidate or harass him. While he commented no more about Fletcher's gait, Garson's loathing grew. He laid blame for the loss of Honor Platoon to Fletcher's bouncing, prancing gait.

Garson continued to coax a bit more muscle onto his slender frame, and while he detested physical training at MCRD, he performed well in all but one exercise – chin ups. He accomplished the minimum number but no more. He was, as always, fleet of foot, and could scramble over the vertical wall and swing across the muddy moat with ease. He had no difficulty with giant arm swings, jumping jacks, deep knee bends and other calisthenics or with the M-1 and bayonet drills. With gritted teeth and a feigned murderous leer, Garson thrust and parried, swinging the nine-pound weapon in horizontal and vertical butt strokes, aiming at unseen groins and chins.

"Come on, you fuckin' shitheads, let's hear you!" Growls and snarls were never loud enough.

"Write that I'm OK, and the food's good," Hupner dictated. Garson scribbled the words on the sheet of Marine Corps stationery. "Tell daddy I made some good friends here who read and write for me." Hupner's illiteracy had still evaded detection by all but a handful of confidants, Garson and Barker among them. By quarter inches, Hupner had been able to notch his web belt tighter about his middle, and he marched smartly with shoulders square and chest taut. He excelled in physical exercise and in inspections. He wore his Expert marksmanship medal proudly. His smile and warm demeanor won him many friends.

"Yeah, did some shootin' back home in Blanco County, but I don't like the M-1 much – all that figuring out how to click them sights. Why, we used to use good ol' Kentucky Windage – if your missin' high and left, you aim low and right and hit the target. No foolin' around with clicks an' such."

Hupner occasionally lamented that he missed his mamma and daddy back home. But in many ways, he appeared to thrive at MCRD. While the rest of the platoon took on the expletive-riven *linqua franca* of the Corps, Garson did recall a time when Hupner uttered an untoward word. He eschewed scatology; blasphemy was totally absent from his vocabulary. Hupner listened carefully and never interrupted a speaker. A Baptist, he attended Sunday services regularly.

"My daddy always said to mind my manners 'specially 'round old folks."

He seemed to take to Marine Corps, as Hal proposed, like a dick to a pussy. For a robust man, Hupner was surprisingly light afoot, agile actually. He displayed an infectious grin that, for some, seemed to connote something more.

"What the fuck's a matter with you, you dumb Texan?" PFC Duff spewed at Hupner's face one day. The junior drill instructor, unlike Corporal Reid who preceded him, took only a bit of pleasure in baiting Platoon 023's larger recruits. Duff stood half a head shorter than Hupner. What was more, recruits from Texas were often singled out, the DI uttered impression was that they were drawling idiots. Hupner never complained about the physical ordeals or the fact that he was the focus for Duff's harassment.

"Ah, nothin', sir," Hupner lazily replied.

"Why's your mouth always hangin' open like that, then?"

"Dunno, sir." Hupner later told Garson he did not understand what the drill instructor meant.

"You don't know?" Garson swore he heard Duff's eyeballs pop. "Well, keep your damn mouth shut 'cause you look like a fuckin' idiot."

"There's some good ol' boys in my outfit," the bulky Texan said as Garson wrote. "I like our right guide, Barker, too; he's from up north in Detroit. We got no colored ones in here, but one Indian. Think he's Cherokee. There're some others who are good ol' boys, too." Right Guide Barker made certain that no one saw that envelopes were addressed in Garson's handwriting.

Hupner's forebears, Garson gleaned from conversations, were from Hill Country, Germans who immigrated to the state in the previous century. His family's farm was located between Johnson City and the Colorado River. He had traveled to Austin a few times, but until he departed for MCRD, he had never left the state.

"Bet your family name was spelled with an umlaut way back when," Garson once interjected. He was trying to display some erudition that he remembered from German language classes.

"Those two little dots over the "u" that change the sound. Hüpner," he said, recalling how Holy Redeemer nuns tugged his lips forward with their fingers to gain the correct pronunciation.

Hill Country was flat farming area, Hupner explained. His family raised cattle and sheep, and he once described the shearing process that consumed his extended family for several weeks.

"Daddy knows Senator Lyndon Johnson," Hupner related. The rangy legislator had been in Congress since 1948, and had recently been elected minority leader of the United States Senate.

"Our people liked to dance and party," Hupner said. "I was always big for my age, and they let me have beer from the time when I was 13. Mama didn't like me having beer, but daddy said it was OK so long as I didn't get tipsy." Garson found similarities of the Texas celebrations to the Belgian Kermisses he had attended with his parents, uncles and aunts near Green Bay. Hill Country was populated with thousands of Germans, Hupner said, and they regularly gathered for Oktoberfest each year, enjoying good beer, *spanferkel* – roast young pig — *sauerbraten*, *kuchen* and *kolache*.

"We have an Easter pageant when folks dress up like bunnies and flowers, Indians and settlers. It's called the Fredericksburg

Easter Fires, and they dance around to teach us about our German ancestors. It all started after the war when I was just a kid." The celebration, Hupner explained, was said to commemorate fires ignited by the Comanche Indians to signify their acceptance of a peace treaty with German settlers more than a hundred years before.

"When those fires burned, us kids got frightened at first, but mama told us that the fires were set by a bunny who was just boiling eggs for Easter. Now we sit in them grandstands to watch the fires. They also tell stories about Indian sacrifices and other history events."

"I got a letter! I got a letter! Hope to hell you got one, too." It was a little lyric that recruits now gave to bugle notes announcing mail call.

"Oh, man, your sister's a real looker," Hal observed as he stared at two candid photos that Garson's childhood friend, Lana, had sent him. Right Guide Barker distributed mail these days, so her letter and snapshots avoided scrutiny by drill instructors. Lana posed in a black leotard and net stockings, her ruby lips pursed provocatively.

"Some legs, man!" Hal admired with a whistle. He asked for Lana's address that he might write to her; but Garson demurred, saying she had a boyfriend. In fact, he would jealously rebuff similar requests from other Marines. Her two-page missive mentioned that she was trying out for a sophomore musical review at Custer, the high school that now occupied a spacious, new building. She would be in its first graduating class.

Garson studied those black and white images many times, thoughts returning to that evening when, like a Peeping Tom, he had clandestinely observed her cavorting before a bedroom mirror wearing only brassiere and panties. She still reminded him of the ballerina Moira Shearer who had danced in one of his favorite movies, "The Red Shoes."

"She doesn't look like you at all," Hal observed. To Garson's chagrin, he now admitted that, save for the little gap between her front teeth, Lana bore little resemblance to Shearer whose head was crowned with flaming henna hair.

"Better hide these or you'll get me in trouble," Barker warned. Garson secreted the photos in the deepest foot locker recess. He had been compulsive about securing the wooden chest since that confrontation with Sergeant Maddox the first month of Boot Camp.

He also received occasional letters from his mother, terse penciled letters with bits of news about the latest winter storm and persistent cold. She also jotted some lines about Deaffy, the wizened crone who prowled Garson's neighborhood, collecting junk and discards. His mother had complained for some time that her hand writing had deteriorated with the onset of arthritis. For too many years, her hands had been plunged in scrub buckets and now in a restaurant sink.

His parents were literate, certainly, and they read the afternoon daily newspaper most nights and occasional magazine articles. But he had never known them to peruse books. The built-in shelves that flanked the fireplace in his home contained few tomes as Garson remembered – three or four random volumes of the *Encyclopedia Britannica*, a pictorial survey of World War II, *Ripley's Illustrated Believe it or Not!* and four or five other volumes.

Garson inquired in each letter if his mother had given his address to Betsy, the wiry-haired girl with the radiant smile with whom he had shared homerooms at Messmer High. She had permitted him to copy her daily geometry homework assignments. He would not have advanced to junior status without her. For two years, he cast furtive glances at her across the desks, and reveled in their brief conversations at the bus stop. He still lamented he had not said some things to her that had come to mind after the encounters; typically, he had ready comments only in retrospect. He hungered to write to her, to pen a poem or something about his feelings.

Pushing his fantasies farther, he thought of writing to his Uncle Vin who knew a man on Milwaukee's east side who sold jewelry out of his apartment. Perhaps he could ask his uncle to look for an engagement ring. His mother liked Betsy even though the two had never met. Her photos in the year book and attendance at a

Catholic school were enough to win his mother's approval. His outlook buoyed when he thought about her.

"Where'd you go to high school?" Jensen asked Liska one evening as they worked on their 782 gear.

"St. Lad, Saint Ladislaw, all through grade and high school. You?"

"Grosse Pointe," Jensen's prominent Adam's apple bobbed. Liska knew the school, he said.

"We had Franciscan nuns. I remember one from grade school, Sister Cunegund — almost like a DI to us altar boys." Jensen nodded; he had been an altar boy, too.

"Cuny, we called her, said the rosary was more powerful than a gun. One time, a kid named Mitchell and his pal were walking down the hall when two nuns approached. 'Watch out,' Mitchell said, 'here come two uglies, armed and loaded for bear.' He hadn't noticed that Cunegund was behind him, and in an instant she shoved Mitchell into the bank of wall lockers and slapped him. She was a tough old nun."

Stretching truth, Garson chimed in that a couple of the Franciscan nuns at Holy Redeemer grade school he attended were holy terrors, too. He admitted to failing as an altar boy because of his inability to memorize the entire *Confiteor* prayer.

"I also got rapped across the knuckles a lot because I held my pencil too tight. Always had a permanent callus on my second finger." He held his right hand aloft to display the knob on his second finger – the social finger as it was called by DIs.

While at Saint Lad, Liska related that Sister Cunegund developed cancer, and the prognosis was bleak.

"Word was she wanted to see all her altar boys before she died." But Liska had developed so much antipathy toward her that he refused his mother's admonition to visit her in the convent hospice.

"When she died, I felt bad about not seeing her." His eyes were downcast at the memory.

Despite his Polish Catholic upbringing, Liska's father and most of the relatives were essentially free-thinkers, he said. His father always told him that the Liskas were not donkeys on a treadmill. One Liska was an avowed atheist, and his mother claimed to be somewhat psychic. Several family members were Masons, including an uncle, a war veteran. Liska enjoyed seeing his Shriner uncle in parades, wearing pantaloons and fez.

"It was funny because the nuns made us cross to the other side of the street when we passed the Masonic Temple in Hamtramck," he said.

"So, I really never believed all of the religion stuff the nuns taught. I thought that Jesus was a real person in history who preached good messages and set good examples. But my dad never for a minute believed he was God incarnate like the Church said." Garson felt an affinity.

Over these final weeks, Garson learned much about the city of Detroit from Liska, Jensen and others. He discovered that the Motor City, the fifth largest in the country with nearly two million people, was much larger than Garson's hometown. Moreover, while Milwaukee's tallest building was the handsome German Renaissance city hall whose bell tower reached 350 feet, downtown Detroit was studded with spectacular skyscrapers that included the soaring Penobscot and Fisher Buildings many stories taller.

"Detroit was once called the 'Paris of the West.' It's got the beautiful Fox Theater downtown," Liska said. The ornate, balconied and brocaded movie palace reminded Garson of the movie venues that lined Milwaukee's central commercial strip. Detroit's famed Hudson's Department Store sounded similar to Gimbel Brothers. Streetcar lines trundled thousands across both towns.

The predominantly Polish community of Hamtramck was two square miles virtually in the middle of Detroit, an almost self-contained area with shopping, movie theaters, banks and more.

"Girls liked to hang out at a sweet shop called 'Sodas' on Conant across from the DeLuxe Bakery," put in Jensen. "Remember the guys parked their rodded- up Flivers and Model Ts?" Liska did.

"They even started building a shopping center at Greenfield and

Eight-Mile before I left home," Jensen said. Other Michiganders observed that Canada was right across the river from central Detroit, a tunnel and the ornate Victory Bridge spanning the waterway. Many families drove there to buy pre-colored oleomargarine not available in America. They talked of the grand homes, including those of the Ford family, above Seven-Mile Road, mansions with broad yards and looping driveways similar to the impressive estates Garson occasionally saw ranked on the Milwaukee bluffs overlooking Lake Michigan.

"Jews live on the west side and colored are in what we call 'Black Bottom.'" A recruit whose name Garson could not recall sneered at the mention. He spoke with a drawl, incongruous for someone from the North. Garson later learned that many thousands who had migrated to Michigan, taking jobs in auto and defense industries, were from West Virginia, Kentucky and Tennessee, bringing with them certain antipathies, particularly toward Negroes. The Detroiter would add many harsh observations when the topic of the 1943 race riots arose.

Belle Isle picnicking and amusement park was situated in the river where crowds sought relief from summer heat; thousands climbed aboard the wooden roller coaster and other rides. Garson interrupted Liska, saying that Chicago's Riverview Park featured three coasters and the torturous Bobs and Shoot the Chutes along with the throat-tightening parachutes. He had during one summer spent a week with his dapper Uncle Hervé and voluptuous Aunt Baccia. They had unofficially adopted their nephew, Garson's cousin Bob. In many ways, Bob, a half dozen or more years older, whose father had abandoned the family years before, emulated his uncle, dressing nattily; lately Garson envied his cousin's stylish Wellington Boots and leather jacket but especially the 1949 lemon yellow Mercury convertible with its rakish, fender-mounted silver air horns. Bob had officially changed his surname to match their uncle's.

As a 13 or 14 year old, Garson enjoyed the Riverview excursions, particularly because Milwaukee's amusement park, State Fair, had no daunting rides that compared. Bob also took him to Brookfield

Zoo and stock car races at Soldiers Field. At a swanky bar afterwards, Bob had introduced Garson to his girlfriend, a willowy brunette who looked like Yvonne DeCarlo – a cloud of dark hair, heavily-lidded eyes, expressive brows and full lips glowing with ruby lipstick.

"Ever hear of the Detroit race riots?" Jensen said he was about eight at the time. His parents were relieved to be out of the city when they occurred. Decades later, in preparing for his narrative, Garson researched the war time cataclysm. It erupted because Negro workers and their families who migrated from the South to fill jobs in the auto industry came in conflict with southern whites.

Housing and other urban needs were strained with the influx of newcomers. Negroes were excluded from virtually all public housing, and many lived in dreadful conditions, paying two or three times more rent than white families. Pent-up anger led to summer street fights involving Negro and Polish youths that spilled into Hamtramck and elsewhere. Liska agreed, for his memory of the riots was clear as well. Detroit seemed on edge for a long time, and it took only a spark to ignite a full-blown confrontation. At one point, thousands of whites stopped work at the Packard plant that manufactured bombers and military boats.

"My dad and uncle worked at Packard back then," put in the recruit whose family had moved from West Virginia to work in Detroit. "They said some niggers, ah, I mean colored who didn't deserve it were promoted over whites. My aunt said she didn't like that colored women were using their washrooms. No wonder the Kluxers got involved."

"It all started at Belle Isle in early June," Jensen recalled, "with some fights between white and colored hoodlums." Rumors about a woman being molested and murdered fanned the tinder, and roving gangs looted and battled along Woodward Avenue, the main thoroughfare that angled from downtown Detroit; cars were overturned and torched. Guerilla warfare overwhelmed the police force and state troopers. It was reported that at one point, a crowd of 100,000 gathered to witness the spectacle. In three days of rioting, 34 people, most Negroes, had been killed. Thousands were arrested. Finally, Federal troops in armored cars and jeeps with automatic weapons patrolled Woodward, cooling the mob's ardor.

Garson could not recall the name of the Detroiter who used the racial slur and placed blame for the riots solely on Negroes. Garson learned that the recruit had, like his teen pal Mellish, been forced to enlist because of a scrape with the law. The armed forces, of course, had been integrated after the world war. He supposed the West Virginian may not have voluntarily served with Negroes but did not have a choice. But, by what Garson could determine from limited observation, the number of Negroes in the Corps was few at that point. Platoon 023 had none while there were no more than a half dozen in the entire battalion.

"Look, we had riots, too, during the war," put in Ridley. Garson felt he tried to defuse the growing tension caused by talk of the Detroit events. Ridley was about ten when antipathies had sparked between servicemen who clashed with Mexican gangs.

"Yeah, I saw that in *Life* magazine. Mexican kids wore Zoot suits — baggy pegged pants, ah, trousers, called ankle chokers, pocket chains down past their knees, with long coats and pork pie hats" offered Liska. "*Pachucos*, right?" Ridley nodded.

Resentment among Mexicans, analogous to what occurred in Detroit, dated back a decade, caused by discrimination in wages, inadequate housing and overt race baiting by newspapers and authorities. Mexican youth developed the unique dress style and street culture. War rationing of wool and government regulations for trimmer cut suits caused them to flaunt their distinctive, blousy style. Marines, sailors and soldiers on liberty found the display unpatriotic and un-American, and looked to settle the issue. Scuffles between the sides led to fights in East Los Angeles. Claiming they had been jumped by the Spick gangs, sailors organized a convoy of taxis carrying hundreds, and they attacked random kids and burned their clothing.

"Yeah, I remember reading about a phalanx of sailors, Marines and others marching abreast down the streets," Ridley continued, "assaulting Mexicans in bars, movie houses – everywhere. The police didn't lift a finger to stop anything." Newspapers lauded the military for clearing the streets of hoodlums. But in a few days, military authorities confined Marines and sailors to their bases, declaring the city off-limits for liberty.

Late one January night, Garson considered such incidents as he marched along the company street that intersected with the Grinder on a midnight to two fire watch. There was no air traffic at Lindbergh Field at that late hour and the landing strips were dark. Streetlights in the San Diego residential neighborhood that rose above MCRD to the east and west sparkled like diamonds in the night sky. The mid-40s temperature was comfortable.

"Why the fuck do we carry M-1s on fire watch?" was how Hal had once put it. "Can't shoot at anybody, man, 'cause we got no ammo." Garson agreed.

Moving the M-1 rifle from one shoulder to another at each end of the 40-yard street, Garson again mused about scaling the chain link fence, sprinting across the runway and stowing away on the first flight out. But, he thought, only a few more weeks of Boot Camp remained; he was a short timer.

He halted, shifted the rifle again and about-faced away from the Grinder. A shock snapped from his neck down his spine. Someone was approaching. The tall street lamp reflected two shoulder bars, a captain, likely the battalion commander. Garson was terrified. It was a cardinal rule every recruit could recite: Challenge any one who neared his post at night. He knew the script, and in those few seconds mentally recited it:

"Halt, who is there?" When the intruder identified himself the dialogue was to proceed.

"Advance to be recognized." When the intruder identified himself, the sentry continued. "Advance, Captain Mundt." But the words were frozen in Garson's throat. He shifted the M-1 to port arms as prescribed, the weapon angling across his chest.

Over six foot, the officer towered over him. He said nothing. Suddenly, Garson's rifle was ripped from his hands. There he stood, disarmed.

"Aren't you supposed to challenge everyone who approaches, recruit?"

"Yes, sir! Sir, yes, sir" Garson kept his focus forward, eyes fixed on the gold bars.

"Why didn't you do that?"

"Sir, no excuse, sir!" His voice quavered.

"And are you to relinquish your weapon in such a manner?"

"Sir, no, sir." Fear gripped his body, and he felt a tremor in his legs. If Sergeant Maddox learned of this, he would suffer serious consequences — bodily harm, perhaps even brig time. But Captain Mundt, noticing how shaken Garson was, gave him a reprieve.

"What's your Eleventh General Order?"

For what seemed like minutes, his vocal chords would not articulate the words. But finally, they spewed forth.

"Sir, my Eleventh General Order is: 'To be especially watchful at night and, during the time for challenging, to challenge all persons on or near my post, and to allow no one to pass without proper authority'."

"Why didn't you follow that order, son?" the officer demanded. His tone, while authoritative, seemed unthreatening, almost avuncular. He called Garson son, not pussy, not shit-bird or any of the other degrading names drawn from a drill instructor's vocabulary.

"Sir, no excuse, sir!" Garson felt trembling spread upward from his legs. After a few moments, the captain popped the rifle back into Garson's hands.

"Now, see that this doesn't happen again," he demanded, turning on his heel and striding off. Nothing ever came of the encounter, and Garson was forever grateful to the officer.

While there were others in 023 who received particular correction for shortcomings, the ungainly Prick among them, Pop, in looking back, worried that his past confrontations with Sergeant Maddox might have serious repercussions. The first incident involved the little Christ child statuette, then the improper clothing stamp. Another time it was the woeful boxing match with Fletcher. While Garson was 17, his face was that of someone younger, a boy almost: In some light, he appeared no more than 13 or 14. Perhaps it was his childlike appearance that attracted attention. No matter the reason, every incident increased Garson's disquiet.

Sergeant Maddox exhibited what Garson considered the most severe action against him when he was pulled from formation, and directed to the quonset designated as the battalion headquarters. He had been assigned as the runner, a messenger who relayed written and verbal orders to battalion platoons.

Garson stood at parade rest for hours, legs splayed, arms locked at the small of his back, moving as undiscernibly as possible to relieve muscle tension. All morning, he delivered only one message. The duty normally lasted for two hours, but for some reason relief did not arrive. Sometime, well after noon chow, Garson's stomach protested the lack of sustenance. Coincidentally, Sergeant Maddox passed, and Garson snapped to attention.

"Sir, the private requests permission to speak to the drill instructor, sir."

When he nodded, Garson informed him that he had not been relieved for chow; the senior DI said nothing but strode to a vacant billet across the walkway. Turning, he crooked his index finger at the subordinate. Garson entered, and before his eyes adjusted to the gloomy interior, the sergeant grabbed him by the lapels, kicking shut the door. He rammed Garson into the hut walls. Because of the quonset's concave sides, his head hit first, then his shoulders, back and finally his tailbone. He was buffeted back and forth for several minutes, Maddox's face grimaced in rage.

"A Marine remains at his post until relieved. You know that, you fuckin' clown?" Garson tried to answer, but the throttling caused him to bite his tongue.

"If I order it, you'll remain on your post for eight or 12 hours, all day even. No chow. No piss call. No nothing." He continued to batter Garson into the wall.

"If I tell you to stay all night, you'd better not fall asleep. Do you understand me?" After several more minutes, Maddox seemed to collect himself. He released Garson.

"Now get the fuck back to your post!" He hurled Garson through the doorway. Catching his balance, Garson scampered across the company street. His throat was dry and constricted; he gasped for breath; the back of his head and backbone smarted; his dungaree shirt was in disarray. He righted his cap and assumed parade rest again. He was not relieved for another two hours, having spent the better part of the day on duty.

There was another incident, not as severe; but Garson worried that the accumulation of such encounters, small and large, may result in his not graduating.

"March into chow at attention." The command meant that until the platoon entered the mess hall, each man was to remain at attention, taking only one step forward at a time, bringing the second foot alongside. Garson could not recall how the platoon had recently displeased the sergeant. In most instances, the DI subsequently departed for drill instructors' entrance.

Garson always had trouble with vexing buildup of ear wax; it was a problem endemic to his mother as well who often probed for relief with the closed end of a bobby pin. Assuming Maddox had departed, Garson poked a little finger into his right ear to relieve the itch.

Suddenly, he was jolted and knocked from the rank. The sergeant had apparently tarried to make certain his order was obeyed to the letter. Grabbing a fist full of dungaree shirt, he shook Garson violently.

"Thought I said, 'March into chow at attention,' clown." Fury laced his words, and sputum sprayed into Garson's face. Like a rag doll, he rocked Garson back and forth as he had several times in the past; the dungaree shirt pulled free from Garson's waist. After several minutes, Sergeant Maddox released his grip with a final shove. Garson scrambled back into the rank, fearful even to straighten his clothing.

I just don't understand it, but my Pop never expressed animus, leastways in print, toward Maddox for any of these altercations. He seemed to be saying that because he was a spoiled only child, an unwashed civilian, he needed physical correction before he could become a Marine, a man. He needed discipline, something that he had lacked in his formative years. At this early point in his career, Garson regarded Maddox as just the authority figure he needed.

"For chris' sake, Maddox even runs his white gloves *under* the fuckin' toilet bowl rim during inspections," cavilled Hal. "Fuck's sake!" The sergeant sought dust on every horizontal surface, door and window ledge, on steel bed springs of racks; he possessed an uncanny ability to ferret out dirt and disarray, his white gloves like dousing rods to water. Garson recalled his mother's obsession with cleanliness, a compulsion that even involved scraping along baseboard edges with a paring knife wrapped in a rag. At least twice in those final weeks, Maddox meted out dreadful retribution for the platoon's shortcomings.

"Sand field day!" The words brought recruits to inexpressible anger. Maddox's order meant that buckets of water and sand were dumped onto the concrete deck of the quonset. Bare-footed, recruits scrubbed with brooms to erase any untoward mark or blemish, real or supposed. Finally, after an hour or more, sand was swept up and shoveled out after which the deck was swabbed. If one stray grain of sand crunched beneath Maddox's shoes, he ordered the onerous cleaning process to be repeated. A few Boots glared almost mutinously.

Likewise, should PFC Duff find displeasure in insufficiently tight bedding or other shortcoming, his retribution took a different form, a nonsense exercise that Garson felt came right out of grade school experiences after the war, the "Duck and Cover" drills at Holy Redeemer. Duff stood, arms akimbo, at one end of the quonset.

"Flood!" he shouted, at which recruits quickly climbed atop upper bunks.

"Earthquake!" They vaulted from the racks and skittered beneath them.

"Fire!" Recruits jumped down, and scampered toward the doorway, assembling on the company street.

"You fuckin' cruds aren't tired are you? We're just getting started. Earthquake!" And on it continued for half an hour or more. Once,

Garson stumbled exiting the hut and sprawled into the bed of ice plants. Several others tripped over him while many leaped prostrate bodies. Garson righted himself and gathered with his fellows in darkness outside. Fire! Flood! Earthquake!

"Now let this be a lesson to you fuckin' skinheads. This hut better be A. J. squared away at all times." Garson tossed and twisted sleeplessly much of the night.

After what Maddox regarded as another failed inspection – several recruits appeared unkempt – the senior DI ordered the platoon to pack all of its clothing into seabags and fall out on the Grinder.

"Clowns, since you can't get things right, we'll have a little seabag drill," the sergeant explained. Filled seabags weighed 40 pounds or more. On the Grinder, the canvas sacks stood beside each recruit, like outsized, green rifles.

"Right shoulder. Seabags," was the sergeant's order. Dare not anticipate the command of execution. The recruits hefted the bulky bags to their sides, and flung them onto their shoulders.

"Port. Seabags!" They leveraged the heavy bags, holding a lower edge with the right hand while the left supported it at a 45 degree angle. After several minutes of such maneuvers, they were marched forward and commands shouted while astride: Right shoulder. Left shoulder. Port. Seabags. Only a few minutes passed before Garson began to flag, his forearms and shoulders virtually wailing in protest. Labored breathing was audible. Several seabags plopped onto the concrete and when they halted to retrieve them, the formation was in disarray. Maddox seemed not to notice, as he simply marched them on, occasionally changing direction by flank or column movement. Garson saw the look of amusement on the faces of other platoons that marched past.

Prick the bulky farm kid, continued to struggle in recruit training. Several in the platoon ridiculed him for the decided Germanic inflection to his words, worse even than Garson's. He also uttered quaint country words like "dasn't" and "daren't," and expressions such as "gone to flinders." He had come to accept his sobriquet, "Prick," among Boot Camp buddies, yet still bristled when DI's bludgeoned him with it.

"You guys don't mean nothin' by it," he said. To ease his buddy's reaction, Garson had earlier told him about a kid he once knew named Neil Fuchs, normally called "Foochs."

"You can imagine what some of us did with that name when we got into a scrap. How'd you like to be called Neil Fucks?" Prick's scowl eased. But there was more that troubled the plodding farm boy. In a private conversation with Garson, Prick revealed what was called a sense of foreboding and fatality that some claimed was a trait of Germanic people.

"Just when you think things are goin' good, watch out, 'cause they'll turn bad on you," he said softly, pushing his owlish glasses back up his nose. "That's what Pa always says." Despite the many weeks that had passed in Boot Camp, Prick seemed to be barely holding on. Introverted and undemonstrative, whatever confidence he brought to his enlistment was badly undermined. He did not possess the inner fortitude of Hupner, the Texan who was another focus of steady harassment.

"Prick, if you don't fuckin' get this shit, we're holding you back," PFC Duff threatened. To be held back, to be made to repeat weeks of Boot Camp, was one of the most dreaded consequences a recruit might face. It was not merely an indication of failure, but adding weeks onto three-month recruit training was nearly as bad as receiving a BCD. Prick, among other Marine Corps deadly sins, had not qualified at Camp Matthews. And like Pop, he had failed to pass the swimming test.

"What the fuck's a matter with you, Prick," the drill instructor shouted. It was an occurrence repeated at almost every formation, or so it seemed to Garson in retrospect.

"Don't know, sir," Prick muttered.

"Can't hear you, Prick."

"Sir, don't know, sir!"

Even when he raised his voice to repeat his response, it was of insufficient volume to satisfy the drill instructor. At times, his chin trembled visibly when confronted or corrected. Garson said he pitied the rural fellow, and at times tried to assist him in folding his skivvies and socks correctly, spit shining shoes and pulling his blankets tight. The drill instructors had numerous times torn his rack asunder for lack of drumhead tautness, strewing about sheets and blankets.

Prick's parents, like Garson's, were immigrants who had arrived in Wisconsin around the century's turn.

"My pa told me he feared for his future in Germany after the First World War. There was lots of inflation and worthless money, then Hitler's Brown Shirts came." Garson did not believe Prick was a Jew. Somehow, the father managed to immigrate, worked as a hired farm hand in Wisconsin for a time before bringing over his wife and children, like Garson's grandfather. It was a story familiar to Garson. Prick, the youngest, was born when the family bought 80 acres in Washington County. They raised dairy cows and a few crops. When Prick came of age as the youngest, it was apparent he would need to find work elsewhere; he enlisted in the Marine Corps after completing high school.

Garson said he often speculated what would become of Prick and Hupner when – perhaps it should have been "if" — they graduated from Boot Camp. Garson feared for his own future in the Corps. Certainly, Hupner's illiteracy would be discovered over time, and that would mean discharge, he was certain. What kind of Marines would these buddies make? Like Garson, Prick and Hupner were classified as basic infantrymen – the 0300 MOS in military parlance. They were slated to be virtual cannon fodder, as the saying went. Yet, other recruits of common background had tested well, and garnered specialized occupation numbers like Preston and Rusty.

Instruction and exams during the latter weeks of MCRD training focused more intensely on combat readiness. No matter the occupation specialty or future duty station, every Marine must learn to be a cog in the fighting machine. There were many practical topics covered in classrooms and field demonstrations. Always with the aid of the *Guidebook*, the ubiquitous Marine Corps "bible," they practiced hand and arm signals, studied military mapping, scouting and patrolling, infantry and tank tactics, and more. Hal, as usual, found a bit of humor after the platoon had been instructed on radio protocol and how to use the phonetic alphabet.

"Peter. Peter," he mimed, holding an imaginary microphone to his mouth. "This is foreskin. I been cut off."

The Corps, instructors proclaimed, perfected the World War II tactic of amphibious assault, the coordinated infantry, naval and air attacks familiar to everyone who had seen movie newsreels and popular war films, particularly "The Sands of Iwo Jima." At MCRD, they viewed documentaries to illustrate and reinforce lectures on combat tactics.

"Saw this at the Ritz when I was a kid," Garson whispered when the screen splashed the vivid color images of "With the Marines at Tarawa," a 20-minute documentary about the horrific island battle that claimed ten thousand Marine lives. Because it was so graphic, the War Department had been reluctant to release it to the public, the MCRD instructor boasted, but President Roosevelt permitted its theatrical showing. It won the 1944 documentary Academy Award. Garson and others were less impressed with the black and white half-hour documentary about Korea. Somehow, in Garson's mind, the Peninsula's "police action" as it came to be known, never measured up to the romance and glory of world war combat in either fact or fiction.

"We don't call 'em fox holes," corrected one instructor, answering a question about the defensive pits that men dug at the MLR as it was called, the main line of resistance. "Foxes hide. Marines fight! They're called fighting holes." In lectures and graphics, they learned how the Corps's fighting force was organized, from four-man fire team to squad and platoon, from platoon to battalion, regiment to brigade and division. But in all of this each individual Marine was vital, responsible to maintain himself in healthy trim.

"Your feet are more important than anything," the Navy corpsman intoned during instructions about first aide and health care. "The slightest sore or blister means you can't march. Then you'll fall out of the formation. Your unit loses a rifle. Keep your feet dry and change socks regularly." Under early winter sun, Garson and

Hupner worked together, practicing the application of tourniquets using bayonets, improvising a sling from a dungaree jacket, fabricating a stretcher from a blanket and stout tree limbs. They watched demonstrations about rendering artificial respiration, how to treat minor wounds and burns, and injecting morphine.

Garson did not recall any discussions among recruits about such topics when they were "off duty." Instead, the focus was entirely on girls, music and movies. Such talk was initiated after chow, when the platoon assembled behind the mess hall to await the DI and the march back to the quonsets. Smokers hurried through meals, anxious to get outside and light up. Since the fraudulent enlistee, McCracken, had been separated from the platoon, no one had tried to smoke clandestinely; consequently, cigarettes had not been confiscated since returning from Camp Matthews. It was also rare these days, for DIs not to kindle the smoking lamp, or to prescribe only one cigarette for the entire unit.

As many readers by now have observed, my Pop constantly tinkered with his manuscript, sometimes without regard to transition. Put it this way: Sometimes you can see the manipulative man behind the screen, the mechanism behind the clock of my Pop's narrative. If you learn how a director shoots and edits his film, uses sets and music to suggest mood and motive, how an actor manipulates his role – the mnemonics of movies — you may lose the magic. It was often obvious to me that my Pop manipulated elements to achieve his end.

When Ridley and Heissen joined discussions about movies, the level of erudition rose dramatically. Both were perceptive and perspicacious about the popular entertainment medium that had been imprinted upon most urban youths of that day. Garson was attentive to his buddies' insights since heretofore he knew only what screen images pleased and moved him, not why.

"You know, the first science fiction film was made over 50 years ago," Ridley said, "by a Frenchman, I think. 'A Trip to the Moon.' The rocket hits the man in the moon right in the eye."

Garson and childhood pal, Leland, had seen the silent science fiction film called "Metropolis" at a little theater on the west side.

The cramped Violet was one of several independent exhibitors in town who retained a collection of worn, old movies that were shown to young, uncritical Saturday matinee audiences. Garson agreed with his pal that the silent movie with its organ music score was a "gyp," although both boys were fascinated with the metallic female automaton. Neither boy liked "Things to Come" because the airships and cityscapes were obviously either toys or hand-drawn. They found risible rocket ships that buzzed across the screen trailing lazy cigarette smoke exhausts. Buster Crabb was just OK in the "Flash Gordon." But Azura, the witch queen of Mars, was someone to oogle.

Ridley agreed that some of recent science fiction releases were inexcusable with awful acting, horrid special effects and laughable costuming like the shimmering one-piece coveralls worn by bug-eyed aliens in "Invaders from Mars." Garson nodded with other recruits who enjoyed the giant ants in "Them!" and the metal creature Gort in "The Day the Earth Stood Still."

Garson would not share the memory of a harrowing night when he sat alone through "The Thing." The movie's eerie electronic Theremin score unnerved him as much as the screen action. The second showing of the feature ended at nearly eleven o'clock. He walked the shadowed vacant streets alone. Each time he neared the intersection of a dark alley, he moved to the middle of the street, thinking if the lurching other-worldly creature stepped out, he would have a running head start. Garson was beginning to understand what moods music and editing could elicit.

Ridley tended to use the words "films" or "motion pictures, which Garson found pretentious," instead of "movies" and "pictures." But the Californian knew much about the construction of the medium, what he called *mise en cine*; he described how directors achieved desired effects with camera angles, dolly and tracking shots, and the overhead crane perspective that foretold doom.

"You see 'The Third Man'?" Garson nodded. "Look, all those tilted shots that heightened the tension in Vienna when Holly Martin's searching for his pal, Harry Lime. The facial close-ups, the zither music." Garson presumed that Ridley had learned it all in college courses. Garson did not mention that he prided himself on understanding most of the German dialogue between the Viennese characters.

"Then there was an entire film using subjective camera. Not a very good one, I thought, but you get the idea." It was a post war Raymond Chandler film noir, "The Lady in the Lake" that Garson recalled seeing as a kid at the new Tower Theater.

In other discussions, Heissen revealed his avowed preference for American popular composers such as the Gershwins, Irving Berlin, Rogers and Hart, Cole Porter, Jerome Kern and others, but did not share Ridley and Garson's appreciation for most movie musicals. Garson's childhood movie memories remained fresh, of him drowsy against his mother's arm during sugary romantic silliness; he would perk up during dance numbers, men in elegant formal wear, women in sparkling, sequined gowns, swirling about art deco sets.

Among more recent films, he enjoyed dramatic Kelly in "An American in Paris" and "Singin' in the Rain." Of course, he was totally captivated by a movie only he among Boot Camp buddies had seen. How could he admit that the star-crossed love story in "The Red Shoes" had planted a seed of fascination for ballet, classical and modern? He was still entranced with the British ballerina Moira Shearer who also starred in one of the three screen tales comprising "The Story of Three Loves."

When Garson later mulled over such Boot Camp discourses about movies, he realized he had not since arriving at MCRD had any of those dreams of tap dancing that he enjoyed back home. He never excelled as a subject of such nighttime visions, never approaching the elegance of Astaire or the athleticism of Gene Kelly; he only displayed a level of competence. Decades later, when he sought its meaning, he learned that the faster the dreamer danced, the more he needed to keep up with the pace of life. The Corps had even intruded on his dreams.

"Know what I hate about musicals?" Hal intruded. "Just when sweethearts are about to kiss and grope, they fuckin' break out in song instead getting it on. Just ain't natural." Garson agreed that the *smaltz* and syrup often ran thick. More, he had become impatient with the diminished role of dancing in recent movie musicals; even though he sat through several of them, he was peevish with Esther Williams and her water-born extravaganzas.

"Know what I miss as much as movies?"

'Feelin' your girl's little titties?" Hal put in.

"Naw, man! Music." Ridley's forehead knotted and pale eyebrows curved down. "Look, we haven't heard a note of anything except 'Marine Corps Hymn' in months." That observation generated a discussion among several recruits about music, of which they had been deprived for nearly a quarter of a year.

The popular music of Garson's generation had evolved but little from the war years – big bands, mellow soloists and harmonizing vocal groups. Italian crooners such as Tony Bennett, Al Martino and others had joined Sinatra on the radio. Early in the new decade, Garson and most of the Villard Avenue crowd had been swept up by the romantic strains of Joni James, particularly her plaintive, popular ballads "Why Don't You Believe Me?" and "Have You Heard?"

Garson was reminded by Ridley and Heissen's mention of the Benny Goodman Carnegie Hall jazz concert, just recently released on records. He remembered one of the cutting edge radio stations airing the lengthy "Sing! Sing! Sing!" with provocative solos by vibe player Lionel Hampton, pianist Teddy Wilson, the rattling drums of Gene Krupa and Goodman himself. Other concert numbers were popular, among them "Body and Soul," "Avalon," and "Moonglow."

Ridley also mentioned Stan "the Man" Kenton, a younger arranger practicing what was called progressive jazz. "Artistry in Rhythm" and "Sketches in Standards," featuring studio orchestras with brilliant brass ensembles, had been released in recent years; Garson had been attracted to such music, jotting down titles he heard on the radio. He had also been attracted to small groups, combos like George Shearing's mellow quintet whose "September in the Rain" gained popularity.

While Garson did not encounter many readers in the platoon, books were important in the lives of a few. He recalled engaging

Ridley in discussions about science fiction, mentioning some of his favorite authors – Bradbury, Heinlein, Norton. In his early teens, he had even started to create a novel modeled after *Star Ship Troopers*, but his, the tale of a female stowaway on a rocket to Mars that included a bit of titillation.

"Thought you said you wanted to be a journalist," Ridley interjected. Garson replied that he had heard that some newsmen wrote books.

Many of such MCRD exchanges occurred on Sundays, respites from the less demanding rigors in the final weeks. Recruits straddled foot lockers, cleaning rifles, tending to equipment and uniforms, or simply idling. There seemed to be fewer drill sessions on the Grinder along with reduced emphasis on physical fitness and exercise; formal classroom instructions diminished. PFC Duff, who usually had the weekend duty, seemed less inclined to demand extracurricular activity. While discipline still remained, it was less severe than the first two months. Perhaps they were becoming veterans, Garson mused.

"Remember my old man's party records?" Preston asked Garson and Rusty. Conversations often veered dramatically from one topic to another especially for those who were impatient listeners. While the three North Milwaukee musketeers were not billeted in the same hut, the growing leniency by DIs permitted them to more freely circulate among the quonsets and spend time together.

Comedians Red Foxx and Moms Mabley had released multi-disk sets, live recordings before boisterous audiences. The records were known to be "blue" – risqué riffs filled with double entendre and suggestive situations. Preston's dad had secreted a set of the heavy 78 records in a hall closet and Preston occasionally played selections for his pals.

"Got a girlfriend?" baby-faced Krupa asked one day when the platoon gathered after chow.

"Well, sort of," answered Garson.

"What do you mean, man?" Garson explained that he was "working on" a girl from his high school. He met her in sophomore homeroom and they got to know one another. He and Franny had broken up for reasons he did not recall, and he became enamored with Betsy. Her bright and generous smile had been the first attraction, what he called "dark, smoldering eyes," and black wiry hair. She was several inches shorter than Garson, but her nascent woman's figure filled out the torso-fitted wool skirts and sweaters. They had never actually dated because she lived a long way from Garson's neighborhood, and he had no car. So, the relationship was little more than flirtation, but to his mind it was more. Yet, he waited impatiently for communication from her.

Despite the fact they had not been fired in weeks, M-1 rifles were inspected regularly. Recruits were expected to maintain their spotless and dust-free condition, not only the bore, but every recess. Stocks were to be burnished by hand-rubbing with linseed oil almost until palms fairly blistered. Any hint of blemish or dust was akin to mortal sin. Rust was cause for brig time, it was rumored. Garson scrupulously tended to his M-1. He pushed many patches through the bore until it fairly shone, and was particularly attentive to dust out the receiver with the shaving brush. He was confident.

The routine for inspections of this kind called for the platoon to open ranks on the Grinder, permitting sufficient room between squads for the DI or officer to walk through. When an inspector passed, Garson now knew, he snapped his rifle from the order to port arms, thumbed open the bolt, then cast a quick glance to insure the chamber was open. He waited rigidly.

"One fuckin' Boot couldn't get the bolt to stay open. It kept slamming shut when the DI stopped. So he made the shitbird open it with his mouth." It was Hal, of course, who offered that anecdote. The bolt and operating spring were heavy and resistant.

"Another clown was told to slam the fuckin' bolt on his nose." Garson winced at the thought. If a recruit's hand failed to let go of the weapon when it was snapped from his grasp, there were repercussions.

"Let fuckin' go of your piece!" The slightest clutch or hitch caused a harangue. Only once in Garson's experience had a Boot dropped his rifle. As might be suspected, it was poor Prick.

In formation that day, Garson held the M-1 across his body as required when Maddox approached, eyes narrowed. In a millisecond, he snatched the weapon from Garson's hands. Like a drum major, the sergeant twisted the rifle this way and that, scrutinizing from butt to muzzle to trigger guard and more before holding the weapon aloft to sight one-eyed through the bore. It was all done with the finesse and panache of a band drum major.

When Maddox looked into the open receiver seconds later, Garson's confidence ebbed, and a knot gripped his throat. The DI paused, finding something amiss. With two fingers, the sergeant delicately plucked a lone brush bristle that had somehow lodged inside and escaped Garson's inspection. Like a man studying a bug in biology lab, Maddox held the bristle aloft between thumb and finger, scrutinizing the foreign object. Then he focused on Garson's face, forcing him to look at the bristle. Garson maintained his neutral stare until unexpectedly, the DI poked the bristle into Garson's right eye and threw the rifle into his chest with a thud.

That night, the entire platoon was ordered to field strip M-1s – disassemble rifles into component parts, about two dozen in all, and with the stock, bayonet and scabbard, strew them onto their fart sacks. Garson was certain it was not he alone who had caused the punishment; others might have been accused of distraction and slack discipline in the changing Boot Camp environment.

"Now, you pussies, climb into those racks," Sergeant Maddox commanded. "You're gonna sleep with those rifle parts. Good night," he sing-songed childlike, extinguishing the lights and slamming the door. Garson at first felt like an East Indian fakir lying on a bed of nails; but, hearing the defiant rustle of metal on sheets in other racks, he pushed his rifle components toward the edge of his bunk. Once or twice during the night, Garson rolled onto a bolt or trigger guard. Before reveille and the sergeant's inspection, the parts were strewn back.

Staff Sergeant Maddox became the yardstick by which Garson measured all other veteran Marines he encountered during his four years in the Corps. Garson had for many weeks observed this man; he knew the senior DI's physiognomy. There were virtually no wrinkles on his sun-burnished face, and only a small scar marked the right corner of his mouth. His tall and taut frame showed no trace of excess. He was eternally immaculate, well-turned out in dress greens and tropical shirt; brasses always glowed and shoes ever gleamed. Correctly, Garson concluded that his superior's service ribbons designated he had seen combat in Korea.

"How're ya gonna live on these peanuts?" Hal's quibble pulled Garson from his private musing. "Made more money selling fishing worms back home, for fuck's sake." Garson agreed, adding his old newspaper route paid him more. Garson counted the pitiful handful of bills and coins repeatedly.

Marine Corps pay days arrived the first and fifteenth of each month. Garson drew no more than few dollars each time, the remainder kept "on the books" to be paid out at the end of Boot Camp. When cash was distributed, a lieutenant sat in the Duty Hut, flanked by an imperious guard carrying a holstered .45 caliber pistol. Stacks of crisp currency, newly printed some said, were piled before him. Each recruit stood at attention before the officer, sounded off his serial number and name. The payroll officer peeled bills loose from the stacks like a Las Vegas dealer.

Usually within a brief time after paydays, the platoon was marched to the Depot exchange to purchase cigarettes, toiletries, stationery, stamps and other personal items. Fortunate the recruit who received coinage in change, for he could literally barter nickels for dollars with a buddy bent on clandestinely acquiring MCRD's forbidden fruit – pogey bait – candy.

At intervals amid the ranks of quonset huts stood vending machines available only to drill instructors and permanent MCRD staff. The dispensers seemed to have as much attraction for some recruits as the magnetic North to compasses, as El Dorado to Ponce De Leon, virtual *fata morganas* of sweets. Many dreamed of the confections, and several schemed to get them.

"Give you a buck for a nickel." As days following pay days increased, the price of a nickel escalated, at one time, Garson clearly remembered, costing five dollars to those who could not resist their craving. Moreover, miscreants needed to be stealthy and fleet of foot, and hope for a sleepy late night fire watch or one who abetted him for a price or morsel. Garson only once received the corner of a Baby Ruth that Rusty shared. He recalled the taste for days.

Then there was the matter of usury demanded by recruit sharpers. A three-dollar loan needed to be repaid on the next payday with an astounding interest rate – five dollars total. A seven-dollar advance cost ten bucks. Like most, Garson steered clear of such transactions.

Immediately after money was distributed in these latter days, some kind of collection or other was invariably announced by the DIs — donations for a Marine veterans' fund, the new Iwo Jima Marine Corps memorial to be erected at Arlington Cemetery or the like. A subscription to "Leatherneck Magazine" was almost mandatory. The fancy silk pillow cover and engraved plaque to commemorate enlistment that he felt compelled to purchase were sent home. Garson hoped these mementoes would assuage his parents' lack of enthusiasm for his decision to join.

"I'll bet DIs get kickbacks for all of this fuckin' shit," Hal groused. "They're always pushing us to buy."

"Get one fuckin' Camel to the Duty Hut!" The order was invariably heard in the days that followed trips to the base exchange.

"Fuck, don't those DIs ever buy their own fuckin' smokes?"

Camels, of course, were the preferred Marine Corps brand. Woe to everyone, smokers and non-smokers alike, if a cigarette was not trotted up to the DI on the double quick. The platoon still might be ordered out for duck walking drill. Worse, DIs might confiscate every cigarette, or fail to light the smoking lamp for days. Hupner, Prick, Ridley and Right Guide Barker were among the few non-smokers remaining in the platoon. If they had not been habituated before, many recruits, Garson included, had taken up the habit since arriving at MCRD.

"What the fuck, you some kinda sick bay commando?" PFC Duff's chin jutted as he questioned Garson who fell out for sick call that morning. DIs projected a view that any Boot who admitted illness or ailment was not truly a hard-case Marine. Minor maladies such as aches, strains, headaches were to be tolerated; simple illnesses such as fever or loose bowels were to be borne. Those, like Ridley, who sustained actual bone breaks or fractures were permitted treatment, of course. But Duff and other DIs were the gate keepers, weeding out those they considered sand baggers, malingerers. Like being called a crud, becoming known as a sick bay commando was a serious insult.

"And what the fuck's a matter with you," Duff demanded of Garson on the company street that morning. It was the only time he had answered sick call, and that one incident cured him for the remainder of Boot Camp.

"Migraine headache, sir."

"Mi...! How the fuck you know it's a migraine? You a fuckin' corpsman?"

"Sir, no, sir!"

"Then get the fuck back in that billet, idiot. I don't want to ever see you out here again."

Looking back on those MCRD days, Garson admitted his presumptuousness that he had little potential for becoming a Marine. Certainly, he would in years after gain promotion, earn a Good Conduct medal and be honorably discharged. But there was always uncertainty whether he would have stood the test of combat, to become a true heir to the Marines of Belleau Wood, Tarawa and Iwo Jima and the Chosin Reservoir.

"He was fascinated rather than repelled, thrilled by the patriotism and heroism of the American Allied troops, and oppressed by a sense of guilt and deprivation because he was not sharing their vicissitudes." That was what a Franklin Roosevelt biographer wrote. "[L]ike a moth to a flame...he felt drawn to the thrilling allure of soldiering and battle."

"Ever read *Battle Cry* by Uris?" asked Ridley one day. From comments and observations, he had discerned that Garson was a modest reader of books. Garson was familiar with the title but had not perused the lengthy novel.

"Look, I read it to get an idea of what was ahead when I joined," Ridley said. He described that the book focused on a Marine raider battalion called Huxley's Whores. The characters come from a variety of backgrounds, just like units in so many war era movies — an all-American urban kid, Indian from the western reservation, poor Mexican from L.A. and others. Told by a hard-bitten veteran sergeant named Mac, the "whores" fight with the 6th Marines at Guadalcanal, Tarawa and Saipan.

Ridley added that an older cousin served with the Corps. Like Liska's uncle, the arms of Ridley's relative were carpeted with tattoos. As a child, Ridley studied them and determined to get one for himself. Blue and red inks revealed skulls, he said, and a black panther clawed bloodily at his cousin's bicep. A vertical scroll proclaimed "Death Before Dishonor." Best, a saucy, nude blonde pinup with bulbous breasts and pert nipples clung to one forearm while her unadorned brunette companion teased from the opposite arm.

"Speaking of tattoos," interrupted Hal, ever ready to amplify a yarn. "Saw a guy once who had a broken line tattooed around his neck with the words 'Cut on dotted line." Several in the quonset raised eyebrows.

"Somebody told me they saw a guy who had train tracks running up the back of his leg and into the crack of his ass. You could see a fuckin' caboose disappearing in his asshole."

"Naw!"

"Did you know Hal got busted by the tax guys one time?" Heissen nodded to his pal, obviously trying to change the discussion. "You tell it, man." Hal needed no prodding to spin another of his fantastical tales. He and his brother, if the yarn was to be believed, decided to sell worms to fishermen. They were handsome youths and were as magnets to fawning town girls.

"We got the idea to hire the girls, five or six of 'em, I guess, and paid them nickel a dozen for worms they picked. They did good job for a while, and we were getting hundreds of worms. Our parents got hold of a wooden kid's coffin, put it in the garage and laid in newspaper and dirt for a worm bed. We sold them for 15-cents a dozen, and were making good money."

As it happened, their customer base expanded from family to the neighborhood anglers. Orders mounted exponentially, especially for the long, juicy night crawlers. Somehow, the girl pickers sucked up their courage and kept at it.

"We had a really big order once, but it was stormy that night. Our girls refused to go out in the thunder and lightening, but we threatened them. They refused until we offered them ten-cents a dozen. We still had a good business. The girls learned to seed the grass with dish detergent to drive the worms out, and even picked in the cemetery. Then, we began selling to a Berlin bait shop, and orders went wild. Just about that time the cops came to check us out. Our dad laughed, saying his boys were just good little capitalists."

"You left out the other part," Heissen added.

"Oh, yeah. That fuckin' crab-ass widow in town who hated every kid spied on us, and complained. The cops checked with the tax guys, I guess, and they said we had to pay because we made too much money. We were a business. So, they shut down our worm operation. You can bet the old lady's house got a lot of attention on Halloween after that."

Garson and others could now see a glimmer of light at the end of the MCRD tunnel. To exhibit their short-timer status, they strutted smartly, the platoon guide-on almost arrogant in the breeze. If Garson ignored the yo-yoing head of Fletcher (when writing about him decades later, the image of gnarled and gnomish Daniel Quilp in Dickens's novel *The Old Curiosity Shop* came to mind) the platoon looked good on the Grinder. Now, Garson came to realize why Marines were called Jarheads. From the rear where he marched, a smartly-blocked dungaree cap perched atop Fletcher's white side wall haircut appeared like a lid atop a jar.

"There are two ways to do things in this man's Corps – the Marine way or the wrong way." That Corps axiom was not merely a Boot Camp lesson for Garson, it had become a life lesson. Now he was approaching the final days of his indoctrination. Perhaps his future held the promise of combat experience. What had begun as a flirtation with the "idea" of the Marine Corps, perhaps a youthful lark the summer before, had now become a decidedly serious endeavor.

***

CHAPTER 6

RELATIVES AND KIN

"I have a belief that a man's real relatives are scattered throughout the universe," Jack Crabb said, "and seldom if ever belong to his immediate kin."

That was one of Garson's favorite quotations. Crabb, of course, was the 111-year-old narrator of Thomas Berger's comic novel, *Little Big Man* who recounted numerous tall tales and yeasty yarns of his life on the Plains until the Battle of the Little Bighorn. Adopted by the Cheyenne, the Human Beings, Crabb encountered such "real" personages as Custer, Earp, Hickok and Calamity Jane. Garson was attracted to the author's engaging story telling, vivid scenes and indelible characters. In his own life, as he often reiterated, he gravitated to people who could regale audiences – anecdote spinners, fabulators. He was quick to lament that his tale lacked Berger's verve and satiric sparkle.

"Your uncle was a lay-about," Garson's mother told him more than once, "and a souse. He and your father didn't work much during the Depression. He mooched off us." The uncle to whom she referred could have been none other than Vin – one of the trio of brothers who had come to Milwaukee in 1925.

Evidence was circumstantial for her assertion, as Milwaukee's directory listed five people in the household in 1939, when Garson was three. He had no memory of who else may have lived there with his parents, his grandfather Guttig and himself. But what his mother considered Vin's mooching was not the only reason for her antipathy.

Vin, a man of modest stature, shorter than his older brother by an inch or more, was always trim. Some might call him handsome. He had light, wavy hair, slightly-puffed cheeks and an overbite. He spoke with a tinge of sibilance, and laughed easily. For many years, he worked as a porter at various hotels on the east side after arriving in the city with his brothers; invariably he rented efficiency apartments on the northern edge of downtown. Gregarious, he knew many people.

He told his nephew on several occasions of experiences among some shady types who were ready with bootleg booze and homemade brew. Such yarns were always out of earshot of his sister-in-law. Until Prohibition ended in 1933, there were numerous hideaways in Milwaukee east of the river where alcohol fueled good times.

"Tried to make gin myself – once," he said with a wry smile. Garson gave his uncle the benefit of the doubt despite his mother's antipathy toward her brother-in-law. Vin sought to supplement meager earnings, and prevailed upon an acquaintance who promised to buy several gallons of homemade hooch from him, he explained.

"I mixed ingredients in my bathtub, and let it cook for a few days" he explained. "Somebody in my building must've smelled something. There was this chubby girl down the hall who always wanted me to take her to a speakeasy, but I said no so she got mad at me. She or somebody else must've called the dicks."

The police rapped on his third-floor apartment door one evening, demanding admission. Vin quickly closed the bathroom door, hoping his concoction would not be discovered.

"I let them in, and they looked around suspiciously. Don't think they knew anything for sure. There were lots of complaints like this all over the city, but many didn't pan out. Lots of the cops drank, and looked the other way. But one of dicks stuck his head in the bathroom."

"What's this?" he called to Vin.

"Oh, I'm making root beer."

"*Root* beer?"

It was not long before the police discerned that the tub contained more than soft drinks. Vin was arrested.

"They drained my gin out, gave me a little fine and threw me in the hoosegow for 30 days." He laughed, a tinge of pride turning up one corner of his mouth.

And there was more for his sister-in-law to disdain: A life-long bachelor, Vin had a girlfriend for many years — slender and pretty woman with Clara Bow lips and a tousled brunette bob. Garson's mother liked Marcella. The woman was "easy-going," she said, and did not "put on airs." As a child, Garson recalled Marcella's pretty dresses, and the scent of Lily of the Valley perfume. He liked her, too, as she smiled and her eyes danced when greeting him. When the couples socialized, the women always had their heads together in private conversation.

"We compared notes on the brothers. I wanted to have her as my sister-in-law." She once asked Vin why he did not marry Marcella.

"Why buy the cow when you can get the milk for free." That was how Garson's mother remembered Vin's riposte, amplified with a nasty cackle, she claimed. Such a response drove another wedge between the in-laws. For her, only married couples were allowed to have carnal relations. And marriage, it was her perpetual belief, was "for better or worse," and "til death do us part." She lived by such morality, and preached it to her son from the time he understood such things.

Garson long speculated that it was Vin who introduced his brother to the couple who loaned money for the down payment on the North Milwaukee house. Cyril knew Uncle Vin from bartending or portering days. This may have created a circumstance that led to Vin's living with his brother – partially in recompense for the introduction.

After Prohibition ended, Vin turned to bartending as a profession. He continued to reside in an apartment building on Marshall Street, six blocks north of downtown, and worked in various hotel bars and saloons. Garson imagined him in a long, white apron and striped tuxedo vest with brass buttons. More, Vin once operated a neighborhood grocery store near the Milwaukee River after the war. But that failed to provide a secure income.

"Too many customers wanted credit," he said; "I was too easygoing and a lot didn't pay their bills." He was forced back to bartending until becoming eligible for Social Security. Vin lived for decades in a rooming house adjacent to one of Milwaukee's fine German restaurants, John Ernst Café, amid a concentration of elegant apartment buildings.

There were numerous other criticisms that his mother heaped upon her brother-in-law, and to Garson, an air of tension between them was palpable whenever they were in the same room. He could not imagine how it had been when Vin lived in the same household – be it for a week, let alone more than a year.

Yet, Garson liked his uncle, despite seeing him only irregularly. He always retained a friendly demeanor, laughed easily and told frothy stories, even though some were inappropriate according to Garson's mother. When Garson was about ten, he received a little token from Vin that became a lifetime treasure.

"When I was a boy younger than you," Vin told him, "my father, your grandpa, took me along to a little town south of Sugar Bush. I don't remember why we went, but we visited two old timers, brothers they were, that he said fought in the Civil War." Vin thought their names were Gottlieb and Wilhelm, and their last name was Turkey or something like that.

"'We was in a Wisconsin infantry regiment,' Wilhelm said."

"'That was in the famous Iron Brigade,' Gottlieb said."

Years later, Garson attempted to verify the tale, and found records of two men from that county who had been drafted into the 6th Wisconsin Infantry regiment in 1864, and served until discharged at war's end. That regiment was part of the most famous brigade in the Union armies; it sustained the highest casualty rate of any such unit in all the armies, North and South. Wilhelm and Gottlieb probably fought in several of the late war battles south of Richmond in 1865, and might have witnessed Lee's surrender at Appomattox.

"The brothers took a shine to me. I was just a little curly-headed shaver, and they were really old then. They showed me a coin, an 1854 half dollar, and said it was a lucky piece that was carried all during the war."

"'If you look close,' Gottlieb said, showing me, 'you can see "ABE" scratched on it.'" Indeed, in the open space at the left hand of the seated Lady Liberty, Vin squinted to see the three, barely discernable capital letters. The coin itself was badly worn when Garson saw it.

"They said that there was a review or parade for President Lincoln who visited the Union camps south of Richmond before he was shot. They told me they just asked him to scratch his name in the coin as a memento, and he obliged." Vin never doubted the credibility of the tale, but Garson did.

"The brothers saw how much I liked the coin, and they gave it to me. I kept it all my life," he said before presenting the piece to his nephew. While the coin's intrinsic value was negligible, Garson retained it for decades, "for the next generation," he said.

Then, there was Garson's other uncle, Hervé, another Belgian miscreant, to hear his mother tell of it.

"Thinks he's some kind of a big shot," she scowled. "Stole your father's name, you know," she declared. While Garson's father did not agree with his wife's criticism of Vin, he sometimes acquiesced to the scorn she heaped upon his youngest brother. In Garson's memory, Hervé was something of a dandy – taller than his brothers with a slicked-back black hair and a razor sharp pencil mustache; he was willowy and well-groomed. Confident almost to a fault, he had a ready smile of pearly teeth. Unlike his brothers, he appeared out of place in casual attire. Garson's image of him was in a glen plaid suit, white shirt with collar eyelet pin, and neatly knotted tie held in place with a gold bar. Garson also envied the two-tone wing tip shoes his uncle favored. While attractive and impeccable, Hervé seemed not to have much time for him or other children.

In summer, Hervé sported those wonderful straw boaters that Cagney wore on-stage in "Yankee Doodle Dandy." He was the only smoker in the family, and Garson was fascinated when English Ovals were brought to life with the intricate, leather-wrapped Ronson lighter that he flicked with panache. His uncle blew out neat blue jets and whirling smoke rings, ethereal donuts.

Hervé left his brothers behind around the time of the 1929 stock market crash, and headed for Chicago. How he managed to succeed is largely speculation. He married in that bustling metropolis, but Garson had no memory of the first wife, not even her name. His mother said, like Vin's Marcella, she was a nice woman. That they were married in a Catholic Church ceremony also augured well. The two wives got on well, and it was a shock when Hervé divorced her. It was about this time, too, that Hervé officially changed his name. He chose Garson's father's given name with a different middle initial, "H" to distinguish himself from his older brother.

"We had our car stolen when we visited them in Chicago one time," his mother told Garson. While the couples socialized in Hervé's apartment, they heard a noise in the street where their car was parked.

"We wanted to look out the window, but Hervé insisted it was just some neighborhood commotion. Next morning, our car was gone. We thought he had something to do with it then, and still do. He traveled in a fast crowd." Garson's father's expression during such statements was usually one of skepticism. Hervé socialized with several who could have played parts in gangster movies – slick and swarthy types, fast talkers and steady drinkers, gamblers even.

"Now we don't know that for sure," Garson's father interjected. Garson recalled his mother's glare.

"Yes, and he used your name to get loans, too," she said angrily. It was another of her claims that Hervé used his brother's home ownership for a credit rating to establish himself financially. He was long-known to frequent the horse track, Arlington Park, in Chicago, and play the slot machines that were legal in Illinois. She refused to call him by the new name he had assumed.

Then there was that second wife, Bacia, Garson called her, with glaring platinum hair whose true color never revealed itself. She reminded Garson of Jean Harlow – shapely in form-fitting dresses. He liked her warm manner and infectious, throaty laugh, but not the wet kisses she delivered with plum-like lips or hugs that smothered his face in a generous bosom. She was given to fur stoles, glittering gold jewelry and mixed drinks in stemmed glasses. It was no surprise that Garson's mother was barely tolerant of the woman, often masking disapproval of the affected manner she claimed Bacia exhibited.

"She's common, just like us," she would say to her husband, "but she puts on such airs."

Not long after the war ended, Hervé owned a well-appointed Lennon Stone house near Skokie, and he drove a new Buick with an automatic shift and plush interior. Chevrolets and Pontiacs, like the one Garson's father drove, were for folks of lower station, Hervé seemed to imply. In time, his preference turned to Cadillac's.

It was perhaps 1946 that the brothers, their wives and Garson traveled to Sugar Bush to visit family and friends, and attend the Kermisse. The country had been relieved of restrictions on gasoline purchases. Garson's mother had settled a gray fedora with a tiny red feather on Garson's head, adding a dapper topcoat to the ensemble along with a crisp white shirt and bowtie. While he in no way resembled the popular singer, Frank Sinatra over whom girls wailed and wept, several relatives called him Frankie. He remembered another of those photos lost in the fire — a candid profile in which his head looked too large on the small body.

In the past, when his father had driven, the family stopped along the way only to fill the gas tank. But Hervé and Bacia were of a different sort. From north Milwaukee, Hervé pointed his heavy sedan east, onto Port Washington Road, Highway 141, that arrowed toward Wisconsin's northern peninsula. Bacia sat in the seat beside him, while Garson and his parents occupied the rear. In not many minutes, buildings on the fringe of Milwaukee thinned and the countryside opened. Hervé maintained a steady pace for 40 or 50 miles, the heavy Buick confidently hunkering onto the macadam roadway.

Garson's father and his brother harmonized with the only tune he had ever heard his father sing – a First World War tune titled "K-K-K-Katy." Billed as the sensational stammering song in that era, Garson's mother disliked it, and often said so when her husband sang the final lines: "When the m-m-m-moon shines over the c-c-c-cowshed, I'll be waiting at the k-k-k-kitchen door." She detested anything that reminded her of farms, barns or cowsheds. Garson was amused, and the brothers laughed; the women were nonplussed.

Hervé clicked on the radio in the middle of the song "Heartaches" by Ted Weems. Garson tapped his foot in time to the rhythm while Elmo Tanner whistled; it was one of his favorite tunes. The radio station also played "Peg O' My Heart," another popular number of the day by Jerry Murad and the Harmonicats. He had seen the group in a movie. The band's musicians performed on a half dozen different harmonicas. A midget with pork pie hat played a huge baritone harmonica, while a tall musician blew a tiny soprano. The little fellow was shoved back and forth between the taller players; he glared up at them, straightened his hat but never missed a note.

"We're stopping at Oostburg," Hervé announced after Bacia leaned toward him and whispered in his ear. They were somewhere between Port Washington and Sheboygan. Oostburg, Garson thought it a funny-sounding name.

"So soon?" His mother's voice was tinged with irritation. Garson and his parents remained in the car while his uncle and aunt entered the gas station. They returned within a few minutes, however. Hervé carried a bottle of Schlitz Beer.

"Bathroom's filthy. I can't go in there." Bacia shook her head in disgust.

They drove on for perhaps ten or 15 minutes before reaching another filling station outside of Sheboygan with acceptable facilities. Relieved, they drove on. Garson was intent upon destination signs, and as he was when traveling to Rubicon to visit his other aunts, uncles and cousins; and he read Burma Shave signs with his mother, who laughed at the funny final rhymes. At intervals, his father pointed to the right.

"See. There's Lake Michigan." The blue expanse spread to the east, low waves sparkling in the afternoon sun.

Garson's mother tsked-tsked when Hervé headed the Buick into a restaurant parking lot near Manitowoc. Even his father evinced impatience with his brother. Everyone went inside. When they returned to the car, Garson was the last to enter, and before he removed his hand from the jamb, his uncle slammed the door. Garson howled in pain as his first finger was caught. His mother quickly reopened the door. Tears streamed as he held his right hand.

"Let's see! Let's see," his mother shouted. Garson displayed the injured finger. There was a bit of blood, and it seemed to swell immediately. The pain was pronounced. It was obvious to her that the fingernail was damaged, and it might fall off in time.

"Get a rag and some ice," she commanded. Now it was Hervé who exhibited impatience as Garson's parents ministered to their son. He sat between them now, crying incessantly as they drove.

"Oh, he'll be OK," said his uncle. Scant assurance to a pained boy.

Garson's mother swathed the cold rag about the finger and held his hand upright. Still, the injury throbbed with each heartbeat, like someone hitting it with a hammer. He was tired and as miles passed, his sobbing continued.

"Can't you shut that kid up," Hervé growled. Garson tried to stop, but pain prevented it. As the August sun began to slide toward the left side of the car, he grew weary and mewled fitfully. Garson had no memory of the remainder of the trip. In Brown County, they visited Grandma Clémence. Already 80, she still displayed merry eyes, Garson thought; but she appeared thinner than he remembered.

While Hervé and Bacia rented a Green Bay hotel room, Garson and his family stayed with another uncle, the one who was a cattle dealer. Like his younger brothers, he was childless, by choice or circumstance was not known. His aunt was a neat and fussy woman who maintained an immaculate house. Garson slept on the couch in the living room; a mantle clock chimed him awake every 15 minutes.

"Remember the Mickey Mouse ice cream?" his mother asked her son in recalling that time. Indeed, the memory of their visit to widowed Aunt Ida who worked as a waitress at a Prange's lunch counter in downtown Green Bay was distinct. They sat in a booth and his mother ordered sandwiches. Ida suggested something called a Mickey Mouse for her nephew. When the dessert arrived, Garson was amazed and excited. The plate contained pancakes, a large one served as Mickey's body and two small ones were ears. A dollop of ice cream with a cherry created a nose while strawberries simulated eyes; an arc of raisins created a smile. Shoes were bananas.

But when his mother encouraged him to eat the creation, he wagged his head.

"Wanna to take it home," he said.

"Oh, it'll melt, Sonny," said his aunt.

He pouted, folding his arms about his chest. He failed to lift a spoon to mar the handsome creature, even as the vanilla ice cream began to melt and run. His mother looked at him, eyebrows raised to reveal sympathy. His father glared from across the booth. Five or ten minutes later, Ida removed the uneaten dessert. In her widowhood, this aunt had assumed the mantle as keeper of the family history.

Save for the oldest son, the new generation of Fermiers was not as fecund as Garson's grandparents. The oldest, born to the first wife, sired two or three children, but among the other five sons, only two had offspring. The sisters each bore two children.

Garson remembered little about the Kermisse celebration in Sugar Bush the year they called him Frankie. There was a lingering impression of his Uncle Hervé, dressed in his Chicago best with a natty straw boater perched on his gleaming hair, shaking hands and socializing with many people he had not seen in years. Some speech was tinged Gaulic accent; even Garson's father and uncle seemed to inflect their words more than normal. From the crowd a tall angular woman with a straight nose approached Uncle Hervé; with her sharp cheek bones and shoulder length hair, she reminded Garson of Katharine Hepburn. Hervé tipped his hat. Garson's mother called the woman an "old flame." She and his uncle had an animated chat for several minutes while Bacia grew noticeably impatient.

Among the attractions at the celebration were little stands selling quilts and handicrafts, beignets, other foodstuffs and Belgian beer. Hawkers tried to attract the men to games of chance.

"Frankie, what happened to your finger?" one of Garson's other aunts asked, seeing the large bandage. When he explained the accident, she glared at her brother. She was the soft-spoken aunt whose sight was dimming and would in time be lost completely. Now she wore thick glasses that made her olive-colored eyes look huge.

Never again would his parents travel anywhere with Hervé and Bacia. But there was a larger reason for antipathy. With some cause, Garson's mother accused her brother-in-law of ruining the family's finances by inducing her husband to abandon the welding trade in favor of a retail business.

I beg reader's indulgence for another elbowing interjection in my Pop's chronicle – for that's what I fear it's becoming, just a chronicle, a catalog of unconnected incidents that don't probe character and advance his memoir. Neither of us ever read more than small parts of Remembrance of Things Past, *that magnum opus many consider the paragon of memoirs, but my Pop may be drifting in that direction with all of these nostalgic late-boyhood details. You'll see that such matters go on interminably in this and later chapters. Almost feeling readers' flagging interest, I was tempted to excise many scenes and sections. But, on reconsideration, I desisted because, after all, this is my Pop's creation. Thing of it is, I can only forewarn what's to come.*

In contrast to trips up North, journeys to Rubicon and his mother's family were never as eventful. They drove to Washington and Dodge counties not only for christenings, communions and weddings, but, during the years of war rationing, to bring back foodstuffs – meat, produce and eggs. They usually departed after Sunday mass.

In the old weathered Pontiac, they drove west on Silver Spring Drive, under the Chicago, Milwaukee & St. Paul Railroad trestle. Barely visible down the tracks to the northwest was mysterious "Black Bridge," a railway span that beckoned like a *fata morgana* to the northeast and played a part in another boyhood adventure. A dozen blocks west they passed the 80-acre farm of a man named Dieterich from whom his parents had long purchased fresh milk. Silver Spring led to Appleton Avenue and Highway 41, bending to the northwest. Within a few miles, they entered a village with a tall-steepled white brick church and a funny sounding name, Fussville.

"It's Footville," his mother always mused when passing the handful of buildings comprising the community. After meandering through nearby Menomonee Falls, the single-lane highway dipped and bent. Garson watched the scenes as if he was standing still while outside the panorama was passing like a silent movie backdrop. It was a feeling, he wrote, best described by John Updike in his novel, *The Centaur*.

Garson knew the route almost as clearly as his father. It was predictable that the steepest grade led to Meeker Hill – a virtual Matterhorn. On one trip, the old Pontiac failed to master the daunting incline; as it increased, Garson's father depressed the clutch and pulled the floor shift lever into second gear. The engine whined and impetus slowed. The car began to balk and buck. His father clutched again, and pushed the lever forward into the lowest gear. The engine labored and clattered.

"Now what?" his mother asked, exasperation accenting those two words. His father said nothing. A shiny car passed the struggling Pontiac, honking; children in the rear seat pointed and laughed at Garson when they drove past. He stuck out his tongue, but too late for them to see.

"You never take care of cars." His mother again, leaving unsaid deeper criticism. His father ignored the admonition, intent upon nursing the Pontiac up the grade, studying dashboard gauges. The red brick Meeker Hill Garage was finally in view at the summit. The road behind was obscured by billows of blue exhaust. The smell of the overheated oil was obvious. The pace was glacial.

"Jesus Christ!" his father blurted.

"No need for such language. Your son's got ears."

"Yeah! Yeah!"

It seemed like hours before they pulled off the road to the left and onto the garage's crackling cinder drive. When Garson's father turned ignition key, the Pontiac clattered in some kind of death rattle before going silent. The hot engine ticked. A man in soiled coveralls exited the concrete block building, wiping his hands in a greasy orange rag.

"What seems to be the problem?" He was a bulky man, a great shock of unkempt brown hair protruded from a brimless cap.

"Maybe a fan belt, but I don't know," Garson's father opined. Garson's mother said nothing, but her body communicated more than words. She had for years, it seemed to Garson, chided her husband about the care and condition of the Pontiac. She complained about the trunk, cluttered with tools, many rusty, two flat tires, a wheel, also rusted, spools of wire, ropes and much unidentifiable debris and detritus.

"Looks worse than Deaffy's yard," she chided. "Like 'Fibber McGee's closet.' Don't know why you can't clean it out."

"Yeah! Yeah!"

They all exited the Pontiac, and the mechanic and his helpers pushed the car into the left hand bay. Garson and his mother walked to a grassy hillock, and sat down. More than a mere fan belt was needed. His mother fussed occasionally, muttering under her breath. She found a hard mint candy in her purse and handed it to Garson. He counted the cars that passed. One agonizing minute followed another. After repairs were finally completed, the sun had tilted toward the west. It was too late to continue the journey. They drove back home, and she telephoned her sister, saying she would visit the next Sunday.

Most trips did not end so prematurely. Half an hour north of Meeker Hill, the road swooped around a sparkling blue lake.

"Pikey Lakey," Garson's mother called out as the road wound past Pike Lake; boats bobbed in the water, and the irregular shoreline was dotted with cabins.

"Belly bouncer!" Garson shouted when the road slipped over an acute little hill with a sensation of going airborne. The route dipped and curved, passing open fields and forest glades. Garson watched as tidy farmsteads with barns, sheds and silos and rectangles of crops with neat rows of corn or hay passed the right side window. He saw tall fieldstone houses with peaked roofs and lightening rods, some accented with oriel windows, their yards containing gardens plots and wash waving on lines propped with poles. Clutches of chickens or white ducks gamboled and pecked in the grass. The smell of manure was pervasive, and sometimes his mother held a handkerchief to her nose. In pastures grazed white and rust Guernseys along with black and white Holsteins, dairy cows, Garson knew, and an occasional black angus.

"Schleisingerville," his mother announced. It was the town founder's name that she knew as a girl; the name had been Americanized to Slinger. In not many miles highway dropped into the prospering town of Hartford, and Garson spotted at little movie house on Main Street, its marquee listing a title he had seen at the Ritz months earlier.

During the war years, Garson noticed a collection of World War II style quonset huts adjacent to a canning factory a few minutes outside of Hartford. And in adjacent fields, men worked, wearing shirts, large white "P's" emblazoned on their backs. They were German prisoners of war, Garson's father noted, who had been shipped to America after they were captured or surrendered.

"Some of 'em like it here. They talk German with the farmers. One said he wanted to stay after the war," his mother added.

Fifteen minutes farther, the steeple of St. John's Church announced the approach to Rubicon on county highway P. They passed Fireman's Hall in town, and Garson's mother repeated her joy of seeing movies and dancing there when she was a girl. They spent the remainder of the day, usually first visiting Garson's younger aunt, the dark one, Terez, he found warm and inviting. Her three daughters, with the olive skin and dark hair of their mother, were reserved in their reception of the younger cousin.

Typically, Garson's older aunt, Eva, served dinner at her farm nearby, setting out large platters of food on a broad oval dining room table with claw feet; extra leaves were set in to accommodate everyone. The meals were virtual banquets with chicken breasts and legs, stuffing, mountains of mashed potatoes, and beans, corn or other vegetables. Dessert always consisted of molded orange Jell-O with carrot shavings imbedded like insects in amber.

This aunt had a brood of six or seven children. Most of these cousins were older than Garson. He liked the girls, especially the two youngest who were so giddy and attentive. They doted on Garson for reasons he did not understand. Some summers, he spent a week on the farm with that family. After only a day, his allergies to maturing hay and farm animals caused him great discomfort. His nose dripped, eyes reddened and watered, and his lungs rattled and wheezed. He yearned for his mother.

The girl cousins took pity on him, asking their mother if they might take him into their upstairs bed instead of having him sleep alone on parlor sofa. Because the allergy plagued him until he returned to Milwaukee, he slept between the girls each night. They took turns rubbing his back. He affected generous sighs and moans, and was comforted by the attention, intoxicated with the aroma of soap-scrubbed bodies beneath nightgowns. He was fascinated by these cousins with their summer-bleached hair, sun-burnished cheeks and merry pale eyes. He smiled at their twittering. He was impatient for the nights to arrive so he could renew the intimacy. Garson could not bring to mind any untoward stirrings, but when he returned home on Sunday, memories of those nights lingered, sometimes holding sleep at bay.

Garson found only the youngest male cousin, a black-haired boy about his own age, companionable. The older boys were rambunctious and rowdy, showing off and teasing the cousin their father called "weak and citified." Garson was just as mischievous and devious as any boy, but he was uncomfortable with some of the things they did. One day, the boys led Garson into the corncrib, empty now of all but a handful of dry cobs; one cousin brazenly pulled down his coveralls, squatted and defecated. To Garson's further amazement, he used a corncob to clean his behind. At another time, they dared him to grab a wire fence that he suspected was electrified; he told his aunt, and she upbraided her unruly sons.

Those cousins took cues from their father whom Garson disliked almost from the first. The name Essig perfectly suited him as far as Garson was concerned. He was a man of modest stature and generous belly behind bibbed overalls. He nearly always wore a striped farmer cap, and when he removed it indoors, the white skin above the eyebrows and on the dome of his head reminded Garson of an Easter egg. His eyebrows and lashes were so white, they disappeared; he was missing a digit on one finger severed while bailing hay, Garson's mother said. But it was that laugh that Garson most dreaded – a reedy cackle that started deep in his throat and burst from his mouth like a volcano. Garson was intimidated when such derision was directed at him.

Essig displayed undisguised scorn for people and things of the city. He called his small nephew *kleine hans wurst* and *schnickelfritz* — little imp. To his recollection, the uncle also took much pleasure in belittling Garson's father by manner or word.

"Dewey's gonna win the next election," he sneered one summer. Essig had a long standing antipathy toward Roosevelt and Truman, declaring they were socialists bent on turning the country from its enterprising ways. He was given to browbeating his brother-in-law at every turn. Garson found it inconceivable that such a man could be the father of pretty and caring daughters, one of whom would later enter a Catholic convent. But, then, he knew his uncle only a little.

The drives home from Rubicon, mostly after sunset, were sometimes an evening adventure. Garson often slept on the mohair rear seat, tired after a day of country air, food and activity. At least once or twice during the miles, he was disturbed by his mother's shout.

"Willie!" Gravel splattering on the Pontiac's underside, and a lurch back onto the pavement awakened Garson from light slumber. He sat up blearily.

"Keep your eyes on the road," his mother commanded. As Garson observed, his father rubbed his face and blinked his eyes; but every few miles his head again sagged toward his chest. As his mother demanded, his father occasionally stopped, and walked around the car to freshen himself. Perhaps he should not have drunk that last bottle of Stork Beer after dinner. Garson's mother maintained her vigil until her husband turned from Appleton Avenue onto Silver Spring Drive; past the farm on 60th Street, city lights finally beckoned.

Garson's house sat on a standard 40-by-120 foot city lot, and contained about 1100 square feet of space, its basement bare and attic barren. Garson's bedroom, on the west side of the house, looked out on the two-car garage and the backyard that featured his mother's wash lines, a vegetable garden and a rectangle of lolling rhubarb leaves. On summer nights, bullfrogs thrummed from the nearby marsh, crickets chirred, and dark brown June bugs zapped onto screen windows and doors; lightening bugs winked, and cicadas whined late in the season;

Milwaukee, still a provincial city by most accounts, celebrated its centennial after the war, immigrant flavors still discernable. When the Boston Braves moved to the city, an Eastern newsman wrote:

"By and large, Milwaukeeans are a gentle, ruminative lot, physically prepossessing in the Wagnerian manner, expansively hospitable in a Polish-Germanic way, polite to policemen (and vice versa), partial to Socialist Mayors and rarely moved by anything other than the remote prospect of owing anybody money...." Garson's mother was a devoted advocate of the latter trait.

Yankee founders and German burghers who followed gridded most city thoroughfares east-west and north-south; the latter, numbered streets, measured over two football fields long while the former, streets with names, were 150 yards in length. Garson paced them both, recording the distances on a map of the neighborhood he was creating, clocking himself at about four minutes for the 210-yard long blocks. Forty-First Street, of course, was roughly that many blocks from the city's main watercourse, and Milwaukee stretched out west about ten blocks beyond Garson's neighborhood. Roads that had been laid out over old 19th century trails such as Appleton, Fond du Lac, Green Bay and others angled across the city grid toward those distant towns.

Also cutting across the neighborhood was the Chicago, St. Paul & Pacific Railroad that sent two or three trains through each day. The freight line rose onto an embankment at Silver Spring where a large marsh spread. In summer, cattails stretched up over six feet, and spiders with quarter-sized bodies spun webs between the stalks; garter snakes prowled the soggy ground, and dragonflies, like iridescent P-51 fighter planes, patrolled the bog.

West of the embankment, Silver Spring Park, one of the finest in the county system, stretched for about two-thirds of a mile and included a kidney-shaped swimming pool. Cinder and paved walkways meandered through the greensward that featured a broad lagoon with boats, ducks, white swans and occasional geese; bullheads and crayfish populated the green water. Impromptu paths ducked in an out of the dense forest of trees, foliage and brambles, a virtual temperate zone jungle where boy Tarzans like Garson might encounter scampering squirrels and rabbits, or hide in the underbrush from menacing white marauders.

South of Custer Street sat a low sprawling factory whose glass windows were invariably opaque with grainy gray-orange soot; the building emitted an uncommon reek. The logo of the Hercules Powder Company, painted on its tall chimney, was a red silhouette of the ancient warrior pulling back a bowstring. Garson and his pals were never certain of what the factory produced, suspecting it was war munitions. It was learned later that the firm actually manufactured less ominous chemicals for the Fox River Valley paper companies. Adjacent to the east stood an expansive athletic field with baseball diamond and practice space for the Custer High football team. Goalposts sprouted each fall and yard markers chalked on the grass.

There stood a huge house on Hopkins and Sheridan unlike any other in the entire neighborhood, reminding Garson of Tara, the O'Hara's plantation manor house. A curved driveway rose from the street to the house. Six columns supported three-sided galleries on both floors, and a fan window topped double doors of the main entrance. While the dwelling gleamed white from a distance, closer inspection revealed a dowdy mansion more like Tara of Reconstruction era – paint had not been refreshed in years, the driveway was rutted and weedy, and ornamental greenery unkempt. Curtains behind the tall windows were faded and frayed.

When Garson collected for weekly bills on his newspaper route, he stood in the doorway, gazing at the tall ceiling and impressive stairway to the upper story. He asked himself if he had actually seen numerous little girls gamboling about that house in dingy pinafores, but was unsure if the scene was only a dream.

A little event occurred within the first year after the war that at any other time would have gone unreported; but it seemed to typify Milwaukee's attempt to turn away from four years of world war and focus on less stressful pursuits. A mallard duck laid a clutch of eggs on a Milwaukee River bridge pile-on across busy Wisconsin Avenue. Newspaper feature writers dubbed her Gertie. The little drama splashed across news pages in story and photo. When eggs hatched, pedestrians threw crumbs to the mother and her little family of five. To the horror of everyone, a duckling fell into the murky river, and a fireboat was dispatched to net the foundling and return it to the nest. In time, the family was rescued from its precarious perch, and relocated to the safety of a park lagoon.

War's end brought numerous changes to Garson's life, that of his family and Milwaukee itself. Boosters long touted their city as the "Machine Shop of the World," with its dependence upon durable goods – heavy machinery, metals fabrication and manufacturing. Over half of the city's workforce was engaged in manufacturing of one kind or another. Where other cities sustained post-war slowdowns, Milwaukee's metal and electric equipment trades rapidly shifted gears into peace time production. Garson's father's brought home almost the same weekly paycheck, perhaps $50 or so, as he had during the war when he worked long shifts that beefed wages. Their house was mortgage free, and a little, gray cashbox high on a closet shelf held a stack of war bonds.

His mother's livelihood was dramatically affected, however, as thousands of veterans returned to resume pre-war jobs. For the next several years, she found work where she could, trading the tan and brown Schlitz Brewery uniform for an apron, scrub bucket and dust mop. Garson did not miss the odor of yeast and hops that once clung to her.

One post-war city directory listed her as a "charwoman." At first, his mother cleaned several residences in a neighborhood along Roosevelt Drive that featured the finest residential housing stock in Milwaukee – single family homes and duplexes, of brick or stone, substantial Tudors and half-timbers with richly ornamented exteriors. Dating from the first quarter of the century, many displayed stained glass windows and arched doors, and interiors with fireplaces, maple floors and woodwork. Furnishings were plush and costly. Doctors, attorneys, businessmen and professionals called this neighborhood home as did synagogues.

"Now don't touch anything," his mother warned Garson, who accompanied her, directing him to sit quietly at a dining desk. During summer months when both parents worked, Garson accompanied his mother to commodious homes that she cleaned. He was surrounded by china cabinets and tightly packed bookshelves. Statuary and bric-a-brac crowded niches and alcoves. He drew for a few minutes, but was invariably bored, occasionally studying swirls on an ornate Oriental rug.

"Jews live here," she once said when Garson asked her about a little rectangular stone in a brass holder tacked at the doorway. She told him it was a mezuzah. A handsome menorah also perched on the dining room mantle. He had occasionally heard his father mutter about Jews, claiming they seemed to control everything.

"I don't care," his mother sharply retorted. "They pay me well, and as far as I know, they're good people. They trust me with their house keys. They know they can leave money and jewelry lying about, and I won't touch a thing." Garson had no knowledge of Jews other than the Bible stories he knew from school. He made no connection between them and his mother's employers.

Impatience occasionally overcame his mother's admonitions, and he surreptitiously opened drawers to fondle fancy pens and letter openers; he riffled the pages of a leather bound notebook, finding nothing of interest. He gazed at small paintings and framed photos of boys in suits, shawls and yarmulkes, men with long, dark beards and black hats.

As far as Garson discerned, she was responsible for all household cleaning – living, dining and bedrooms, but not kitchen work. His mother mopped, polished and scrubbed floors, and she was brisk and meticulous in her chores, as meticulous as in her own home. She even draped a rag over a paring knife, and on hands and knees, scraped dust and grime from the intersection of floors and baseboards. He knew no one else to do that.

Garson also accompanied his mother when she cleaned the office of a chiropractor on the number 27 streetcar line. He was ever fascinated with the collection of what he regarded as machines and contraptions, thinking they were like the apparatus seen in Doctor Frankenstein's laboratory. When late summer allergies flared one year, his mother asked the chiropractor if he could do anything to relieve her son's suffering. Neither parent, Garson knew, frequented doctors; they simply bore up to maladies, often subscribing to folk wisdom and remedies.

"Don't walk on the cold floor with your bare feet," his mother often pronounced, "it's just like 'poisant'" – she meant poison, of course. Vick's Vapo Rub and a warmed flannel cloth on the chest was a cure all. Garson was made to lie under a gooseneck sunlamp during deep winter months.

When reflecting upon the experience in the chiropractor's office years later, Garson wrote that the practitioner was something of a charlatan. He asked Garson to remove his shirt and lay on a padded table; he wheeled over a machine, pointing its bullet nozzle at Garson's narrow chest. The doctor flipped a toggle switch. The machine's tip glowed red and hummed ominously. Garson felt nothing, yet he was uncomfortable, thinking about the dreadful monster and his shrieking bride, Boris Karloff and Elsa Lanchester, and their betrothal on storm filled night.

The treatment provided no relief from the sneezing and wheezing. From late August or early September until the first frost, he was plagued with respiratory distress. As expected, Garson also contracted the entire gamut of childhood diseases – there were no inoculations to ameliorate them: Measles, chicken pox, whopping cough and mumps. Toby told him that he had to be careful when his cheeks were puffy because he had an uncle whose mumps descended to his testicles, causing them to enlarge like inflated balloons. And his mother chided him about picking at chicken pox scabs lest they leave a scar to disfigure his face.

When he contracted one of those illnesses, he and his father traded beds so his mother could provide succor. He remembered the high-pitched shriek in his ears, like a swarm of cicadas; during another sickness, he experienced a sensation of seeing everything through the wrong end of a telescope.

The chiropractor's waiting room where Garson usually sat while his mother cleaned was laden with numerous magazines. Most were dog-eared copies of *National Geographic*, medical journals and more. He once happened upon an old issue of *Life* magazine, containing a section of photos from the glorious World's Columbian Exposition in Chicago, published on an anniversary of that event.

Garson was awed by images of that soaring alabaster city on Chicago's lake front, its gleaming buildings and domes, watery basin, bridges, promenades, triumphal statuary, numerous exhibition halls and pulsing machinery. It had all evoked ancient Greece and Rome to him just as the nuns described them. He read that the exposition spread over 630 acres and attracted millions. The towering Ferris wheel with large gondolas carried people more 260 feet into the air; they could see Wisconsin and Iowa from the apex, it was said. Garson wanted to experience that ride and see the magnificent city, to walk among the exhibits and sample the exotic foods, to feel the crush of people. But as he read, he was deflated to learn that the spectacular collection of buildings had burned decades ago and now no longer existed. It was like the Mickey Mouse dessert he could not take home.

Garson had likewise been deflated to read that a glorious old movie house in downtown Milwaukee had been bulldozed. Printed in afternoon newspaper's *Green Sheet* supplement, the story and photos told of the Butterfly Theater on Wisconsin Avenue with its opulently ornamented façade. The box office sat in an arched entryway; above which glowed beautiful leaded glass windows. Two faux columns with female figures flanked the entrance. Most striking of all was a female figure, perched on a pedestal atop the facade, arms outstretched into butterfly wings. After dark, thousands of incandescent bulbs sparkled in a dazzling display. Once again, he had been born too late for such glories.

Like his mother, he loved such marvelous movie houses — temples of diversion, palaces of pleasure, meccas of entertainment and education. Most of the best ones beckoned from Wisconsin Avenue. Anticipation of the show days before, queuing up, purchasing a ticket and being absorbed into the environment was a significant part of the experience.

"Anticipation is always better than the realization," someone once told him. Plush carpeting and brocaded draperies and tapestries, marble stairways, ornamented ceilings, statues and freezes of Egyptian gods and Buddhas, and thematic décor from Venice, the Middle East and other exotic locales transported Garson from the prosaic environs of the city into exotic realms, promising romance, adventure and more.

There was also a very special experience at the magnificent Warner Theater downtown. Someone his mother knew began inviting her and her son to pre-release screenings. Weeks before the films were introduced to the public, theater owners were invited for previews. Despite the fact that there was only one feature, no cartoons or coming attractions, and no popcorn, soda or candy, he felt superior, telling his pals about what they could expect to see.

Other post-war changes were as much psychological as physical. After the death of his grandfather, the cadence and tone of the house changed. Garson often wondered how his father had felt about

Guttig's long presence in his house. His grandfather had been the dominant male presence for eight years, not only caregiver for his grandson but role model as well. In some ways, Garson's father had resided in the background; but now he gradually reasserted primacy.

In fact, Garson may have begun to notice his father for the first time – as if he were almost a new presence. By then a man of 44, he had grown "fleshy," as the saying went, his waist thicker, and facial lines craggier, particularly the crease between his prominent, gull-wing eyebrows; his eyes were nearly as dark as coal. Garson's father shaved virtually every morning, running the razor over his face twice; still, by day's end, cheeks and chin bore a blue shadow. He used a shaving mug and double-sided blade whose edges were honed with a mechanical strop that Garson found fascinating. If his father had been taller, Garson thought, he might appear to be related to the actor Tyrone Power, who had served as a Marine aviator. Then there was that peculiar serration across the bridge of his father's straight nose – as if someone had once scored him with a bread knife. Facial pores were large, and his thick black hair, once parted neatly down the middle, was now often unruly. Unlike his son, he never in more than 80 years lost a hair from his head.

He still worked a welder at a small firm across the river from the Pabst Brewing Company. The company, Krasonya, assembled boilers and vessels of all sizes. During the war, Garson liked to tell his pals that his dad had been too old to be a soldier, but he made boilers for Navy ships – destroyers, cruisers, carriers and others that helped win the war. The largest of these containers could not be housed within the building's confines, and were assembled in the enclosed yard on the riverbank. Curved sheets of steel were welded together until the vessel took shape; then his father crawled inside to seal the seams. Sparks showered down, pocking his shirt and trousers, and, his father always claimed, destroying the pigment in his hands. He was good at his trade.

"I can't do anything with these rags," Garson's mother often complained, displaying the tattered garments. What was more troubling, welding flame heated the boiler's interior, causing his father to perspire; when he emerged after several hours bathed in sweat, his body chilled in the outside air. He told his son that such conditions caused incipient arthritis in his back and shoulders that, in time, would nearly paralyze him in pain.

Then there were his father's voluble personal habits that contrasted with the taciturn, undemonstrative Guttig. Like him, Garson's mother usually held most emotions in check while his father often put feelings on display. He was impetuous while she was observant and diligent. He was easy-going and gregarious while she was self-controlled. Garson exhibited characteristics from both.

"Willie!" Garson's mother shouted out when her husband urinated without closing the bathroom door. "Were you born in the barn?" Her thin brows knit fiercely. Soon she was criticizing her young son for the same failing. To no avail, she chided them both to lower the seat after they finished their "business." His father called it the toilet instead of the more polite term bathroom that his mother preferred.

But there was more. Garson's father flatulated brazenly, not limiting himself to the toilet. It seemed to Garson that he forced gas from his body to amplify the sound, the resonance of a tuba. Garson seemed to think all of this had something to do with those days of his father's youth when he and his rowdy younger brothers slept in the attic bed. Garson's mother was disgusted by such displays.

What was more, other bodily functions were amplified by a veritable symphony of sound. Every cough, sneeze, yawn and sigh was embellished with verbalization. Blowing his nose sounded like a trombone. His snoring was the thunderous cataclysm of a summer storm. When arthritis settled in his joints and back in late age, he virtually screamed whenever he arose from a chair. Then there was the simple matter of sipping hot coffee: He slurped it noisily and greedily. Garson and his mother wagged their heads.

Yet there were many things Garson liked about his father. He could free-hand sketch respectable rabbits and squirrels, and was ready with a laugh, even though an occasional derisive note was discernable to an impressionable boy. His father owned a fine Gibson banjo from his youth, and he could still haltingly plunk out a tune. As he worked on chores about the house, songs ushered from his mouth in a kind of low-range whistle or "dee dee, dee dee da."

"Bix Beiderbecke, now there was a player," his father proclaimed. "Hot, sassy music. Played with a guy named Howdy Quicksell who could plunk a banjo like no one else." Garson's mother frowned. She had no interest in such syncopated tunes, enjoying instead the crooning songs of Bing Crosby and lately, Nat King Cole. Garson would come to favor Bix.

In some ways, however, Garson was uncertain of his father, measuring his tolerance for a son's mischief; he often pleaded with his mother not to reveal misdeeds. Much more lenient with her son, she had struck him only once in anger that he could recall.

"For god's sake, hit him on the hinder," his mother shouted when her husband applied corporeal punishment. "You want to hurt him?" Garson smiled inside when she came to his rescue. For one misdeed, his father slapped him so hard across the face that his head snapped; when he ran into his room, an ear was red and ringing.

"Yeah! Yeah! You baby him too much." He did not hear the ensuing argument between his parents, but that was the last physical punishment he recalled receiving from his father.

On another occasion, Garson heard his father say that his son looked sickly and weak. It was a conversation that was not intended for his ears.

"Look at those eyes: They're so slitted and sunken. That chest of his is so narrow, like a pigeon. Why he's chicken breasted." She huffed at the observation, angry. But hearing his father's denigration, Garson's ears reddened. Afterward, he raised himself on tip toes before the bathroom mirror to view his upper body. Compared with Toby or other boys, he had to admit, his chest did appear narrow and compressed. He also came to see his eyes as disfigured, especially when he laughed or smiled broadly.

Yet his mother had always told him he had a "cute little shape" with an "apple cheeked *Kiester*, not like your father's flat hinder."

He dwelled upon his physical deficiencies, maybe even deformities, for all he knew. He thought of himself as emaciated almost like those death camp survivors American armies had found in Germany, Poland and elsewhere. Thereafter, he declined to enter the Silver Spring Park swimming pool with his friends, instead observing the frolic from outside, fingers clenched in the chain link fence. Now, when bathing, he locked the bathroom door lest someone see him unclothed; he no longer permitted his mother to smooth Vick's on his chest when he was sick. In not many years, he would be too embarrassed to exchange street attire for gym clothes at school. Much later, having to disrobe with other recruits for the Marine Corps physical mortified him; he worried that the deformities might forestall his enlistment.

He detested a Holy Redeemer school photo taken about this time that he thought reinforced his father's observations. Garson agreed that his eyes were too narrow and their lids drooped at the outer edges. He hated the hideous knit sweater his mother insisted he wear, depicting a stag, doe and snowflakes. Like short pants when he was younger, Garson could not wait until he grew out of the sweater and was even tempted to "lose" it somehow. His hair in the pose was long at the top but trimmed tightly above his ears – what he would one day call Marine "white side walls."

As he grew older, he feared his deformed state was as repulsive to girls as was Charles Laughton's Quasimodo to beautiful Esmeralda, Maureen O'Hara, in "The Hunchback of Notre Dame." He had seen that movie a second time at the little Elite Theater on Green Bay Avenue, and wished he might look like the handsome Gringoire, Edmund O'Brien, instead. He several times tore out advertisements for the muscle building program of Charles Atlas. He was the skinny boy in the cartoon at whom bullies kicked sand until he completed the Atlas regimen and turned the table. But Garson never had enough money to send for the program.

Because both of his parents worked full time, his mother virtually without interruption until the day she died, Garson experienced many solitary hours, learning to enjoy his own company. He was free to speculate, to daydream, to fantasize at length, becoming a boy of his own devices.

Following the war, it seemed that several people, kin and others, came to displace Garson and occupy his room for varying amounts of time. Among the first of these was a relative from Rubicon or Hartford. Garson could not dredge her name from memory. Just out of her teen years, she apparently came to Milwaukee to find a job or enroll in school, he was not sure which. What he did remember was the presence of a young female in the household.

He recalled with some clarity that she wore glasses. Her pudginess was held in check by a girdle. She was aloof and paid Garson little heed, finding him a nuisance. Bathroom facilities were shared, of course. Garson was fixated with the stockings that occasionally hung over the bathtub to dry; the odor of flowery perfume lingered after her ablutions. Once, when he rushed in after she left the bathroom, her girdle lay on the commode. Garson fingered the fabric and garters, feeling warmth that lingered from her body. He was about to pick it up when she rapped like a woodpecker. Frustrated, he opened the door; she pushed past him and scooped up the undergarment.

There were others who lived with Garson's family, cousins perhaps, "shirt-tail kin," some were called, who stayed for weeks or a month or more. Occasionally, when visitors used the room, Garson and his father were consigned to the attic where a lumpy double bed was situated. Roof rafters were barren and without insulation, and Garson often stared at the bare bulbs that illuminated from the ceiling. When it was cold, he and his father heaped on two or three quilts. But Garson most often slept on an uncomfortable roll-away bed, loose metal stays beneath the thin mattress poking his ribs whenever he turned over; the bed creaked with each move.

Victory in Europe and Japan had not passed too long, and a remnant of soldiers, late war inductees, still resided at what had been the County Correctional facility north of Silver Spring Drive. Known as the Army Disciplinary Barracks during the war, it was still utilized for some military activities, including incarceration of minor military offenders in actual cell blocks as seen in "Brute Force" and other prison pictures.

Garson's mother explained that she had met "Spot" on the bus. A corporal, he was a florid man with thinning red hair and an abundance of freckles even on his upper body; his shoulders bore thatches of red hair. His eyes were merry blue, and when he unleashed a hearty laugh, silver fillings in his back teeth were visible. He was a gregarious Irishman like Corrigan the bus driver.

"He asked me one time if I knew of a place he could rent," his mother explained to her husband. She and the soldier regularly rode together, and struck up a conversation. Spot roomed somewhere else in the city, he told her, but he wanted to find something more proximate to the military installation. Men were being regularly discharged, he said, and it would not be long before he would be out of the army.

Garson knew his mother had poor sales resistance, and in a moment of weakness she said she might be able to rent him a room. While Garson's father was still making good pay as a welder, her income had declined considerably since war's end.

"Got a buddy who's looking for a place to rent, too," Spot said when he visited the house. Soon, strangers took possession of Garson's bedroom, and he had nothing to say about it. What Garson's father made of this, he did not know. His wife had decided without consultation, likely convincing her husband that extra income during such changing times mitigated for the boarders.

Where Spot was reddish and trim, Paulie, his roommate, was dark and rotund. While Spot was brawny and well-proportioned, Paulie was doughy and pear-shaped. Paulie's pitch black hair was slicked back severely on a large round head, and eyebrows arched dramatically as if they were painted with a brush. Spot was gregarious; Paulie was reserved. Spot was a clerk, Paulie a cook.

Wardrobes also distinguished the two soldiers. Spot was given to casual attire, often wearing military khaki trousers with undistinguished shirts. Paulie, in contrast, owned an extensive wardrobe – several suits and many trousers, numerous shirts and ties and shoes; Garson's mother called him a clothes horse, and he took up more than half of the closet. Everything was arrayed in an orderly manner, reminding Garson of his grandfather's fastidiousness. Paulie quickly discarded military attire at day's end.

Spot often sat home evenings, reading the newspaper or other material. Paulie, dressed to the nines, as it was said, walked to Villard Avenue or took a streetcar downtown. He sometimes returned before Garson went to bed, eyes red and bloodshot, tongue thick and tie askew. At such times, his normal reserve was replaced with jocularity. He tousled Garson's hair and called him "buddy."

In time, Spot met and married a slender woman he knew from his hometown, Reedsburg, a few hours north of Milwaukee. Her name might have been Estelle. Garson's family was invited to the nuptials; Paulie was the best man. So the roommate packed his considerable wardrobe and moved away, and a woman took up abode. Garson found her regular facial lineament attractive if not beautiful; her eyes and straight hair were the color of caramel; he liked her mid-range voice.

Spot seemed generally in good spirits, often passing time reading, and listening to a kind of jazz he called bebop. Garson was familiar with that style, having heard some of Benny Goodman's Carnegie Hall tunes on the radio. There was also an impression from late in the war of an added movie attraction, as short films were sometimes called, featuring an aggregation of Negro musicians performing jazz and blues; Garson was transfixed by the artfully composed creations. About the time he began jotting notes for his memoir, the Library of Congress Film Registry had selected the ten-minute film titled "Jammin' the Blues," as "culturally, historically, or aesthetically significant." Among the musicians were Illinois Jacquet, Lester Young, Marie Bryant and others. Garson remembered seeing it in his boyhood.

With chin propped on his hands, Garson also watched Spot at the kitchen table, fascinated as the soldier carved figurines from bars of Ivory soap. One subject was a couple embracing on a park bench that he painted silver, creating a tiny Rodin sculpture. He left it behind when he moved away; it perched on the dining room mantle for a long while until it broke when Garson's mother dusted it. Spot also carved a striking female nude with jutting breasts and generous bottom. Garson wanted that soap statue, but when Spot offered it, his mother responded predictably:

"You just take that with you."

The couple lived with Garson and his family for what may have been months, but might have been a year or more. Children measure time differently than adults, of course. Spot finally earned his discharge when, coincidentally, Garson overheard a whispered conversation between his mother and Estelle about missing her period. They moved away, presumably back to Reedsburg. Years later, his mother learned that Paulie, who seemed to have been a perpetual bachelor, had gotten married to a girl from Chicago. Garson's mother and the couples traded Christmas cards for a few years.

And, so, once more, Garson took possession of his room, moving clothing and other possessions from the attic. The roll-away bed was folded up and stored away.

Garson's mother was also given to bringing home stray cats and "discarded" dogs, and Garson grew up with a series of pets. Dogs were invariably cocker spaniel mixes with black curly hair called "Topsy." Cats bore luxurious gray hair and were named "Mitzi." He supposed the latter name came from the Lubitsch movie, "One Hour With You" in which Maurice Chevalier sang "Oh, that Mitzi!" Garson had been bored by the movie, but thought Jeanette MacDonald was beautiful.

Garson admitted his unkindness to "Mitzi," prodding and teasing her to distraction until the animal avoided him entirely. There was another creature that Garson also taunted unmercifully, an unconscionable treatment that would cause him much anguish and self castigation.

Garson's father had been an avid fisherman since his youth, and he occasionally he took his son on outings to nearby lakes. Garson enjoyed casting his bamboo pole for the most part, watching the bobber to reveal a nibbling perch, crappie, blue gill or sun fish. One of his mother's brothers who resided on Okauchee loaned his brother-in-law a boat for angling. Garson was not along when his father inadvertently snagged a snapping turtle. Solid and compact, the creature must have weighed five pounds or more. His father brought the turtle home, much to his wife's chagrin.

"What you going to do with that thing?" she frowned.

"Gonna make soup with it," was the reply.

"*I'm* not cleaning it!"

The creature lived the remainder of its sorry days in the garage, scuttling about the unnatural environment, lurking under a derelict trailer or in a shadowed corner. Initially, as Garson recalled, his father put out a pan of water, but the fetid liquid was rarely refreshed. An occasional sprig of lettuce or a worm or two were all the nourishment provided.

The creature frightened him. He squatted down, studying it at a distance: Its head and pointed nose were brown and olive, its shell dark and spiky. Thick legs were heavily scaled, and its claws long. The long tail bore three rows of scales. It was never determined whether it was a male or female. Later, Garson read that such creatures traced ancestry to the time of the dinosaurs. He learned, too, that when removed from their natural habitat, snapping turtles became aggressive.

So, he avoided approaching the doomed captive too closely because its long, accordion neck shot out in an instant. Its jaws can sever a finger, his father warned. Yet, Garson tormented the poor creature nearly every day after school, poking and prodding it with an old broom handle to trigger its menacing attack. It was going to be killed anyway, he reasoned. At a safe distance, Garson gazed at it. The turtle sometimes gazed back, perhaps protesting its ill treatment.

As days passed, the turtle's reactions to the torment grew torpid, and Garson became confident that he was quick enough to avoid any lunge. On one occasion, it clamped its jaws vise like on the broom handle. Trying to wrench the prod free, Garson twisted it with all of his strength, tearing the turtle's beak; crimson flowed from its mouth. Garson was taken aback, realizing for the first time that this creature could bleed, that it could feel pain. It scuttled away slowly into the darkness, trailing a smear of blood across the concrete.

Sadness and regret gripped Garson and he blinked away tears, vowing to leave the poor creature in peace. He waited a day or two before entering the garage again, and when he did, the air was laden with putrefaction. He gagged. In a pool of afternoon light the turtle lay, tiny flies and maggots swarming over its body. He felt that he needed confess this sin, to tell Father Dolan of his crime. He was responsible for the turtle's death that was certain. He had goaded it into submission, caused pain and death. Garson feared that his behavior marked him with a serious character flaw. He was cruel and selfish.

That creature haunted him, and the event recurred in dream and reverie over the course of years. It grew to symbolic proportions, like the final sequence in Fellini's "La Dolce Vita" when the crowd of sybarites study a strange sea creature washed up on a beach. In its death throes, it stared one eyed at the observers – just like that snapping turtle did when Garson harassed it.

As Garson grew older, he became more sensitive to his city's weather. Winters seemed to last many months. Sometimes in January and February fearsome days-long periods of sub-zero temperatures gripped the city. Those months might bring wind-borne snow from the Plains, or "Panhandle Hooks," snow enforced with moisture from the Gulf. In late winter, "Lake Effect Snow" was created by wind blowing onshore from Lake Michigan, blanketing Milwaukee miles inland.

In the small candid black and white photo taken by a neighbor, Garson's mother stood in front of the house, piles of snow reaching nearly to her chest. She wore that dark mohair coat that made her appear quite rotund, her head covered with a kerchief. She had shoveled the entire side- and service walk all alone. When Garson wrote about it, he felt guilty: As a ten-year-old, he should have helped his mother with the hours-long chore. Snow had drifted over the backyard fence, and lay so heavily on the arbor vitae tree in the front yard that its trunk drooped near to breaking.

The snow began just before New Year's Eve, 1947. It piled up rapidly, driven by horrific western winds; more than a foot and a half created drifts of ten feet and more. Streets became impassable, cars, trucks and streetcars were trapped on nearly every thoroughfare. Many workers trudged for miles to get home. Milwaukee was virtually paralyzed.

For days, newspapers were filled with stories, of people using toboggans and skis to shop for groceries, of nights spent aboard streetcars, in taverns and bowling alleys all over town. There were accounts of kindnesses by strangers, good Samaritans, who gave succor to those stranded, of folks providing sandwiches and coffee to people they did not know. Garson studied photos of people laboring to cut narrow paths through towering drifts, of stalled streetcars blasted with snow and festooned with ice. Ultimately, more than a month of the new year passed before Milwaukee returned to normal.

"Played *Schafeskopf* all night," Garson's father said after he trudged home the next day. It was the whist-like card game he had learned from his father- and brothers-in-law.

Spring normally teased the city in March and April for a day or two, thermometers rising as the sun's angle decreased, only to retreat into another icy shell. Pity the poor migrating robins that flew into southern Wisconsin too early. When summer warmth finally arrived, sometimes suddenly, high temperatures and humidity could prostrate the city.

"It's really close today," Garson's mother cavilled, wiping perspiration from her brow and upper lip. Many families, Garson's not among them, flocked to the Lake Michigan shore to find relief. It was, indeed, "cooler near the lake." Others drove to nearby inland lakes for respite.

Other changes after the war occurred rapidly. One minute, it seemed, food and other goods were rationed, and the next Garson's mother purchased numerous items not seen in years.

In addition to Magdalena, Garson knew several families with only one child. During the later Depression years almost a quarter of all families had lone offspring. Decades later, when population cohorts were labeled, Garson's generation became known as the "Fortunate Few." Both Toby and Larry as well as several others on the block might have been considered "only children" like Garson because of the age gap between them and older siblings. Some people called these latter arrivals "surprise children," and they were all very close in age, having been born before economic times suffered a second downturn in the late 1930s.

Garson recalled only one or two mothers on his block who did not have regular jobs outside the home. Each day, most women boarded buses and streetcars and traveled to work like their husbands. Magdalena's mother was one of the exceptions, at least until the death of her husband. Likewise, there were few large families among his pals.

During the war, the threat of polio infection was first raised, particularly among children. In time, the danger became pronounced. Newspapers warned pregnant mothers and children under 12 they were in the most acute danger. A quarantine was declared in Milwaukee. Garson, Toby, Larry and others were confined to their houses and yards. They had all seen photos of afflicted children, heads protruding from massive iron lungs, kids with braced legs and crutches. At the Ritz and other theaters, canisters were passed, collecting coins for the March of Dimes. Some kids groaned when the house lights went on, and the ushers passed down the aisles.

Since Larry was next door, it was easy to toss baseballs and footballs across the bushes during quarantine. Toby lived across the street, so the boys needed hefty throws to reach one another. When the ball fell onto the pavement midway between their yards —typically one of Garson's anemic efforts — it was invariably the daring Toby who shot a quick glance before dashing out to retrieve it. Garson always envied his brazenness. He was the oldest of the trio, and he celebrated his birthday liberation before his pals. Garson and Larry had to wait enviously several weeks longer.

Garson thought Toby was obsessively meticulous. He owned a wondrous assortment of possessions: Lead soldiers, a tropical fish tank, marbles more beautiful than Garson had ever seen, an intricate three-masted schooner in a bell jar his grandfather had constructed, Indian projectile points, two cap guns, a Red Ryder BB rifle, stacks of Superman comic books and much more. When

Garson picked up an item for inspection in Toby's bedroom, his pal demanded it be replaced exactly where it had been; many times, Garson was unable to find the precise position, so Toby tore the item from his grasp to set it back in place.

He also owned an extensive stamp collection, and Garson was envious of the colorful scenes and unusual shapes of foreign issues from exotic lands. The triangular stamp of Tanu Tuva, a place that had ceased to exist after 1944, was particularly fascinating. Garson had to satisfy himself with prosaic United States issues.

Most impressive of all was Toby's electric train layout — not one of those fake and unrealistic Lionel sets with triple tracks. His was an expansive HO gauge setup that his father had constructed in a corner of the basement; it was replete with buildings, bridges and tunnels, a water tower, foliage and trees, a town and tiny figures. Garson's eyes danced when the trains came to life, steam engines chuffing up grades, rounding curves, speeding along straightaways and through tunnels. Garson remembered a tiny oval train set, now long discarded, he had received as a child; it was nothing like this.

Toby invariably received interesting gifts for Christmas and birthdays from his parents and grandparents – an erector set, an ant farm, handsomely illustrated books — nothing like Garson's parents had ever given him. Toby's birthday was in spring, or so Garson recollected. He was envious when his pal unwrapped the Gilbert Chemistry set. The box contained beakers and test tubes, scores of vials and measuring utensils, a small scale and numerous containers of powders and liquids. The boy depicted on the box cover was awed with delight as a tiny explosion mushroomed in an atomic cloud.

One afternoon, Toby determined to make something special; he would not reveal what. According to instructions, he meticulously measured and weighed ingredients for ten minutes or more, finally siphoning shiny black grains into a quart mason jar. Garson observed intently, saying not a word.

"Let's go try it," said his pal. On the sidewalk before his house, Toby slowly poured a thin line of powder. Garson recalled scenes like this from movie serials when Lash Larue or Rocket Man were trapped in caves and shacks, bad guys determined to blow them to smithereens. Garson's heart tripped rapidly. This would be something. The line of powder extended ten feet along the concrete.

Toby withdrew a wooden match from his pocket, and as it flared to life, his eyes widened in anticipation. He cupped a free hand about the flame, and slowly bent over the powder trail. He winked at Garson just as he touched it off.

"Oh, boy," Garson shouted as the grains whooshed in a blinding light, like a camera flash bulb. The ten foot trail seemed to burn in an instant, white smoke billowing. But somehow, a spark jumped into the glass jar containing the remaining powder. There was another whoosh, much larger than the first, as bright as the sun. The jar rocketed into the air then smashed in the street. Toby was knocked backward onto the seat of his trousers. Stunned, Garson's mouth formed an "O."

Toby sat for a few moments, dazed. Garson was frozen.

"I'm OK, I'm OK," he murmured heroically. Garson was uncertain as Toby's eyelashes were singed black. His eyebrows had been obliterated, and his cheeks and nose turned crimson, looking worse than Garson's Uncle Essig in summer. He helped his friend into the house where his mother gasped. She shrouded his face in a wet dish towel.

"You better go home now," she directed Garson. No serious injury had occurred, and after a few days, Toby was almost himself again – except for the missing eyebrows and rosy face. He admitted that his parents had confiscated the chemistry set.

Without question, Toby was daring and adventurous, given to climbing trees, swinging on ropes, jumping from garage roofs and more. He once broke his right arm on some leap or other; the limb was set in a cast and he carried it in a sling. But to Garson's amazement, Toby learned to startle pals when, like a quick-draw cowboy, he withdraw his broken arm from the sling to brandish a cap gun. He was also better at the border shift with two pistols than anyone. When the boys played war, Toby carried an army canteen on a webbed military belt; a musette bag was slung over his shoulder.

Only once was Toby disappointed by a gift. When he and Garson saw war movies at Saturday matinees, he told his friend he wanted a pair of those neat canvas army leggings. A helmet, he knew, was out of the question. Garson, of course, used his father's Air Raid Warden helmet, but Toby belittled it because it was white and from the Old War.

"My dad said my grandpa was in the war," Toby announced, "and he said he had leggings." In a week, the grandfather had rummaged through an old attic trunk, and found the items. When Garson asked him how they looked, Toby frowned.

"What a gpy! They weren't leggings like they had in 'Bataan,'" he grunted. "They were like the ones in 'Sergeant York,' puttees, just rags wrapped around your legs." Garson laughed inside. For once, Toby had not gotten what he wanted.

Forty-first street and all of North Milwaukee for that matter was populated with tall, elm trees whose upper branches arched across residential streets, providing cathedral shade in summer. In spots, a few other hardwood trees, maples and oaks, towered up. On Garson's block, in the green space between sidewalk and curb in front of the large old house where Widow Klatsch lived, sprawled a catalpa tree. Each fall, the tree bore fruit – inches long, green growths that reminded Garson of giant beans. They hung like verdant icicles, stretching as they expanded during the summer.

"Indian cigars," Toby explained. "When they fall off and dry out, we can smoke 'em." In fall, the grass was littered with the brittle tobacco-colored fruit.

Neither of Garson's parents smoked. Only his Uncle Hervé and a few relatives did, so smoking was something exotic, not much seen outside of movies.

"I got matches," Toby told Garson and Larry one day. "Let's smoke!" Garson was reluctant; but because he was fearful of Toby's reaction, he assented to the daring experiment. Larry, as expected, wagged his head from side to side.

"My dad smokes," Larry began, "and he said I mustn't do it

because I'm too young, and I gotta wait until I'm 18, and my mother said it makes your breath stink, and..."

"Larry!" Toby held up his hand, "shut up!" Sitting on the grass, the boys studied the cigars, rolling them in their fingers. They smelled oddly.

"Break off the tips," Toby instructed. "Ready to light up?" he asked Garson. Garson tentatively stuck the brittle pod between his lips, holding it with two fingers of his right hand, as his Uncle Hervé and others did. Toby dragged a wooden match across the sidewalk, and reached the flame toward Garson.

"Suck in now," Toby said, "suck it in deep." Sulfurous smoke billowed from the glowing end. Garson took a long pull, inhaling. He felt the acrid smoke searing his throat. He coughed deeply; tears welled in his eyes and he spat several times. The taste was dreadful. Toby snorted at Garson's discomfort. Larry merely watched, mouth agape. As Garson coughed, hacked and spat, he noticed that Toby had failed to light his cigar. It was all a ruse; he had been gulled by his pal once more. He hated him, wondering why a best friend would do such a thing.

Unaccustomed to having the upper hand in anything concerning Toby, Garson found it curious that the only thing he could do that Toby could not was whistle, oh not like Elmo Tanner, of course. Instead of pursing his lips and blowing, Toby produced a shrill sound from deep in his throat, a high-pitched shriek that was distinctive, and he usually summoned Garson from across the street with the unique trill. Yet, it was Garson who Toby's dad called "Squeaky" because of the squealing laughter that proclaimed his amusement.

Toby's dad was a mailman. When he drove home at day's end, he continued the war's fuel-saving practice of turning off the car engine many yards short of his house and coasting to a stop. Garson noted, too, that he failed to affix stamps to his utility bills, explaining that Milwaukee Electric and other utilities paid the postage. Garson's mother frowned at such ideas.

But something about his pal's father that excited Garson: He was a ham radio operator. A large antenna rose alongside the chimney, and a special basement room contained apparatus – radios, amplifiers, transmitters, receivers, all bearing a wonderment of dials and gauges. Garson was never permitted in the walled-off inner sanctum, but he occasionally spied Toby's dad wearing a headset and speaking into a microphone.

"This is W9KRM. Over," he uttered authoritatively. Sometimes, he worked on a Morse Code key, swiftly clicking dots and dashes. Toby boasted that his dad had contacted people all over the United States, and in Canada and Mexico, and even Europe. Scores of postcards tacked to the room's walls had been sent by ham operators he had contacted, Toby said.

Adjacent to the radio room, Garson was enthralled with wooden crates filled with old magazines that he later learned were called pulps. They were about the thickness of a school notebook, but the ragged-edged, sepia pages were brittle. The magazines, Toby explained, belonged to his older sister, who had left them behind when she moved away after high school. All had daring, brightly-colored covers, some depicting moony-eyed or weeping women and handsome beaus. But there were many with titles such as *Thrilling Wonder Stories*, *Black Mask*, *Planet Stories*, *Spicy Detective* whose covers thrilled Garson. He had never seen their like.

Printed on heavy, slick paper, most covers were enticing, invariably depicting voluptuous women, mouths agape in screams, threatened by villainous goons in robber caps with five o'clock shadows and lantern jaws. Other lurid covers featured weird, tentacled creatures with multiple eyes, firing ray guns or seizing nubile beauties, tearing dresses. Bosoms heaved against tattered bodices, and thighs were visible under torn skirts.

Garson knew the answer before he uttered the request, but he asked Toby if he might borrow several issues to read the stories; he promised to return them quickly. Of course, Garson had little intention of perusing the texts. He had a passing thought to steal a few publications, but never found an opportunity. Instead, he slowly pawed through the crates when chance presented itself, less than satisfied because he wanted to scrutinize every cover in detail. But, thinking about it, Garson rationalized that he could not secret the magazines from his mother anyway. Thus, the pulps were all a hopeless tease.

"What're you doing," his mother asked one day when she returned from work. Trying to duplicate his pal's feat, Garson attached a wooden crate he had found onto a three-foot long length of two-by-four. He had badly nailed wheels cannibalized from his roller skates to the underside of the board.

"Gonna be a scooter," Garson declared proudly. Indeed, he had observed while Toby's father assembled his son's scooter. But Toby's skate wheels were screwed in place, and sturdy conveyance was painted silver. Lighting bolt decals adorned the sides. Toby virtually flew down the street, pumping his right leg furiously to propel the clattering conveyance like the Little Rascals. In contrast, Garson's scooter never seemed to run true, the nails holding the wheels usually loosening. The wooden crate, filled with knots and cracks, was never painted. Toby was always in the lead with such things – scooters, a bicycle, motor scooter and finally a car.

Toby's red Schwinn bike was the envy of the block with its substantial frame and shrouding, white sided balloon tires and gleaming chrome. Despite its perfection, Garson's pal was a constant tinkerer; he wanted to make the Schwinn look better, adding lights to the handlebars, mud flaps and reflectors. He even had a generator for the light.

Garson, as might be expected, never owned a new bicycle. His had been assembled from various parts by his father – frame, wheels, fenders, handlebars and seat never perfectly mated. Garson painted it blue with white trim, but his usual impatience prompted him to remove masking tape too quickly; the lines delineating colors blurred. Garson attempted to maintain the bike with limited success. The handlebars, which he tightened constantly, were usually slightly misaligned with the wheels. The front tire incessantly rubbed the frame, and Garson rarely replaced broken spokes.

He tried to improve its appearance, saving paper route money for a chrome lamp like Toby's to mount on the handlebars. After weeks, Garson accumulated sufficient funds to purchase the light from the Villard Avenue sport shop. With money wadded in his pocket, he peddled in anticipation down the block. When he turned to head south on Custer Street, a heaved-up section of the pavement caught his front tire, wrenching the handlebar from his grip. He was literally launched headfirst into space; for less than a second, he flew like Superman until smashing his face into the street. Not many years before, he would recall, another bike had played him false and caused injury.

Thousands of sparkling lights whirled about his brain before everything went black. When he roused, two adults were lifting him from the pavement. They led him to the water fountain at the football practice field.

"Hold your head over the bubbler, kid," Garson was told. His lip was bleeding. The cold water provided momentary soothing. He tasted blood, and his tongue explored his upper lip; the abrasion was painful. His shirt front was bloody.

"You OK?" the strangers asked. "Where do you live?" Garson nodded down the street.

"Wanna go home," Garson replied through the broken lip. His bicycle was mangled, handlebar wrenched to a 45-degree angle. Woozy, he staggered home, stopping once or twice to clear his head. When his mother returned home from work and saw him lying abed in the bloody shirt, she screamed. She studied the mangled lip, now the size and color of a purple grape. Between throbs of pain, he described the accident.

"Got to get you to the hospital right now!" This was beyond the skills of Viv, the neighborhood nurse. But he knew well enough that at the hospital, a doctor would need to stitch the ugly cut. He was adamant: He would not go because, like tonsil removal, needles were involved. The abrasion knitted, but for weeks, the scab tore open every time he laughed; he tried not to stretch his lips. When the injury finally healed, his upper lip was misshapen and would remain so for a lifetime.

"She's got money in there," Toby reported. He always had information that no one else did. "Hundreds maybe." They were sitting on his pal's front steps when the subject turned to Deaffy, the neighborhood tatterdemalion.

"How'd you know?"

"Saw her on Villard once. Buying bread and things at Pittleman's. Pulled out a wad of paper money to pay for it." Garson did not believe it, but was typically reticent about challenging his pal.

"They said that when she moved on our block, she had a baby that died." Garson's mouth hung open at that information. How could Toby know about that since he was not even born when Deaffy took possession of her shack? But, neighborhood boys took that intelligence as a matter of faith because Toby seemed always to know what he was talking about.

There were other rumors, too, that circulated on the block – a marriage and a man who spurned her, and more. Deaffy continued her neighborhood rounds, sometimes pushing an old baby buggy with its top removed, collecting items and storing them in her weedy yard. She was slower now, and favored her left leg. It could only be guessed what her shack contained, in addition to all the money Toby claimed was inside.

"Look at this," Garson's father said, holding up *The Milwaukee Journal*. The daily printed a story about two reclusive brothers in Harlem who had lived in a brownstone mansion filled floor to ceiling with newspapers, uncounted books, musical instruments, tapestries, human organs in jars, even a Model T Ford and tons of other useless impedimenta. Decades past, the house had been in a fashionable New York City neighborhood that was now dowdy and dolorous.

The brothers, Homer and Langley Collyer, were both found dead inside the manse, his father said. One had been killed by a falling pile of newspapers, and the other, blind Homer, had died without food and assistance. The city ultimately removed 19 tons of junk from their dwelling.

"Reminds me of Deaffy," Garson's father remarked.

In the summer after the war ended, the great neighborhood battlefield and playground, the vacant lot next to Mrs. Hexe's house, was obliterated, leaving behind what appeared to be atomic devastation, at least to hear Garson's pals tell of it. Workmen backed a massive bulldozer off a flatbed trailer, and steered the machine onto the vacant lot. It knocked down stunted trees and shrubs, and scraped away ground foliage. A day or two later, a huge steam shovel was brought to bear, and as a crowd of neighbors watched, two rectangles were excavated, the foundations for houses. Simultaneously, similar catastrophic events occurred at the south end of the block where another wild space was tamed.

Over ensuing weeks, concrete was poured and blocks laid for basements. Carpenters assembled a wooden skeleton, nailing on floors and the frames for walls, ceiling and roof. Slowly, square and compact houses emerged; each structure measured some 900 square feet – two bedrooms, kitchen, living room and bath, the rooms tiny in comparison to Garson's house; interior materials were of a lesser quality than pre-war Milwaukee bungalows and older houses on the block. Garson heard his father mention something about hollow core doors and wallboard instead of plaster; negligible ornamentation was visible. They were designed, Garson's father observed, as inexpensive dwellings for returning veterans who qualified for special low mortgage rates.

"To call those houses Cape Cods is a joke," he observed. "They're just cookie cutter houses." Indeed, builders were erecting thousands of such homes all over the city, creating sprawling new neighborhoods from former empty spaces, separating houses and people with driveways. The farm where Garson's parents had once purchased fresh milk soon bloomed with rows of new houses. *The Milwaukee Journal* printed an aerial photo of the unnatural checkerboard.

One day, cabinets and other interior components were unpacked from huge crates and cartons which were left on the building site. Garson could not recall who suggested using the abandoned containers, but it was probably Toby. The neighborhood leader, he was a boy of vision and action.

"Let's make a clubhouse," he announced to a group of three or four, including Garson and Larry. After carpenters vacated the site for the day, two large corrugated containers were pulled together, and Toby cut a doorway between them, creating a closet of space. He always carried a pocket knife wherever he went.

"Meet back here tonight after dark," he directed. Toby brandished a flashlight that evening, and someone brought a candle, illuminating the interior. Garson ate from a box of Cracker Jack, sharing it with Larry. They talked about movies and events that had occurred at school and on the block. Then, abruptly, the conversation turned.

"Hey, let's show our wieners!" Garson was long uncertain of the source of that suggestion, but, as usual, concluded it had been Toby. Larry and another boy looked startled. Garson was mute. Why would anyone want to do such a thing?

"C'mon! I saw my sister's thing once. It was different. She didn't have a wiener."

Toby stood up, and brazenly dropped his trousers and underpants. His penis looked odd, Garson thought, different than his own, skin concealing its tip. Minutes passed, then another of the group followed Toby's lead. Two now stood, trousers and shorts bunched about their ankles. For years after, Garson avoided thinking about the incident, ashamed that he had taken part. Much more might be made of all of this overtime, he feared. Fearful lest he be accused of being a sissy, he reluctantly stood and unbuttoned his trousers, dropping them over his shoes. He was uncomfortable. The boys tried to appear nonchalant, to avert eyes from one another.

Larry was now the lone holdout. Garson almost predicted what happened next.

"Oh, I don't want to do this." Larry's head wagged. "My mother said I shouldn't touch my 'thing.' except to go to the bathroom. She said it was nasty and dirty. She makes me use toilet paper when I make water, so I don't get my underpants yellow. Why are we doing this? Oh..."

"Larry!" It was Garson now. "Shut up! Don't be a drip." His pal slowly uncrossed his legs and stood. With fingers on his trouser buttons, he hesitated, looking at the others. Suddenly, he bolted from the corrugated clubhouse.

It was a curious little episode that was never repeated. And none of the boys spoke of it afterward. Garson failed to confess the deed, as he did not know how to categorize it for Father Dolan. Was this one of those impure actions? Was it a sin at all? Within days, the containers were flattened and removed by the construction workers. The boys now played inside of the rough interiors of the new houses, swinging from horizontal two-by-sixes like Tarzan until doors and windows were installed, and the entire structure closed off.

Garson thought about the episode for several nights until one afternoon Magdalena and her mother visited his house. As the mothers chatted in the kitchen, he asked the girl to join him in the basement, saying that he wanted to show her the new automatic stoker, a marvelous device that shuttled coal from the bin to the furnace. Magdalena followed. She had, after all, been in the basement before, with Garson, Johnny Klatsch and others. He pulled the overhead chain and a bare bulb illuminated the area between the furnace and coal bin. She looked at the stoker without interest. He had a plan.

To Garson's eye, Magdalena had grown a bit prettier. He still found fetching that little gap in her front teeth. Her eyes were the blue of a summer sky, he noticed, and her dark hair was cut in a neat butcher boy style favored by her mother. She wore a pleated party dress with short puffy sleeves, white anklets and patent leather shoes. That they were both only children also counted for something. Yet, he still disliked being called her little boyfriend.

"Can I see your 'thing'?" The question just popped out of his mouth unbidden. Magdalena responded with a half-lidded stare, imperious, seeming not to hear; perhaps it was a pretense.

"I'll show you mine if I can see yours." Incredible as it may seem, Garson thought "hers" might look different, like Toby's sister's; he had only a vague notion of such anatomical differences based upon what Toby had said. His mother then and ever after failed to discuss such things; he had to learn on his own. While never having seen any female anatomy completely disrobed, he knew only that breasts grew when girls got older.

Slowly, he unbuttoned his trousers and pulled them down along with his undershorts. Magdalena's eyes widened to saucers as she gazed at his genitals, stunned into silence.

"C'mon." He affected the best vocal modulation in his repertoire. Long seconds and minutes passed. Garson grew uncomfortable, basement dampness chilling him. Anticipation was ebbing. Then, Magdalena's fingertips fondled her hem. With agonizing deliberation, she lifted the ruffled dress as if in a tease. Her face was without emotion. Garson watched, breath caught in his chest. He saw her thighs now, and her white underpants. She was going to show him! She slid her fingers into the elastic waist, and pulled it away from her body. Garson's heart seized.

"Magdalena!" Her mother called from upstairs.

She jolted and shuddered, then blinked, as if snapped from a trance, like a marionette whose strings were cut. Garson's heart started again. Her dress fell to her knees, and she gazed straight into Garson's eyes for many seconds. He thought he saw something there, some distant promise. But he only interpreted that in retrospect.

"Gotta leave now, *Liebschen!*" came her mother's voice from the rear hallway. Magdalena pushed past Garson, and scampered up the stairs to the back door. Deflated, Garson pulled up his trousers, remaining in the dank basement for many minutes.

"Never happened!" Lana declared flatly fifty years later when Garson asked her about the incident. She had long since eschewed the Biblical Magdalena that her father had given her. She was adamant that his recollection was but a figment of his fevered imagination. She was so emphatic, in fact, that Garson began to doubt that the incident involved her or even occurred at all. He wondered how she would react to his written account.

Magdalena and other girls were beginning to intrude upon Garson's boyhood attentions with more emphasis.

On one of the trips to Green Bay, Garson happened upon a comic book that fueled that attention. He was not given to comics as a rule, caped crusaders and flying heroes holding little interest for him. But at a corner grocery near his uncle's house, he absently twirled a rack of comics. On the cover of *Jumbo Comics* appeared a striking woman, "Sheena, The Jungle Queen" she was called. Swinging at the end of a vine, dagger poised to stab an attacking eagle, she was adorned in an animal hide frock that hugged the contours of her lithesome body. Long, golden hair flowed. She wore hoop earrings and bangles – incongruous, Garson had to admit.

She was the first female comic book heroine, Garson would learn. Imitators followed, but for Garson there was only one Sheena. Of course, Garson knew about Tarzan, but this white goddess was sensational. She had been raised from childhood by some African tribe which worshipped her. Like other comic heroes, she was strong, courageous, resourceful and resilient, always aiding weak and oppressed African natives.

Quite by coincidence, coins his Uncle Hervé had given him at Kermisse remained unspent in his pocket, and he paid a dime for the colorful publication. Knowing his mother would frown on such licentious publications, he rolled the paper book tightly, carrying it inside of his topcoat. On the drive home, he could think of nothing but Sheena. He carefully secreted the comic in his room, and poured over each exciting panel, as Sheena wielded her knife to kill crocodiles, lions and other predators and vanquish villains and marauders. When the cartoon heroine gained her own exclusive publication, Garson found more issues at the Villard Avenue drugstore, purchasing them eagerly.

As nearly every boy in America, Garson was exposed to a myriad images and photos that helped fuel fascination with the female form. Depicted regularly during the war were images of the aircraft pinup paintings – flirty, teasing and perfectly proportioned girls. The work of commercial painters like Gil Elvgren, George Petty, Alberto Vargas and others were proliferate in advertising and promotions – even in patriotic appeals. Garson scrutinized such images at length, captivated by the thrust of breasts, the curve of derriere and hints of nudity. Skirts and dress hems were invariably raised or caught on some object, revealing thighs and stockings. While not given to movie magazines, Garson liked many of the stars who posed for photos and artwork – sweater girls like Betty Grable, the dark and alluring Hedy Lamarr seen in "Algiers," enchanting

Dorothy Lamour, and angular Veronica Lake, Alan Ladd's co-star in "This Gun for Hire" and "The Glass Key" with her peek-a-boo blonde tresses.

While at the chiropractor's office paging through publications as his mother cleaned, he happened upon an old issue of *Life* dating from the war years. Inside, the actress Rita Hayworth posed beguilingly. She had danced with Fred Astaire in a movie he had not seen, but he did recall her in "The Strawberry Blonde."

In the full page photo, she kneeled on a bed, auburn hair framing her beautiful face. She wore an alluring peignoir, its dark lace bodice cupping her breasts. Years later, it was revealed that the photographer suggested she take a deep breath before the camera flashed to amplify her bosom. By war's end, more than five million copies of the iconic image were sold; only the Betty Grable photo in a white swim suit outsold Hayworth. Decades later, the negligee Hayworth wore was auctioned at New York's Sotheby's for tens of thousands of dollars. Transfixed by the provocative photo, Garson clandestinely tore it from the magazine, and carefully folded it. He secreted it in his room with the Sheena comics and several other images, anxious at what his mother might say should she discover them.

But there were other boyhood fixations and passing fancies. Milwaukee's ballpark did not look at all like photos of Wrigley Field or Yankee Stadium that Garson saw in movie newsreels. With its green wooden walls and fences, Borchert Field looked rickety. Sitting on a rectangle of a city block about three miles east of his house, it dated from the last century, and was home to the Brewers of the minor league. Its mascot was a beer barrel swinging a bat.

Garson remembered attending a game or two, but once in particular with his father and Uncle Hervé who was visiting from Chicago. It was a warm sunny Sunday after Mass, if memory served, almost a scene from the Robert Redford movie, "The Natural." Hervé wore the raffish straw boater and dark glasses, a seersucker suit and canvas summer shoes. They sat in the shade of the grandstand, and often had to crane their necks around spindly roof supports to see all the action. The Brewers played a team called the Minneapolis Millers that day, a traditional rival, and the stands were packed. Hervé purchased the tickets, and soda and bag of peanuts for Garson; shells crunched beneath their shoes. The men drank Schlitz beer from paper cups. But Garson recalled his uncle's demeaning comment that the Brewers had not the stuff of the Chicago Cubs.

Garson was indifferent to baseball, as played by the hometown Brewers or even major league teams for that matter. In 1947, things changed, albeit briefly, when Jackie Robinson was added to the Brooklyn Dodgers. Garson was somewhat repelled by all of the hoopla surrounding the first Negro major leaguer. But his interest was piqued months later when a quiet unassuming player named Larry Doby joined the Cleveland Indians as the first Negro in the American League. He was a handsome fellow of over six-feet with an even dusky skin tone and gentle smile. His quiet humility seemed to contrast with Robinson's flamboyance. The next year, Doby and the Indians won the World Series over a team that would, in not many years, move to Milwaukee.

Never given to collecting baseball cards, he did purchase several packets of bubble gum to obtain a card for Number 14. He studied Doby's statistics from the Negro Leagues where he had played for the Newark Eagles before and after military service.

I found it implausible that my Pop liked baseball at any time. Thing of it is, he told me he never even went to County Stadium when the Braves moved to Milwaukee, or when the old Seattle Pilots became the Brewers. Curiously, I knew he read novels about baseball, once writing an essay about them. By far, he told me, his favorite was The Universal Baseball Association, J. Henry Waugh, Esq., Proprietor, *by Robert Coover. Similar to fantasy players of today, the reclusive protagonist created his own eight-team league along with athletes, maintaining statistics. Games were played by the roll of dice. Waugh gradually lost his ability to differentiate his game from reality. My Pop's bookshelves also contained Philip Roth's* The Great American Novel *and* The Natural, *by Bernard Malamud. Maybe I'll read one of them someday. I apologize for this irrelevant digression.*

Because it played better on radio, Garson developed a pronounced interest in football, particularly Notre Dame Football, likely after he saw Pat O'Brien's movie portrayal in "Knute Rockne, All American." He had a clear recollection of being glued to the kitchen radio when the Irish played Southern Methodist, cheering for the Catholics, then coached by Frank Leahy. He also tuned in each August to the College All-Stars game, pitting collegians against the professional champions at Soldier Field. The All-Stars usually lost, but in 1946 and 1947, the squads shut out the Rams and Bears in successive years. The Green Bay Packers were in one of the team's sorry eclipses in this era.

More, Garson and others preferred football because the sport's rough and tumble seemed manly. The Northside Tigers was an impromptu aggregation who played teams from Granville and other areas a few times each fall, using Custer High's neighborhood practice field. Garson often watched the school players prepare for games, envious of their red and white helmets, imposing shoulder pads and cleated high top shoes that clacked on sidewalks as they ambled to practice.

In fact, Garson whined for weeks, begging his mother to purchase him a pair of football shoes. She was reluctant, even after he promised he would try out for the school team when he reached high school. Proudly, he laced up the black high top shoes, and carefully walked on the grass to the field so as not to wear away the hard rubber cleats. He had purchased a two-tone football helmet, and inked "N. SIDE TIGERS" across the front.

Because of his short, underdeveloped stature and unpronounced skills, Garson was invariably the last to be called into a game. On kickoffs and punts, when he was allowed to play, he often muffed catches to the groan of teammates; but if the ball did not bounce from his bony chest, his fleet illusiveness produced long gains and occasional touchdowns. Once, he was waved into a defensive huddle, positioning himself behind the line. When ball was snapped, he knifed through a gap in blockers and tackled the runner, a sturdy boy from Granville, for a huge loss. He smiled at the memory of being roundly cheered by teammates.

One post-war change in Garson's life had major ramifications for him and his parents, causing far-reaching household financial stress. The residual effects churned for decades after.

At the time, Milwaukee boosters prided themselves in calling their city the "Machine Shop of the World." The community's manufacturers, foundries, and fabricators fairly hummed for four years during the war. Some expected peace time production to slow as it had in many metropolitan areas. But such was not the case. The transition to a normal economy barely missed a payroll. A. O. Smith quickly shifted from munitions to producing auto frames. Allen-Bradley, Falk, Allis-Chalmers and others likewise rapidly re-geared.

His father, as far as can be determined, left his job as a welder within a year or so after war's end. Despite good paychecks from Krasonya, he told his son that years under the helmet with sparks flying in cramped quarters caused physical problems, exacerbating a predisposition for arthritis. Until he knew better, he thought his father was rationalizing. About the same time, Hervé suggested an alternative for his brother that would be far less physically taxing.

In Chicago, Hervé had taken up a new enterprise, producing and selling popcorn to retailers. For a small investment, Hervé proposed, his brother would receive a franchise encompassing Milwaukee and portions of southeast Wisconsin. Garson's mother was reticent, ever suspicious of her brother-in-law, a man who, after all, had assumed her husband's give name and used it for financial gain. But Garson's father was convinced such a dramatic change would benefit the family.

Thus, he turned his back on factory work, cashed in several thousand dollars in war bonds that had accumulated during the good war economy and became an entrepreneur. His father purchased equipment and heavy bags of raw corn grown by Iowa monks, he claimed. Garson and his mother spent Saturday's producing popcorn and filling large bags the size of pillows. At first, Garson found it exciting as the kernels, oil and salt churned in the hot kettle, and burst forth as plump, pale yellow popcorn. He liked the smell and taste of the fresh snack, and was proud to tell his friends about the new family venture.

By fits and starts, Garson's father convinced retail establishments – taverns, bowling alleys, arcades — to install dispensing machines and purchase popcorn. Each week, he made his rounds, delivering the product. The business adopted the name Hervé had selected in Chicago – ABC, "A Better Corn." He called his snack "French Fried Popcorn."

To house the business, his father rented a small commercial building. On the southern approach to the long Sixth Street viaduct spanning the Menomonee River Valley to downtown, the cramped storefront was situated amid a block of dingy brick residences. As Garson explored the immediate neighborhood, he met a few of the dark-faced children with accents, Mexicans, and was captivated by two giggling sisters with bright smiles and shiny hair; he thought they liked him, a new boy from the other side of town.

More, Garson soon located the area's movie theaters, walking a block south on Saturday afternoon to attend matinees at the World Theater, an unassuming third-run house near National Avenue. He also had a dim recollection of taking the Number 17 streetcar west to the National Theater, an old house seating more than a thousand whose lobby dazzled with faux marble columns, ceiling frescoes, and a grand staircase to the balcony. However, he ignored the hints of shabbiness.

But after little more than a year, his father decided more space was necessary for an expanding business, and he purchased a story-and-a-half commercial property on Galena Street, a former grocery store of discolored Cream City brick with enormous front windows. Garson soon discovered this older area of the city dating from the century's turn lacked the freshness and space of his own neighborhood. Weathered multi-family houses were tightly packed together with postage stamp yards. The entire area was gritty and noisy with traffic, 20th Street serving as a major north-south arterial. Even foliage was different from his block, old trees looking less robust and greenery trampled and under stress. Instead of wooden pickets marking yards, stark chain link fences divided property lots, trapping wind-blown debris.

Across the street stood an unmatched pair of long and narrow, frame buildings, gray paint flaking. One housed the popular "Stop & Go," the local watering hole, as Garson's father had it, a working man's gathering spot that made no pretension as a bar or tap. It proudly proclaimed itself as a saloon. Its tongue and groove ceiling rose 20-feet above the linoleum floor. Even when it was swept, mopped and cleaned, the imbedded odor of tobacco smoke and stale beer assaulted him.

Its bar was long, spanning 15 yards or more with a collection of mismatched stools. From a perch, Garson studied bottles of rum, rock and rye and other whiskeys, brandy, gin, vodka that shared the back bar with gallon jugs of pickled eggs and pigs' feet, jars of beef jerky and tiny sausages along with typical snacks. Schlitz and Gettelman were the featured local brews. A dime bought a six-ounce shorty glass.

In the open space stood a snooker pool game and a dozen Formica tables and chairs, the latter for nightly chicken dinners and Friday fish fries. Décor consisted exclusively of lighted beer signs. Despite not serving what many considered an effete brand, Miller, the image of the brewery's girl seated on a quarter moon hung above the cash register. At any hour, the Stop & Go hosted ten or a dozen habitués, old retirees or late shift workers during the day, and regular laborers afternoon and evenings.

Above the tavern's high ceiling were a half dozen apartments, reached by a narrow, dark stairway. Flanking that building stood what looked to Garson like an actual tenement house, a narrow gangway separating it from its neighbor. If Charles Dickens had seen the building, he might have described it as "grotesquely out of the perpendicular [with] a feverish bewilderment of windows." This structure contained perhaps a dozen or more rental units; like its neighbor, it appeared tired and worn down. Peeling planter boxes were usually devoid of color or greenery, and wash lines spanned the buildings. To Garson, it seemed a virtual human warren, evoking scenes of movie tenements in "Dead End," "A Tree Grows in Brooklyn" and "I Remember Mama."

"We saved so hard for that money," his mother objected. To a boy of 11, resignation was evident in her tone. She knew her objection to cashing in the remainder of their war bonds would be overruled. But there was something more ominous: In addition to yielding the savings, she had to consent to a mortgage on their house, once fully paid off – an event that in not many years led to family financial catastrophe.

For Garson's part, the Galena Street neighborhood was populated by rough and tumble kids, quite unlike his pals and neighbors on his own block. Like those movie Dead End Kids, many of the boys appeared scruffy and frayed, collarless shirts often stretched so far that they drooped over a shoulder. Hand-me-down pants were belted tightly, waists looked like puckered paper bags. Some wore black sneakers, others scuffed shoes with no socks. "Ragamuffins," declared his mother.

One family in particular typified the blue collar milieu. The parents claimed to be Slovenes. Most of boys reminded Garson of his Uncle Essig's brood – sturdy, hard eyed and daring. The Fuchs family numbered six or seven as far as Garson knew; he had seen the oldest boy boil over in anger when anyone called him Neil Fucks. Garson was scrupulous in using the preferred pronunciation, "Foochs." Neil, after all, was a defensive lineman for the St. Michael grade school team. If truth be told, however, none of the Galena Street denizens were any worse than the North Milwaukee crowd, Garson concluded, given to no more than petty mischief and misdeed.

"That brew's got a little caramel in it," his Uncle Vin once joked when he saw the youngsters; Garson was uncertain of that metaphor, but years later concluded his uncle's snide comment had something to do with the inconsistent skin coloration and dishwater hair streaked with darker hues evident among neighborhood kids.

With unaccustomed bravado, Garson assumed a new mien among this crowd, introducing himself as "Blackie," taking the daring name from the radio detective, Boston Blackie; Garson thought a new name and identity were more suitable in the gritty milieu and his place in it. He invented a personal history, too, describing to new acquaintances his many wondrous possessions, including a Gilbert Chemistry set and a large HO train layout. Most prized, of course, was his grandfather's sword with its long engraved blade and elaborate basket hilt like the ones wielded by Errol Flynn in "The Sea Hawk" and "Captain Blood." Garson also talked about exploits with the North Side Tigers football team, and other more fanciful adventures.

To give himself a harder edge and prevent Fuchs and others from thinking him a softie like the prissy rich kid in the picture "Dead End" who was set upon by hoodlums, Garson fabricated a few stories, including one that had elements of truth.

"Me and the gang was walking down our alley one night, throwing rocks into neighbors' backyards just for the fun of it. I picked up a big stone, and shot-putted it. Something smashed in the dark. It was Bauman's bird bath." Garson tried to affect a streetwise banter.

"'Scatter!' somebody yelled, and we all hot footed it outta there. Next day after school, old lady Bauman comes over and says to my old man that he had'a pay 'cause her bird bath was busted. Somebody must'a ratted on me — which I thought ain't fair. It cost twenty bucks. My old man gave me a real whippin', I can tell ya, and took the money from my bank." Garson hoped such affected tales would burnish his reputation, give him cache to match the new *nom de guerre* on Galena Street.

Truth be told, Garson felt himself superior to these Galena kids; for certain, he lived in a much nicer house and cleaner neighborhood. He believed himself to be smarter, too, despite some recent failures at Holy Redeemer school. More, he had a sense of relief, gratitude almost, that he did not live in a neighborhood with such shabby tightly-packed flats, noisy traffic and withered greenery. But when his mother discovered the name kids and adults called her son, she protested vehemently.

"Blackie! Where'd that come from?" she asked one woman.

"He told us!"

When Garson's mother enunciated his true given name, everyone was taken aback. Despite that setback, the neighborhood kids accepted Garson, rarely treating him as anyone other than one of the crowd. He once got into a scuffle with a boy that grew from friendly chamfering to serious fisticuffs. Garson was winning the contest when an older brother intervened, knocking Garson to the ground. He arose, dusting off his trousers and glaring at the antagonists. To his surprise, hands were extended in friendship, and nothing more was heard of the altercation. These were good kids, he concluded.

He spent several summers and many weekends in that neighborhood. While his mother worked at her cleaning jobs, his father was responsible for his care. As a result, there was even less supervision and more freedom in the new neighborhood. Street savvy was more daring than in his neighborhood, and Garson's education into the lore of the alley expanded quickly. Girls really had seven holes? Much to his mother's chagrin, even his vocabulary took on a sharper edge.

"Futzing around" was what Garson told his mother when she asked what he had done during a day on Galena Street. She was taken aback by his response.

On the tenement's second floor lived a family with one daughter, to Garson's eye, an utterly golden girl in a gray neighborhood. Long after the Marine Corps, he was reminded of this girl when he saw Betsy, Cybil Shepherd, appear for the first time in the movie, "Taxi Driver." Glowing in her white dress, she strolled in that drab and gritty cityscape, utterly transfixing Travis Bickel, Robert DeNiro. Garson had to know this girl, and he thought of means to impress her. When writing of her at far remove, he chose the name Roxy, hoping it might connote what he remembered of her. He thought the curled tresses that hung about her shoulders were the color of summer sunshine. Like Lana, Roxy's mother cosseted her daughter, attiring her in fluffy dresses and patent leather shoes.

At first, she exhibited interest in Garson, the new boy in the neighborhood. He always tried to get close to her, and once she did not object when he sat next to her during a matinee at the Colonial Theater. But she avoided him thereafter for reasons he never discerned. And as time passed, and his stock of yarns became depleted, she grew aloof — like the girl at Holy Redeemer who wore the faux leopard coat and muff.

One of the boys who befriended Garson was Leland. His real family name ended in "icz" or "wiak" or something similar, claiming his parents were Slovenes. His voice was croaky, reminding him of radio's Froggy the Gremlin. Shorter by an inch or so and loose-limbed – his sisters declared him double jointed — Leland occasionally unnerved Garson when he exhibited a gloomy gaze. Each summer, the boy's sandy hair was trimmed in what was called a "Butch" that looked like a broom full of stiff bristles.

"Don't like, don't like, my hair like this," he said, rubbing an open palm over his dad's handiwork. Along with his peculiar voice, Leland had a habit of repeating phrases.

"That's a great, a great picture." An avid movie fan who possessed a storehouse of information, he became Garson's closest pal in the Galena neighborhood.

There were now new movie theaters to explore on what was known as the west side, a once prosperous neighborhood established by German immigrants a half century before; their offspring had moved to more prosperous environs, leaving the area to newcomers from farther east, among them somewhat disreputable Bohemians, Croats and Slovenes that his mother disliked.

The Colonial movie house on Vliet was large, the size of the National; its exterior and handsome interior appointments made the 20-year-old theater inviting. While it featured a balcony, that section was closed during matinees to prevent kids from throwing popcorn and other items on main floor audiences. A dozen blocks west on Vliet sat the smaller Liberty Theater with its recently modernized marquee; it staged Saturday amateur variety shows along with movies. It was the unassuming Violet Theater a short distance away where Garson had several hair-raising experiences. "The Beast with Five Fingers" with Peter Lorre, even viewed in that cramped and uncomfortable environment, frightened him into bad dreams.

Like many independents, the owner retained hundreds of canisters of old titles, even some silents that rolled for uncritical Saturday audiences. The threadbare theater only operated on weekends, screening scratched movie prints with jarring jump cuts and erratic sound. Seats were hard and uncomfortable. Someone told Garson he had seen rats in that vest pocket theater, munching on discarded snacks. Admission was only a dime, but the nickel popcorn was invariably chewy. It was the perfect gloomy venue for the re-releases and sequels of Frankenstein, Wolfman and Dracula pictures.

It was at the Violet that Garson belatedly fell in love with Jean Harlow through the scratched and badly mended copy of "A Dinner at Eight." He loved Kitty Packard's nimbus of platinum hair, penciled eyebrows and candied lips; she seemed to jiggle when she strolled in those sparkling, form-fitting gowns.

"See," Garson's new pal, Leland, leaned over and whispered "she don't wear no brassiere, no brassiere. Betcha she don't wear underpants neither." The Legion of Decency frowned on such things, Garson was certain. And there were more situations and suggestive dialogue that Garson was beginning to understand. Leland had seen the movie before, and he knew about the final scene as Kitty and Carlotta walked arm-in-arm toward the dining room.

"I was reading a book the other day," Kitty declared.

Carlotta, the dowager actress Marie Dressler, lurched at the statement, turning in disbelief that such a woman might actually read.

"Reading a book?"

"Yes," replied Kitty in her high voice, "it was about civilization or something. A nutty kind of a book. Do you know the guy said that machinery is going to take the place of *every* profession?"

"Oh, my dear," Carlotta responded, eyeing Kitty's body from top to bottom. "That's something you need *never* worry about."

The Catholic Church's censorious Legion was critical of every Harlow movie, it seemed, especially such pictures as "Red Dust" with Clark Gable in which she bathed naked in a barrel, nearly revealing her breasts. Once a year during Sunday mass, the congregation rose to take the Legion's annual pledge: "I condemn all indecent and immoral motion pictures, and those who glorify crime and criminals." Further, everyone vowed to protest the production of such movies, and promised to stay away from those films and the theaters that screened them. To view a condemned movie meant committing a mortal sin; a venal sin resulted from seeing one that was morally objectionable in part.

"The Sign of the Cross" was another of the condemned movies despite the fact that it featured Christian martyrdom in Rome's Coliseum. Such a movie would never be played at the Ritz, Garson concluded after seeing it with Leland at the Violet. Typically, it was another of those poorly mended prints from the early 1930s, with jump cuts and flashing cue marks. By now, Leland did not need to point out that Claudette Colbert who played Cleopatra wore nothing under the revealing lamé gown or bathed naked in a pool of milk.

"Look there" Leland pointed to the screen when Christians were torn apart by lions. "The women are naked — naked!" Garson missed some of details, but Leland agreed to stay for part of another showing so they could concentrate on the fleeting background shots of unadorned bodies. Even though the background figures were tiny with as much suggestion as actual depiction, this was Garson's first view of nudity. It was exciting.

In those post-war years, another movie, a *cause celebre,* was held out of Milwaukee for a time. It was Howard Hughes's infamous Western, "The Outlaw," the story of Billy the Kid and the man who killed him. However, it mattered only a bit that the female lead was buxom, raven-haired Jane Russell, and that some suggestive scenes earned a condemnation.

"They say, they say, you can see her bazooms real good," Leland related. It was Russell's first starring role, it was said. Garson was uncertain of the source for another rumor, the most compelling one, for seeing the movie.

"They say 'damn' over and over, over and over." That hearsay piqued the interest of most boys, even more than reputed racy depictions and suggestions. There was not a second thought given to the Legion of Decency's condemnation. Small, neighborhood theaters would not tempt the ire of the Catholic Church in scheduling the movie. Despite that, Garson and his friends knew details long before its appearance in Milwaukee.

In "Gone With the Wind," the daring curse had been uttered only once – to the gasps of many audiences. "The Outlaw" promised something more. Finally, the Esquire Theater on Wisconsin Avenue announced the scandalous movie would be shown, defying the Milwaukee archdiocese

"What a gyp!" was all Garson could say as the pals exited the theater one Saturday. Garson and Leland had boarded the Walnut Street bus to the Number 12 streetcar line, and rumbled downtown expectantly. The Esquire's façade had recently been refurbished, and its marquee removed; its interior was utilitarian. Having seen hundreds of movies, Garson thought himself sophisticated about them. He had unknowingly absorbed the medium's semiotics, as later critics would call them, of film making, and was beginning to see how editing worked, how miniatures were used and the way movie music raised emotions. From the start of "The Outlaw," both boys were put off by the actor who portrayed Billy the Kid.

"He's too pretty, too pretty to be an outlaw," Leland whispered when Jack Beutel made his first appearance; Billy was usually depicted as a Western criminal of unkempt mien. It was also readily apparent even to these boys that his acting abilities were limited.

"Nobody can do that — shoot a hole to make a whistle, a whistle," Leland whispered after Billy's incredible six-gun feat. What was more, the dialogue was unconvincing, as if the actors were not giving their best performances. There was also the predictable whooping Indian chase with white men playing Apaches, of course. Garson was titillated by the suggestive sequences involving Rio McDonald, dark-eyed Russell. Yes, her bodice did almost burst to overflowing several times, and the heavy-eyed, wet lipped close-ups and blackouts said a lot. Most disappointing, however, the word "damn" was not uttered even once. Not one time! Garson wanted to know who started the rumor about the profuse use of that word in the movie. Yes, it was a gyp.

Together, Garson and Leland sat through hundreds of hours of movies in west side theaters. They shared their views, generally agreeing on what they enjoyed. They studied how Hollywood constructed scenes, the way real action was projected against pre-filmed backgrounds, how miniatures and stop-motion were employed, and how everything was stitched together. They shared evaluations about actors, which ones, like Wayne, Mitchum and others usually played themselves while such actors as Tyrone Power and Richard Widmark could modulate performances.

While he idled long hours near his father's business, Garson continued to attend Holy Redeemer School. Milwaukee's Catholic grade schools educated students through the ninth grade with diocesan high schools beginning in the sophomore year.

"When I was in school, I walked over a mile in rain and wind, snow and cold." That bromide from parents and other adults was heard by almost every child. Fact was that Garson walked a mile and a quarter to his school on many days; but when the weather became too severe, his mother gave him bus fare.

As later grades passed, Garson's scholastic achievements waned. For years, his mother boasted that her son had wonderful powers of concentration; he was able to complete homework while listening to radio.

"He's smart," each year's teacher agreed with Garson's mother. "He just doesn't apply himself." In middle grades, report card grades slipped to a point that there was a danger he might be held back. Yet, Garson excelled in some subjects, those he liked – U. S. history and literature; his grades in German were always good because of his childhood familiarity with the language. On the other hand, Bible study and church doctrine held little interest for him. He struggled with Latin.

"Know how to conjugate 'to spit'?" a school yard wag asked after a Latin class. Heads shook.

"Spuo. Sparé. Act-too-ay-splatus!"

One thing Garson craved was to be a mass server. He envied the altar boys every Sunday, traipsing and genuflecting in their black cassocks and white chasubles, ringing bells, swinging censers, carrying tall crucifixes and mouthing Latin responses to the priest. Altar boys served as interlocutors for the congregation, said Sister Cletus, the older nun who trained the new servers.

It was perhaps in fifth grade that recruiting for replacements to graduating ninth graders took place. Garson's mother was excited about the prospect. While she had never mentioned a desire to see her son, like one nephew, enter the priesthood, she was pleased that he would be on the altar during Sunday masses. Garson was required to remain after school two days each week to study the handbook with all its Latin responses; each Friday candidates were tested. He quickly memorized the *Kyries* and early mass phrases. But then in the third week of instruction, he encountered the daunting "*Confetior*," the prayer of penance, and struggled for several days to master it.

"*Confiteor Deo, omnipotenti et nobis, fraters, quia peccavi nimis cognitationeco, verbo, opera, et omissióne: meu culpa, meu culpa, meu maxima culpa. Ideo precor...*" Here he invariably stammered, his power of memorization played out.

"Once more," Sister Cletus ordered. She was tall and serious; her eyebrows were thick behind frameless glasses.

Garson began again, but could not make the breakthrough to "*Mariam simper Virginem.*" Sister Cletus's impatience was evident in the way she held her body. She had him skip the "*Confiteor*" and memorize later responses. He accomplished these not with ease, but acceptably. It was simply the menacing *Confetior*," the eternal blockade, his *bete noir*, that frustrated both student and instructor. At the end of only the fourth week, the nun sent him home with a note, asking for a meeting with his mother who joined her son in the school office on Saturday.

"I'm afraid your son can't be a mass server." His mother's mouth opened and did not close. Her eyes formed the question.

"Well, he simply can't remember all the responses." She paused, tenting her hands before her face. "I think he tried, but he just can't." Garson could see his mother's thoughts. She had long anticipated seeing her son up there, in front of all the parishioners each Sunday; she had told relatives and friends about anticipating that day. But now, hopes were dashed. Her son had failed her. She never expressed criticism and opprobrium, but this was a bitter disappointment, and Garson could see it in her face.

For Garson, the Roman Catholic faith was not a matter of true belief, he seemed to think in retrospect, but one only of habit and ritual. It was something that he had always done, something his mother insisted upon. His father seemed less devoted to it. He knew from deed and word that his parents bore strong moral and ethical senses. They believed in giving an honest day's work, contributed to the church as much for appeals to charity as for maintenance of the institution. By action, they were fair in their dealings with anyone and considerate of neighbors.

"When you shovel snow," his mother instructed her son, "always clear a few feet over your property line." She even did this for Mrs. Hexe next door despite lack of reciprocation. Garson's mother never cheated or stole. Some employers may have tested her, leaving money and valuables lying about; she was never found wonting. Moreover, she upbraided him for the few minor thefts he admitted, and admonished him when some inadvertent blasphemy or curse word slipped from his mouth.

"Don't say 'Damn.' Say 'Darn' instead," Garson recalled her advising him. One of her worst epithets was "gawl darn." She detested her husband's angry outburst of "Jesus Christ!" She advised saying "Jeepers Creepers" instead, and suggested other euphemisms for swear words. Garson found amusement in the W. C. Fields expletive, "Godfrey Daniel!"

Daily mass was mandatory during the school year; Garson and his parents also attended every Sunday and holy days. He detested interminable Sunday high masses. He practiced meatless Fridays, but sometimes clandestinely ate candy and sweets during Lent. For weeks the approach of Good Friday caused him much ill ease. His mother demanded attendance at *Tre Ore* services, the dreaded Stations of the Cross, three hours of endless prayers and reflection on the suffering and death of Jesus. The 14 events of His agony and crucifixion were depicted in small niches along the church walls. Altar icons and statutes of saints were ominously shrouded in black until the Easter Sunday service when the altar blossomed with lilies and bright flowers.

The celebrated 41st Street religious war started innocently. Several boys and girls sat on a porch one summer evening; it may have been at Veronica's house. She was one of the new girls, her parents having moved on the block after the war; older and a head taller than Garson, she had hit him in the cheek with a split pea fired from a blow gun during some fracas; a welt was raised. He was since wary of her.

The ramble of topics included Garson's dislike for the "Katzenjammer Kids," and Ernie Bushmiller cartoon "Nancy and Sluggo."

"You like Schmoos?" Garson had not warmed to the curious cartoon creatures introduced into Al Capp's "L'il Abner" daily newspaper strip. Shaped like a baked ham with trusting eyes and scraggly mustaches, the critters reproduced quicker than rabbits, adored humans, laid eggs and gave milk and happily died to provide sustenance to owners. Some adults claimed the cartoon satirized the ominous promises of Rooseveltian liberalism.

The front porch gathering also talked about movies, and which "Lassie" picture everyone liked, and which was better – "My Friend Flicka" or its sequel, "Thunderhead." Garson thought the best of those animal movies was "The Yearling;" he recalled his sadness at the death of Fodderwing, the crippled kid who had a way with critters, and when Jody shot "Flag," his beloved pet deer. The episode echoed his unease caused by his treatment of the turtle.

"I liked Tin Man best," Garson opined, referring to "The Wizard of Oz," a movie recently re-released in Milwaukee. Someone's head nodded in agreement, while others mentioned Dorothy, Scarecrow and even the flying monkeys. Then, for reasons Garson did not recall, the conversation took convulsive detour.

"Do you know there're secret tunnels where priests and nuns live," Veronica declared. "Priests sneak through them every night, and sleep with the nuns." Aghast, Garson asked where that information had come from.

"For me to know and you to find out."

"Ain't so," Garson retorted.

"How'd you know?" Her face tightened and she glared at Garson.

"'Cause I know."

"You watch the convent all night?"

"Course not."

"The nuns have babies, too, and the bishops kill 'em and bury 'em in the basement," Veronica continued. Garson was incredulous.

"That's some stupid Lutheran crap."

"Naw-huh. The Catholics're stupid."

"Dumb Lutherans," another of the kids chimed in, reinforcing Garson. Castigations and aspersions escalated, epithets bounced about the group. Garson and two or three others stood up and backed from the porch.

"Mackeral snappers!" Veronica scowled. The crowd slowly separated into contending factions, sidling into the street. Antagonists stood ten yards apart, shouting epithets, hurling charges at one another, each more outlandish than the other. Voices rose and tempers flared.

"Martin Luther was a dope."

"Oh, yeah! The pope's a baby killer." For 15 minutes, the feud continued. Fists were raised, fingers jabbed like rapiers and faces contorted in rage. Suddenly, a neighbor burst from her front door. She was followed by a woman across the street.

"Stop this right now!" the first woman demanded. She glowered at one group and then the other. Her ally pushed two or three of the contestants. "Go home! All of you!" demanded the second neighbor. "Go home right now!"

Sheepishly, Garson and the others turned and, heads bowed, shuffled apart. When Garson's mother heard about the incident, she was mortified. She asked if he had instigated the confrontation, but he wagged his head. He simply could not remember how it all started.

"I don't want to hear about such nonsense ever again," she chided Garson. "You better go to confession. You hear me?" In a day or two, the fracas was forgotten, and Catholic and Protestant alike gamboled in games and adventures.

Garson thought it was later that summer that a large, striped carnival tent was erected on a table of land above busy Silver Spring Drive, an east-west arterial. "Revival Meeting Tonight," proclaimed a billboard. For reasons he could never discern, he was attracted to the gathering and determined to investigate. That night after supper, from across the highway he watched people file inside the canvas — men in Sunday shirts and slacks, women wearing dresses and neat little bonnets but only a few children. Strings of bare light bulbs illuminated rows of folding chairs, and strains of organ music wafted on the evening air. He timorously entered with a small crowd. Two people in long robes holding Bibles smiled broadly as they greeted people. The smiling woman patted Garson's head. Bare bulbs swayed in the evening breeze. On stage, a man coaxed hymns from a portable organ. Garson sat down in the middle of one row, and waited until what he thought was a minister drew himself up behind the podium.

"Brothers and sisters, welcome," announced the balding man from the dais. "I'm Brother Trooper, and this is Sister Faith," he continued nodding to his companion.

"We came all the way from Ohio. Stopped in dozens of cities and towns to bring the word of the Lord, to bring souls back to Jesus."

"Praise the Lord," the audience responded. Garson noticed two other children in the crowd, but he was the only one without parents. His concentration strayed many times during the service as he shifted his gaze from the swaying lights to the generally rapt faces of those seated near him. Uncomfortable, he dangled his feet. The preacher's words grew louder, and his gestures became more dramatic. He paced back and forth across the stage, sometimes glowering at the audience, waving his thick Bible aloft. He described the fires of Hell that awaited those who were dishonest and stole, those who drank to excess and those who fornicated, whatever that was. White spittle foamed at the corners of his mouth, and he occasionally sprayed when his voice rose.

"To be saved, you must accept Him as your personal savior."

"Amens" and "Hallelujahs" rained. Garson wanted to leave the tent. Time passed glacially. Finally, at the close of service, the woman, Sister Faith, shuffled down the aisle with a collection plate and colored sheets of paper announcing tomorrow's service. He took one then asked for another – for his mom and dad. The woman complied, likely hoping the boy would bring his parents the next night. Garson thought no such thing; he knew his mother's loyalty to Catholicism.

Garson wanted to return the next evening to get more of those papers, but did not want to sit through more preaching. At about nine o'clock, he returned to the tent. It was darkened now, the entryway flaps tied shut. For a time, he had been fascinated with collecting things of this sort, like those cash register receipts when his father worked at the Wadhams station. He just wanted the colored sheets. He crawled under the tent's edge and entered the gloomy enclosure, wary that someone might discover him. Streetlights provided some illumination through the canvas, and he tiptoed carefully to the stage. Inside the lectern, he found stacks of the colored sheets – one side filled with dates, announcements, and Bible citations with the verso blank. They were all neatly stacked and aligned. A little chill washed over him when he grabbed several sheaves from each stack, perhaps 30 in all. Then he peered out from where he had entered, and crept away down the slope.

Back home, Garson counted the sheets, and stored them in a box under his bed. He smiled, hoping to use the purloined paper for drawings or writing music, or just to have them. In time, he used one or two sheets, hoarding the supply lest it be exhausted too soon. He gave thought to returning to the tent to secure more, but a wedge of guilt nagged him. Before he could shake the feeling, the revival ended and the tent was gone. He never confessed the theft.

"Where'd you get this junk?" his mother demanded weeks later while she cleaned his room. Garson hunched his shoulders, and she did not pursue the matter. She later added the stack of purloined papers to newspapers for the school scrap drive.

"Nocturnal emissions." That was what Father Kelly called them during religious instructions in one upper grade. Garson shuffled nervously behind his desk. The priest exhibited no noticeable change in tone or expression while addressing the boys about such a sensitive subject. It was part of a class that was segregated by gender, girls likely listening to similar instructions about their changing bodies and urges, Garson guessed.

From somewhere in the back row, the term nocturnal emissions caused a snicker followed by a deep-voiced guffaw. It was that brazen athlete, Garson saw. Father Kelly lifted his chin and glared, and his spectacle lenses reflected sunlight streaming into the classroom window, creating a fleeting image of some alien creature, Garson thought. Another boy coughed before silence returned.

About the time of such lessons, a new girl began attending Holy Redeemer. She had come from a public school, it was said. She was blonde, of course, and tall – and the only girl in the entire school, it seemed to Garson, who had breasts – generous protrusions that stretched the fabric of sweaters she invariably wore. Not one of the other girls bore any hint of budding. He felt uncomfortable staring at her chest, but almost all the boys ogled, sometimes slack mouthed. On the playground after lunch, knots of boys positioned themselves proximate to her. She noticed the attention, Garson thought, and seemed to enjoy it even while the other girls did not.

Not surprisingly, her name was the same as that of a salacious little ditty common among older boys at the time: "Charlotte, the harlot, the girl we adore," went the lyric, "the pride of the prairie, the cowpunchers' whore." She insisted on being called Cherry.

"She does it, you know," whispered one of the older boys the spring after Cherry came to Holy Redeemer – "*IT!*"

"Dyes her hair, too." Near the end of the term, rumors such as those circulated. They were probably correct about her hair, but Garson refused to believe the other matter. For Cherry exhibited an uncommon intelligence and courtesy in class, and the nuns seemed to like her. Her hand was invariably among the first raised when a question was posed. Taller than Garson, she hardly knew he existed and paid him scant attention. Yet he admired her from afar, refusing to believe what they said about her. Several times, he saw her apply ruby lipstick after she left school at day's end; the nuns did not permit cosmetics in the classroom.

He found her resemblance to the buxom young actress Janet Leigh almost unsettling. He could see Cherry as Aline de Gavrillac opposite Stewart Granger in "Scaramouche." The good sisters often admonished students to "avoid the occasion of sin." It was sometimes difficult to do. Garson once awoke halfway through the night, pajama bottoms slightly damp, certain his dream had featured her; he was sad at his inability to summon the dream's details, but concluded that he had one of those emissions.

In these years, Garson began his first job, a summer one, as a caddy at Brynwood Country Club far north of the city, exclusive for Jews. He was paid 75-cents to carry a single bag for 18-holes, two bags for $1.50; generally there was a 25-cent tip. Caddying was one of his favorite early jobs though carrying two bags on his bony shoulders caused soreness. He especially liked the women golfers in their shorts or tiny skirts; they always smiled and tipped well no matter their scores, more generous than the boisterous men.

When Garson turned 12, he purchased a *Milwaukee Journal* newspaper route. Papers were picked up at a small tin structure some blocks south of his house. His route had about 50 customers, and he picked up newspapers after school each day, usually with his battered bike. Sundays were a different matter. He arrived at C-11 at four in the morning, pulling his undependable wagon. If his father was available, he drove to the station and along the delivery route. It took 45 minutes or an hour. When his father accompanied him, they would often drive to the Spudnuts shop on Green Bay Avenue after delivering; the aroma of fresh donuts and coffee were invigorating. Father and son shared laughs.

The memory of one arduous Sunday remained for years, of the time when his father was out of town on business. Coincidentally, Toby and his parents were on vacation, and Garson agreed to deliver his pal's newspapers. While it meant extra money that week, he could not have anticipated the grueling work load. His wagon was broken, so he needed to literally manhandle the heavy papers, leapfrogging the four bags almost a half mile to deliver his own route before then returning to the station for Toby's papers.

Normally, Garson prided himself on finishing deliveries before six in the morning, conscientious so customers could read the news at breakfast and hopeful for weekly tips. But with the double route and no vehicle, he slumped into his bed, sore of foot and shoulder, after nine. No matter that he made $15 or $20 extra that week.

The C-11 station manager was a man who amazed Garson and carriers with the rapidity with which he counted currency. Using a rubber finger, he riffled through bills like a machine, talked as rapidly as he counted.

"He's a Jew, you know," one carrier whispered. Indeed, the manager had a knob-like nose, thick lips and dusky skin tone. Garson was certain he did not live in the expensive west side enclave where his mother cleaned, however.

The station captain was Mellish, the kid in kindergarten whose incessant fidgeting caused his image to blur in the class photo. Now tall and handsome with pomaded brown hair piled atop his head, he was in charge of the station and responsible for handing out newspapers to the carriers as well as assembling the bulky Sunday edition whose feature sections were delivered during the week. Garson would develop a close friendship with Mellish, another of those story tellers of youth to whom he was attracted.

While Mellish was now more in control of his energies, he still displayed small nervous quirks. Tapping his fingernails on his upper teeth and working his mouth as a kind of resonator, he created amazing tunes. Garson thought he could be a featured player with loony Spike Jones and his City Slickers.

There was another boy, considerably younger, with who Garson had a fleeting friendship. The toe-headed, somewhat obsequious boy would become the most famous person Garson ever knew. He was attracted when he delivered papers to the boy's house, a prim, white Cape Cod, from which emanated strains of piano music. He saw the boy in his yard only rarely.

Unlike his own pals, the boy still wore shorts in summer, and shirts with collars; his hair was always neatly combed. Garson could not pry from memory how the relationship was initiated, but he had a clear image of watching Ralphie in a sunny living room, playing a baby grand piano with such ease that it took Garson's breath away. Invited inside, he sat cross-legged on the gleaming hardwood floor, observing the tiny pianist whose fingers fairly flew across the keyboard. Garson listened to strains of what he later learned were compositions of Chopin, Strauss, Bach and others waft about that house. Ralphie seemed to spend most of his time practicing, Garson concluded, and had no pals. He sometimes appeared lonely to Garson.

The pianist's house was ever in perfect, immaculate order, an image from a home-making magazine, and his mother a model for a beauty magazine with coiffed curly hair, wearing pretty print dresses and lace-trimmed aprons set off with a pearl necklace. The house contained more books than Garson had seen outside of the public library. There were encyclopedias and tomes with fancy bindings often seen in movie libraries as well as shelves of "real" books not simply part of the décor.

"Ralphie," his mother said in a soft but firm voice, "tell your friend he must go home now. You need to concentrate on your music." Garson visited the diminutive musician occasionally over the course of time, always transfixed by such wonderful tunes produced by so small a boy. Coincidentally, Garson heard about a Toronto teenager named Glenn Gould, a piano prodigy who was thrilling audiences with his incredible performances. Garson wondered if his new acquaintance would reach such heights. Gould was only four years older than Garson.

Ralphie would go on to study at Julliard and become a world-renowned performer; Garson read about concerts and awards and accomplishments over the years. Then, decades after, they met as adults when Garson interviewed the fair-haired musician for a television station; Ralph had returned to Milwaukee to arrange a deferment from the Vietnam War draft. They shared a few pleasantries about days past.

Three years after the war, Frank Zeidler, whose brother had been elected to Milwaukee's highest office but died in the Navy, was elected the city's mayor. Dark, spectacled and bookish in contrast to his gregarious baritone brother, the younger Zeidler would be reelected to three four-year terms, continuing the city's Socialist tradition of solid public works and corruption free government. Garson's parents voted for him only once. To their son, they repeated an unsubstantiated rumor by political opponents that Zeidler had ordered signs erected in the Deep South, encouraging Negroes to come to Milwaukee for good jobs and housing.

Garson met and came to know Zeidler much later in life. He was in complete accord with an historian's assessment that Zeidler was "reflexively honest, personally forthright, and frequently at odds with the Common Council." He was a "self-taught intellectual," and considered public libraries the "universities of the streets." When Garson knew him after he left office, the mayor was considered a Milwaukee treasure, his knowledge of history and state politics prodigious. Garson would acknowledge the former mayor in one of his books.

Other events outside of Garson's home intruded upon his consciousness. Headlines were made by sweaty, glowering Joe McCarthy who ran for the United States Senate against a Wisconsin saint, "Fighting" Bob LaFollette. Garson was also conscious of the presidential campaign that year, the first in his life without Franklin D. Roosevelt on the ballot. Unprompted, the 12-year-old renewed an antipathy toward the Republican Dewey who four years before had the temerity to run against the president. Garson still found the candidate's narrow face, prissy mustache, scattered teeth and overbite repulsive. He also disliked the cocksure air the candidate projected in movie newsreels and in radio addresses, and the predictions that President Truman would certainly be defeated.

The Cold War, of course, was a topic on many lips. Delivering *The Milwaukee Journal,* Garson read headlines about the Berlin airlift. And the nuns at Holy Redeemer led discussions about the march of Soviet Communism. The gentle Hungarian cardinal, Jozsef Mindszenty had been imprisoned and tortured for resisting the invasion of his nation. At his teachers' urging, Garson purchased several comic books depicting the dire Hungarian situation – religious persecution and political oppression, starvation and worse

– and clandestinely left them on streetcars for the uninformed. Hungary, after all, was the country of his mother's birth.

Despite the peace, the world war continued on movie screens, and would for several more years. But there were new signs of conflict. Supported by muscular Communist China, the Korean peninsula was divided. Many predicted a war might result. Still, overshadowing everything was what Garson considered his growing maturity. He would soon be out of Holy Redeemer school. His mother insisted he not attend Custer High with most of his pals and associates, but Messmer, the Catholic school a long bus ride from home.

***

Chapter 7

SEMPER FI

"From the Halls of Montezuma to the shores of Tripoli...."

Garson's vocal chords were seized by the billowing acrid gas. His raspy voice would not permit him to utter more lyrics. He shuddered in a paroxysm of coughing and gagging. Around him milled the other recruits, all retching and weeping. As the whiteness thickened and enveloped him, Garson's gas mask slipped from his hands and fell onto the wooden floor. He slumped to his knees. Tears cascaded down his cheeks. Garson was blinded, all but paralyzed. And that was the point.

"A gas attack can be disastrous if you're not prepared for it," the instructor, a thick-necked buck sergeant, had intoned minutes before with words out of the *Guidebook for Marines*. It was one of the final Boot Camp exercises, a "hands-on" lesson about chemical warfare, teaching nascent Marines how to prepare for imperiling gases that might blanket battlefield or bivouac. The names sounded ominous — mustard, hydrocyanic acid, phosgene and other agents, blister gases that acted primarily on the eyes, skin and respiratory tract, choking agents, blood and nerve poisons, frightful vomiting compounds and, of course, tear gas with which Garson now had intimate contact.

"When the word 'GAS!' is heard, stop breathing immediately and don your masks," the Marine had said. Garson practiced holding his breath for 30 seconds, the time needed to retrieve the protective device from canvas carrying bag, thrust his chin inside, checking charcoal-filled canister and clearing the rubberized face piece. Scratched and blotched vintage film images depicted a simulated battlefield attack and response. Garson was unnerved, recalling newsreel footage at war's end, of horrific Nazi death camps, of Auschwitz gas chambers where Zyklon B cyanide killed tens of thousands — Jews, gypsies and other undesirables.

With masks in place, the platoon was herded into a windowless structure on stilts. They crowded together shoulder to shoulder, back to chest. Garson saw Prick's eyes, wide behind the plexiglas bubble, like a terrified insect with a large proboscis. His fear reinforced Garson's.

"Now, we'll drop a few pellets into the burner here so you can see what tear gas looks like in closed conditions. Then, when I give the command 'All clear,' you will remove your masks and sing the first two verses of the 'Marine Corps Hymn'."

Thick white smoke billowed immediately, and in seconds it puffed and swirled about the enclosure, a debilitating fog, Garson knew, filling every inch of space. Recruits milled and bumped into one another. Anxious minutes passed.

"All clear!" the instructor's words were muffled as he did not remove the protective mask. Reluctantly, Garson pulled the canvas and plastic device from his face, holding his breath as long as possible, hoping to avoid the inevitable.

He began singing the Marine Hymn, but his vocal chords were wrenched by gas. He swallowed, dragging drafts deeper into his rebelling lungs. He retched. The stench was putrid, of sulfur, rotten eggs and rancid butter. A swarm of bees seemed to sting his tongue and throat, fire ants bit his eyeballs. His nose dripped mucus, sputum drained from his mouth.

"Can't hear you!" the Marine shouted. No more than one or two voices were heard now. Time seemed to stop. Then, the large double doors to the outside burst open. Like cattle from a burning barn, the recruits nearest the doors stampeded into the sunlight. Regaining his feet, Garson only shuffled, virtually borne outside by the maddened herd. The wraith of smoke rapidly dissipated in the afternoon breeze. Many, Garson included, fell to the barren ground, hacking and coughing and spitting, trying to clear the clawing fumes. There, a photographer snapped photos of the ordeal, images of bawling recruits with anguished faces that were later printed in the platoon's memorial volume. Several corporals passed around canteens, directing the afflicted to flush their eyes and rinse their faces. It took many minutes for Garson to collect himself. It was painfully obvious what devastation such tear gas could do to fighting men.

While some of the rigor of recruit training ebbed in these latter days at MCRD, there were still new exercises. Sergeant Maddox, many surmised, hoped his unit would make an Eleventh Hour dash for Honor Platoon. He had 023 on the Grinder as much as possible.

"To the winds.... Haar'!" It was a maneuver Garson took to with aplomb. At the command of execution, the four squads literally dispersed from one another – the outside units marching to right and left flanks while the third squad continued on its line of march and the fourth pivoted to the rear. When the disparate components were separated by some 20 yards, Maddox commanded them to reassemble.

"To the rear.... Haar!" At that command of execution, the squads turned 180 degrees and strode back toward one another. At a pace apart and still in cadence, they reassembled and resumed the original line of march. It was a marvelous maneuver, something fit for a proper drill team.

With the exception of Fletcher's bouncing gait and Prick's plodding stride, Platoon 023 gained proficiency and confidence in close order drill. Garson made certain to roll back his shoulders and puff out his narrow chest, taking to heart the incessant harangue of the DIs.

"Lean back, swing those arms, six to the front, and three to the rear! Heels! Heels! Heels!" Garson had by now developed a unique strut, careful to point his toes fore and aft, avoiding what his mother called a "go to me, come for me" gait.

A few of Garson's Boot Camp comrades called him "Hunchie" because of his carriage. Despite some physical development, he remained self-conscious about his narrow chest. When Garson rolled back his shoulders on the march, his body took on a distinctive posture. Even after his discharge years later, that martial stride was evident. One morning while walking to a Milwaukee transit stop, he crossed a busy intersection. The driver of a car hailed him. Garson bent down to peer into the window.

"Were you in the Corps?" the stranger asked. Garson assented.

"Thought so. I'd know that walk anywhere. You were my NCO at Pendleton!" Garson would spend the final six months of his enlistment at the southern California base, assigned as a Troop Handler, leading companies through months-long advanced combat training. On the march, trainees were burdened with full combat gear – steel helmets, 40-pound packs, cartridge belts and canteens, and carried either nine-pound M-1s or 15-pound BARs. A tight and taut 145-pound corporal then, Garson wore only a blue helmet liner and carried a walking stick; he set a blistering pace in that hilly coastal terrain. With only months remaining before discharge, he bore the air of a cocky, short timer. Most Marine trainees despised him, calling him bandy rooster and worse.

"Man, I hope we're this good when Mundt's watching," Garson mumbled on the Grinder.

There was also a flurry of activity in the days before graduation including the formal unit photo. Platoon 023 was arrayed on a five-tiered bleacher, drill instructors seated lower center. Sergeant Maddox, campaign hat nearly touching his nose, laid his NCO saber across his lap. He exhibited an expression of indifference, as if this platoon, one of many he had led through recruit training, was of a lesser quality than its predecessors.

The recruits were attired in their new dress greens and barracks hats, shoes glossy after many hours of spit shining. Those who had qualified at Camp Matthews pinned on shooting medals, the majority marksman. About a dozen, Garson included, exhibited sharpshooter medallions, and a few displayed expert awards. Every recruit wore the National Defense Ribbon authorized by President

Eisenhower, a tiny bar with a yellow band flanked by two red ones. Since it was issued to every enlistee, the award was pejoratively known as the "Fire Watch Ribbon," signifying nothing other than enlistment.

The smaller recruits, the "short rounds," flanked the DIs on the bench in front. Garson's red-headed pal, Rusty, ears more prominent because of his white side wall trim, had modified his former insolent expression, appearing benign. Nearby sat Brtek, short and broad; Garson had teased him as a "beach ball with legs" months before. But the Michigander's puckered uniform blouse indicated he had shed many pounds since October. Garson and Krupa, the "Baby Marines," still looked their parts as innocent, uncertain youths. To Garson's left stood Prick wearing a blank expression behind owlish glasses.

Right guide Barker and the burly Texan, Hupner stood together at top left of the photo. To Garson's eye, they, like Preston and several others, represented the image of Marines – tall, broad of chest and shoulder, lips stern, chins jutted forward with steely gazes under low hat brims.

Days before graduation, Springer and Buchman, who had been without dentures for nearly a dozen weeks, were summoned to the dental facility. They returned in a few hours, fitted with sparkling new Marine choppers. The appliances amplified Springer's oval head and the black thatch of hair to equine proportions; the falsies somehow seemed outsized, unsuited. When he smiled, Garson saw a white, gaping bear trap. He was reminded of this, decades later during a scene from the movie, "Never Cry Wolf," when the Inuit hunter, Mike, displayed new pearly teeth purchased from the sale of a wolf pelt.

"He just doesn't look like the old Springer anymore," Garson told Prick.

Buchman's new choppers were less dramatic, but the upper and lower plates puffed out his normally sallow cheeks. And they clacked when he enunciated certain words. Both he and Springer, to Garson's watchful eye, seemed to have difficulty manipulating the new fixtures, chewing unnaturally. Garson still awaited his lower partial.

Platoon 023 was now one of the older training units at MCRD, gaining altitude in the pecking order. Garson cultivated a sneering air of superiority, emulating disdainful looks directed at him months ago. He felt he and his buddies now merited that right. While watering and raking the sandy plots between their quonsets one morning, Garson witnessed a sight that awakened distant memories.

"What the fuck is this, a fuckin' Chinese fire drill?" exploded the same receiving barracks corporal who had herded Garson and others across the Grinder in fall. Wearing those dowdy grey sweatshirts and dungaree caps sagging over their ears, the fresh fish were bunched together back to breastbone. Poor fucks, Garson thought in relief.

"Whadaya think? Which is tougher, MCRD or Parris Island?" That opened discussions between Marines no matter where they were in the world. Agreement was never achieved. Normally, enlistees from east of the Mississippi River were sent to the South Carolina recruit camp, but this had been changed when Korea erupted.

"See Parris and die they say," offered Krupa, the baby Marine. "Had a cousin who went there. Said it was completely in the boonies, surrounded by swamp with millions of mosquitoes, gnats, sand flies and snakes. You sweat all the time. Said the DIs there are a lot harder on skinheads than MCRD. If that's true, I'm glad they sent us here instead."

Later in his Marine years, Garson would bristle at being called a "Hollywood Marine," implying that his training had been less rigorous. He reasoned that MCRD was actually more difficult psychologically because civilian normalcy was evident in the low San Diego hills surrounding the California base – houses, traffic, people living normal lives. Lindbergh Field, within virtual walking distance, was also a constant reminder of how proximate departure might be.

"Know what I miss – a lot?" the gadfly Hal often turned discussions in his favored direction.

"Squeezing your girlfriend's little titties?"

"Naw, man. I miss Vegas action. Craps, Twenty-One. When I'm done being screwed, blued and tattooed here, I'm headin' for the desert, bright lights and easy money. Gonna shake hands with Vegas Vic." Garson recalled Hal's story of having hitchhiked to the desert town from Wisconsin years before; he had been apparently bitten by the gambling bug. Several of his humorous yarns involved the desert town.

"Did I tell you the one about super sex?" Hal's black eyes widened as he forged ahead before objections might be raised. "Yeah, there was an old guy whose wife had died, an old widower, and his health was failing. Eyesight was poor and hearing worse. His son wanted to get to know him after many years on his own and before the old man croaked." The son suggested going to Las Vegas together.

"We'll have a good time, Pop, do a little gambling, see some show girls, hang out, you know." During the drive from Phoenix, it became apparent that the old man's hearing had deteriorated to near deafness; the son had to often repeat himself. He secured a room at the Pioneer on Fremont.

"Pop, stay here. Relax a bit. I'm going downstairs to check things out." Preston and Rusty exhibited impatience with Hal's narrative. Was this another of those shaggy dog tales?

In the casino, the son approached a fiery redhead whose voluptuous body was wrapped in a dress like a sausage casing. She was obviously a pro, or, as Hal had it, a "business" woman. She agreed for a price to go up to the old man's room and give him the time of his life.

Like Mellish, Hal was an expert at spinning waggish webs — gesticulating, adjusting modulation, pausing, pulling in his audience.

Later, the old man lay abed relaxing with his shoes off when he thought he heard someone knock. A more insistent tattoo on the door finally roused him. He opened the door.

"The red head was stacked like a fuckin' brick shithouse," Hal continued, voice high and nasal. "With one hand leaning on the door jamb and the other on her hip, she murmured like a contented cat.

"'I'm here for super sex.' Old man's eyes slowly traveled from her strappy shoes, up her stockinged legs, pausing at her hips and tits, before looking straight into those feline green eyes. Minutes passed. He swallowed, then said: 'I'll take the soup.'"

"Aw, man," the audience to Hal's tale groaned in unison, and several departed with dismissive waves. But the Berlin gadfly rapidly launched into another yarn, hoping to detain some of his listeners.

"Hear about the guy who went to Vegas, gambled for three days, lost all but a few bucks, got in his car and headed for..."

"Yeah, yeah, we fuckin' heard it before, Hal: 'Bet on 27 red? Well, whadaya know?'" Garson interrupted. Hal grinned.

Often, Garson tried to draw out others about their lives before the Corps. He hoped to gain insights from their experiences. He found Ridley, the Californian, as fascinating as Liska, Hupner and a few others. His skin seemed permanently burnished, perhaps from Pacific beaches, Garson surmised. His hometown was Van Nuys in the San Fernando Valley, not far from coastal haunts.

"Why'd you join?" Garson asked.

"Something to do, I guess. Got bored with college and decided to enlist. Look, my dad wanted me to go into the Air Force, but I thought, naw, let's do it right."

"Another John Wayne Jones, huh?" Garson laughed. Since Christmas, Ridley had captured Garson's attention with stories of campus escapades. He had been a frat boy, and the stories of continuous parties with plenty of beer and babes were mesmerizing. Ridley also amused him with a frat house ditty that stuck with Garson the way a piece of Kipling poetry was retained by the erudite.

Collegiate, collegiate, yes, we are collegiate, nothing "intermedjut," no, man. Trousers, baggy, all our clothes look raggy, but we're rough and ready. Yay! Sigma, Dogma, Delta-a-hand-a-poker, tomato and potato, college gentlemen are we! Slickers, Knickers we can do without. And we couldn't care if there were no suspenders. Neckin', muggin', all our girls like huggin', last night on the back porch. Real collegiate are we.

Garson thought he had heard the tune somewhere, likely in a movie or on radio as a kid. There was a similar tune Garson found interesting, "The New Ashmolean Marching Society and Students' Conservatory Band" that Heissen mentioned.

"Frank Loesser wrote that," put in Heissen, who had established his *bona fides* about popular American composers and music as well as movies. When asked how he knew so much, Heissen explained that he was always attentive to movie credits, liking best when they rolled at the end of pictures as audiences vacated theaters; he studied them carefully.

In youth, Garson usually preferred seeing movies alone, away from pals and distractions. Leland had been an exception. Garson wanted to be absorbed in larger than life screen images, sometimes wishing himself into the sequences. Even as a teen, he had viewed pictures that pals considered slow and dull, movies like "Sunset Boulevard" with its portrait of an ossified Hollywood of long ago. Before his enlistment, he had been romantically transported by Audrey Hepburn in "Roman Holiday," aching that the princess, "Smitty," as she called herself, could not abandon royal duty and convention to consummate her love for a common reporter, Gregory Peck's Joe Bradley. Garson yearned to be such a newspaperman.

When neither Ridley nor Heissen were involved in discourses about movies, conversations were far less incisive, lacking analysis and erudition. These tended to deteriorate into "what-happened-next" discussions of plot lines and stars.

"Remember when those old Frankenstein pictures were re-released when we were kids?"

"Yeah, 'Frankenstein' and 'Bride of Frankenstein.' They were great."

"Then they made sequels during the war where the monster and Wolfman fight to the death in a castle, but then are found frozen in the next picture. Karloff didn't even play the monster in a couple of those. There was also one where all of those monsters – Wolfman,

Dracula and the rest – come together." But the monster sequels were finally debased, Garson thought, by comedians Abbot and Costello.

"I always liked the Wolfman's ma, that little woman with the accent and face like a prune."

"Maria Ouspenskya." To Garson's surprise, it was normally taciturn Prick who offered that detail.

"Ous…? How'd you know that?"

"She wasn't the Wolfman's mother. Just a gypsy woman who knew about the curse. Name was Maleva or something like that. Showed those pictures in Hartford when I was a kid, usually on Saturdays when me and my brother got to go. Ouspenskya had that crackly voice and said, 'My, son. My, son.'"

"Yeah." Garson surmised that Prick was like his own rural cousins who rarely sat in movie theaters, burdened as they were by farm chores. It became clear that while he had not seen many movies, he, like Heissen, was attentive to detail. Prick recalled other sequences, including the one "Son of Frankenstein" that always generated laughs: When Krogh, the militaristic Prussian inspector poked darts into his stiff artificial arm while he played a game against Wolf, the monster's latest rejuvenator. They all guffawed with Prick as he recounted the ludicrous climax when the maddened creature ripped off the policeman's wooden limb.

Later, when Garson listened to Ridley's informed disquisitions, he came to see that the first two Frankenstein films, directed by James Whale, borrowed visually from German Expressionist directors of the Weimar era like Fritz Lang. And these influenced America's post-war film noir directors.

"What's your favorite oater?" Typically, conversation shifted to Westerns.

Garson thought for seconds, mentally running through dozens of Westerns that had captivated him in youth. The John Ford cavalry trilogy, even "The Three Godfathers," all set in Monument Valley, were among his favorites. He sat through "Red River" more than once because he felt Howard Hawks directed a better picture; Wayne's portrayal of Tom Dunson was meatier than his Nathan Brittles or Kirby Yorke roles. While Garson did, none of his Milwaukee pals agreed that Monty Clift was not credible as gun-handy Matthew Garth, even when, in a celebrated sequence, he sucked arrow poison from the heroine's breast. To Garson's surprise, the usually circumspect Ritz exhibited the titillating lobby poster of that provocative scene. Times were changing.

"Shoulda stayed in those pictures like 'A Place in the Sun' and 'The Heiress.' Monty's just too fuckin' handsome," Rusty had opined.

Garson counted among his favorites "My Darling Clementine" and the brooding "The Ox-Bow Incident;" both were devoid of sprawling settings; stories were more deliberate and nuanced, he thought. Garson liked the symbolic manner in which the latter picture opened and closed with Henrys, Ford and Morgan, riding into and out of town as an old bloodhound trotted across the dusty street. The movie challenged Garson's sympathies for the Confederacy's "Lost Cause" engendered by "Gone with the Wind" and other films that portrayed all Rebels as honorable and gallant. He silently celebrated the deserved end of Major Tetley who led the lynch mob in his gaudy grey uniform.

In such discussions, actresses drew most focus, of course. But Garson began to realize that his boyhood infatuations with sunny blondes and redheads like Betty Grable, Lana Turner and Maureen O'Hara, even Jean Harlow, were shifting. He was developing deeper attractions to sultry brunettes, actresses such as Hedy Lamar, Dorothy Lamour, Merle Oberon, exotic actresses with smoldering darkness beneath seductive lids. He held back airing such preferences, however, after listening to Buchman one day.

"You know Lamour had some colored in her," he proclaimed to Garson's disbelief. "Yup, that's what they say. She's from Louisiana, you know, and there are lots of Cajuns and Spanish and coloreds mixed together. They said her dad was colored, but Hollywood kept that secret. Maria Montez was part Negro, I heard, from some Caribbean island. Just look at those eyes and cheekbones." Garson was unpersuaded.

Of course, Garson enjoyed the epic adventure stars like Wayne,

Stewart Granger, Power, Cooper and he appreciated the versatility of Cary Grant and Jimmy Stewart, and was attracted to tarnished and edgier characters portrayed by Robert Mitchum and Burt Lancaster, in movies of crime and retribution, of capers and prisons, especially "Out of the Past," "The Killers" and "Brute Force." He was sympathetic to Sterling Hayden and Robert Ryan, the weary Stoker Thompson in "The Set-Up," a boxing movie that took place in real time. He was conflicted by Fred MacMurray and Barbaba Stanwyck in "Double Indemnity," and John Garfield and Lana Turner in "The Postman Always Rings Twice," yearning for sunnier climaxes.

"Remember this?" Ridley put in, "The cheaper the suit, the gaudier the patter."

"Bogie in 'The Maltese Falcon,' right? Sam Spade? Always got the drop on Wilmer, the gunsel. Elisha Cooke, Junior." Ridley nodded.

"That was one of those movies they call 'film noir.'" He drew upon a college course about contemporary movies. "Most scenes are filmed at night, and directors and set decorators used lots of shadows, had interior shots with window blinds. They say it all represented dislocations after the war. Fatalism, I think." Garson hung on every word. Bogart, Mitchum, Lancaster, Ryan, Hayden and others were consummate noir actors, set against, as they were, femme fatale actresses such Ava Gardner, Yvonne DeCarlo, Gloria Grahame, tough and tawdry temptresses given to erotic innuendo.

"Milwaukee didn't like those movies. We had some kind of commission. Kept Howard Hughes's 'Outlaw' from playing in town." Garson knew about the controversy, and the notoriety that piqued his and Leland's determination to see Jane Russell.

"Was the movie 'M' a film noir?" Garson wanted to know.

"You mean the Peter Lorre silent, about the guy who killed kids?" Ridley asked.

"No, the one a few years ago with David Wayne playing that part."

"Looked a little cheap to me. Think it was shot right in downtown L.A." The subject matter had troubled him. He had several times mulled over scenes — when the criminal gang discovered a closet full of kids' shoes, and put the molester on trial in that underground garage. Garson, one of only a handful in the Ritz audience, had briefly shifted sympathy to the sniveling killer. Character actors Martin Gabel, Luther Adler, Howard Da Silva and others were convincing, Garson thought. Not even Ridley had seen that version.

Ridley and Heissen, waxed eloquent about factors Garson never considered, such aspects as pacing, symbolism and the way music heightened tension and prompted emotions. Garson was attentive to conversations about subjective camera, tracking shots, rear screen projection, montage, *mise en cine*, crane shots and more.

Ridley, Heissen and others all agreed that the many science fiction offerings of the current decade had been lamentable, larded with stop-motion fakery, stilted acting and ridiculous special effects. But a few titles stood apart, among them "The Day the Earth Stood Still" and "Them!" but especially "The Thing," as it came to be known.

If I was my Pop's editor – which I'm not – I'd advise that he excise most of the preceding tedious disquisition. Sure, I know how important films were in his formative years; he's made that abundantly clear before. Thing of it is, I know a little about classic films, the American Film Institute and top one hundred lists. I've heard about the golden age of Hollywood. At my Pop's urging, I've seen several of these old black and white titles, some film noir – well, only a couple, I admit, and I fell asleep part way through. Take "Casablanca," for instance, said to be near the top of any critical list. I don't think Bogie and those actors compare favorably with performers of my generation. Stars of my Pop's era just didn't have the chops, didn't have the skills of today's actors. For me, Bogart and the others simply spat staccato dialogue back and forth. I saw some scenes of one of my Pop's favorites, "His Girl Friday," and Grant and Russell actually talked over each other.

As January at MCRD waned, it became apparent that the pace and intensity of Boot Camp slowed even further. In retrospect, it seemed that Garson's umbilical cord to his past life was all but severed now, that the three-month incubation was ending. Some recruits speculated that Sergeant Maddox might even be preparing for a new platoon. In only a matter of days, despite nagging doubts, Garson hoped to be reborn as a Marine.

Winter daylight was short, now, the San Diego skies darkening about the time of evening chow. After meals, recruits gathered behind the mess hall to smoke and converse, and Right Guard Barker more often than not marched the platoon back to its billets. While the time for unfettered idling was not yet at hand, there were hours when other interesting exchanges occurred. From Ridley, Garson hoped to gain a better understanding of campus life, perhaps with the expectation that he might experience it after the Marines. While he was committed to the Corps, second thoughts had crept into his mind. Perhaps military life would be only temporary. He had become something of the Californian's acolyte, and Ridley disquisitions usually fascinated Garson, especially the idea of pursuing knowledge for its own sake.

"There was this philosopher, Zenon of Greece," Ridley explained, "who wrote about philosophical paradoxes. One involved looking into one's past with mirrors." Garson screwed up his face skeptically.

"No, listen: When you look at yourself in a mirror, an infinitesimal amount of time passes when light travels from you to the mirror and reflects back to your eye. So, you're looking into the past, right?" Garson nodded tentatively.

"Look, Zenon said if you set up a large enough number of mirrors, each reflecting the preceding one, you can theoretically see backwards in time – perhaps all the way back to your childhood." He smirked, and Garson walked away.

There were other times when Ridley talked about his life before enlisting. Van Nuys was located northwest of downtown Los Angeles, a town that literally exploded into existence during and after the war. His father had come west from Chicago before the war, attracted by defense plant work; he had married and worked his way up to engineer. The suburb was studded with manufacturing, including the sprawling General Motors assembly plant. Most of the metro area's auto dealerships were situated downtown, along Van Nuys Boulevard.

"Everybody cruises the boulevard on Wednesday nights, showing off rods and customs, picking up girls, parking at drive-ins." It certainly sounded much more spectacular than cruising the Burg with Toby and Belcher back home. It seemed like something out of the Felsen novels and *Hot Rod* magazine images. Decades later, of course, Garson compared Ridley's descriptions with scenes in George Lucas's "American Graffiti."

"Unlike you snowmen from Wisconsin, weather's always great here. Sun and easy living. Beaches aren't too far either, maybe three miles to Malibu. Which reminds me. This is one Hal might tell: A Jarhead stopped a guy who sashayed along the beach. 'Where can I find the Catalina Island Ferry,' the Marine asked. The guy jutted a hip, set an arm akimbo, blinked and lisped, 'Why, you're thpeaking to him!'" Garson snorted.

Garson was fascinated with the lives of other recruits, compared their colorful cities with ordinary Milwaukee, to measure their zestful experiences against his mundane ones.

"Grampa was shot in the leg on his wedding night," Hupner put in.

Garson stopped shining his shoes, and shot a quizzical gaze at the large Texan.

"It was a shivaree." He went on to explain that the Texas newlyweds had been married in a little Baptist church near Plano, and the bride's parents arranged that the couple would spend their first night in a cottage on a neighbor's farm.

"After everyone ate dinner and danced a little in the yard, my grandpa and grandma walked to the cottage with everyone behind. Some men had guns to celebrate, and they began shooting up in the air," Hupner said. "Others shouted and waved their hats."

"Grampa said he and gramma were waving at our kin from the little porch when he felt something sting his leg. He looked down to see his pants leg bloody. It was only a little .25 caliber pistol, and the wound wasn't too bad. But he had'a have it bandaged up. I guess that was a wedding to remember."

Hupner often talked about his family. He was the only boy after his grandfather, and his family had high hopes for him. He must have had something like dyslexia because he never learned to read or write properly. Garson asked him how he had passed the multiple choice tests for the Marines.

"Oh, I just guessed. Put x's in the boxes where I thought they should be." He was uncomfortable with the topic.

"Hey, Liska," Hupner turned to the pale-eyed Detroiter, "remember when you talked about going to Alaska when we was at Matthews, when you visited your kin or friends or whatever?" Liska nodded. "I was wondering what got those folks up there?" Liska responded.

"Some years after the second world war, a neighbor of ours heard of a Federal program to get folks to relocate up there. You could get a square mile homestead, but the deal was that you had to clear at least 20 acres, build some kind of house – many used those surplus quonset huts, like the ones we got here – and stay there for two years. After that, the land was yours." Despite the friendship that had developed between them during many weeks, Garson still could not long gaze into Liska's pallid eyes.

"Several families from Hamtramck, second and third generation Poles, seized the offer," the Detroiter continued. "The owner of Mirek Buick in the town, hearing about those families migrating to Alaska Territory, offered to help. He bought some army surplus bulldozers, caterpillars and other heavy equipment, and hired a man to take them to the territory. But when the man got to Whitehorse in Yukon Territory, he sold the equipment and absconded with the cash." Liska obviously enjoyed describing his experiences back home.

"A real *'cwaniak'*," Liska said, a "*'Scheister*, as you call him.' Anyways, when they found out all the equipment had been stolen, half of the settlers turned back and went home. The Golombowskis, our shirt-tale relatives, and some others stayed, and hacked workable land out of the forest and tundra up there. Because of the awful mosquitoes and thawed permafrost, they couldn't clear during high summer – July, August. So they stayed in Anchorage, working in stores and gas stations to earn money. Then when the ground hardened up in early fall, they'd go back to their land."

"What about that trip," Hupner asked. Liska ran a palm down one cheek of his pocked face as if sorting his reminiscence into an orderly narrative.

"After my junior year, summer of '52, my dad said he wanted to visit the Golombowskis, and decided to drive all the way. He owned a solid car, a '50 Chev station wagon. Put on six- or eight-ply tires, and we took along extra ones and headlamps because they told him the Al-Can Highway was so stony that headlights got smashed and radiators and gas tanks were damaged. My dad was prepared though, and we had no problems. Even had a sign painted that we put in the side window – 'Detroit, Michigan to Alaska,' it said." The elder Liska planned to reach Anchorage before the rainy season when roads turned into a quagmire, so father and son departed July Fourth.

They posed for snapshots standing at Mile 0 marker, Liska noted. The sign read 918 miles to Whitehorse, 1523 to Fairbanks. The route followed old Indian trails, logging roads and the like, skirting east of the coastal range. The road had been constructed just ten years before by about 10,000 U.S. soldiers, mostly Negroes. But the route had not been properly maintained, and chuckholes, gravel breaks, poor shoulders and gulley washes reduced speed to 30 or 40 miles an hour. The elder Liska feared loosening motor mounts and other engine parts.

"They told us to watch out for airplanes that sometimes made emergency landings on the road. Gas, food and lodging were maybe 50 miles apart. Longest stretch was about a hundred. Saw bear and moose every day," Liska related. "I remember we covered our luggage in the back with old sheets. Every night, I had to shake the yellow dust off, then wipe down the bags before they let us in tourist cabins.

"Served moose steaks at local restaurants. One cook told us they only used young moose because the meat was nice and sweet. It was, too." Garson, many times thinking he had lived a prosaic life, longed to have such adventures. When Liska talked about the Yukon, Garson could only relate to movies he'd seen about such places – "Call of the Wild" with Gable, even the Crosby and Hope picture, "Road to Utopia."

"When we got to Anchorage, we stayed with the relatives from

Hamtramck, the Golombowskis. They rented a house from an old cowboy named Henry Olmstead until their own cabin was built. He used two war quonsets. In his 90's, I guess, wrinkled like a prune. Told me he was born right after the Civil War, and came west from Indiana. Panned in the Dakota goldfields. Said he'd seen Wild Bill Hickock in Deadwood once, but don't know as I believed him. Worked cattle in Montana.

"Showed me his old Colt six-gun. I asked him why he carried that instead of a cartridge pistol. 'You can stoke this with a lot more powder than a cartridge gun, and that'll drop a steer sooner. Old Wild Bill carried a .36 caliber Navy like this one, you know.' Olmstead told me he didn't carry the gun to shoot people. Said he'd never do that. 'Guns're fer shootin' cows when they charge your pony. Losing your mount was the worst thing that could happen to you out West. 'Without a mount, you couldn't get work,' the old man said. I believed him.

"The old codger told me some fantastical stories during the week we were in Anchorage; I didn't believe half of them, but I found him interesting. Said he'd seen five people killed over the years. In Deadwood, he claimed he saw a whore, a chesty blonde, gun down a miner who beat her up. Right in front of the famous Gem Saloon where she worked,' Olmstead said; 'that was one lawless camp, I tell you.'"

While his dad remained in Anchorage for several more weeks, Liska and one of the Golombowskis boarded a train to visit a high school chum, Danny Pentkavich, whose family had settled further north, near a town called Talkeetna.

"When we got off the train, it was like walking into Dodge City or someplace in the Wild West. Everybody was armed – handguns, rifles, shotguns. It was a Western town with false front buildings like you see in the movies. Grizzlies and moose were all over the place not far out of town, sometimes even wandering close by. You had to carry a gun for protection. Funny: There in the middle of nowhere were these Polish people from Hamtramck working the land. It'll be interesting to see how long they'll stay up there. Talk is that statehood may come to Alaska someday, but many said they didn't want to see things changed."

Garson reminisced about all of this a few years later when his military plane laid over in Anchorage en route to the Aleutian Islands. He had been transferred from the Naval Air Station in Washington's Puget Sound to a desolate volcanic rock of an island where he spent a year. Marines euphemistically called Adak, way out in the thousand-mile string, the "Playground of the Bering Sea" where there was a woman behind every tree. The problem was there were no trees. As it happened, however, when the army was stationed on Adak after driving back the Japanese invasion of the islands in 1942, it planted a tiny copse of firs and fitted up a sign: "You are now entering and leaving the Adak National Forest." The anemic soil prevented the trees from growing taller than three feet in a dozen years.

"You got a one, you got a many!" That was a bromide offered by a Milwaukee street philosopher, said Buchman, the recruit who, along with Springer, now displayed a new set of Marine-issued dentures.

"You know, you were talking about 'Black Bottom' in Detroit where the colored lived," Buchman nodded to Liska. Buchman had a childhood memory about Milwaukee's minority area that brought forth laughs. The city's Negro community was largely confined to a neighborhood a mile north of the central business district whose commercial and entertainment heart spread along several blocks of Walnut Street near Schlitz Brewery. Called Bronzeville, the street contained nightclubs, a tiny movie theater called the Regal and small businesses. Garson was somewhat familiar of the main street as he and Toby had once played the part of detectives, hired by a neighbor to spy on a philandering spouse.

Whites, absentee landlords of their day, owned most of the buildings on Walnut. Buchman's dad owned a modest commercial building with apartments above. The storefront was leased to a Negro barber, and as a child Buchman sometimes accompanied his father to collect rent money. One of the habitués of the barber shop was a man of indeterminate age always attired in finely tailored suits, pocket handkerchiefs and Hamburg hats with tiny red feathers peeping from the bands. The man's skin was light and his hair slicked back like Cab Calloway. They called it a "conk." His nose was narrow and straight, and his baby blue eyes were startling.

Buchman said the man was something of a street philosopher, folklorist and occasional pool hustler named Luster Dapp. He pontificated about the news and rumors of the day, editorializing with an arsenal of quips and aphorisms that were legendary.

"Some people get *magna cum laude*, and some *summa cum laude*. I got 'thank you, Lawde!'" Buchman remembered several of those Dappisms even though he and his dad often failed to understand their meaning. But some made perfect sense.

"Can't do no more than the hand can take" was a favorite. Buchman's dad maintained a good relationship with the Negro proprietor, and was warmly welcomed, sometimes with a cup of coffee or other times with a more bracing tonic kept in the back room. When Dapp was in the shop, the Buchmans often tarried for a half an hour to listen. Garson wondered if Dapp played to the white folks in his audience.

"If you wanna get a politician's eye, get his wife a vicuña coat." As a kid, Buchman did not know what a vicuña was.

"You're ridin' the gravy train with biscuit wheels," he would pontificate about anyone who found good fortune.

"That's right, Luster. You got it there, man." The response from listeners, called testifying, Garson later learned, characterized parishioners in many Negro churches.

"Givin's for the needy, not the greedy," Dapp said of charity. Voices of shop patrons lowed and heads nodded in agreement.

Dapp was also given to malapropisms and misused words. Like many, he applied the Depression era term *hoi polloi* to the wealthy instead of common people. And he invariably mispronounced hoax as "ho-axe," pronounced foliage as "foilage," generating gentle guffaws among barber shop denizens for reasons Dapp never understood; and no one ever corrected him, so that humorous gift kept on giving.

"You know what Moms Mabley said, right?" Dapp referred to the Negro comedienne whose Harlem performances were earthy and popular.

"'The good old days?' she asked. 'Where *were* they? I was here!'"

Buchman also recalled another Milwaukee character, more benign than Luster Dapp, but, for Garson, just as fascinating. He lived on the west side, in the largely Jewish neighborhood in which Garson's mother had cleaned houses after the war. His name was Grushka, as Buchman remembered, an immigrant from Eastern Europe who had somehow escaped the Nazis.

"On summer afternoons, his wife helped him into a chair on the front lawn, and here he'd sit for hours. He had long white hair and a walrus moustache, and played the harmonica. He sat with a blanket over his legs even in the heat, said nothing and played old world tunes, I think. Kids watched."

My apologies to readers for yet another intrusion here – seems to be a habit now — but I must challenge my Pop about the foregoing character. Frankly, I think he borrowed that old man from the childhood of my sisters and me. I don't know the old man's name, but the one I knew sat out on the lawn on a high-backed kitchen chair, creating gentle airs with a harmonica on summer afternoons. He was never seen going to any of the synagogues in the neighborhood. I'll say no more than this, but ask the discerning to consider what additional implications this has for my Pop's narrative.

Daily mail calls for Platoon 023 were no longer the formal affairs of earlier days. Several of Garson's buddies had set words to the bugle call notes that announced the mail.

"I got a letter. I got a letter. Hope to hell you got one, too." Right Guide Barker distributed letters and packages to each squad leader who handed them to recipients. This late in recruit training, DIs no longer monitored, censored or confiscated contents or made recruits chew envelopes.

"This is my girl," said Krupa, holding two small snapshots for Garson to see. "Name's Lisa, Lisa Cannoli. Goes to Holy Angels." Garson was familiar with the all-girls high school, housed in a two-story gargoyle festooned gothic building on the streetcar line to downtown. He had traveled that route numerous times to the grand Wisconsin Avenue movie palaces.

"Wait a minute, Krupa," Garson blurted, "wait just a fuckin' minute. Thought Heidi was your girl, Heidi Bedusek."

"She is." Garson was stunned. Krupa had two girls? Where was the fairness in the fateful scheme of things? When Hal heard of the "Baby Marine's" girlfriends he put forward the supposition that Krupa was either pulling somebody's leg, or he had a "giant *Schwanz*."

"Does Heidi know about Lisa, and vice versa?" Garson asked Krupa.

"'Course not. Whadaya think I am?" Garson studied the black and white photos for several minutes. Lisa wore abbreviated white shorts, a Betty Grable sweater and high heels, sat on a bed with one knee drawn up in a simulated cheesecake pose. She had a pretty face, right enough, but her nose was a bit blunt and her cheeks displayed some blemishes. What was more, her legs were not particularly shapely. But as a girl in her mid-teens, she exhibited a pinup's bosom. Garson was envious. He had had no letter from beguiling Betsy, the dark-haired school girl he fancied, and whose face and figure often flitted through Boot Camp daydreams. Krupa snatched the photos from Garson's grasp.

"When we was kids," Krupa put in, "we heard there was a sea monster in Kloetsch Park lagoon." Garson knew that sprawling greensward in the northern Milwaukee fringes. As a kid, he had harvested wild asparagus along the vacant interurban right of way near there.

"Yeah, one night we hiked out there to see it," Krupa continued. "Me and my little brother and a pal sat on the shore all night, waiting for the monster to show up. He was scared shitless, but we never saw nothin'."

"Never fuckin' heard of such a thing," Garson remarked. The platoon's designated "Baby Marines" also compared respective neighborhoods and schools.

In those latter days at MCRD, Garson received another letter from his mother, longer than preceding missives, filled with neighborhood news.

"They're building a new little house on the corner where Deaffy used to live," his mother she wrote. It would probably be like the other Cape Cods constructed after the war. Garson had not thought about that neighborhood tatterdemalion for some time. To say he had "known" the mute denizen was not accurate. But she had threaded her somber way through his life since childhood, frightening him and other kids while attracting sympathy from some neighbors such as his mother. City authorities had taken her in hand the year before, and condemned her property.

That night, Garson dreamed of Deaffy, cleaned up and coiffed, wearing new clothes; she rang the bell at his house, and handed him a cake made of peanut butter and jelly. There was a confusing segue in the dream to a scene of his grandfather, Guttig, on the day he departed for the hospital. As he was helped into an ambulance, he turned to study the bungalow that had been home for eight years. He weakly waved farewell.

The letter from Garson's mother also contained a troubling request. Did he remember the insurance policy that she had initiated when he was an infant? He recalled her crossing the street each week to the insurance agent to turn over a dollar and a quarter. When Garson turned 21, the policy would come due, paying him a thousand dollars.

"For college, I hope," his mother had promised. His parents, however, now needed that money as they were in dire financial straits. The double mortgage payments on the bungalow they had purchased decades before and paid off during the war, and on the Galena Street commercial property bought six years past, were overdue. Good man though he was, his father's inadequacy in business was now manifest. Neither his popcorn franchise nor his mother's restaurant salary was sufficient to hold creditors at bay. They could retain title to the Galena building, as his father insisted, but at the loss of the family home. That financial catastrophe would drive a permanent wedge between wife and husband.

"Please sign the insurance policy so we can get the money to pay the mortgage. Sorry to ask this. We'll make it up to you." Garson thought his mother's longhand seemed somewhat shaky when she apologized. Of course, he signed the enclosed document, and posted it as quickly as possible. Like his grandfather, Garson would never see his childhood home again.

"Uniform of the day'll be dress blues, tennis shoes and a light coat of oil," quipped Hal as the recruits dressed and prepared for the graduation ceremony. Dress greens, barracks hats, cartridge belts and rifles were the actual order of the day.

January 14th was a typical San Diego day. While the season's sun struggled to gain winter footing, the morning temperature was comfortably in the 50s. The battalion assembled on the north side of the expansive Grinder early that Thursday morning, the platoons, comprising two hundred recruits, arrayed in three rectangles. Attired in dress blues, a drum and bugle corps played military airs, brass horns gleaming in the morning sun, snare drums rattling sharply. Platoon guide-ons fluttered lazily in the soft breeze.

Before the assembly were gathered officers, DIs and other personnel. Bleachers had been erected in front of the Spanish colonnade; parents, family and friends observed the ceremony. Ridley's family and a pretty girlfriend had driven down from Van Nuys to offer congratulations. Garson's mind drifted during the MCRD commandant's address, and he recalled only a few words – of country and Corps.

"At ease disease, there's fungus among us," Hal whispered irreverently. Garson grew attentive to remarks by battalion commander Mundt, for he would announce the winner of the three-month competition. While the designation would not reflect upon his personal status and achievement, Garson fidgeted inside during those pregnant minutes; he felt that he and most others had worked hard to gain that signal reward.

"The second recruit battalion banner of Honor Platoon goes to," the captain hesitated, passing his eyes over the assembly, "Platoon 022." Garson and others deflated visibly. Barker, someone said later, grimaced. The winning right guide stepped forward smartly, pride evident in his expression and bearing. Mundt tied the long yellow banner to the lowered guide-on.

"Pass in review!" The band immediately struck up the Marine Corps Hymn. Senior DIs marched their platoons to the right, Platoon 022 in the lead. Sergeant Maddox led his unit forward, then at about 20 yards ordered two turns by column. The familiar notes of "The Star- Spangled Banner" caused Garson's throat to tighten. What was more, Platoon 023 had never marched so well – more than 60 new Marines molded into a unified body, every stride and arm movement in harmony; it was almost as if every heart beat as one. Regardless of losing Honor Platoon, he was proud of what he and his buddies had accomplished. He personally had succeeded in the most demanding experience of his life. Soon, he would be a true Marine. Ahead was the reviewing stand, officers saluting.

"Eyes...right!" Maddox barked as they neared the dais. Rifles at the right shoulder, Garson and the rest snapped their heads. The sergeant swept the NCO sword from his shoulder, thrusting it forward. After the ceremony ended, several agreed with Garson that the alignment of 023 had never been better. There was not a waver or hitch; every footfall sounded as one. The DI did not even call cadence. Somehow, even bandy-legged Fletcher's barracks hat failed to break the uniform plane or disrupt the platoon's rhythm. All was perfection.

Despite his disappointment, Maddox exhibited a magnanimous demeanor that afternoon when his recruits were lined up before the Duty Hut for the final encounter. The normal protocol for entry had ceased, and they were called in one by one. For reasons he could not explain, Garson was confident when he stood at attention before his drill instructor's desk. Maddox shuffled through Garson's recruit file, then looked up, bidding his subordinate to stand at ease.

"I see here you shot sharpshooter. Good." Did he not recall the minor confrontation they had had on record day Camp Matthews after Garson had improved his score to 218? Don't you remember the little religious statuette? Garson wanted to ask.

"Pistol range gunney at Matthews jotted a note here that you were good with the forty-five. That bodes well, too."

"Thank you, sir!" Maddox looked up, his wide mouth more relaxed. He appeared almost benign. Garson's narrow chest swelled.

"No need to call me sir, anymore."

"Sir, no, sir!" Garson stammered, slightly unnerved. Garson found it difficult to let go of "sir" after the past 80 days. "I mean Sergeant." His fingers fidgeted at the small of his back. Had the DI forgotten those throttlings delivered because of the improper clothing stamp, or the time Garson had served as battalion runner, even that more recent episode in the chow line? Perhaps these would not to be held against him, not noted in his permanent record.

"Congratulations, you've been promoted to private first class."

"Thank you, s..., er, Sergeant!"

"I wish you success for the rest of your Marine career," he glanced again at Garson's record, "four years, I see." He suggested that Garson consider studying for his GED, and taking correspondence courses from the Marine Corps Institute. He stood, then, and offered his hand across the desk. Garson stood rigidly once more, and clasped Maddox's hand, confidently responding to the DI's firm grip with one of his own. They smiled at one another. It was the last time the two met.

"Semper Fi, Marine!" Those were the final words Garson heard from Sergeant Maddox. When, in later years, Garson reflected on his four years of Marine Corps service, Maddox stood prominently, his image, demeanor and comportment emblematic of the Corps as Garson knew it. He later served under numerous superiors and commanders – NCOs and officers. None left a stronger impression upon him than his Boot Camp leader. The senior DI was the benchmark by which all future leaders were measured. More than a half century later, Maddox stood as tall in memory as Garson's grandfather.

"This is a bunch of fuckin' bullshit," Rusty complained almost mutinously, reverting to the peppery demeanor Garson knew from Villard Avenue that had been suppressed for three months; he was once again a feisty, confrontational gremlin. Another collection was being taken, this one a parting gift for the platoon's DIs. The new

Marines were expected to pony up for several cartons of Camel cigarettes.

"Jesus fuckin' Christ, they make ten fuckin' times what we do," Rusty groaned. "Whyn't they buy their own fuckin' butts?" The five-dollar collection came after a long series of demands on a private's poor pay.

"Ain't giving fuckin' shit! Saving my money for Vegas," Hal groused.

For three months, Garson and the others had been paid $78 a month; they drew only a little of that each payday for toiletries and incidentals. Now, those who had been promoted to PFC earned a raise of about eight dollars. He mused that was about what he had earned on his newspaper route as a 12-year-old.

"But think of all the great fuckin' chow we get and the wonderful living quarters!" chimed Hal.

Garson and the others felt virtually invincible now, almost able to take on a company of Gooks or at least handle a pair of Swabbies in any fight. As graduates, they were permitted to open the top buttons of their dungaree jackets just like DIs and other MCRD permanent personnel. They were accorded a few hours of base liberty.

"Hey, look, man, they're BAMS, just like Hal said."

"Well, I'll be fuckin' damned," Garson replied as he Preston and Rusty sauntered across the Grinder en route to the post exchange. A rectangle of young women in Marine green jackets, skirts and caps marched smartly on the north flank of the parade ground. Officially Women Marines, they were referred to colloquially, perhaps pejoratively, as "broad-assed Marines – BAMs."

For weeks since Platoon 023 had returned from Camp Matthews, Hal insisted that he had spied females across the Grinder; but at such a distance, no one could verify: They were only tiny figures in dress greens. Since Hal had strained credibility with incessant scuttlebutt, rumors and suppositions, few believed his wishful fancies.

Yet here, up close, smart and trim BAMs, hair bobbed beneath their caps, strode confidently, M-1 rifles at their shoulders. A female three-striper barked cadence in a low-register voice. They may not have rivaled movie stars, but they were young women, a gender remembered only in a few snapshots and fantasy. The trio of buddies slowed their pace, transfixed by the sight. Garson lifted his nose, hoping to capture any stray feminine pheromone.

With money in their pockets, they were intent on purchasing cigarettes, and sundries denied for long weeks. They also bought small grip sacks, "AWOL bags" Marines called then, in preparation for their departure.

"Gonna get some fuckin' nickels, man," Rusty had proclaimed when they first received their pay. He was determined to plug the nearest candy bar machine whose sugary riches had beckoned all of those weeks. Like a miser with pieces of gold, the diminutive redhead later cradled a half dozen Baby Ruths and Butterfingers; he overcame his notion to eat every last one, giving bars to Preston and Garson.

Garson was dispirited the day his recruit buddies dispersed to other duty stations. When they vacated the quonsets, they proudly wore crisp dress greens while Garson remained in dungarees. Because his denture was not yet completed, he was temporarily assigned to what was called "Casual Company." Ironically, in his previous life, "casual" had been a word used to describe things cool and informed. But the amorphous unit in which Garson found himself was comprised of transients — Marines without orders, awaiting discharge or in transit. Among them were veterans, several displaying Korean combat ribbons; one wore a Purple Heart and, Garson thought, bore mental scars. He heard incessant nighttime murmurings from the Marine's bunk. Garson felt hollow.

For the next several weeks, Garson and the other casuals conducted deadening police duty, detailed to clean administrative facilities and vacated quonsets, preparing the latter for new recruits. Duties were completed before noon chow with the remainder of the day left for idling. Perhaps the only beneficial aspect was that the casuals ate in the Sea School mess hall, a facility separate from recruits, and on whose tables sat jars of peanut butter and jelly. He had not tasted those delicacies since he departed Milwaukee.

During those dolorous weeks, it seemed, Casual Company habitués spoke of nothing beyond liberty and the Arabian Nights delights of Tijuana. Conversations reinforced Ridley's disquisitions about the Mexican town and its "attractions." Garson had no interest in bullfights, however. After being locked away for months in the Corps's celibate seclusion, he determined to secure an overnight liberty pass and wander "south of the border, down Mexico way," as Gene Autry sang, determined to end his days as a hapless virgin.

The smarmy tales had been alive in Garson's mind for a long time, since the past summer when Toby and Rowdy returned from their trek to California. Their experiences coupled with Ridley's descriptions of the fabled city of booze, broads and bawdy houses, firing Garson's flammable imaginings into a fevered conflagration; he was anxious to visit a town said to be filled with nubile senoritas anxious to please Marines. In Garson's mind, Tijuana was a virtual *fata morgana*.

Garson awoke one morning, in a clear state of arousal, thinking he had dreamed of Maria Montez, the exotic narrow-eyed star of B movies. Buchman's assertion that MCRD chow was laced with salt peter was clearly false. As a new salty Marine, he needed to relieve his "Blue Balls," get his fucking ashes hauled, or as another euphemism had it, dip his wick.

When the trolley wheels shrieked away from the San Diego station, he settled into the long rear seat with four Casual Company buddies, one of whom he later named Bauer, a tall Milwaukee youth who said he had graduated from the city's all-male Jesuit high school, Marquette. A tuft of thick, sandy hair was set off with eyes the gray of a ship's hull. He was awaiting orders for a permanent duty station.

"Brought some French ticklers," Bauer boasted. "They drive whores wild. Want one?" Garson had heard Buchman and others wax at length about such sexual stimulators — ribbed protrusions that supposedly enhanced a girl's sexual experience. He shook his head at the offer. He had enough to worry about just now. For some minutes, Garson dampened his apprehension about what he expected at the destination, distracting himself by studying the sleek, streamlined trolley car, like the ones in Chicago. His home town still clung to those decrepit orange rattlers.

I beg indulgence once more, forewarning tender readers, especially my youngest sister, about what's to follow – an account of his first sexual escapade. Thing of it is, I think he generated far too much verbiage on the simple fact of getting laid for the first time. My generation will regard him as uncommonly naïve, a virtual naïf. What's more, the episode might be challenged because some evidence suggests it occurred later in his Marine career, perhaps while he was at Camp Pendleton a month later. Now, I'm no moralist, far be it, so I'll let it stand with fair warning.

The trolley trip took about 30 or 40 minutes, and before the car had trundled too far, Garson's fantastical visions born of Hollywood-created harem delights pushed to the fore. The nervous night before, his febrile mind had re-run scenes from "The Thief of Bagdad" and "Sinbad the Sailor." He yearned for dark-eyed Catana Perez in "Captain from Castille," or fiery Pearl Chavez in "Duel in the Sun." Even dreamy-eyed, plum-lipped Katy Jurado might be waiting.

The car line terminated yards of the Mexican border gate. The Marine quartet ambled past the guards, exhibiting ID cards and passes. They had a 24-hour liberty – a day of R and R, relaxation and recreation. Garson recalled Colonel "Chesty" Puller's demand to authorities to "Give my Marines booze and broads."

Just as Ridley had described, beyond the border gate stretched a long concrete viaduct that spanned a wide ravine — a Tijuana neighborhood crowded with small shacks. Drying clothes hung limp in late afternoon calm; children scampered about the dusty lanes in the winter gloaming.

"Reminds me of the tin roofs of Plymouth," Bauer observed as they ambled across. Garson, as did most Milwaukee males his age, was familiar with the Wisconsin town's repute. A community of several thousand, it lay an hour north of Milwaukee and was said to be dotted with cat houses. Word had it that the town's leaders, cops and politicians, depended upon speed traps and bawdy houses to enhance the city's coffers. Kickbacks and protection from brothel owners also supplemented salaries, it was claimed. Garson never thought to ask why such establishments had tin roofs.

As Garson trudged along, more apprehension gnawed at his stomach, fear almost overwhelming anticipation. He was obviously not as experienced in these matters as his roistering buddies. He had had a few daring moments with Franny in the backseat of Toby's old Buick, but he had never developed the courage for "stink finger" or "dry humping." Franny, girlfriend of his youth, would certainly have easily resisted; Garson knew himself. He once saw a bare breast when Chet ham-handedly fondled that trailer park girl in that backseat. As a kid, he had a few times gazed goofy-eyed at the posters of strippers outside of Milwaukee's Empress Burlesque until a doorman waved him away. Then, during the journey to MCRD, he clandestinely perused eye-opening articles in the journal *Sexology* furtively purchased at Chicago's Union Station. That was the sum of his concupiscent caperings. All else was fancy.

"At night, T-Town's a carnival of lust," Ridley had noted to rapt a Boot Camp audience, "all wild with blinking neon, bars, nightclubs and strip clubs at almost every turn, hawkers trying to steer you inside with promises of beautiful girls, people selling all kinds of trinkets and junk, carvings, rugs, paintings on black velvet. Little kids grab you: 'Hey, meester, want to screw my seester? She's a virgin. Only three bucks.'" He advised that they resist such blandishments, and patronize proper brothels.

"Just ask any cab driver, and he'll get you to one for a few bucks." Garson had three or four five dollar bills in his pocket with several singles – two weeks' pay.

The Casual Company buddies stopped under the marquee of the Copacabana, life-sized photos of scantily clothed girls flanking its entrance. But on more careful inspection, Garson noted that the images were of world-renowned strippers like Blaze Starr, Ann Corio and Lili St. Cyr who, he was certain, would not perform in such tacky environs. A man with shiny hair, pencil mustache, white slacks and red jacket importuned with promises of pleasures inside.

The Marine quartet sidled into the club, murky and redolent with smoke; brassy Mexican music concussed Garson's ears. The strippers' stage was empty, however. In scant minutes after perching on the bar stools, a girl sauntered to Garson's side. She almost immediately snatched his barracks hat, and perched it on her head with a rakish tilt.

"Buy me a drink, Marine," she said in a voice that might be described as small and sugary. He ordered a rum and coke for himself, and motioned the bartender to give the girl what she wanted.

Wow, she's really stacked, Garson thought, like a brick shit house. A powder blue fuzzy sweater strained to contain her generous bosom, a taut, calf-length skirt caressed hips and buttocks. She was pretty, of course, dark, neck-length hair curled loosely, revealing gold hoop earrings; perfect white teeth and glossy lips complemented tawny skin, high cheek bones and cocoa eyes. A floral zephyr teased his nostrils.

From far remove, Garson's memory would not yield the girl's name, but he liked to think it was Dolores since she reminded him of the exotic, raven-maned silent movie actress Dolores Del Rio whose photos he had seen in old magazines. Garson's Dolores jutted the last finger of her right hand from the tall, high ball glass, nail polish glistening. Ruby smudges clung to twin straws rising from the iced drink. Other than sharing names – he called himself Steele, Rip Steele – he could not recall much conversation.

Expectant minutes passed while Garson's mind raced ahead to some cinematic assignation. He tried to disguise his anticipation, to remain calm like a proud seasoned Marine should. She delicately rested her left hand on his knee. He inhaled deeply, trying to slow his respiration, and audibly sipped at the tasteless rum and coke. Then, almost imperceptibly, Dolores's finger began tracing its way along Garson's trouser crease. He affected an expression of nonchalance, but had difficulty controlling his breath. He hoped he convinced her of his battle-tested maturity. Dolores knew better. Her wandering finger reached Garson's groin. His thoughts exploded like fireworks.

"Oooh," Dolores purred, languidly drawing out each word, "do you like me?" Was she trying to mime Mae West who had once said something like that in an old movie? No, West had asked her foil: "Are you happy to see me?"

She plucked the cherry from her glass and gazing at Garson under dreamy eyelids, touched her tongue to the fruit, then caressed it with plumy lips. Trying to force himself into flaccidity, Garson called extraneous visions to mind, of Sergeant Maddox, decay and death, of God even, of his mother. He should not succumb to seduction so easily.

"Want my picture?" Her words were breathy. Alcohol was toying with Garson's brain, but he formed more mean mental images until the arousal was subdued, and he was able to follow her. Dolores guided him to a back room containing a photo booth. Under the glaring lights, she was still pretty but he observed that her lipstick was applied a bit too generously. For a dollar more, she said, he could buy her an orchid wristlet. She was persuasive, saying that she liked him a lot.

That photo still rests in Garson's album. It could be the sepia image of two young lovers: He and Dolores seated with backs to the camera, heads turned over their shoulders. They posed cheek to cheek, his skin sun browned and hers only slightly paler. The barracks hat brim, a regulation two fingers above the nose, shadowed his eyes. She curled her left wrist over his shoulder, displaying the flower; with slightly parted lips, her expression was languorous, well-practiced and promising. When displaying that photo to Marine buddies in the years ahead, he often boasted that he had had a memorable tryst with the girl, but never clarified she was a Tijuana bar tart.

Back at the bar, he purchased her a second highball. Emboldened by alcohol, he asked if they might go somewhere for a few hours or spend the night together. She assented with a fetching smile. After one more drink, she said she needed to call someone to say she would be coming home late. With a smoldering gaze, she sucked the final dregs of her drink before slowly swirling from the bar stool; she brushed her lips across his cheek, then strolled to the back of the room, hips swaying in the tight skirt, buttocks beckoning under the fabric. She sauntered through a draped doorway. Garson ordered another rum and coke, smugly satisfied at his suavity and sophistication. He sipped at his drink, and grew headier amid the smoke and music. He would not need a whore house.

"She ain't comin' back, man," Bauer said many minutes later. "She got what she wanted. She gets paid by the drink and a cut on that picture you took back there." Garson desperately wanted not to believe Bauer; his mind fought against it. Dolores had found him appealing and interesting; perhaps it was love at first sight as in the movies. Twenty minutes later, Garson conceded that it was all a come-on, a tease like Lana back home.

Garson and his buddies finished their drinks at the Copacabana, and then sauntered outside into the clamorous, neon-flooded street. Unsteady, he wavered; Bauer slid a hand under his armpit to steady him. His memory of what occurred next was hazy, the effect of the cheap rum taking a toll.

"Lookin' for some *chiquitas*, Marines?" A taxi driver leaned against a battered, old Chrysler at curbside. A polished smile of spectacularly bright teeth lighted his scarred face. Bauer, somehow wise to these ways, negotiated a price. The girls, the driver assured, were all beautiful and young, and the price was cheap. For ten minutes or so, they drive about, Garson's head reeling as they jostled over unpaved streets. Only occasional incandescent bulbs cast cones of illumination.

At a shotgun shack on a narrow alleyway, the driver stopped, and honked. A rectangle of yellow light poured out as a large woman swung open the door with a beefy arm. Bauer went inside, but returned in only a few minutes.

"Fuck, man, nothin' but old broads and scuzzies in there," he sneered at the driver. "Can't you take us to someplace better?" For an additional few dollars and after another ten-minute ride, they arrived at a larger establishment, a one-story bungalow with shuttered windows and a rose-painted door. Bauer again reconnoitered, and within minutes waved them in.

Inside, a dozen or more women and girls sat on sofas and chairs arrayed around the living room; some conversed, others sat and smoked in solitude. They were of varying ages with skin tones ranging from alabaster to dark Indian. Most wore airs of disaffection or boredom, paying little heed to the new arrivals. Even in his bleary state, Garson was devastated that none approached images of movie trollops he carried — the like of Vantine, Jean Harlow's portrayal in "Red Dust," Ona Munson's Belle Watling in "Gone With The Wind," Garbo's "Camille," even Crawford's Sadie Thompson in "Rain."

Suddenly, Garson was confronted by a beefy woman. She stood inches taller and outweighed him by a dozen pounds. She grabbed his arm, pulling him toward a dim recess of the house, pendulous breasts swaying beneath the gaudy dress. He resisted, but she was uncommonly strong and insistent. His soles skittered across the linoleum while he tried to extricate himself from her iron grip. The whore turned, and flung her hand into his crotch.

"Come on, cherry boy," she scowled, clutching at his groin and kneading it vigorously. Garson was shocked into sobriety; he had not the slightest sexual urge now. He wanted a woman, his first, to be petite and pretty like the movie maidens about whom he fantasized, not someone larger and older than he, someone almost maternal with conjoined Frida Khalo eyebrows.

"What's a matter, you a queer boy?" she burbled, feeling no erection. "I give you good fuck anyway." She tugged at him again. His buddies laughed at the antic *pas de deux*.

"Go on, Boondocks, mount her for the Corps! Put a flag over her face and go for 'Old Glory'!"

After several minutes, she desisted and turned him loose, disgust written on her face. Garson straightened his uniform blouse, attempting to regain his composure. He glanced about the room just as a comely young woman swept aside a beaded curtain and stepped into the common room. He guessed she may have just serviced a client. She wore a gauzy dress that revealed shapely legs and a petite figure. Garson thought he could see the hint of nipples, but it may only have been his imagination. He signaled the madam and counted a pair of five dollar bills into her meaty palm. She nodded toward the girl. His buddies had by then disappeared down dark hallways.

It might have been poetic, of course, if Garson's initial sexual encounter had been at the hands of some heart-of-gold prostitute who gently introduced him to mysteries of her body and wonders of passion. Garson had dreamed of the moment when a girl would sense something in him that she had never found in any man before, something romantics described — emotional residue left on young hearts forever. Such was the stuff of movies, of writings akin to his own memoir even.

Some inches shorter than he, she seemed trim and narrow hipped. Preceding him down the dimly-lighted hallway, she shook loose her dark hair, cascading it about her shoulders. She led him into a small room, and motioned for Garson to pull the curtain closed. A tiny table lamp illuminated a single bed with a mattress as insubstantial as a MCRD rack, hard and unpliant. For some minutes, Garson stood uncertain; perhaps she expected that he merely bare his loins. But daringly, he disrobed completely, clinging to that notion of romance, and sat on the rumpled sheets. A guttural grunting emanated from an adjacent room, and the odor of unwashed bodies and antiseptic filled his nostrils.

In a well-practiced gesture, Pearl — for that was the name he gave her — shrugged off her gauzy shift and stepped free of her panties, unashamed to reveal her body. Breath caught in Garson's throat and his heart battered his ears. He peered at her breasts and her fan of pubic hair. As his brain whirled, he saw only perfection, Maureen O'Hara's "Shireen" to Fairbanks's Sinbad, his "burning bright." Minutes may have passed while he was frozen in the vision. But when reliving the experience much later, he had to admit that, while she was diminutive, her breasts sagged, belly protruded and upper thighs were unusually fleshy. She held out her hand for a dollar when Garson requested a rubber; the image of those Boot Camp venereal films and the need for protection had been etched in his mind. With the ease of a clinician, she unrolled the prophylactic on his erection.

Insouciantly, she lay on the bed beside him, thighs wide, beckoning with both hands. He kissed her sweaty forehead and warm cheeks, ran his shaking hands over her breasts and belly; he felt her nipples respond. Pearl smelled faintly of rosewater. She rolled him atop her, and with a well-practiced gesture pulled him inside. He moaned lowly as warm tissues infolded him; he thought afterward that she winced. Every nerve ending seemed to be focused there. The sensation was overwhelming, overpowering, like nothing he had ever known or suspected. His entire body shuddered as her hands played along his backbone.

"Ooh, *querido*! Ooh, *chico*!" Pearl cooed in his ear.

His heart thundered uncontrollably. He did not recall how he had done it, but suddenly he found himself under her, her knees at his hips, their loins slapping rhythmically, audibly. It seemed he had been preparing for these moments all of his years, and did not want them to pass too quickly. He was anxious for the realization to be better than the anticipation. Perspiration beaded his brow.

"Ooh, I'm coming. I'm coming." Pearl burbled.

Ignoring her, he plunged on, and on. Many minutes passed, 15 or more, perhaps; it might have been hours, for all he knew. Once again, he rolled her under him. Her body was sheened with perspiration; the pungent odor of rut emanated from her. Her fingers, like claws, scored his back; he winced as salty perspiration run into the cuts. Red welts were visible the next day. Eyes wide, he lifted his torso and studied her in the dim light, drinking in details, trying to lock everything in memory, lest he never experience this again. She cried out about repeated climaxes, and tears ran from the corners of her eyes.

Finally, he was overcome by an inexorable upwelling, a release he had only imagined before. He hugged her tightly as every nerve and fiber concentrated in his groin, and he lunged violently, seeming to explode. Guttural utterings spilled from his throat; timpani thundered in his ears. As if he had run miles, he was breathless, collapsing upon Pearl; bones failed to support him, muscles and tendons jellied.

With only momentary pause, she rolled him roughly from her and arose. Walking to a small basin, she unceremoniously swabbed a wet rag between her thighs and over her groin before stepping into her panties and draping the gauzy shift on her body. Tying her hair in a bandana, she left the room.

The tryst had passed too quickly, of course. He had hoped for much more, yearning for foreplay and romance as well as raw carnality. Garson long proclaimed there was nothing more ravishing than sitting across the table from a beautiful woman with fine food and wine, pleasant conversation – the opening airs of an evening's sensual minuet.

But when the Marines strolled back across the viaduct to the border well after midnight, Garson was once again locked in his own thoughts. If he was realistic about that experience, he had to sadly conclude that Pearl's responses were studied, measured and lacked spontaneity. Yet, he liked to think that he had surprised her, perhaps even pleased her a little with his stamina and insistence. He desperately hoped she might have shown some sign, a smile or gesture, indicating there was something special about this encounter. There had been none. It was certainly unlike anything he had intuited from movie scenes of his youth with crashing waves and symphonic crescendo, or even fade-to-black.

When he reflected, he concluded that he was only a faceless, unremarkable client, a "John." Despite her youth, Pearl had been there so many times before, he knew, with uncounted men and boys. For her, a *puta* after all, it was merely, as one wag characterized it, a plumbing exercise.

It's sad, really, when you think about it – my Pop's first sexual encounter. Sure, it wasn't one of those furtive, fumbling couplings in the back of a car, or in a girl's bedroom when parents were away. But it wasn't much better. Myself, I'd never pay to get laid; I don't think any guy I know would. More, I've read those stories about young guys being introduced to the joys of sex by patient and gentle working women. Put it this way – I think it's tawdry, degrading, depressing, disgusting even, especially for someone like my Pop.

When the Marine buddies re-crossed the viaduct toward the border gate into California, Garson and the others unconsciously stayed in step. And to the tune of "Colonel Bogey March," they sang the verse over and over again:

"Horse shit — what makes the brown grass green. Horse shit — what makes a good Marine." Silently, of course, Garson assayed his first sexual encounter on the return trolley ride. Two things were certain, he concluded: He was a cherry boy no more, and he needed a long hot shower.

Drowsing in his rack some nights later, he reviewed the swirl of activity that had constituted that final day as Platoon 023.

"Got a ten-day leave, then I report to the 'Stumps.'" Hal meant the base of Twenty-nine Palms in the Mohave Desert where Marines trained for artillery duty. Heissen and one or two others would join him.

"Man, arty school!"

"Lucky fuckin' bastard!" Garson proclaimed when he heard about Hal's leave.

Like all but a few new Marines, Garson was now comfortable with the Corps's multi-purpose word. It no longer carried the potency of his younger years so recently passed when four letters formed a verbal assault weapon. Now, it was just another piece of vocabulary.

"Going back to Berlin?" Garson asked Hal.

"Naw, Vegas. I hope soon to be rolling along across the desert at a high rate of deliberate speed. Fremont Street, here I come."

The Detroiter Liska, Milwaukeeans Springer and Buchman and "Baby Marine" Krupa with his two girlfriends, and others were bound for Camp Pendleton, a quick bus ride up the coast, for advanced combat training. Garson would follow in a few weeks, but never caught up with them again. From there, Heissen and others had further orders for Pickle Meadows in the Sierra Nevada Mountains for cold weather training. The Corps apparently believed the Korea Peninsula was insufficiently pacified, and needed to remain prepared for battle in such a frozen clime. Over the years, Garson would wonder about the big Texan, Hupner; certainly his illiteracy would in time be discovered and lead to discharge. And what of Prick, the gentle bumbler who did not earn his stripe?

Garson did not learn where his mentor Ridley was ordered. He had been released from MCRD early to be with his family. He speculated that the college boy would receive a good assignment, perhaps something that involved intelligence and writing like public information. The Californian could be a great spokesman for the Corps, Garson mused. The army long carped that Marines were publicity hounds, assigning more writers and cameramen than infantrymen to every unit.

Barker, the polished and proud Right Guide was assigned to Sea School, the spit and polish training unit that prepared Marines for duty aboard ships or at embassies the world over. Only the best gained entry into that elite cadre, and Barker was among the best. He would be issued natty dress blues and, with his fellows, personify in the public eye the few, the proud, the Marines. Garson was confident he would have a sterling career.

Rusty and Preston secured enviable post-Boot Camp duty as "airedale pogues." The little redhead was to report to the Marine Air Station at Cherry Point, a lengthy trip across the country to North Carolina. Preston was assigned to the Corps's California air base at El Toro not far up the coast. Both would remain at those installations for the duration of their three-year enlistments. When they said their goodbyes the next day, decades would pass before they met again.

Among those remaining in the quonset that final night, a few conversed in hushed tones, still cowed by former proscriptions. So that was it, Garson reflected. Platoon 023 would tomorrow cease to exist, its members, recruits no more, dispersed to the winds, like that close order drill maneuver they had lately perfected. For him, Boot Camp had begun as an adventure, even something of a lark. In retrospect, however, it had been a serious endeavor that had inculcated discipline and purpose. He had survived one-sixteenth of his enlistment.

"Know what *déjà vu* means?" Hal queried as he closed a lock on his packed seabag, preparing for departure. Garson was often amused recalling the scene.

"Yeah, it's the feeling that you'd somehow been here before," he returned.

"So, do you know what vuja de means?" There were only blank looks.

"Means, you never want to come back here again. Semper fuckin' Fi, Gyrenes!" The silver fleck flashed from his smile as Hal, now PFC Faltschaft, snapped everyone a crisp high ball salute, shouldered his sea bag and strode from of the quonset.

***

Chapter 8

VILLARD AVENUE GANG

"Gonna change my name to 'Rip Steele.'"

That was what Mellish, eyes dancing, proclaimed he intended when he came of age. Obviously, he was influenced by second feature and B movie actors like old cowboy stuntman, Bob Steele, and younger Rip Torn. Garson found amusement in that avowal although he did not let on. A few years before, of course, he had himself briefly assumed the alias "Blackie."

What distinguished Mellish from most of Garson's other youthful pals was his repertoire of family adventures with which he captivated audiences, especially Garson. His voice changed inflection, eyebrows swooped like gull wings and hands gesticulated. He might have been a shaman in preliterate society.

When Mellish worked as the newspaper station captain, Garson volunteered to help assemble the bulky Sunday edition in predawn hours when the final news and sports sections arrived. It was called "subbing." Mellish was at his best during those times because he had a captive audience.

"Did I tell you that time my brother Davy and I were fighting in the back seat of my dad's old car," Mellish began. "My little brother was mad 'cause I teased him about something, maybe that Alfalfa cowlick of his. When dad nosed the car into our garage, Davy suddenly jumps out. That car, a '34 Hupmobile, had suicide doors

– you know, hinged at the back instead of front. When he jumped out, the car door caught on the garage door and tore it off!"

Garson admitted that he had undeveloped verbal skills, and was envious of pals like Mellish who could hold an audience recounting experiences about which Garson only dreamed, like episodes out of movies. He was always attracted to pals with large families who seemed to live lives filled with incessant mischance and misadventure. He remembered his father's stories about growing up in northern Wisconsin. Garson lived vicariously in such tales.

"Did I tell you about the time," Mellish usually began his yarns. "My folks were gone, and we were playing war in the house. I was showing off with my dad's 12-guage. Didn't know it was loaded. When Davy ran up the stairs, I pulled the trigger and was knocked on my ass. Blasted the ball on top the banister to smithereens. Wasn't a ball exactly. Think it's called a finial.

"'Oh, cripes, Dad'll kill us!' Davy goes. 'What'll we do?' I came up with the idea to mix up plaster of Paris to patch the ball back together. Actually, it looked pretty good when we finished painting it. We touched up little dings in the wall where birdshot hit." Mellish chuckled in the telling, amusing even himself. Clownish expressions begged the audience to respond.

"We thought we'd done everything to hide the damage. But then, my folks came home. 'What've you boys been up to?'" The brothers, who had cowed their little sister to silence, wagged their heads.

"When dad started to go up the stairs, he put his hand on the bannister, and the ball fell off and smashed to pieces on the floor. We got a lot of hell for that stunt."

Mellish was one of about a half a dozen children, the youngest of whom was a little girl of about eight or nine who Garson named Perdita; she had a lazy eye and a testy temperament. She liked to kick boys in their shins, and Garson caught more than one of those blows. The oldest brother was studying to be a policeman like his father and an uncle. The two brothers nearest Mellish in age were unapologetic scamps, at least in his recounting.

"Did I tell you about the time we got into the prison at the

Disciplinary Barracks?" Mellish, often spinning off in tangents, took some time in getting to that yarn. First, he described bow hunting in the large open space across from their house, near what was once called the County Correctional facility, the community prison. The multi-acre site was dotted with small woodlots and open spaces of wild foliage. Barns and farm fields were visible to the northwest. Davy, the brother who often sustained most injury or punishment, once downed a large owl with an arrow.

"It wasn't dead, and we felt sorry for it," Mellish remembered, and Davy wanted it for a pet. So he wrapped the bird in a jacket and carried it home, hoping to nurse it back to health. The boy attached a makeshift bandage to its injured leg, and over time the bird improved. They kept it in the basement, tethering it behind cabinet, and fed it mice they caught and night crawlers they dug.

"One night, Dad was working down in the basement, reloading shot gun shells, I think." Mellish ran his hand over his mouth and his body trembled in amusement at the recollection.

"He heard a funny sound behind him, some kind of whooshing. When he turned, that owl was flying at him, eyes glaring, claws clutching. Dad grabbed a hunting knife from the bench, and flailed at the bird, cutting off one foot. He killed Davy's pet owl. Geez, we all got hell for that one, too."

Mellish never seemed to exhaust his storehouse of stories about such escapades. Nearly all seemed to end on humorous notes. How, Garson wondered, could so much happen to one family, to one person? Why, it was right out of "Our Gang" or "Bowery Boys" movies.

"Hey, let's make a trek to Black Bridge sometime." That was a suggestion Mellish put forward one day as he was closing the C-11 newspaper station. "Maybe Toby and some others can come along, too."

Black Bridge was a railway trestle on the Chicago, St. Paul & Pacific line visible in the distance on clear days, a dark, brooding presence, mysterious *fata morgana* on the far horizon. The distance to the span may not have been many miles from the neighborhood, but it seemed a world away, a trek such as the one taken by Walter of Gurnee, Tyrone Power's character in "The Black Rose." The structure was rumored to hold secrets – a hobo camp, buried treasure somewhere nearby, and things ominous.

"Gypsies," some said. "They hold kidnapped kids captive out there." Garson envisioned matters less foreboding, of girls in colorful dresses and dangling earrings dancing by firelight – something right out of "Golden Earrings" with Marlene Dietrich. But the thought of the Wolfman's protector, Maleva, the gnomish Maria Ouspenskaya gave him pause.

Several boys, fellow carriers and others who hung out at the paper station, liked the idea, and all agreed that after deliveries the following Sunday, they would rendezvous at the Mellish house and head out.

"Bring your bows." While Toby and others owned weapons of deadly power – 60- or 70-pound pulls – Garson's boasted no more than 40 pounds; it was a second-hand acquisition from a cousin, attained over his mother's objections.

"It's only a little bow," his father had said, overruling her. "Let him be a boy, for Christ sake." Garson was further mortified because the bow was lemon yellow. He had purchased a nondescript quiver and half dozen cheap arrows from the Villard Avenue sports shop. He briefly flirted with the thought of becoming a champion archer like Howard Hill who made all manner of fantastic trick shots in a movie short that accompanied "The Adventures of Robin Hood."

On the appointed morning, Garson draped the quiver and arrows on his shoulder, strung the bow and walked to Mellish's home, a high-peeked, two-story structure with four or five bedrooms. Garson recognized the dirt-floor garage from a story. The parents and Perdita were at church.

In the kitchen, Mellish and his brother, Davy, were assembling sandwiches, toasting Wonder Bread and spreading on mayonnaise. Mellish fried eggs in an old encrusted iron skillet. They offered Garson one, and he bit into it reluctantly, uncertain about the flavor combination.

"Fried eggs and mayo?" his mother frowned when he told her about his newly discovered delicacy. "What a combination." It was an uncommon combination that Garson added to his culinary repertoire, joining another favorite, peanut butter and baloney on white bread.

The trek to Black Bridge would not rival the adventure depicted in a future generation's film, "Stand By Me"— no pursuing thugs or corpse to be unearthed. With three or four others, Toby arrived, and they climbed the embankment and rail bridge that spanned Silver Spring Drive to begin the Sunday odyssey.

The Chicago, St. Paul & Pacific operated a single-track line that meandered from the Menomonee Valley marshalling yards near downtown, through the city on a private right of way, coming to grade near Hampton with crossings at Villard and Custer Avenues. The sun was sufficiently high when the band set out, light glinting from the distant dark steel span. They passed on the west side of the Disciplinary Barracks complex with its water tower and collection of low structures, the main building reminded Garson of a castle. They trooped along, alternately, striding on rail ties or stone ballast, occasionally balancing on the rails. Garson walked with a light step, fantasizing about Robin Hood's Merry Men. When he thought about it, Toby bore a slight resemblance, minus the mustache, to Errol Flynn

After trudging for 20 minutes or so, a garter snake that had been sunning itself beside the track wriggled toward the weeds. Since childhood, Garson had an aversion to snakes for reasons he could not explain. His mother may have transferred phobias of such creatures to him. The reptile was less than a foot long, and Garson had to admit that its reticulated coloration of greens and tans was handsome. Yet, he withdrew an arrow, and fitted in nock onto the bow string.

"Don't shoot! Don't shoot!" Toby shouted. "Wanna capture it." It was what Garson feared – Toby carrying that snake for the remainder of the trek. Once, his pal had captured a small serpent no more than three or four inches long. Daringly, he dangled the immature creature above his open mouth. Garson's stomach churned.

Garson let loose the arrow, and to his surprise it struck the snake at mid body.

"Crap!" Toby glared. Guilt gripped Garson immediately. Why did he do that? It was a harmless creature, like the snapping turtle. The boys circled the wounded serpent as it writhed, pinioned by the arrow. Blood oozed from its jaw as the sinuous body coiled and flailed futilely, trying to free itself, to cling to remnants of life. Garson guiltily pulled out the arrow, wiping the missile clean in the weeds. He gazed momentarily at the snake's death throes, feeling not at all like Robin Hood.

"Let's go," Mellish interrupted. "Got a long way to go." The party strode off once more. A few yards on, Garson turned to watch the snake's final shudders, its tail quivering. From a solitary scrub oak he thought a pair of crows carped at him.

Garson felt a tremble in the rails. A train appeared on horizon, lumbering from the northwest toward the city. Since Garson lived so proximate to the line, he was accustomed to the freights, even comforted at night by their wayward horns. But Garson was wary of the massive engines and string of swaying cars, always stepping well back when they trundled by. He had intense fear of getting a foot caught or tripping, and several times awoke from a dream of being mangled beneath the screeching wheels. He was timorous when the warning signals came alight and clanged; there were no barricading gates on Hopkins Street. Some of his pals placed pennies on the tracks as trains approached, picking up the warm compressed copper after the parade of cars passed. Garson never had the courage to do even that.

He was the first to scramble down the dirt embankment to the flat below. The engineer blasted his horn. Garson's pals daringly scampered aside spare minutes before the heavy diesel rumbled past, steel wheels screeching, clacking on rail seams. A string of 20 or 30 cars swayed behind – box cars in brown and Tuscan red livery; black ore cars; empty flat cars. After many minutes, a yellow caboose passed, and a man leaning on the rear railing waved. Garson returned the gesture.

The group regained the tracks, and trudged onward as the sun climbed higher into the sky. The day was windless. It grew warm under a few stray puffy clouds. The shiny rails shimmered with heat rays, distorting the lines of steel that converged miles ahead. Toby drank from his military canteen. Garson was thirsty, but did not ask his pal who, he expected, would turn him down anyway.

"Whyn't you bring your own?" was his pal's expected response.

Barns and silos, chicken coops and animal pens came into view. Cultivated farm fields were interspersed with stony pasturage where cows cropped wild grass, raising their heads and chewing as they watched the wayfarers. Copses of trees and underbrush sprouted between the fields. There were smaller rail bridges across major thoroughfares – Florist Avenue and Mill Road – but none had a superstructure like Black Bridge.

A covey of pheasants flushed from a thicket as the boys marched past. Toby, who carried an arrow at the ready, let the missile fly, but it was well short of any bird. Others loosed arrows at scampering rabbits, or squirrels that skittered up trees. Later, Mellish said he spied a deer peering from a nearby woodlot, but he was the only one who saw it.

Black Bridge loomed larger, and its particularities became more distinct. Garson had never seen it this close. It spanned the divided lanes of Good Hope Road. Thick steel beams angled upward, defining huge "W's" and "V's." None was vertical. Years later, Garson learned it was of a style called a Warren Truss Bridge. Much to Garson's chagrin, Black Bridge at this proximity was actually rusty, appearing almost decrepit and dangerous to a boy's eye. The structure measured more than 30-feet high. Garson studied it in detail, noting the huge bolts that dotted the beams, struts and girders, almost like giant steel candy drops on strips of paper.

Suddenly, Toby stripped quiver and canteen from his shoulder, grabbed the flanged edges of an angled girder, set his feet in place, and slowly clambered his way upward. Garson watched in amazement. Like Johnny Weissmuller's Tarzan, his pal ascended effortlessly, then stood triumphantly atop the horizontal high steel. Arms exultant, he emitted an unimpressive Apeman yell. A frightened flock of pigeons arose and wheeled into the sky. Still,

Toby had performed an astounding feat.

"Look," Toby pointed from his aerie. "Over there." Heads turned in the direction he pointed. Across the road and below the embankment, a copse of willows and birches shadowed what looked like an abandoned encampment.

"Hey, wait up," Toby shouted as the adventurers scrambled down and crossed a turbid creek. They paused at a blackened fire pit. Rusty tin cans, empty pint whiskey bottles, soiled clothing and shoes, and other debris were strewn about. The pals rummaged about, toeing aside discarded blankets, rags and other leavings. Toby joined them, his hands and seat of his pants smudged with bridge rust.

"Hobo camp," someone said. "Might be gypsies," Mellish replied.

Singly, they surveyed the site, picking up items for inspection before tossing them aside. Under a wooden crate, Garson spotted a small newsprint booklet, perhaps four inches by two. He knew immediately what it was: An "Eight Pager." Such cheap, salacious publications had passed through his hands before; they depicted famous cartoon characters like Nancy and Sluggo, Blondie and Dagwood, and others engaged in sexual congress, penises the size of baseball bats. This one featured Betty Boop and assorted paramours.

"What's that," Toby startled Garson's scrutiny.

"Aw, nothin'." Garson sheepishly folded the grubby pamphlet and quickly slipped it into his back pocket. If his mother ever found this, he worried, he could not guess the consequences. She had long since discovered his cache of pinup girls, including the purloined *Life* magazine clipping of alluring Rita Hayworth in her revealing peignoir, and destroyed them without comment. Perhaps she recognized that healthy boys were curious of such things, Garson guessed. But this was entirely beyond the pale. He would later leaf through the salacious pamphlet several times before tearing it into tiny pieces.

The wayfaring band soon exhausted its survey, finding little of interest and nothing of value. Several lay down in the weeds beside it, weary after the miles-long tramp. Head propped on his palms, Garson watched the parade of puffy afternoon clouds — fair weather cumulus, he thought they were called. Because of the overnight subbing and morning delivering, none of the boys had slept Saturday. Garson's head lolled and his eyes fluttered; he fell into a light slumber. When he awoke, the sun had tilted toward horizon.

As if by unspoken agreement, the pals, successful in their quest to solve the mysteries of Black Bridge, turned toward home. In an hour or so, they finally dispersed from the Mellish house. Garson's bold pal would lead another memorable undertaking whose implications were right out of the movies.

"White Heat," just then in theater release, and other films fired youthful imagination about prison life. With Leland, Garson recalled seeing "The Big House" at the dingy Violet Theater, the 1930 movie with Robert Montgomery, Chester Morris and Wallace Beery that established not only the gritty *mise-en-scene* of incarceration, but also a whole new glossary of slang terms and a menagerie of movie "types" – from the kindly prison chaplain to the benign old lifer and unrepentant gangster.

Once called the Milwaukee County House of Correction, the sprawling facility on Hopkins Street across an open field from the Mellish house had been transferred to the federal government during the war years. It was marked by a mushroom-shaped water tower and two-story armory building that featured ominous barred windows. Tall elm trees paraded in front, and the main entrance was flanked by a pair of stone towers with crenellated crowns. Former army roomers, Spot and Paulie, had worked there after the war, but now the facility appeared lifeless.

"There's a cell block in there just like the movies," Mellish announced one day as they sat on his front porch, gazing at the collection of buildings a few hundred yards across the way. They had been conversing about "Brute Force," the prison movie. Garson had left the theater devastated that the con, Joe Collins, sympathetically portrayed by Burt Lancaster, and his band had failed to break out; partial satisfaction was felt when the sadistic Munsey, the guard captain portrayed by pinched Hume Cronyn, received just desserts.

"Been in there lots of times." Mellish replied to Garson's query about knowledge of the cell block. That triggered another daring undertaking that registered vividly in his mind for years. If memory was accurate, there were about four who took part in the new escapade, but, for reasons he could not say, Toby was not among them.

Mellish and his brothers hunted for birds and small animals in the scrub land on Hopkins Street that fronted the armory building. Sometime after the army had released or transferred soldiers from the facility, Mellish and his brothers had stumbled onto the steel access portal. Adventurous as they were, they lifted the heavy hatch to discover a long maintenance tunnel that led directly to the prison building.

"After the soldiers left, it wasn't used anymore. Ain't no prisoners in there now, only a watchman." The pals chose a suitable night to explore the tunnel and cell block. The trek through the subterranean passageway was long, perhaps a third of a mile of dank and claustrophobic toiling; the dripping ceiling hovered no more than a few feet above their heads; concrete walls closed in tightly. While only Mellish was tall, the entire troop stooped as if in a submarine. Intermittent low watt bulbs cast dull yellow light; heavy electric conduits closed in on the tiny band. The clank of steam pipes initially startled Garson. His thoughts had wandered to the climactic scene in "The Third Man" when police chased Orson Welles's Harry Lime in the sewers of Vienna, or when Paul Claudin, Claude Rains, the man who became the Phantom of the Paris Opera, escaped into the city's sewers after being burned with acid.

Garson's reverie was interrupted when the boys reached a steel ladder set in the concrete wall. Mellish motioned, and climbed up. The metal cover was not as heavy as the field access port, and Mellish handled it unassisted. Hinges squealed. The boys filed out into a sleeping bay. Cots lined each side of the long room. Beyond opened an immense dining hall that once served prisoners and guards. The image of Cody Jarrett, James Cagney, boiling in rage at the death of his mother in "White Heat" momentarily came to

Garson's mind.

Then Mellish motioned his followers down a long corridor which led to the cell block. It was just like Alcatraz, Sing Sing and prisons depicted in movies. Three tiers of cells rose high above, ladder ways connecting them at each end. Even in the dim light penetrating the windows, it was obvious that gray paint peeled from the walls after years of disuse. Here, the companions separated, each set out on his own inspection. Grit crackled underfoot as they prowled about.

Large levers, visible at each end of the row of cells, controlled sliding doors. Gripping bars, Garson poked his head inside a lower level cell. Had his Uncle Vin been incarcerated here for bootlegging? he wondered. A solitary cot hung cockeyed from the wall, its metal stays rusty and crooked. It was apparent that at least two prisoners lived in each cell, sleeping on tiered bunks. A dirty sink and toilet jutted from the back wall. This was how Collins, Jarrett and those other film convicts lived

"Go on in!" Davy motioned. Garson hesitantly stepped inside. It would be claustrophobic to live here. From the corner of his eye, Garson noticed Davy push on the cell door; it screeched and began to close, the sound reverberating from the concrete and steel confines. He darted out, fearing entrapment.

Mellish glared from across the way, putting a finger to his lips. Suddenly, a beam of light pierced the gloom and swept along the floor. Footsteps crackled along the gritty concrete. Night watchman, Mellish mouthed *sotto voce.* He pointed toward the cells. Garson ducked back inside, crouching under the barren cot. The flashlight beam daggered inside the cell block, crawling up one wall and along the ceiling. Garson's heart hammered and his armpits dampened. His thoughts gyrated.

If discovered, what would it mean for the boys? What would he tell his parents? His dad would be particularly vexed. Would he tell the cops to let his son sit? Would he go to jail? After what seemed like an hour, the light winked out. The sounds of his footsteps diminished. Frozen, the boys waited for more minutes. Finally, Mellish waved his arm, and the band followed to the access portal. They trudged back through the dank tunnel, careful not to trip over scattering of tools and other impedimenta. Finally, after an interminable walk, they reached the entrance, and four hands lifted the heavy steel covering. The sky was alight with stars. Everything was silent and normal.

Abed that night, Garson smiled, satisfied that he had participated in another daring escapade, even courting danger this time. But such boyhood larks were soon to end. As he entered his teen years, the time for bolder undertakings was at hand.

Garson completed Holy Redeemer six months into the new decade, but his grades had barely qualified for graduation. He stumbled to the term's end only because of an interest in U. S. history especially the Civil War period, American literature and the good graces of the cloistered teachers. Two sadly faded color photos marked the bright June graduation day in 1951 – his thickset father posing in a dated double-breasted brown suit, and Garson in black cap and gown. It would be the only time in his life that Garson wore such garb and participated in a school year-end ritual. In her mid-40s, Garson's mother avoided the camera, self-conscious, now, of her plumpness. It was obvious how dresses strained around her stomach and behind.

Garson hoped to join pals and acquaintances at the nearby public high school, but his mother insisted he enroll at Messmer, the Catholic school a 40-minute bus ride distant. Garson's father was concerned about the cost of tuition, recommending the public school. Their campaign in favor of Custer was of no avail.

"I want you to have a Catholic education," his mother emphasized. Garson was impressed by the handsome school building on Capitol Drive with its three brown brick stories punctuated by tan terra cotta motifs; from its corners soared tall Gothic spires; its main entrance featured massive cathedral doors. The interior was laden with rich oak woodwork, decorative ceramic tiles; a chapel and swimming pool were complimented by a domed green house and observatory.

The School Sisters of Notre Dame were the school's teaching order. Habits of stiff and flaring wimples contrasted with the softly flowing garb of the Holy Redeemer nuns. No matter the difference in attire, Garson had long been comfortable with these teaching women. As in grade school, he encountered several who encouraged him despite his indifferent academic performance.

After Garson began attending Messmer, the time spent on Galena Street neighborhood declined markedly, and the friendships he had cultivated there ebbed. Roxy and her mother had moved from the decrepit tenement, and his unrequited romance was forgotten. More, he felt the loss of his movie mentor and pal, Leland. Once each week, Garson was still expected to travel to Galena to cook popcorn for his father's business. There was no time for more than these chores. He was uncomfortable returning home on the streetcar, self-conscious that he reeked of oil and popcorn. No matter that he arrived home late, he rarely completed homework assignments anyway.

Garson's Messmer years were memorable less for academics than for a nascent romance and for disciplinary incidents. While several former Holy Redeemer classmates attended the school, Garson rarely entered their social circles. Vito, the boy who delivered the morning newspaper along Garson's route, was an exception. His Swiss-born father, like Garson's mother, insisted on a religious education. Broad shouldered but doughy, Vito sprouted a thick crop of black hair and heavily-lidded dark eyes; his mouth opened on large, chisel-like front teeth. Gregarious and confident, he was also more academically conscientious than Garson.

The two shared a bit of history. At the insistence of his father, Vito, despite a soft boxy body, participated in gymnastics, and he coaxed Garson to accompany him. On one or two occasions, the pals reluctantly worked out in a second-story facility on the west side run by the Swiss *Turnverein*. While Vito exhibited competence on some apparatus, Garson's arms and legs flailed like a rag doll; he was unable to support himself on parallel bars or hoist his body on still rings; he banged bony shoulders on the tumbling mat. More, he was uncomfortable exposing his underdeveloped physique in the showers. Like many such activities, Garson quit after a few fitful months.

It was about that time, too, that Garson nearly severed Vito's middle finger during a mock knife fight. They had both honed small hunting knives to razor sharpness, and challenged one another to a duel. The pals parried and thrust, tossing the weapons hand to hand like gypsies. They avoided contact, but at one point, Garson swiped his blade to the left while Vito swung to the right. Blood spurted from Vito's hand, splattering the basement floor. Shocked, Garson wrapped the gaping wound in a soiled towel from the laundry chute. His stomach convulsed as he guided Vito to the neighbor, Viv, the impromptu emergency nurse who had patched up his head a decade earlier.

"I can't do anything with this," she stressed grimly when unwrapping the towel. "He needs a surgeon." She staunched the gaping wound in a swath of bandages, and summoned Vito's father. When they drove away, Garson fretted, worried that his foolishness ended traumatically. The finger healed but with an unsightly knuckle knob and permanent crook. When Vito became frustrated or angry with Garson, he invariably folded back three fingers and thrust the deformed one into the air in the "social finger" salute.

While Garson's fascination with what was called the fair sex grew, his interest was largely one of mere fancy. As a youth, a Walter Mitty romantic, he concocted strategies to attract girls only in fantasy. He and Magdalena had danced around each other in childhood, but that relationship, he knew, could never be brought to fruition because she regarded him as a putative sibling. More, she was attracted to worldly boys. Still, she was a presence in his life.

"You know Magdalena's dad died," Garson's mother informed him of that tragedy. Her father, the butcher, was horribly maimed in an accident at his east side shop, and a mangled arm was amputated. He succumbed when Magdalena began her teen years. Subsequently raised by her widowed mother, the girl insisted upon being called Lana, a name her father, a courtly man of the classics, would have never permitted.

She stood no taller than five-feet-four on a trim frame and slender legs. Like most of the neighborhood girls, she was small of breast. Auburn hair was worn full to the neck, sometimes pulled into a pony tail, other times swept up at the back of the head. Her lips were ungenerous, but her eyebrows arched provocatively. The childhood gap in her front teeth had closed, but only a little; Garson still found that space fetching. Lana now affected slight speech sibilance when circumstance warranted. And, then, there were those eyes: As a boy, Garson made only passing note of them, but now he observed their incredible shades of blue – cobalt and cerulean. She had the ability to alter their shading depending upon mood.

When Garson read Jack London's *The Sea Wolf,* he was thrilled that the author knew exactly what he saw in Lana's azure eyes – an ocean whose shades changed with deepening depths:

"The eyes themselves were of that baffling protean [color]... which was never twice the same; which runs through many shades and colourings...sometimes of the clear azure of the deep sea...eyes that could brood with the hopeless somberness; that could snap and crackle points of fire like those which sparkle from a whirling sword; that could grow chill as an arctic landscape, and yet again, that could warm and soften and be all a-dance with love-lights... luring and compelling...."

In time, Garson was also struck by her resemblance to a famed British ballerina. More, like Jane Austen's Emma Woodhouse, Lana exercised "the power to having rather too much her own way." She could be kittenish and coy one minute, and unknowingly exude sexuality in the next. Doted upon, she blossomed from girlhood to become strong willed and willful.

"Jeez, Leora!" Lana said sourly when she learned of Garson's date with one of the neighborhood girls. If he cared to admit it, Leora was far from the epitome of pulchritude that he favored. She had a high forehead, and eyes the color of Mrs. Hexe's backyard currants; they complimented her olive skin. She wore her pitch black hair to the bottom of her ears. Her family name sounded Slavic. But there was something else about her background he had overheard – that her mother was Puerto Rican. That seemed as exotic to him as the smoky-eyed girls from Italian neighborhoods he observed at Messmer.

"Want to go to the pictures with me — downtown?" Garson asked Leora in a moment of uncharacteristic brashness. It was customary when traveling to one of the downtown movie palaces to wear one's best attire. On that fall Saturday, Garson pulled on voluminous powder blue slacks called drapes, argyle socks and blue suede loafers. Over a shirt with a flaring collar, he proudly donned his prized tuxedo jacket with a roll collar. To Garson's recollection, Leora wore an ankle-length, buttocks-hugging skirt with a fuzzy sweater and scuffed white buck shoes — common attire among local girls.

Garson was uncomfortable for he was not completely certain of what was expected on a date. He had studied such things on screen, of course, but was unsure how to implement them in real life. The pair took the usual route downtown – Hopkins Street bus to the streetcar terminal, boarding the loud, jostling conveyance to Wisconsin Avenue. Numerous sailors on liberty from Great Lakes patrolled sidewalks of the mile-long commercial strip. They wore winter blues at that time of the year, but reminded Garson of Gene Kelly, Frank Sinatra and Jules Munchen in the joyful musical "On the Town."

Under a dazzling Warner Theater marquee with its ribbons of neon, Garson paid a dollar for two admissions. The opulent venue boasted two thousand seats and three balconies. Garson and Leora climbed to the top balcony where sweethearts and smokers congregated. Garson was so overwhelmed, he could not remember the movies they saw; he may have purchased popcorn and soda, stretching his meager budget.

In the gloom, he cast furtive glances at Leora, but she did not return the attention, riveting her eyes on the screen. Sometime during the second feature, he stretched his left arm and gently laid it upon her shoulder. It was a daring maneuver, and he grew smug with his success. But 15 or 20 minutes into the black and white picture – he remembered only that much about it – his arm began to tingle. With each passing minute, it grew painfully numb; to no avail he made infinitesimal adjustments to his hand, hoping to ease the increasing discomfort. When the music convulsed in a crescendo of strings and horns and "The End" blazed across the screen, Leora and Garson arose. His arm was lifeless. Not wanting to alert her to his plight, he excused himself for the restroom, and there, massaged the prickly limb back to life.

He had not tried to caress Leora or even kiss her, fearful lest she think him too bold. He felt she was pleased with their date nonetheless. He could not recollect any conversation on the ride back to North Milwaukee, but he walked her to her front door. He strolled home several inches above the pavement, reveling in the memory of that first date. They chatted amiably several times thereafter at the Smith Park social club, but he did not ask for another date. It appeared she liked him well enough, and he thought others considered them a couple. His narrow chest swelled when he thought about it.

Life's dominos fall predictably in retrospect. Isaac Sager, called Shorty for a diminutive stature, had long operated a hamburger parlor on Villard Avenue; he had recently constructed a new restaurant on North Milwaukee's mercantile thoroughfare, Villard Avenue. Garson's mother had discarded her mop and scrub bucket, securing steady employment as dish washer at the new restaurant. The eatery quickly became a popular north side dining spot, filled to capacity on Sundays and holidays.

Leora cared for the toddlers of a night shift waitress who lived in one of the new Cape Cod houses on the Garson's block. He and Leora had occasionally passed time together during her duties, conversing on the concrete front stoop. He glowed during those meetings. Then, one Saturday night matters took tumultuous turn. Garson rapped at the front door in a state of anticipation. Leora bade him enter. Inside, he was thunderstruck by a scene he would replay innumerable times. Seated with his arm draped on Leora's shoulder was Garson's best pal, Toby. Garson's heart lurched, and bile bubbled in his stomach; he felt his face flush and his scalp tingle. He had once again been betrayed. How could Toby have done such a thing after all of these years? Where was the loyalty, the friendship?

Garson bolted from the front door, agitated and breathless. Abed that night, he twisted in the sheets, mind whirling about the loss of his girlfriend – to someone he supposed his best pal. He reviewed the date with Leora: If only he had kissed her, been bolder. She must have found him wanting. Surely, she would tell Lana and the other girls, and soon he would face ridicule. Fitful for the next several nights, he tried to find some countervailing reasons, some positive aspects to losing his first girlfriend. That was it: Leora's mouth was too wide, and she showed too much of her gums when she smiled. What was more, her eyebrows were too thick, and her chest was flat as a pancake.

As do many only children in crisis – for this was, indeed, a crisis in his life — Garson withdrew into himself, determined to stand strong against life's buffeting blows. He would employ similar tactics when he was beset by future emotional trauma.

The relationship with his pal Toby was strained, of course, and the boys would never again be as close as before. The betrayal seethed in Garson for many weeks. It would be Lana, his ersatz sister who pulled him from his funk. As always, movies were the source of balm.

Like the lead actor in "Cinema Paradiso," Garson studied with great care the manner actors kissed on the screen. Osculation, he called it. He did not like the tight lipped kisses, little more than friendly busses. Gary Cooper kissed that way, and even Cary Grant, perhaps because they were married to other woman in real life, Garson surmised. Lana readily avowed that she was disgusted with those open mouth screen kisses, most notably when Athos, Van Heflin, nearly devoured Milady DeWinter, Lana Turner in "The Three Musketeers;" and in "The Prisoner of Zenda" when Rudolph, Stewart Granger, kissed Princess Flavia, Deborah Kerr – strings of saliva glistened between parting lips. Garson was not repelled at all, and, in fact, yearned to experience such intimacy – if only he were brazen enough.

"Hate the way Toby kisses," Lana vituperated. "Yeah, keeps his mouth open and tries to stick his tongue in my mouth." Because of their unusual relationship, she exhibited uncommon candor with Garson, a friend she had taken to calling "little brother." It was troublesome that Toby dated Lana now, his friendship with Leora having ruptured after only a few months. Still, Garson's thoughts of Lana often registered uncommon emotional stirrings that seemed to belie mere filial attachment. He was frustrated that Lana did not think of him in the same way.

"She likes you, you know," Lana said of one of her best friend. No, Garson did not know. He long lamented that it was impossible to read the minds of girls; he thought one way while they seemed to think another.

When he wrote about those days in time's long passage, Garson thought to call Lana's best friend Melody because of the name's connotations. She was pretty and demure but far from glamorous. He chose Franny instead, something of a popular name. Two inches over five feet, she had a moon face, thin, arching eyebrows, eyes the color of cocoa, soft brown hair and a sprinkling of freckles, like cinnamon on pie crust, across the bridge of her pert nose. Her lips were ripe and pouty. Somewhat introverted, she had a musical laugh that rarely gave way to haughty cackle. Garson knew little else about her.

As they came to know each other more, Franny told Garson about her beloved grandpa who had taken her to the grand Pabst Theatre downtown for concerts and musicales. Franny remembered the opulent interior with its two balconies, red and gold appointments and immense crystal chandelier – something right out of "The Phantom of the Opera," Garson thought. She also told Garson that she had often danced around the parlor (she used that word) as her grandfather played the violin.

Friday nights each fall, students from Custer High walked to football games at North Stadium. Not having its own sports field, Custer's team scheduled home games at that venue adjacent to another city high school, Rufus King, on Capitol Drive. Many students and fans walked more than a mile from the Villard rendezvouses along Teutonia Avenue to the stadium.

As Garson strolled with a coterie of students one Friday, Lana hung back a step or two, motioning. Take her hand, she mouthed, pointing emphatically to Franny. Garson wrinkled his eyebrows in quandary. Lana glared at him, gritted her teeth and rolled her fingers into a fist. Reluctantly, Garson matched Franny's gait, and slipped his hand into hers, amazed at his own daring. She seemed unabashed and failed to withdraw her hand from his. And just like that, they were matched. Like Emma Woodhouse, Lana smiled in satisfaction.

After Toby and Leora's relationship ended for reasons unknown, the boys imperfectly patched their frayed friendship. While they were not estranged, there were distractions. Just before Toby turned 16, he sold the dashing Cushman motor scooter that Garson had long envied. Toby had long lavished much attention on the little vehicle, repainting it and cruising about the neighborhood in ease. In the scooter's place, Toby acquired a 1936 Buick Roadmaster from his elderly grandfather. The ponderous four-door was immediately dubbed the gangster car fit for Al Capone.

Unsatisfied with its staid appearance, Toby immediately set to work modifying the 15-year-old sedan; he wanted a daring hot rod similar to those depicted in magazines, giving it an appearance that would make a dramatic statement on Villard Avenue. He stripped away much of the chrome, removed taillight mountings and in their place pushed through straight exhaust pipes. New taillights were inserted adjacent to the bubbled trunk lid, and the favored blue dot lenses added. What was more, Toby shrouded the rear wing windows with metal. He spent untold hours in his garage, molding, sanding and shaping. Garson lent a hand for a day or two that summer, filing and sanding until his arms grew weary. Finally, in preparation for a new coat of paint, Toby primed the car in matte gray. It would remain in that livery for years. Some called it the "Gray Ghost."

Toby now became a Villard Avenue cruiser. More significant, the Buick gave him freedom of movement; he was no longer bound by busses and streetcars, limited by bikes or scooters and to cadged rides. He trundled about with his pals and local "babes." Garson was surprised when Toby and Lana became a couple. As dictated by girls' scripts, Lana insisted that she would not travel without Franny.

On a few summer evenings, Toby drove the lumbering Buick to Bradford Beach on Lake Michigan. En route, depending upon solvency, they sometimes stopped at Capitol Drive's famed Pig 'n' Whistle custard stand, the popular drive-in that perched on the lip of the Milwaukee River. On summer nights, young people from the entire north side and contiguous suburbs congregated there. Scrubbed and polished new cars, modified vintage roadsters and coupes and other glistening vehicles were on display. Mufflers burbled, and yards of chrome glared under the drive-in's ribbons of colorful neon. Roller skating car hops in short skirts buzzed about the lot like bees. The scene, of course, was later immortalized by George Lucas's seminal "American Graffiti."

After cherry Cokes, Toby drove to Bradford Beach where they parked at what was known as "Necker's Point." Young people with romantic inclinations frequented the spot. Police patrolled.

"Shoulders above the window line," patrolmen warned, directing a spotlight at one car after another. Great Lakes sailors took liberty in friendly Milwaukee, and it was said they parked at the spot to watch "submarine races." The innuendo was clear.

When Toby parked, Lana scooted over the floor shift; she and Toby scrunched down, heads barely visible about the front seat. Moonlight poured through the windshield. Typically, Garson was apprehensive, struggling to muster back seat confidence.

"Franny wonders why you never kiss her," Lana asked after several double dates. She did not shrink from bluntness. Garson had no answer, of course, fearing her reaction to his timorousness. Franny's body language was clear: She begged to be kissed. Garson and his girlfriend – for that is what she was now called – slid down in commodious back seat. Clutching Franny's shoulder with his left arm, he kissed her temples, then her right cheek. He could feel her shallow breathing and anticipation. He ached to put his lips on hers. But he was distracted. Instead of kissing her, he inched his fingers down her back. After pausing for incredible moments, he slid his hand under the hem of her blouse, worrying it above her waist. By inches he wormed his hand up her spine, feeling a line of perspiration there. Her skin was silky, he thought. Then a finger felt the brassiere strap taut across her back. Franny did not resist. After breathless moments, he inched his hand around her side, feeling the undergarment's cup. Franny stiffened. Without a word, she grasped his wrist firmly, and pulled away.

"She thinks you're very fresh," Lana related after that night; her eyes sparkled in revelation. The two girls obviously compared notes on such matters. Garson's chest inflated. Touching Franny's brassiere was the stuff of fantasy, ecstasy even. He relived those daring moments in dreams for many nights; the memory of that incident remained fresh for decades. As with Leora, his mind churned with potential scenarios.

"Franny'll find someone else if you don't know how to dance. Gotta at least learn to waltz." During the school year, Custer scheduled monthly dances called "sock hops." Most boys, limited in dance floor abilities, attended the socials merely to pose and kibitz, gathering as spectators at the periphery of the gymnasium floor. While Garson was initially one of those wall flowers, Lana was determined to transform him into an Astaire or Kelly. An impatient instructor, she guided Garson's reluctant feet in the basic box waltz. One hand clasped his, the other perching on his shoulder. Her breath was sweet. This was the closest Garson had ever been to her since that basement incident as kids when he asked her to show her privates. He became a bit light headed.

He moved his feet at her urging – shuffle one step to the right, pull the opposite foot next to it; shuffle a foot forward, and bring the other alongside. In eight such movements a box was formed. The voice of Joni James singing "Have You Heard" burbled from Lana's record player. He gazed at his feet. She stopped abruptly, expressive cobalt blue eyes darkening at her reluctant pupil.

"Don't look at your feet. Feel the music," she declared, words larded with frustration. Garson heard the admonition, but his thoughts were elsewhere, trying to get a grip on something that welled inside — some inchoate emotion he had not felt before. He tuned his gaze from her eyes to the windows as they proceeded with the lesson. Garson fumbled, finding it difficult to transfer the melody to his recalcitrant feet. What was more, he was discomfited feeling her hand and waist. He fantasized about the two of them dancing at the Roof or Eagles Ballroom downtown where big bands led by Goodman, the Dorseys, Artie Shaw, and the local Steve Swedish combined with sparkles of swirling light, wafting perfume, the rustle of crinoline and the murmur of conversations in a romantic tableau.

"Come on, little brother, you can do this." Garson was jolted from the distraction. Little brother! After all, he was older than Lana. Was he always to be regarded only as a sibling? In time, he mastered the square waltz steps, and under Lana's tutelage, also became proficient at the "Apple Jack," a popular new dance that featured rapid heel and toe footwork but lacked any physical contact with a partner. Lana loved to dance. As a vivacious teen, she sought boys who exhibited dance floor polish. In time, she became attracted to ethnic dancing, rounds and reels; and in her final years at Custer, she would be featured in musical reviews. Light afoot and precise of posture, she showcased her talents on stage, often attired in daring costumes. She would send him provocative photos when he was in the Marines.

Toby failed to live up to Lana's ballroom expectations. So did a boy named Kowalski. With a pack of Camel cigarettes rolled in the arm of his tee shirt, he was another of those Garson envied. Like Brando in "Streetcar Named Desire," his biceps bulged; his neck was thick and his torso blocky; a Superman tress curled on his forehead. He was a running back for the Custer football team. Garson retained a candid photo of him cradling Lana in his arms like a child, diminishing her. She peered at the camera, hair tousled on the windy fall day, with an expression of discomfort. Kowalski spoke in a low-register voice, raspy from smoking. One evening on his walk home from the Ritz, Garson heard noises from Lana's house. Unbidden, he climbed the steps and entered the enclosed sun porch. The corner streetlamp provided spare illumination.

"Little brother!" Lana welcomed. Garson detected relief in her voice. The couple lay side by side on a rattan couch, her head in the crook of Kowalski's left arm. Even without realizing it, tension between the boys centered on Lana. Kowalski flexed his bicep, and her head bounced. Despite her demand that he stop, he continued. Garson found it unamusing, but he was impotent to intervene. He wished himself in Kowalski's position.

"She goes with a whole bunch of different guys," was common conversational coin in segments of the Villard Avenue crowd. Garson was discomfited by the innuendo that Lana was a "loose" girl even while his suspicions were aroused. Most threatening in the parade of her dates was a guy from Brown Deer, an upper-class suburb north of Milwaukee. Information about him was sketchy: He was older, some claimed, and a member of the air force reserve. One fact was indisputable: He drove a shiny new Ford convertible. Garson actually recalled more about the car than about the guy. The two-tone blue Sunliner sported rakish molded headlights and torpedo tail lights. Chrome shimmered everywhere. The V-8 engine and three-gear column shift made the car fast and agile.

Toby seethed. For reasons unexplained, he had grown protective of his estranged girlfriend. This new guy in her life bore watching. He asked Garson to accompany him on "surveillance." He determined to clandestinely trail Lana. When she climbed into the sparkling Ford, the boys waited in ambush a block away. Toby followed at a discrete distance, the heavy Buick lumbering behind the new car. When Lana's date was stopped by a red light, Toby pulled to the curb, the Buick's straight pipes growling with menace. When the light changed, the two-door leaped forward, rear tires screeching and billowing blue smoke. Toby clutched and levered the floor shift through the gears, but the old sedan struggled to keep pace.

"Bet they're going to Necker's Point,' Garson suggested. Toby frowned.

The Ford slowed as it neared another controlled intersection, attempting to play the light and trap the pursuer on red, but Toby darted through the yellow. It was obvious that Lana had spotted her pursuer and his well-known "Gray Ghost." At a crosstown arterial, the Ford screeched to the right, accelerating dramatically. Toby geared down to make the turn, and when he straightened the wheel, only blue dot taillights appeared purple in the distance. Toby labored to catch up, but the convertible was too nimble, like an eland eluding a bulky lion's charge.

"Where'd they go?" Garson was unable to provide an answer. Toby drove to Capitol Drive, then east toward the lake, where they prowled the Bradford Beach parking lot; later, they scoured the bustling Pig 'n' Whistle drive-in but failed to find their quarry. After about half an hour, Toby and Garson abandoned the hunt. To Garson's memory, Toby dated sparingly and without enthusiasm thereafter. The erstwhile pals would in time conduct a more dramatic surveillance.

In the new decade, Lana's house became the nexus for considerable youthful socializing – parties, dances and more. The crowd sometimes gathered there early on New Year's Eve, attracted by alcoholic offerings. Lana's mother concocted hot toddy drinks, adding no more than a thimbleful of whiskey to each cup.

"I'd rather you drink here than on the street where you'd get into trouble," she often proclaimed. Her face was usually alight with welcoming warmth. She was a respected parent, raising a daughter under difficult circumstances. Lana may have exhibited a wild and unfettered streak, but she never caused her mother true heartache.

"Oh, she's just a P.T.," a prick teaser. That was Rusty's glib assessment of Lana. He was one of two pals with whom Garson had recently associated. He did not recall just how they met, but the henna-headed youth chummed with Preston who had been Garson's classmate at Holy Redeemer years past; Preston was the boy in the second grade class photo who wore the laced, high-topped boots.

As evidenced by that photo, Preston invariably displayed a haughty expression and manner. A curl-lipped sneer was his hallmark. Taller than Garson, he was slender and square shouldered with straight dark hair coiffed in a shiny pompadour and duck tail. He was invariably adorned in the prescribed fashion of the day – jeans, A-2 aviator jacket and spade shoes.

Rusty, whose name was apt for his coppery hair and heavily freckled pale skin, was known as a "wiseacre" by many who disliked him because of his penchant for hurling insults and combative challenges. Typically, Garson concluded, he tried to compensate for his short stature with bravado. Even Garson's mother thought Rusty had "a mouth on him." What was more, he spat incessantly, and could accurately hurl a pearl of saliva for several yards. To avoid retaliation he, like Garson, was fleet of foot and illusive. He lived somewhere west of Silver Spring Park in one of the expanding post-war neighborhoods. The flame-haired red terrier had a bevy of sisters who bore his coloration. Because of the disparity in their heights, detractors referred to the Rusty and Preston, both Custer students, as Mutt and Jeff after the cartoon characters. When Garson joined them, they were called the Villard Avenue Musketeers.

The preeminent area where North Milwaukee youths gathered and socialized was Villard Avenue. Youthful habitués called it "The Burg," a name supposedly derived from German word, *Bürgher* — citizen. Once the heart of a town annexed by the city years before, the street and its environs were a vibrant commercial strip. By the early 1950s, numerous merchants, taverns, eateries, grocers, retailers of every stripe did brisk business there. The Ritz's Theater's modest marquee beckoned at midpoint along with a Carnegie-style bank building.

In the years after the war, Villard developed a reputation as a dangerous place, the hangout for an infamous group of hoodlums named after the street. Brawling, drunkenness and petty crime characterized the area. *The Milwaukee Sentinel* printed lurid stories of the Villard Gang's exploits and arrests. When Garson and his pals began patrolling The Burg, only a few of the former miscreants were seen, the majority having been subdued by prosecutions and incarcerations. Garson and others concluded that Brusowitz, the heavy-handed Villard cop, helped nail them.

"There's Elmo," one of Garson's pals nodded toward a short, powerful man ambling across the street. While none of the pals actually knew him or any of the other toughs who once roamed the street, it was a badge of honor to point them out. Further, when outsiders asked Garson or his pals if they were part of the Villard Gang, the boys always answered affirmatively. They basked in the dubious reflection of those hoodlums.

"Saw 'The Indian' the other night, too," put in one friend,

referring to a swarthy man with a barrel chest, shiny black hair and drooping eyes who they occasionally encountered. "Think he just a souse now 'cause I spotted him crouched in the gangway next to Art's Liquors with hooch in a sack." They saw others from the old gang lingering about from time to time, the swagger of palmier days reduced to shambling.

"Somebody told me they still carry shivs and brass knuckles," swore another acquaintance. Garson's eyes were nervous when any of the old toughs were evident. He had long been fascinated with slum life and gang activities, traceable to the movie "Dead End," with the scruffy young hoodlums featured in the film. He was relieved that he did not live in such a rough-and-tumble milieu amid dismal tenements and debris-strewn streets; he had briefly brushed elbows in such a milieu on Galena Street. In successive years, Hollywood softened the Dead End Kids. Anarchic anti-social behaviors were modified along with their identity to the East Side Kids and finally, to the blousy Bowery Boys. Hollywood transmuted them from hoodlums to ruffians to ragamuffins.

Garson was frustrated because the neighborhood public library did not list Irving Shulman's controversial gang novel, *The Amboy Duke*. Some called it a milestone, depicting contemporary urban life and despair. Rumored to contain controversial descriptions of teen fashions and sexual escapades, Garson determined to find a copy. "A novel of wayward youth in Brooklyn," the provocative paperback cover proclaimed. Garson was fascinated with the story of the eponymous gang, devouring its pages in the secrecy of his bedroom. He was frustrated, however, with the movie version titled "City Across the River" with young Tony Curtis.

Softer in tone and less controversial were novels by Henry Felsen. *Hot Rod* and *Street Rod* revolved around hopped up cars and the teens who enjoyed them. Like Shulman, Felsen wrote of youthful alienation, danger and immorality. Garson found, however, that the books failed to deliver completely on the promise of cover art.

In addition to Villard Avenue, there were several other nodes for teen socializing. One of the rituals was Friday night at the Ritz Theater where Garson joined the crowd. He remembered his mother paying a nickel for his childhood admission, but it was now a quarter. Adults eschewed those nights because the double features attracted packed teen crowds. Ushers roamed the aisles, flashlights at the ready for any untoward behavior that might result in ejection.

"Hey, man, it's the Gong Man," Rusty blurted when the British J. Arthur Rank studio's iconographic oiled muscle man slowly swung his huge mallet at the bronze cymbal, the sound overwhelmed by youthful hubbub. Traffic to the concession counter was steady. When movie scenes lacked action, boys streamed from their seats, intent upon the noisome basement lavatory where cigarette smoke billowed. This was far different from the Dish Nights when Garson had accompanied his mother as a child.

It took some time for Garson to acclimate himself to the incessant murmur of teen nights. He was accustomed to concentrating on the movies, and studying the "Coming Attractions." With his peers, distractions abounded but by degrees, he grew more comfortable in the environment. Yet, he occasionally returned to the Ritz alone or traveled to another theater to see a favored movie without interruption. He never admitted it to his pals, but most movies still presented another reality for him; he wanted to scrutinize them carefully, to absorb their truths and possibilities.

Garson envied the antics of Preston and Rusty, and was amused by their ready wit; devilish and daring, they played off one another. Garson lamented that his mind and mouth never worked with such precision. Invariably, his retorts were hours late, long after the appropriate moment had passed. Neither Garson, Preston, Rusty nor Vito had close associations with particular girls at the time. Garson's relationship with Franny had ended in a whimper, likely because he had no dependable means of transportation; she had found a better suited boy, one who probably kissed her often. Mellish was dating a girl from another neighborhood. Toby was widening his circle of friends and had little time for Garson. The unattached youths, like young male lions ousted from a pride, they became mere scamps and kibitzers.

"Whyn't we grab a case of beer from Pittleman's," Preston suggested one night as the boys strolled along Villard Avenue, bored with the lack of purposeful activity. More frequently now, Garson was swept up in impish behavior and devilment. Next to Wilbert's Bakery, Pittleman's Market often displayed a pyramid of beer cases outside its store windows – Schlitz, Blatz, Gettelman's and Oconto from that northern Wisconsin city. Neither Garson nor any of his pals drank beer or alcohol to any extent; but like smoking, quaffing brews was an affectation. Because he was among the fleetest, pals designated Garson as the one to snatch a case from the storefront that night. He stealthily made his way through the gangway between bakery and market. On all fours, he crept to the stack, and slowly removed the top case. Cars passed along Villard, but no alarm was sounded. Awkwardly carrying the booty, he sprinted down the gangway between buildings to the alley where Rusty, next in the theft relay, grabbed the beer; he, in turn, shuffled it to Preston.

The pals rendezvoused some time later in Smith Park where bottles were opened and beer consumed. Garson took a swig or two — that was enough. From childhood trips to Rubicon, he recalled the bitter taste when uncles offered him sips of a local brew called Stork. Now, he went through the motions lest his pals spot him out or "signify" on him. The pals boasted of the little caper to anyone who would listen. There were other escapades, including the time Garson determined to retrieve errant baseballs and footballs from the roof of the Custer High entryway.

"Let's see what's up there?" He was hoisted onto someone's shoulders, and shinnied up the copper downspout. Indeed, there were half dozen balls up there and he began throwing them down. Just then, a spotlight struck his body like a lance. The boys below froze.

"Get the fuck down from there!" It was Brusowitz, the despised, heavy-handed cop credited with demolishing the old Villard Avenue gang. Now he constantly harassed a newer generation of teens, preventing them from loitering or congregating; he herded them like cattle until they dispersed. Obediently, Garson eased his way down.

"Wha'cha doing up there?" The policeman, well over six-feet, towered over him. The badge gleamed on his barrel-chest. Garson's lowered eyes fell upon the holstered revolver. The hulking officer rapped a night stick in his palm repeatedly while his companion played the light beam from one face to another. Using his most obsequious tone, Garson explained he was only looking for abandoned balls. Instantly, Brusowitz bunched Garson's shirt front in a fist and pulled him face to face.

"Just get the fuck outta here!" Beads of saliva spewed. The patrolman shoved him away, rending the garment; two buttons popped free. As the boys sullenly trudged away, Garson displayed the damage.

"Go back there, man, and tell Brusowitz about it." Garson was hesitant, still shaking over the confrontation. He had determined to live with the damage. Still, he needed to prove his worth to his pals.

"Go on, man," another voice urged. Reluctantly, he walked back to the policeman who stood next to the patrol car.

"You tore my shirt, officer," Garson said meekly.

Brusowitz's mouth gaped in disbelief. Pausing for only a moment, he poked a stiff finger into Garson's narrow chest. It was painful, and menace was clearly in the cop's eyes.

"Just get the fuck outta here!" he growled, almost like a large dog. His partner grinned.

In addition to Toby, the only other of Garson's acquaintances who owned a car was an older fellow with benign but curious habits and inclinations. He name was Belcher. While not yet of age, he was known to regularly consume beer purchased by an older sister. His name was apt, evocative of Shakespeare's indulgent Sir Toby Belch. Belcher sprouted a crop of dingy yellow hair and pale, beady eyes under glowering brows. The intersection of teeth and gums was gray-green, and he often breathed the sweet odor of decay. His body was the shape of a potato. Expectantly, Belcher was unkempt, clothes appearing as though they had never seen an iron. Baggy jeans hung below a prominent belly, shirt tails invariably billowing from the belt line. A gentle soul, Belcher displayed a rollicking sense of humor and a raucous laugh. He was a distinctive Villard Avenue denizen.

Some in the crowd reported that Belcher apprenticed part time in a local tool and die shop; he had dropped out of Boy's Tech, then studied at Vocational School for a year, they said. Those assertions were never verified. He liked most of the girls in the crowd, but none offered more than purely Platonic association in exchange for rides.

Belcher drove a 1938 Ford coupe with a burbling exhaust that roared like a semi-truck when he popped the clutch and roared away from stop lights. He was the recipient of many police citations for loud straight pipes. With the floor shift lever, Belcher was deft at rapid gear changes; the pearly steering wheel knob facilitated tight turns. Garson was amused that Belcher seemed to follow the same rules of car care exhibited by his own father: The trunk was a virtual Fibber McGee's closet of detritus and impedimenta, and the rear seat was usually cluttered with discards – candy wrappers, empty bottles and cans, balled newspaper and other items that defied description. The ersatz white sidewall tire accessories were invariably scuffed and dingy. Mellish related that a year or so before, Belcher had affixed a sparkplug near the end of his exhaust pipe to create a dramatic impression when he drove along.

"Yeah, he'd turn off the ignition and let some raw gas build up, then hit a switch to spark the plug. Man, a jet of flame wooshed out behind. They said he once melted something on a car behind him. Cops nabbed Belcher and made him remove the thing."

"Cruising The Burg" it was called. Normally, the activity involved driving repeatedly along various thoroughfares. But for Garson and others who were typically afoot, it also meant ambling aimlessly along the commercial strip on any suitable evening. Simply to be seen was reason enough. Only Toby and a few others owned cars, so cadging rides was infrequent. For the most part, pedestrian cruisers were segregated by gender; only a supremely self-confident youth strolled with his girl. Whistles and wolf calls were loosed when knots of girls were encountered. No matter the group, Officer Brusowitz waved the young people along, and discouraged loitering and congregations larger than a half dozen.

"Man, he's an asshole," was one of the lesser assertions.

"Let's get something at Militzer's," someone suggested. It was the refurbished restaurant next to Kozoll's Dry Goods. Five or so of the gang crammed into a booth. Few carried more than scattered coins. Waitresses detested the young customers.

"I'll have a pine float," Rusty ordered as the waitress testily surveyed the young people, pad and pencil in hand. Her thin eyebrows were drawn low, obviously distressed at having to serve such despised denizens.

"Tooth pick and a glass of water," Rusty answered her unarticulated question. It was one of his typical smart-assed *bon mots*. The waitress was not amused.

Drivers and pedestrian cruisers often shuffled east to Teutonia Avenue where Town Pride Custard blazed with gaudy neon. During one summer, Lana, much to Toby's discomfit, donned a hop's skimpy skirt and roller skates, attracting numerous lascivious male gazes. She told Garson she did not care because she accumulated a pocketful of tips most nights.

As one of the few car owners, Belcher invariably offered rides along The Burg; but, when his budget was strained he demanded that male passengers chip in quarters for gas. He charged girls only smiles and kind comments. In all seasons, he rode with the driver's side window lowered, elbow jutting out like a giant jack knife. Because of the airflow, it was desirable for riders to avoid the rear seat behind him in cold months.

"Aw, man!" moaned Garson. Usually the first to enter, he was shoved behind Belcher. He pulled up the collar and muffled his face with gloved hands.

Young people who frequented The Burg in those years were slavish to the changing flavors of fashion. Latter day social observers proclaimed Garson's generation as the first to establish clear prescriptions for youthful attire. Levi jeans were *de rigueur* for boys and girls; not to have the brand's tiny red tag displayed on the back pocket was decidedly déclassé. Tight Levis with narrow cuffs, in a season or two, gave way to blousy carpenter jeans replete with a ruler pocket and hammer loop. No matter the style or cut, it was "required" that new jeans be soaked in an effort to fade the indigo blue to a lighter shade; only the manufactured patina of age was acceptable.

"What's that blue ring around the bathtub?" Garson's mother asked after he had soaked a new pair of Levis. Jeans were not permitted at any Milwaukee school. Blousy drapes of various dark shades were the uniform for dress, and Garson fondly recalled a favorite pair of powder blue with dark stitching along the outside seam. Shirts were of lesser importance, but for a time a style with a looping collar worn by singer Billy Eckstine was the rage. "Mister B shirts," they were called. Garson traveled downtown to the only store, Johnny Walker's, that sold them. He held the distinctive collar in place with stick pins.

The orientation to teenage style also focused much on shoes, a particular brand sold by Flagg Brothers. Called "Spades," the soles resembled the shape of the playing card suit. Only two cities, according to a feature in *Life* magazine, took a fancy to those shoes – Milwaukee and Pittsburgh. Black leather Spades rapidly gave way to brown, then, blue and black; the buyer received a nickel change when paying ten bucks. Sneakers were seen only in school gyms. It was all part of the mandatory youth uniform.

The *piece de resistance* was the so-called A-2 leather flight jacket worn by World War II aviators. Of dark brown leather, the garment featured cargo pockets and epaulets; collars were always pulled up at the nape. If Garson recalled aright, the price was $30 or $40 — well beyond his youthful financial resources. Once again, he employed persuasive wiles with his mother, pleading with her that he "needed" such a jacket for his junior year. Similar tactics had been successful in times past – she had purchased the football shoes, typewriter and other "necessary" items.

Finally, she succumbed, offering to accompany him to Gimbel's downtown. Concern lodged in his chest; he knew his pals purchased theirs at a leather specialty shop. His stomach churned as she fingered through the department store's rack of leather garments, choosing one without epaulets or cargo pockets. Garson was mortified because the collar was wool.

"It'll keep you warm," she said, pulling the collar about his ears.

Observing his image in a mirror, he was chagrinned; he could not wear such a garment among his pals.

"It's this one or none," his mother demanded, deaf to his coaxing and pleading. So he owned a leather jacket. But it branded him as a Rube. At her insistence, he wore it in winter during the bus ride to Messmer. To no one but himself, he admitted that the wool collar did keep winter wind at bay while he waited at the transfer point.

Garson recalled fewer prescriptions pertained to girls' attire. They favored jeans, white buck shoes and rolled down socks with tanker jackets and kerchiefs. For school and dress, blouses and sweaters topped fulsome or form-fitting skirts, hems falling to ankles.

Some in Garson's crowd insisted that a few girls, Lana among them, padded undergarments to amplify their chests. There was abroad at the time a sassy ditty that ended with these lines:

So round, so fully packed, you soon will get the knack.

So fellas, before you wed her, please investigate her sweater

Or your wedding night will end up all in tears

'Cause they're wearing lots of falsies in brassieres.

There was another facet of youth style that for a time was adopted by the Villard crowd – shiny jet black hair. It emanated, Garson supposed, from the parade of Italian singers whose tunes gained radio play and sold thousands of records. Girls were captivated by such crooners and balladeers as Dean Martin, Tony Bennett, and Al Martino in the same manner as the previous generation had simpered over Frank Sinatra.

This affinity to black hair, it seemed, was also wrapped in the matter of ethnicity. Milwaukee had two distinct Italian communities. One centered on the pink Pompeii Church south of Wisconsin Avenue and another along Brady Street on the east side. These enclaves of Sicilian families staged street festivals each summer, each dedicated to a patron saint. Under undulating strings of light, the celebrations featured ethnic food, games and carnival rides. Garson, who had assisted his father selling popcorn at a few such events, found them fascinating – foreign and exotic. But his

Uncle Vin, who long lived and worked on the city's east side, had a warning:

"You shouldn't go to those places. They're lots of dangerous types down there, and sometimes trouble breaks out."

Predictably, Lana was among the first to dye her hair black, to emulate the swarthy and edgy types. Over her basement laundry tub, she helped Garson daub dye into his hair; but to his chagrin, the coloring failed to darken his coiffure. He would not look like any of those singers.

"Why you want to look like an Italian?" his mother complained, chiding him about smudged pillow coverings. She preferred her son's normal brown color and the youthful hair style. He and his pals had turned their backs on the tight military cuts of adult men, and grew their hair long. Slicked and shiny with pomade, locks were swept back along the sides, and into a "D.A." – a preened duck's ass at the back of the head. Garson's father had hung a second mirror on the bathroom wall opposite the medicine chest, permitting a simultaneous front and rear view.

It was rare for Garson or any of his pals to see a girl's legs, save when they wore bathing suits at the Silver Spring pool or Bradford Beach where he often admired toned thighs, shapely calves or trim ankles. Few in his crowd compared with the cheesecake poses of Grable, Hayworth or other pinups.

"Hi, little brother," Lana chirped one summer day. She had strolled up to Garson at the Silver Spring pool as he observed swimmers and bathers from outside the fence. He had long avoided the pool, self-conscious about his skinny body. With fingers poked through the chain links, he watched divers, bathers and swimmers. Lana stepped to the fence, blocking his view. She wore a new white suit that gleamed in the sunlight; it revealed a nascent womanly shape. She was small of breast and narrow of waist. Her legs lacked the fine contours of later years and her feet were tiny

"Whyn't you come in swimming?" Those cobalt eyes gripped his; they seemed to change colors like the lens of an automatic camera. Lana shifted her stance from one foot to the other, and as she did, her pelvis rocked. Then Garson's gaze dropped to the crotch of her bathing suit where a few stray auburn pubic hairs peeped out. His throat tightened as he struggled to free his eyes. He was shocked that her privates, like his, sprouted hair. While he tore away his gaze quickly, he was certain Lana noticed. They chatted for a few minutes more.

"Well, gotta go now, little brother." He would never become comfortable with the role she prescribed for him — "little brother." The fingers of her right hand wiggled as she turned and ambled back toward the green water, her wet feet printing the concrete. He was convinced she affected her gait to amplify her buttocks. Garson smiled at those taut undulating melons before they disappeared in the pool.

Despite his fascination, Garson's knowledge of the female form was, by his own admission, much less than most of his pals. He knew, of course, the basic aspects of their anatomy having carefully scrutinized photographs of movie starlets and pervasive pinups of painters Elvgren, Vargas and others. He had viewed air brushed breasts, but rarely glimpsed unadorned nipples and areolas. One of his friends had shown him a pack of playing cards with 52 nude photos; but these were so small that crucial features were mere pinpricks.

His knowledge of sexual congress, pregnancy and birth was largely academic, of course. More was learned from whispered back alley conversations and from suppositions about what followed fade to black movie scenes. The blatant "Eight Pagers," of course, provided crude cartoon images of fanciful fornication. All of this seemed to explode into reality for Garson one night when he was awakened by his mother who slipped into the other twin bed in his room. Noticing that he sat up in bed, she whispered:

"Your dad tried to get funny with me." Garson was shocked by the sudden realization that his parents, his own mother and father, engaged in such disgusting, animalistic behavior. Neither parent had ever even hinted at such matters. From Father Kelly at Holy Redeemer, he remembered sketchy lessons of nocturnal emissions and self abuse. Now everything tumbled upon him. Like a jackhammer, his pulse pounded in his ears.

Nearly breathless, he arose and walked into the living room. He sat on the mohair couch, trying to resign himself to the unsettling revelation. When Garson revealed that trauma to Lana at decades remove, she was amazed at his naiveté.

"Every guy in the crowd had the hots for you," Garson told her decades later. "You dated Toby, Kowalski, that guy from Brown Deer, others I don't know. I.., we were all envious. Some guys thought you were putting out."

"Why, that's not true at all." Her eyes darkened to roiling sea blue. "I was a virgin when I got married." By then, to Garson's disappointment, the fetching little gap in her front teeth had been closed by orthodontia. When they discussed these matters at a far remove, she had recorded three ill-advised marriages, claiming she wanted what those men were incapable of giving – romance.

"Ram, bam, thank you ma'am's OK – sometimes." She could be surprisingly candid. "But I want candles and wine, frilly boudoir frocks and languid lead-ins. The guy could at least shower and brush his teeth before he jumps into the sack with me!"

In her youth, Lana had once unknowingly seduced him through a bedroom window, but he never told her of that circumstance. Some weeks before the incident, Garson was impatient to see "The Red Shoes," a British movie based upon Hans Christian Anderson's fairy tale. Starring the comely ballerina, Moira Shearer, he had read that the movie had been greeted with lukewarm reception in England. Garson studied stills in magazines, despairing that it would never play in Milwaukee. He was pleasantly shocked months later when the glorious poster appeared in the Ritz Theater lobby. The movie preview enchanted him.

Garson knew that none of his pals would see such a sissy film; he knew their views about movies with too much singing and dancing. A movie almost exclusively focused on the life of a ballerina was beyond their pale. The Ritz programmed the movie for two mid-week showings. It may have been a slow time for regular Hollywood movie releases because the Villard Avenue venue would not have booked such a title under normal circumstances. He knew also that the Legion of Decency had trouble with the pretty dancer's climactic suicide. That frowning proscription gave him no pause, however.

From the opening scenes, he was mesmerized by the film and smitten with alluring Victoria Page — her flaming hair and brilliant blue eyes, her taut body, narrow waist and hips and shapely legs. In one sequence, while she practiced at the barre, her tights bunched, revealing the bottom of her buttocks. Yes, pretty "apple cheeks." Garson studied the scene more carefully at the second viewing.

The central ballet sequence was based upon the fairy tale of devilish shoes that forced the heroine to dance endlessly against her will. Page whirled and pirouetted, leaped and bounded, wide eyes blazing in terror and pain. The ballet became an allegory, Garson saw, for the real-life ballerina. He was heartsick when beautiful dancer, torn between the love of her husband and her passion for ballet, flung herself from the railway overpass. The climax unsettled him.

He returned the second night, sitting apart from the few dozen other viewers. It was as if he had not seen it before, fixated anew by the backstage setting, the choreography and the narrative. He was immersed in the glorious color. He became infatuated with Shearer. Then, something else struck him: She bore more than passing resemblance to Lana — those penetrating blue eyes and fetching little space between her front teeth, even the manner both dancer and friend applied lipstick – slightly over-lining natural upper lip lines. Lana's slender legs, narrow waist and, yes, curvaceous behind were similar, he felt. Coincidental, too, Lana had an inchoate affinity to dance.

So rapt was Garson, he barely stirred when key light illuminated the theater. The mundane walk home was filled with a symphony of thoughts. He rekindled the movie's thrilling moments, basking again in its emotions, reanimating the beautiful ballerina. But it was Lana who crowded out all of this.

It was after eleven when from the alley behind Lana's house, Garson noticed light in her bedroom. He strode silently into her back yard, attracted like a moth to the glowing window rectangle.

It was almost a movie frame. Clandestinely, he inched closer. Lana was dancing – undulating, pirouetting and prancing before a full-length mirror. She swayed rhythmically to some tune, arms undulating like seaweed in the surf. Most astonishing, she wore only a white brassiere and panties. Eyes wide, he drew closer, careful to avoid stepping into the light splashed on the grass. His pulse drummed; breath was shallow. Was Lana autoerotic? Was he a voyeur? Occasionally, when the angle was right, he saw two images of her — real and reflected.

Seeing her like that was something out of a dream, a desire. Analyzing the scene later, Garson could not be certain if it was Lana who attracted him, or just a girl exhibiting herself. No, he told himself, she was performing for him, only for him — his own Victoria Page. Lungs clutched, and he stifled a murmur.

Fleeting thoughts turned to her boyfriends, swarthy types and menacingly muscular ones like Kowalski. He recalled that night he interrupted Lana on her sun porch: He and Kowalski figuratively circled one another, like competing males – one a large-chested rooster, the cock of the walk; and the other, a skinny bandy, overmatched and intimidated.

During those reflections, the light in Lana's bedroom suddenly went out. Startled, Garson jumped back, fearful she might discover him there, a despicable Peeping Tom. He retreated from the yard, and walked home. In fitful sleep, his mind conflated visions of Lana and Shearer, whirling in dance, smiling at him, crying, running down a long flight of curved stairs. A train horn blared. Steam billowed.

"Take off the shoes," the dancer said. Garson's heart pained as he sat beside her, removing the bloody slippers. He could not breathe. She lay in his arms. Garson awoke in a tangle of sheets.

This chapter, obviously, is longer than all the others because his memory was clearer about these days. My Pop also had more photos from this period to guide him – images that were reclaimed from his parents before the house fire that destroyed the family's irreplaceable cache. Like me, readers may weary of these windy recollections of teenage travail and fitful groping for maturity. I don't know if he's typical of that era or not.

Garson's formative years included those which many critics considered the second golden age of cinema. The prestigious American Film Institute Top 100 list included some 20-percent produced from late 1920s through the 1930s. However, nearly a quarter of the listed titles were released during and immediately after the world, the era when Garson was most influenced by a steady diet of four to six movies weekly.

War movies remained a staple well beyond the peace. "Battleground" ranked among the best for Garson. John Wayne's portrayal of Sergeant Stryker made a particular impression upon him, more than the actor's earlier screen combat roles. For Garson, Stryker stood as tall as Taylor's Bill Dane and Bogart's Joe Gunn as heroic enlisted leaders. He recalled the public furor when President Truman attempted to merge the Marines with the regular army after the war. The Corps, after all, had won a permanent place in the nation's heart. The president's plan was scotched by Congress. Marines proved their worth scant years later in less glamorous Korean War combat.

Garson did not fare well in high school years. His mother was distressed that some grades, particularly in geometry, were absolutely abysmal; performance in only a few subjects was passable. Classroom boredom increased to such a point that he measured five-minute increments of time with notebook hash marks. Worse, he earned innumerable detentions, those infamous five-by-three inch yellow slips handed out for various infractions like tardiness, truancy and more. Each required an extra hour in study hall. He accumulated so many that, with other miscreants, he traveled to Messmer on Saturdays to mow grass and other chores for the nuns.

Most distracting for his parents were two suspensions – both for smoking. Garson simply could not lie to the nuns. Smoking was prohibited, but many boys lighted up in the lavatory after lunch and between classes. Standing at the row of urinals, one student lighted a cigarette, took a puff then passed it on. Soon, the heated end glowed fiery red, threatening to burn fingers. Among the last to take a drag, Garson waved a hand before his face in a desperate gesture to dissipate the reek before he exited the lavatory. Sister Benedict, the assistant principal, stood outside the door, arms crossed under her bosom, pale eyes magnified behind thick spectacle lenses, wide thin-lipped mouth curved in an ominous frown.

"Were you smoking in there?" she glowered. Others who had exited ahead of him, smokers too, simply said "No, S'ter" when questioned. But Garson, eyes nervous, could not summon such deception. Pregnant seconds passed.

"Yes, S'ter," he admitted. He was led to administration room, and a suspension issued. His mother, a life-long proponent of higher education for her son, was mortified by the incident, one more in a growing litany of indiscretions. She directed her husband to face the consequences with his son.

"I don't know what to do with him," his father's head wagged from side to side as he sat in the Messmer office. He was also informed about Garson's sinking academic performance and apparent indifference. Surprisingly, his father's anger did not flare; it seemed he had become resigned to such behavior. Garson was issued 25 detentions and readmitted to classes. Toward the end of the junior year, he once more encountered Benedict outside the lavatory door. This time, there was no hesitation before his confession.

It was likely a day during their junior year that Garson and Vito, despite consequences of truancy, determined to quit school after lunch. They malingered on Villard Avenue during early afternoon, confident because Officer Brusowitz worked the second shift. Bored, they strolled the two blocks to Custer High, determined to meet their pals inside. They spotted Toby and a few others in the hall between classes, but there was little time to pause and socialize. The bell jangled and classroom doors closed.

"Where do you boys go to school?" They turned toward the questioner – an assistant principal in blue suit, white shirt and bow tie. Garson replayed the scene in his mind many times after, and wondered from what untapped reservoir he had summoned such chutzpah.

"Why, we go to reform school," Garson blurted, almost unthinking. The official glared.

"Oh, yeah, come with me," the man snapped. He grabbed Garson's upper arm, and led the pals to the school office. Police were summoned. In a short while, the truants found themselves seated on a hard bench at a district station. The burly-chested desk sergeant, a distant cousin of his father, recognized Garson. When he phoned, Garson's father was adamant, refusing to pick up his son.

"Just let him sit!" was the terse response to the sergeant's request. In contrast, Vito's father arrived within an hour to take his son home. Alone, Garson occupied the bench for hours, watching policemen and detectives at their work. Sometimes, handcuffed criminals were ushered in and sent back to jail cells. He worried about his fate, about his father's reaction to his misadventure. He castigated himself for spewing that smart remark. Why did he open his mouth at all? Might he be in jail tonight? Well after the dinner hour, the shift changed, and a younger desk sergeant conferred with a lieutenant. Within several minutes a policeman led Garson to a patrol car, and he was driven home. His stomach, empty since breakfast, rumbled as much from hunger as apprehension.

"Gawl darn," Garson's mother growled at him, "why can't you behave. Your dad called me, and said you should sit until you learned your lesson." Garson suspected, too, that his mother was most mortified that a squad car with her son inside stopped in front of the house. He read her mind: What would the neighbors think? His father merely shook his head.

Neither Garson nor Vito participated in extracurricular activities at Messmer; the school was too far from home. As always, they socialized on Villard and its environs. During his high school years, Garson was befriended by one or two teachers. Sister Providence, the American literature instructor, reinforced the pleasure of reading that had been kindled in grade school with Eliot and Hawthorne, even Shakespeare. The Notre Dame nun identified short story writers he might enjoy — G. K. Chesterton, Edgar Allen Poe, O. Henry among them. When he mentioned his interest in writing, she encouraged him to create his own stories. He would take her advice.

Similarly, Sister Immaculata stimulated Garson's nascent interest in U. S. history. He had a clear memory of her presence – a face that bore a gentle expression of empathy and interest in him. She nurtured in him a nascent fascination in the Civil War that was born in the movies, recommending Fletcher Pratt's one-volume history of the conflict, *Ordeal By Fire*. He read much of the paperback for extra credit.

But by far, the most telling experience in his two Messmer years concerned a classmate. Shorter than Garson by a few inches, she was trim of figure. A thick helmet of wiry chestnut hair curled under her earlobes; caramel eyes, crowned by fine brows, turned almost liquid in some light; her nose was pert. Her skin was olive, and for a time he thought she might be Italian. Most captivating of all was her smile – perfectly proportioned lips that framed radiant white teeth. Beautiful smiles had always been magnets for him. In the homeroom they shared, Garson often studied her clandestinely, noting the neat, ankle-length skirts, crisp white blouses and sweaters. Decades after, he recalled her compelling aura, and determined to name her Betsy.

How Garson, ever reticent in such matters, made her acquaintance remained a mystery to him then and when he wrote about her. Perhaps she took pity on his poor scholastic performance, pity that may have began when he needed to borrow a sport coat for the class photo. Since grade school, his wardrobe never included suit or sport coat, his father concluding that such items were expensive and superfluous.

Betsy lived nowhere proximate to Garson's neighborhood, so they would not socialize until Garson was half-way through his Marine career. Occasionally, they tarried at the end of the school day, conversing while they waited for buses. He was lost in her smile and eyes, the charming way she inclined her head when listening; her voice was a breathy rasp like crocus cloth, and her laugh burbled. A wispy scent of citrus hung about her. He ached to kiss her generous lips.

Garson had the distinct recollection of Betsy permitting him to copy geometry assignments — to no avail, however, as he invariably failed quizzes and exams. She was an excellent student. She signed Garson's sophomore yearbook with her nickname, "Tiny," and an ironic note: "To a geometry brain." While Garson was smitten, she remained an enigma, a girl out of his reach. He would attempt to make contact before he departed for California, hoping something profoundly emotional might develop.

Garson's life remained anchored on The Burg. The social event of that final summer involved another of Lana's friends. Dolly's name was appropriate since the top of her head did not reach five feet. Every aspect of her body was diminutive. Winsome, she had a moon face and a blunt nose; Garson could not recall the color of her eyes, but her hair was tawny. She was a steady smoker with the laugh of a much larger person; her voice was husky, and, in fact, reminded Garson of a popular singer of the day – Mel Tormé known as the "Velvet Fog." Some of Garson's pals called her Polly because she could not abide dead air, compelled to fill any conversational pause with chatter.

Dolly's sixteenth birthday approached toward the end of the spring semester. Because her parents were adamant about hosting her party for that special day, she turned to Garson whose basement was expansive and largely uncluttered. Could he ask his mother if she might hold the celebration at his house? Garson was excited. His Sweet Sixteenth had passed largely unnoted save for a card. Holidays and such events had not been significant in his household for many years because of his parents' uncompromising work schedules.

"Aw, Ma!" In his best wheedling voice, he attempted to convince her that Dolly's party would be safe and without problems.

"Please don't call me Ma," she pleaded as always. "No drinking, understand?" she demanded. Almost as soon as he obtained permission, Dolly and Lana arrived with decorations to create a festive environment: They draped colorful paper streams on bare basement rafters, wound crepe around columns and water pipes and set card tables along the walls. Garson's mother admired the girls' handiwork.

The morning of the event, Dolly's boyfriend, older than she by some years – she called him a "professional musician" who played in a jazz combo — arrived with instruments; he his pals had consented to provide live music. The trio, a rhythm section, set up drums and vibraphone; the bassist would arrive with his instrument.

On the birthday evening, the basement brimmed with neighborhood youth. Garson had surreptitiously tapped some rock and rye whiskey his dad had stored on a high pantry shelf, filling a mason jar with the "juice." In a light-headed state, Garson was mesmerized by the musicians. The vibe player's mallets struck metal keys, electric resonators purling notes in pleasant vibrato. The bassist's thick fingers thrummed the heavy strings, anchoring tunes while the drummer's brushes whisked the heads and cymbals delicately. Garson had a recollection of talking with the vibe player during a break, aware of his slurred words.

He did not even attempt to dance that night; typically, few of his pals did. He was intent on the tunes. He never liked music as background, intent to concentrate on every note, to be completely engrossed and undistracted. He fancied himself something of an aficionado.

"I like Hamp, Lionel Hampton," he said with the conviction. "When he played with Goodman in Carnegie Hall, you could hear him kinda hum when he hit some notes." Garson boasted that he often called the local radio station to request "Sing! Sing! Sing!" and other concert numbers. He prattled on about the solos — Hampton's purling vibes, Teddy Wilson's distinctive piano, Gene Krupa's pounding drums and Dizzy Gillespie's blaring trumpet. Dolly's boyfriend was unimpressed.

The popular music of Garson's generation was but a slight evolution from the world war's big bands. Goodman, Tommy Dorsey, Artie Shaw and others still visited the city, playing at the Roof and Eagles ballrooms downtown. Big band singers like Rosey Clooney, Patti Page and others regularly released popular recordings, as did balladeers Martino, Martin, and Bennett, and harmonizers such as the Andrews Sisters, the Ink Spots, and the Mills and Ames Brothers.

Encouraged by cloistered school teachers, Garson serendipitous reading habits flowered. He had warm recollections of books he had perused in the storefront public library near his home, fascinated in youth by books about Indians and pirates. In the final years before his enlistment, paperbacks packaged in evocative covers proliferated; publicity and notoriety attached to certain authors and themes. While he failed to finish every title pals recommended, he did scan Erskine Caldwell's sensational *God's Little Acre* and *Tobacco Road*, searching for rumored sensational passages, "the good parts." Similarly, he was fascinated by Mickey Spillane's hard-boiled Mike Hammer mysteries that expanded the boundaries of sex and violence beyond the writer's more literary precursors, Dashiell Hammett and Raymond Chandler.

Since the days when he poured over the lurid pulp magazine covers in Toby's basement, Garson was also attracted to science fiction sagas – whirling suns and planets and thrilling interstellar flights, dashing heroes and nubile women, robots and bug-eyed monsters. He had read Robert Heinlein novels and the E. E. "Doc" Smith "Lensman" series, and had poured over Isaac Asimov's "Foundation" trilogy. He could cite the "Three Laws of Robotics" from the *I, Robot* stories. He believed himself to be sufficiently conversant with the genre's methods and conventions that he determined to write his own novel. Tangentially, this led him into a latter-day escapade fraught with a bit more peril than previous adventures.

Employing well-oiled guile from childhood, Garson convinced his mother he needed a typewriter. It was necessary if he was to become a journalist. She purchased a neat, Remington portable. He was diligent, pecking the keys steadily, progressing from one or two fingers to a speedy five or six, turning out sentences and brief paragraphs. Movies had taught him that reporters wrote that way.

He was briefly sidetracked from reportorial intentions to take up the task of writing a science fiction novella, using Heinlein, Smith and others as exemplars, employing their tropes and memes. Garson began to enjoy the process of writing, gathering ideas, creating characters and fashioning a narrative. Unlike speaking, writing permitted him time to consider and order his thoughts, to make changes and expunge errors. He was free with snappy retorts and brilliant *bon mots*. Over time, more than a score of pages rolled from the Remington. He could not recall the title of the inchoate opus.

Across the street stood a house, something of an oddity to Garson's eye, a large residence with peculiar exterior wooden scroll work and detailing. Someone told him its style was Carpenter Gothic. He knew the family only from delivering newspapers. The father, considerably older than his own parents, was said to be a German immigrant; he and his son worked at Ladish on the south side. The younger man was named Wolfgang, and Garson admired his cherry red Chevy sedan and the meticulous care Wolf lavished on it: Paint glistened with waxy brilliance, chrome sparkled and wide sidewall tires were as bright as bed sheets. Toby's dull, gray Buick suffered in comparison.

Wolf was perhaps a decade older than Garson. His eyebrows were uncommonly straight upon a narrow face; his bearing and manner brought to Garson's mind the B-movie actor, Louis Hayward. Over time, he discovered that the neighbor read science fiction books. Wolf loaned Garson two paperbacks — a breezy novel by Andre Norton called *Starman's Son, 2250 A.D.*, a cautionary post-apocalyptic tale of an albino hero and his empathic hunting cat that he read quickly. But he was deterred by A. E. Van Vogt's turgid novel *Slan*. When he returned the books, Garson informed Wolf he was writing a science fiction story, about a young girl, Electra, who passed herself off as a man on a Mars space mission. While the heroine was making ablutions in the cramped ship, a male crewmate named Roy Batty discovered her secret. Wolf offered to read what Garson had written, and promised to provide suggestions and guidance.

"Idea's very good," Wolf critiqued some days later, asking where Garson planned to take the plot from that point. "Your description of the space ship, the hardware and the encounter between Electra and Batty are well done. I'll read more later, but keep writing now."

Wolf had recently married. While Garson's mother had not attended the wedding – she refused to burden the pew of any non-Catholic Church – the family walked across the street to offer congratulations at the back yard reception. Family and neighbors gathered there in the June afternoon. Wolf's new wife was younger than he, Garson thought.

The couple lived in the parents' house across the street after the wedding, but Garson's conversations with Wolf became irregular. They waved at one another and exchanged occasional pleasantries. Garson was discomfited that Wolf had not returned the pages of his story. Perhaps a year passed when one evening, the neighbor beckoned Garson across the street. They stood on the sidewalk, and older man spoke in a low tone.

"Interested in making a few bucks?" Garson drew up his eyebrows.

"Your friend Toby's got a car, right? That old gray Buick. Think you guys might like to do a little, ah, detective work for me?" It sounded mysterious, conspiratorial, but appealingly dangerous, like the cases of those sleuths, Boston Blackie, Sam Spade and Mike Hammer. As arranged, Wolf, Toby and Garson met a day or two later at Shorty's Restaurant to discuss the proposition. Wolf bought them Cokes.

"Think my wife's stepping out on me," Wolf said. Garson caught Toby's furrowed brow from the corner of his eye. "Can you follow her and see if there's some guy, some assignation going on?" That was a word neither Garson nor Toby had heard before. "Give you 20 bucks a piece and a tank of gas if you find anything."

The trio discussed details, and slowly Wolf overcame their reluctance, convincing them that they could handle the challenge. He told them that his wife – Garson remembered her name as Melvina or Alvina — said she met her girlfriend at the Ritz Annex bowling alley on Villard Friday nights. She told Wolf that they went dancing sometimes, somewhere on the west side; she was vague about details.

"If it's some guy, let me know where they go and where he lives if you can," Wolf continued. "Just follow them though, but don't let her see either of you." One might surmise that Alvina was one of those shapely blondes who crammed herself into tight dresses like

Joan Blondel or Shelley Winters, jewels dangling, perfume wafting; or like his Aunt Bacia in Chicago who wore outfits that hugged her generous curves. Garson long carried the memory of her hand cupping his chin, puckering her plumy lips, and in an affected voice teasing, "Oh, rooty toot toot, you're so cute!"

But that was not Alvina. She was a mousy woman with thin brown hair and eyes whose color was undistinguished. Far from shapely, she was slender, without the alluring swell of hips, buttocks or breasts. Even her attire was unattractive, and Garson considered her only ordinary, almost unappealing.

It was perhaps the following Friday that Toby and Garson climbed into the ponderous "Gray Ghost," and parked in the shadowed Wilbert's Bakery lot. While Garson's anticipation was high, that first night of surveillance was fruitless. Alvina and her friend walked to the bowling alley and spent a few hours inside, likely at the bar. Before nine, the two women reappeared, chatted on the sidewalk for minutes before parting. Alvina walked home, high heels clacking on the sidewalk. The next time the "subject" – that's what Toby called her – went out, the same pattern prevailed; it continued that way for a few weeks. Toby and Garson grew bored.

"Jeez, man, nothin' happenin' again," Toby complained. "We ain't gonna get that double saw buck."

But then, one night, matters took a dramatic turn. After a half an hour at the bowling alley, Alvina departed alone, and walked to Hopkins Street four blocks west where a dark, DeSoto sedan idled, chrome grill grinning. Holding her dress tight to her bottom, she slipped inside the expensive vehicle. The car traveled south for many minutes, finally pulling up to a tavern on Fond du Lac Avenue. Ribboned multicolored neon identified it as the Wind Up Saloon; a lighted key revolved above the script. Garson and Toby waited down the street, carefully observing, much taken with their clandestine roles. Still, they were fearful Alvina might discover them and jeopardize the surveillance.

Around ten o'clock the couple emerged from the tavern. The man appeared swarthy, Italian or Mexican they thought. He wore a two-tone jacket, dark shirt and tie with pointy white and black shoes like Garson's Uncle Hervé favored. As they followed the dark sedan, Garson was exhilarated, feeling akin to Bogart tailing suspects as Philip Marlowe. The trailed the DeSoto at a distance of a half block. Apprehension seized Garson as they entered the city's Negro section, what some called Bronzeville, with its blaze of neon announcing taverns and night clubs along Walnut Street. The sidewalks were busy with white and Negro pedestrians, well-dressed for an evening of revelry.

The car pulled to curb near the Regal movie theater. The marquee displayed "Pinky," a three year old movie starring Ethel Waters and Jeanne Crane. Garson remembered the story about the mixed race girl from the Ritz; he had been impatient with the weepy drama. Toby slowly drove past Alvina and the man as they strolled arm-in-arm toward a night club pulsing with music.

"What'll we do, man?" Garson asked. Toby said they he would drive around the block a few times. Ultimately, they pulled into an empty space on the south side of Walnut, opposite the line of bars and clubs, the Buick's wheel lurching onto the curb. Toby winced: He had scuffed his white side walls.

They hunkered down again, locking the doors. Garson's brow and underarms felt prickly. For an hour or more, they huddled, listening to the chatter and laughter of passersby; occasionally, from their scrunched postures, they spied the tops of fedoras, robber caps and shiny black hair. Fragmentary notes of jazz and blues wafted out when the club doors opened and closed. Toby occasionally raised his head, timorously monitoring the scene.

"Man, I hope these colored guys don't see us," Garson muttered. They often heard rumors of back alley crap games, knifings and brass knuckle confrontations in these environs. Finally, as the clock inched toward midnight, Alvina and her companion reemerged. He was laughing, white teeth contrasting with dusky skin; she hugged his upper arm and leaned into his body, eyes alight. Once again the couple climbed into the four-door DeSoto and drove east. Toby lumbered behind. The sprawling Schlitz Brewing Company complex of Gothic buildings laid just ahead, its towering smoke stacks exhaling into the night sky.

"Remember that time when me and you tailed Lana and that guy?" Garson tried to ease the tension he sensed in the car. Toby retorted with only a scowling glance. In light late night traffic, Toby followed, quickly clutching and shifting his Buick into third to maintain the pace. They followed for many minutes, making turns onto other streets until they traveled along broad Teutonia Avenue. They passed the ornate Egyptian Theater where Garson had watched many features; it was darkened at this late hour and he missed the marque's movie title. They crossed Capitol Drive where the roadway divided, a grassy median separating the avenue's lanes. Bored, Garson grew impatient, perhaps unconsciously wanting to precipitate some drama.

"Pull alongside, man" he said as they drove adjacent to Lincoln Park. "Let's see if we can get a handle on this guy." Toby's eyebrows drooped when he reluctantly inched up on the DeSoto's right side, adjusting his speed to pace it. The suspects were at first oblivious to the dull gray sedan pacing their car. Garson momentarily had a vision of Bogart and Bacall in that gray Plymouth coupe Marlowe drove in "The Big Sleep." Just then, Alvina glanced to her right. Garson was horrified as an expression of recognition played on her face. Her mouth hung open. He scrunched down in the seat.

"She sees us! She sees us, man! Turn! Turn!" Garson screamed. At Hampton Avenue, Toby wrenched the large steering wheel to the right, down shifted and roared into sprawling Lincoln Park; they sped east along the winding parkway.

"I think she knows us, man!" Garson was breathless.

"Just shut up, man!" Toby grunted through clenched teeth.

They ended the surveillance and returned home. Typically, Garson often capped such drama in sleepless nights, his mind whirling with doubts and anxieties; dark's dread demons pressed tightly in upon him. For days, the pals did not talk about the night's errand. Nor did they report to Wolf that his wife had spent an evening with the dark guy. Garson never learned the outcome, but some months later, Alvina moved out of the house. Neighbors reported they were divorcing. Toby and Garson avoided one another again, and memory of the incident faded. Soon, another incident commanded Garson's attention.

"He's only after one thing — getting inside girls' underpants." That was Lana's assessment of a new acquaintance Toby had made. Tall and square-shouldered, he displayed what Lana called "dangerous good looks." In retrospect, Garson wanted to give him a connotive name, and so settled on Rowdy. Older than Toby by a year or more, Rowdy had narrow, almost Asian eyes, dark hair carefully groomed, sideburns that drooped below his ears and prominent eyebrow ridges. He was one of the few in the crowd who needed to scrape whiskers from the point of his chin every few days. Because he was as a serious and committed smoker – unlike others who only affected the habit as circumstances warranted – his right index and second fingers bore yellow stains, and the odor of tobacco hung about him incessantly.

"You can also tell something's wrong with him because he bites his fingernails to the bone." Lana said. She considered him louche, to use a word uncommon back then, and maintained a wary distance, warning friends of predatory proclivities she discerned.

"You got a face I just don't like," Rowdy blurted to Garson after they first met. He browbeat and belittled Garson, calling him a "little punk," invariably adding the potent four-letter adjective; he challenged Garson to stand up like a man. Conversely, he was deferential to parents, invariably responding with "Yes, sir" or "Yes, ma'am." Adults thought well of him, but peers knew better. What was worse, Rowdy brought out facets of Toby's character that Garson disliked.

Garson saw much less of his neighborhood pal in those days; the association with Rowdy took precedence. They incessantly traveled to other parts of the city, appearing at the late summer State Fair and Western Days. But they seemed to prefer the east side Italian festivals, and, some claimed, were seen in the company of dark and shady types.

After Toby graduated from Custer, he convinced his parents to permit him to drive out to California with his new associate. Since the singer Nat King Cole had popularized the Bobby Troop tune, "get Your Kicks on Route 66," the way west had attracted the fancies of many youth.

The pair must have been away a month, and when they returned, Toby and Rowdy regaled anyone who would listen with adventures and experiences driving to California and back. Garson was glued to the tales, of course, of a lengthy trip — more than two thousand miles out and the same back.

"Not much to look at past St. Louis," Toby said. "Man, everything after that is flatter'n a pancake." The fabled Route 66, he observed, was just as the song lyric had it: Joplin, Missouri, Oklahoma City, Amarillo, Gallup and Flagstaff. Mountains rose ahead. From Kingman, Arizona, Toby and Rowdy veered to Las Vegas.

"Yeah, Fremont Street's great – 'Glitter Gulch,' it's called," Rowdy boasted. "A large neon cowboy named Vegas Vic puffs smoke, waves and says 'Howdy, Partner.'" Garson hungered to be there with them. They also told of wandering through busy casinos packed with gamblers around the clock. They recalled the Salsagev, the Las Vegas and Pioneer Clubs, and one spot that displayed a giant shiny nugget of raw gold. It was the Golden Nugget, Garson later discovered, a gambling hall whose façade was ribboned in neon. He learned that the street was so garish it was almost audible.

"Played roulette and craps," Rowdy continued, "and plugged one-armed bandits." After a day, they continued west. As advised, they carried extra water across the desert, and had to quench the steaming radiator somewhere beyond Barstow. Then, certain as the song, they reached San Bernardino – with an air of superiority, they called it "San Berdoo" – and into Los Angeles. They slept in the car a night or two, saw the towering Hollywood sign, and followed a "Star Map" to some of the movie star homes. They rolled along the famous thoroughfare lined with palm trees and heavy foliage that screened massive mansions like the one depicted in "Sunset Boulevard" and owned by Norma Desmond, the silent movie actress played by Gloria Swanson.

"Saw Tony Curtis and Janet Leigh," Rowdy claimed, "when we ate at Nate 'n' Al's Deli on Beverly Drive." Toby said he was not sure it was those stars, but the couple at least looked like them. They cruised past Schwab's Drug Store, and stopped across the street from Paramount Studios entrance, its fancy wrought iron gate guarded by uniformed men.

"Slept on the sand at Laguna Beach one night," Toby put in. Even he could not suppress the excitement of seeing the Pacific Ocean, watching the insistent waves plunge; the surf lapped them to sleep. Over the course of several meetings, more details emerged. They had returned with several packs of Mexican cigarettes of harsh, dark tobacco. A puff or two made Garson nearly wretch as his stomach gurgled in rebellion. Toby displayed a painting he had purchased for a few dollars — a bullfight scene rendered on black velvet tacked to lath boards. Garson was most attentive to their Tijuana sojourn. Leaving the Buick near the San Diego transit station, they paid 99-cents for the streetcar ride to the border, then walked across a concrete bridge into the garish town.

"How're the Mexican girls?" Garson was impatient to know. The story tellers knowingly looked at one another.

"They got bar girls who'll sit on your lap for as long as you buy drinks. They feel you up, too." Garson was aghast. He envisioned lusty, sultry senoritas with flashing smiles and ruby lips like Pearl Chavez, Jennifer Jones's character in "Duel in the Sun." He wanted to know more, and Toby and Rowdy obliged, explaining that a cabbie had driven them to a whorehouse with a roomful of beautiful, dusky women.

"You just take your pick!" Rowdy smirked. Toby, Lana averred later, returned to Milwaukee as "experienced" as his worldly friend. More reason for her to make a wide berth of them. Garson had all but dismissed Toby's friendship, when, to his amazement, his old pal and Rowdy invited him for a disturbing evening. Analyzing the incident at a later remove, Garson saw that Rowdy was intent on embarrassing him, on exposing him to a life lesson just as John Steinbeck's Caleb Trask did to his brother, Aron, in *East of Eden*. Predictably, Garson failed.

"Whyn't you come along with us tonight," Rowdy queried during a surprise visit to Garson's house some months after they returned to Milwaukee. Garson saw Toby only rarely these days as he and Rowdy traveled in wider circles and, Garson presumed, among more worldly associates. Garson asked where they were going.

"Let's just say you're gonna have a good time." Rowdy winked, and uncharacteristically threw an arm around Garson's shoulders. Garson's antipathy to the youth gave him pause; he wondered why he, the "little punk," was invited.

Trundling across town in the big Buick, Rowdy said he knew of a girl he wanted to take on a date. Garson suspected more. They rumbled over the long Menomonee River viaduct to the south side, then gaped as they passed the showy neon of Leon's Drive-In; its carhops skated about despite the chill evening. Finally, they departed the city onto the highway toward Chicago. A sign lighted by headlights announced "Seven Mile Road," and a short distance farther they turned up a long, stony lane toward a trailer park. Garson knew the things that were said about girls who lived in trailers.

Rowdy was admitted to the narrow abode. After ten minutes, he returned to the car with the girl. While apprehensions distracted him, Garson found her not particularly pretty. She wore heavily-rimmed glasses and her hair, falling past her shoulders from under a kerchief, was mousy brown. Garson blocked her name from his memory. Rowdy motioned Garson into the passenger's seat, and climbed into the rear with the girl. Toby drove back onto the highway, then west onto some country road. Garson found it unsettling that they were not stopping for cokes or malts or anything, not even a semblance of a true "date." Was the plan all along to simply pick up the girl, drive into the countryside and "get it on." It seemed so sordid and clinical, as cold as the night.

Garson felt sorry for the girl even though she seemed to understand the expectations. With hoar frost sparkling on the moonlit farm fields, Toby drove into the chill night. He turned off the engine in a secluded lane. In the backseat, Garson heard the rustling of clothing as Rowdy and the girl apparently disrobed, at least partially. Garson turned his head, peering into the gloom of the back seat. Rowdy reached up, and flicked on the dome light. The girl's sweater was bunched up under her armpits. In another of those rare instances when his mouth seemed to verbalize almost unbidden, Garson blurted:

"I'll bet those tits ain't even real." With a look of disgust, Rowdy interrupted his fondling, unfastened her brassiere and took a handful of breast, displaying it like a fruit peddler squeezing a melon.

"See this, you little punk!" Rowdy growled. The breasts were enormous, pale skin contrasting with areola the size of half dollars, nipples erect in the chill. It was the first time Garson had seen real tits. His throat was instantly dry, and he coughed. He mustered a wan smile as she seemed to enjoy the attention, proud of her endowments, Garson thought. Rowdy switched off the light, and Garson turned away, scrunching down in the seat, folding his arms around his chest as night air crept into the car.

Backseat jostling increased, and grew rhythmic. Rowdy and the girl were actually screwing back there, Garson's mind cried out. He was a voyeur, but there was no titillation. No more than ten minutes passed before motion ceased. Rowdy climbed outside, hitched up his jeans and zipped his fly, then nodded for Toby to exchange places. Rowdy backed the Buick out of the lane and drove to the highway while Toby set to work, preparing himself for "sloppy seconds." Now, Garson's apprehension bloomed as he realized he was meant to be the third with the girl. Back seat rustlings grew more urgent, but the girl seemed reluctant, resisting Toby's fumbling "seduction."

"Can't we stop at Leon's, or somewheres" she asked, "get a malted or something?"

"Let's go to Hog an' Horn, the Pig 'n' Whistle – after," Rowdy promised unconvincingly. Garson's mind whirled to find a way out of this. It took minutes to concoct a story, to gather his words.

"Got no money," he said. Moments passed. "Think I'm going home." Rowdy shot a glance of disbelief, but said nothing. Surprisingly, he drove back to the block.

"Bye, bye, you fuckin' little punk," Rowdy spat out as Garson exited the passenger door.

"Nice to meet you," Garson waved at the girl. What a thing to say, he castigated himself later. What would Toby's parents say if they saw him back there with the girl? What would Garson's mother say? Both houses were dark, however. He was relieved when the Buick pulled away from the curb in a cloud of blue exhaust. That episode was the final adventure he and Toby shared. Their friendship had frayed beyond mending now. Garson gravitated to others in the crowd.

He was shocked to learn that his pal, Mellish, had had a run-in with the law, and was now confined to juvenile hall. Mellish and his younger brother, Davy had smashed the rear window of the store on Silver Spring, and made off with several cartons of cigarettes. They were caught selling the booty. His father, the police sergeant, and mother were heartsick. Their elder son was no more than a rapscallion. Ultimately, the judge gave Mellish and his family a choice: Incarceration in juvenile hall until he was 18, or enlist in the military. He joined the air force, and in a matter of weeks, it seemed, departed for Texas without saying goodbye.

Mellish returned to Milwaukee from Lackland Air Force base two or three months later. He was home on a ten-day leave. His once proud hair style had been reduced to stubble, but his carriage and demeanor were decidedly different – military. Sitting on the cement steps outside the Mellish home, Garson, Preston and Rusty listened intently to their pal's experiences.

"Yeah, they were tough on us, right from the first. My recruit sergeant got on us a lot, making us do pushups when we fucked up." Garson found Mellish was looser with profanity now, and sprinkled in the four-letter word with abandon.

"It took us weeks to learn to march well. There were 50 of us in the recruit platoon, and I was picked to be squad leader." He explained that he was given the responsibility over the dozen men in the unit, and he had done a good job of it. He earned his airman's stripe after basic training. Over the course of several nights, Mellish's descriptions of military life registered something in Garson's mind.

In Garson's era, military service was an integral part of the passage to adulthood. After high school graduation, almost every youth volunteered. Some even signed up prematurely when they came of enlistment age. The military, it was said, provided a learning experience, a chance to see the world and to rub shoulders with youths of high and low station. After serving three or more years, a soldier returned to civilian life and took up a trade or found a job in one of Milwaukee's expansive manufacturing facilities. The GI Bill afforded veterans a chance to purchase a house and, for those so inclined, to study for a college degree. There were others, like Mellish, who enlisted under duress. Still, he was optimistic about his prospects.

"When I go back," Mellish said on one of his final evenings home, "I'm headed for Florida. They said I'll be an airplane mechanic, and may even work on jets. When I get out, I can go work for some airline like Republic here at Mitchell Field." When he prepared to depart, he looked outstanding in the crisp blue uniform and peaked cap, brass medallions shining, shoulders square and chest taut. He saluted his pals as he strode away.

"Ya know, we should think about joining," Preston stated after Mellish's departure. He and Rusty, Custer students, were not performing much better than Garson. Their minimal interest in school, never robust, had been depleted. There were adventures out there – in Texas or California or somewhere – to be had by young men with gumption.

Garson swiped sweat from his temples. Early in that steaming summer, he sat in the large study hall at North Division, one of the city's public high schools. On several days, newspapers reported that the thermometer rose to nearly 100 degrees; humidity was as heavy as a wet wool blanket. Only movie theaters, a few other public venues and homes of the wealthy east siders featured air conditioning.

After his junior year, Garson's sad academic report listed a pair of failures along with several Ds. He was obliged to attend summer school. But weather and boredom prevailed, and he stuck it out for a week, watching the wall clock's glacial progress.

"Ma...Mom, think I'm going in the service," he told her one evening.

"The service! Why, for heaven's sake?" He gave her many reasons and much rationalization, but she was unmoved. Disappointment was clearly written on her careworn face.

"You know I want you to go to college. Whyn't you just finish school, then go in?" Garson countered, acknowledging that he was failing several subjects; he doubted ever catching up. He did not reveal that he had already quit summer school.

"Besides, I can get my GED in the service. Then when I come out, I'll go to college and study journalism. I promise, Mom." That was the line of attack he chose, and over the course of week or more — thrust by him and parry by her — a well-practiced duel played out. He felt confident in his offensive.

"Ask your dad," she waved off further discussion. His father was nonplussed by his son's decision. While he wanted the best for his son, he never pushed the idea of college. His stated goal was for Garson to take over the business one day. Garson rebelled silently, a fleeting vision of himself at 30 in such a life; there was no way he wanted a job selling popcorn.

A coincident event also precipitated Garson's decision to enlist: He had quit as a busboy at Shorty's. With Preston and Rusty, he was briefly employed at the A & P store's regional bakery. They were grease jockeys – the demeaning assignment of preparing cake pans for the bakers, and cleaning encrusted mixing machines and dough vessels. The trio, scamps playing off one another, joked and horsed around, played pranks, often bombarding one another with cream filling. They were summarily fired after trapping an apprentice baker, a weaselly, young German immigrant, in an open freight elevator, bombarding him with vanilla cream filling. As a parting insult, they stole a beautifully decorated cake from the walk-in refrigerator. They had burned bridges to much of civilian life.

"They said they'd sign," Garson informed his pals even before he gained his parents' consent. In time, Preston and Rusty secured approval. None of the Musketeers' prospects seemed promising. There was only the decision of which service branch to choose.

"Think the air force sounds too easy," Preston averred. Garson and Rusty nodded agreement.

"Yeah, I'm for the real thing – the Marines," Garson proposed. "They make you a tough." He had long been fascinated with the Corps, attentive in the past to its defense of Wake Island and the heroic Pacific Island landings – Guadalcanal, Tarawa and especially Iwo Jima, even the recent Chosin Reservoir. The Marines were the first to fight, and they always accomplished their mission. The Corps would make them men. All of this was personified in John Wayne's portrayal of Sergeant Stryker.

"'Sides, girls love those dress blues," he emphasized. "When we get home, they'll be all over us." Preston and Rusty's expressions revealed the dubiousness of that claim. The pals discussed matters further.

"Maybe if we go in for 20 years right away," Rusty opined, "we'll get good deals – you know promotions and good duty and stuff." Garson and Preston agreed that sounded plausible. Since Garson was the oldest, he was the first to visit the Wisconsin Avenue recruiter's office. His father sat beside him that September Saturday. The Marine wearing glamorous red-striped blue trousers, a crisp khaki shirt, sergeant stripes and gleaming brasses greeted the pair, skeptically at first. For as long as he remembered, Garson appeared tender for his years. Photos of that period reveal the visage of a youth years younger. After lengthy discussions, the three-striper asked the fateful question.

"So, how many years are you thinking of – three, four or six?" Garson paused, reviewing Rusty's suggestion – 20 years for a good deal. But that was not one of the proffered options. Garson chose four.

"Well," the handsome Marine responded, "I'd recommend you take three. Then, if you find it's a life for you, you can always re-up, reenlist, for more." Garson's father nodded in agreement. Undeterred now, Garson was intent upon the agreement with his pals. He and his father signed a preliminary document contingent upon reaching his birthday. His father was stony as they drove home. His mother was silent when she heard the news.

Long self-conscious about his rail-like frame and narrow chest, he worried that the sickly features his father had once observed might be impediments; Preston and Rusty would leave him behind to an uncertain future. The physical loomed. He was sleepless for nights, worried he would not measure up, dashing all those hopes and plans for quitting school and starting a life of adventure. The jostling streetcar ride downtown unnerved Garson, each clack of the tracks pushing his heart rate higher; the two-block walk to the cavernous commercial building adjacent to the river tightened his chest. Scores of recruits gathered that mid-morning, and Garson's stomach gnawed audibly; he had been too nervous for breakfast. Shunted from one queue to another, he was poked and prodded, made to cough and bend over, to display his privates in front of a flashlight; he felt humiliated and vulnerable in the line of enlistees, trousers and shorts bunched at their ankles. His mind whirled: His mother had always chided him not to sit on concrete steps.

"It draws you know," she warned. "You'll get piles." Would that disqualify him? When he could, Garson folded his arms over his bare chest, shielding his underdeveloped torso, hoping examiners would not take note of his deficiency. He knew he had little discernable muscle anywhere. Waist 24 inches. Height five-feet-seven. Weight 120 pounds. Vision 20-20. He had never known his blood pressure or heart rate before medical people recorded them. When queried, he had no idea about his family's medical history – illness, cause of grandparents' deaths.

"Gonna need some dental work on those back teeth in Boot Camp," he was told. His rare visits to dentists during his life had been traumatic; now another painful encounter was added to the coming mental burden. Later, Garson sat on a stool for the hearing test.

"Turn your head away from me," commanded another white-coated medical man. "I'll whisper a word. You repeat it." He heard the man mumble something, and instinctively turned to face him.

"Wha'd you say?" Something grated in Garson's throat. Jeez! The man harrumphed, ordering Garson to turn away again. Preston and Rusty were amused when told of the incident.

That afternoon, he found the intelligence tests unchallenging, and was among the first to complete the batteries. As the day progressed, his confidence rose, and when he walked back to the streetcar line amid the tall downtown buildings, he murmured the first stanza of the Marine Corps Hymn to himself. "From the Halls of Montezuma...." It seemed he would be a Marine after all!

Preston and Rusty's birthdays were a few weeks later, so Garson waited impatiently. In the meantime, his father contacted Messmer when the new school year began, informing them of his son's impending enlistment. Truant officers would not seek him out. During the weeks before departure, Garson visited some of the Messmer nuns that he held in regard, Providence and Immaculata in particular. Despite the abysmal academic performance of his junior year, the suspensions and the demerits that would never be served, both teachers had exhibited patience and confidence in him.

"I want you to get your GED now," the imposing Immaculata admonished in that rich voice of hers, echoing his mother's wish, "so you can go to college – to be a writer as you wished." He acknowledged that he would try. As she spoke, his mind wandered a bit. The skin of her face, pinched tightly by the starched Notre Dame habit, was without flaw; her deep brown eyes were lustrous, eyebrows thin and perfect. He wished he could see her hair, surmising that with a little lipstick, she would be an attractive woman. As they parted, her long fingers clasped his for a few seconds. When he passed from the stately entrance of that handsome sandy brick building, he hoped he could return one day, meeting her again, this time in dashing dress blues, proving that he would be successful in life.

Before Garson's departure, a convoy of vehicles – two squad cars and an ambulance stopped next to the shack of Deaffy, the neighborhood recluse and scavenger, the *eminence grise* who had wandered benignly through Garson's entire life. Rumor proclaimed that the reclusive tatterdemalion was being evicted for failure to pay property taxes. Garson did not recall seeing her on her normal appointed rounds in alleys and byways in recent months. But, then, he had not paid particular attention to her wanderings since boyhood; she was merely part of the neighborhood fabric.

While he did not witness the event, some described Deaffy as being bundled in blankets. From rheumy eyes, she gazed mutely at the knot of curious neighbors who had gathered to observe her departure. Her hair was badly matted, and her skin looked more creased and leathery than usual, it was said. She was emaciated. Little food had been found inside her tiny abode.

Neighborhood gossip about her was roused once more. People retold the stories: Deaffy was a foundling who had been raised in an orphans' asylum. When she came of age and was released, some insisted, she had married a sea captain who plied the Great Lakes. One neighbor said Deaffy had a baby, but another contradicted, averring that the child had never come to term. The seaman left her about that time, and took up with a woman near Lake Erie. A bigamist, he never returned to Milwaukee. Despondent, Deaffy became addled and reclusive, it was said.

After all of those years, city authorities carrying a court order now took her in hand. A doctor and nurse led her from the sad abode. The revolving red light of the ambulance cast strange shadows on her creased face.

A week later, a ponderous bulldozer churned through the yard like a scythe to ripe wheat, and carved a swath through the debris-strewn yard and decades of Deaffy's valued accumulations. The tiny shack at the alley was destroyed as easily as a child tearing apart a Lincoln Log house. Within two days, trucks carted off every scrap, obliterating any remnant of the old woman.

It might be poetic to relate that when authorities combed through the shack before it was flattened, they discovered thousands of dollars in cash squirreled away, just as Toby had claimed, or a cigar box filled with gold coins and stock certificates. Even something like Charles Foster Kane's childhood sled, "Rosebud," would have added a melodramatic coda.

Finally, there was a rumor that a city worker found a curiosity in a corrugated carton – a gallon jar with a fetus floating in formaldehyde. It seemed to corroborate a story of years ago that Deaffy had been pregnant when the sailing man deserted her. Afterward, she bore a premature child without benefit of doctor or midwife, and retained the tiny body as a reminder of the captain's perfidy. The container and its content were taken to the city's medical examiner.

"Naw, naw, ain't true at all," grumbled Mrs. Clennam, Veronica's mother. Her family had moved onto the block after the war, and she had taken on the mantle of neighborhood gadfly after the departure of Widow Klatsch. Mrs. Clennam, however, never appreciated the lore of the neighborhood and Deaffy's significance in it.

"Wasn't a fetus at all," she corrected, her voice authoritative. "Just a tiny bisque doll in a pickel jug." When he wrote of those years, Garson discovered that Deaffy's true name was Vera Hollenbeck. He often wondered about her fate.

During his final days, Garson bid perfunctory farewells to Toby, despite the antipathy that remained between them, and to Lana. She promised to write. There was no embrace, not even a handshake. He was too intent at some coming prospect. The balmy October temperature of the previous week had plummeted into the 40s. It was windy and drizzling. As he climbed into the family car that morning, he recalled his mother's story about Guttig's final departure.

"Remember, I told you that your Grandpa turned to look back before he got into the ambulance. You could see him thinking: This was the last time he'd see the house." In those final minutes Garson felt guilty, having sold the Hungarian army sword his grandfather has once carried. Certainly the plain, old weapon had been battered from boyhood thrustings, and its hilt was loose. But when Garson had pocketed the pair of ten dollar bills, a gloomy foreboding engulfed him, as if he was betraying his childhood mentor and caregiver. Garson never mentioned the sale to his mother.

But now, he was on his way to become a Marine, the "first to fight" as the Corps proclaimed. Scenes from similar departures by movie servicemen flickered in his mind. When the car pulled from the curb, he turned his head, gazing back through the rear window. The house quickly grew small.

COMMAND OF EXECUTION

So there you have it, my Pop's decidedly minor opus. You might agree that it's more memory than autobiography, more review than examination. A more accomplished writer might have done more justice to the material. I used a lot of energy and time with his scribblings – more than I foresaw or wanted. Put it this way, it cost me valuable time away from family, my bands (rock, of course) and golf. As recompense, I demoted his title to the subtitle, substituting mine in its place.

Looking back, my Pop said it was presumptuous of him to believe he had the makings of a Marine. His four years were wedged between the end of the Korean War and the beginning of Vietnam; the French defeat at Dien Bien Phu occurred during his first year in the Corps, just after he was transferred to the Naval Air Station on Whidbey Island in Washington's Puget Sound. Perhaps, if he'd shipped over, re-enlisted in 1957, he could have been a veteran NCO when U.S. involvement in Southeast Asia heated.

"Might be pushing up daisies in 'Nam or Laos right now!" he smirked.

He had wanted to test himself – not necessarily as Tom Dunston or Sergeant Stryker, as Pedro de Vargas or Walter of Gurney, as Alan Quartermaine or Scaramouche, as Peter Blood or Robin Hood, but at least as one of the Merry Men.

But to his stated discontent, my Pop would serve as a peacetime Marine, a stateside pogue who spent most of his career in guard and security duty in the Pacific Northwest and in the far Aleutians. He wondered aloud how he might have measured up, stood the test of blood and guts as did his brethren before and after him; he never felt he was a worthy heir to the Greatest Generation or later Marines who sacrificed in Southeast Asia and the Middle East.

When he returned to civilian life in the fall of 1957 much had changed. With $500 in savings, my Pop found a disconcerting swarm of kids twirling hula hoops – the leading assault battalions of the Boomer generation — as well as a deranged Wisconsin farmer named Ed Gein who crafted cadaver skins into lampshades, providing Hitchcock with inspiration for his best movie. My Pop said that the great American songbook was losing favor to a new musical stew; simultaneously and fortuitously, blues and jazz were ascending in the popular mind, their pinnacle of popularity only a few years ahead.

In a post scriptum, my Pop wrote that my grandma left the restaurant kitchen and began cleaning a bowling alley from late at night until morning. She and my grandpa were able to purchase a tiny Cape Cod house and pay it off in seven years. She died of complications from diabetes before reaching her eightieth birthday. She detested medications.

My grandpa retained a fragment of his snack business near decade's end, confined to a handful of Milwaukee taverns. The Galena Street property went into foreclosure, deteriorated in a long vacancy and was finally demolished by the city. He ended his work years as a school bus driver before dying while asleep on a living room couch at age 82; my grandma didn't even realize he'd passed away while she watched television. My Pop refused consent for an autopsy. To the end of his days, my grandpa believed the Apollo moon landing was only the production of a television studio, skeptical of the new technology like George Amber Minafer's antipathy about automobiles.

Uncle Hervé sold the ABC popcorn business and parlayed profits to purchase a Florida savings bank. He and Bacia, she of the soft, wet kisses, lived out their lives in comfort. Uncle Vin, contrastingly, was nearly as impecunious as my grandfather. A lifelong bachelor, he resided in a multi-bedroom apartment, subletting to tenants, acquiring rooms full of ratty, left-behind furniture, finally dying in his early 80s with less than a thousand dollars in hand.

Lana and Pop had one date after his discharge. At evening's end, they tarried on her familiar sun porch — a place she claimed to have held suitors at bay — they overcame the taboo of putative siblings. It began innocently enough with a goodnight embrace and a buss or two, then progressed to lingering kisses. Before he knew it, his alcohol-fueled hands slipped under her sweater. He yearned to fulfill a fantasy of years past when he peered into her bedroom window.

"Don't try that salty Marine stuff on me, little brother!" Lana's words, as usual, ultimately deflated him. By then, she had found an accomplished partner who shared her enthusiasm for ballroom and ethnic dancing. Garson imaged them as Astaire and Rogers.

"Clarence and I embrace but never kiss," she had informed Pop over dinner. "He's not into girls, you know, and I have nothing to worry about." Lana and Pop saw each other sporadically over ensuing years while, like her movie namesake, Lana discarded three husbands during her unsuccessful search for the perfect romantic partner.

After his return home, my Pop contacted Betsy, the comely Messmer High classmate whose looks and charm captivated him beyond all others. She had sent him a beautiful tinted graduation portrait in a handsome leather frame; fellow Marines at the Whidbey Island barracks said he was a lucky guy. He returned home on leave midway through his career, and they dated, much to his mother's delight. She told her son that he'd made a perfect choice in the Catholic girl. Through an acquaintance of Uncle Vin's, Pop purchased an engagement ring with a miniscule diamond, and presented it to Betsy on their final evening together. She demurely accepted his proposal.

While my Pop was stationed on desolate Adak Island in the Aleutians, he received a Dear John letter from Betsy. She would return the engagement ring to his mother. The devastating missive caused many sleepless nights, and distracted days over many weeks during which he reread her words. Still, after his discharge, Pop visited Betsy in her cramped west side apartment; his breath became shallow when she radiated that smile. The distinctive scent of citrus he remembered had been replaced with an earthier, more mature aroma. He gazed at her new baby, not many months old, but did not recall the man she had married among his Messmer classmates. He envied the husband, whoever he was, wishing he were that man.

But Pop mused years later that her Dear John decision permitted him to use the G.I. bill to gain his university degree instead of marrying after the Marines and entering the unskilled work force to support wife and family. He also laughed aloud to think he'd never even seen her legs, always incased as they were in slacks, jeans or ankle-length skirts.

When Pop had asked Betsy to marry, they double dated with Mellish and his girlfriend, a pretty Custer High senior Pop had not met before. Mellish was still a storehouse of stories, and banged out some jazz tunes on a battered upright piano in the beer bar north of Milwaukee. Mellish married not long after, the couple raising two accomplished daughters, and celebrating their golden anniversary shortly after the new century turned.

Toby had married, too, and Pop returned to Milwaukee permanently, the couple lived in a trailer park on city's fringe. They ultimately relocated to Alaska where they raised a large brood, each child's given name beginning with the letter T. Toby became a fishing boat captain who was once held by Russian authorities for straying into Soviet waters beyond the Bering Sea. He wrote a book about those and other adventures. After a diligent search, my Pop unearthed a copy; it was larded with what he considered too much religious cant.

During his brief stint as a television reporter, Pop interviewed a childhood chum, Ralph Votapek, then a renowned international pianist, perhaps the most famous person he ever knew. Votapek was in Milwaukee during the Vietnam War, dealing with a deferment from the military draft. He recalled my Pop, and they reminisced about the old neighborhood; his mother still lived in the tiny Cape Cod bungalow on the city's north side where my Pop had several times sat spellbound by the little boy's keyboard mastery.

Preston and Rusty were discharged after three years of service, both, as related, seeing duty on Marine air bases. Preston remained in California and worked many years in the aerospace industry, accumulated what he said was a "shit load of money," only to lose it in the 1987 stock market slump. He and my Pop had fitful contact over the years. Rusty, meanwhile, settled somewhere into rural Wisconsin, but he and the old buddies never rekindled their friendship.

Heissen, who married his Berlin high school sweetheart while in the Corps, returned to Milwaukee after discharge, and enrolled in Marquette University's school of journalism where he and Pop became reacquainted. Because both were over 21, they occasionally rendezvoused with other veterans at an off-campus bar called the Avalanche. As senior editor of the school's literary quarterly, Heissen named Pop his assistant; but when it came time to designate the next editor, Pop's application was denied in favor of a student from New York who wore a long Harvard Yard scarf and smoked a pipe. Heissen ultimately became a successful school administrator and union organizer in the Pacific Northwest. Nearing the end of his long career, Heissen met President Clinton who visited his school after a student shooting.

Hal Faltschaft had a successful career as a Great Lakes merchant mariner, spending the frozen months in Brownsville, Texas. He thoroughly enjoyed the off-beat movie "Lake Boat," based on playwright David Mamet's experience aboard those long fresh water cargo vessels. He continued frequent treks to Las Vegas and Reno where he long engaged in the futile effort to find an edge at casinos. After leaving the Lakes, he located permanently to Nevada where he admitted there was no edge in gambling except for the house. He penned a terse missive to the Las Vegas mayor that read, "I give up!"

Pop was left to wonder at the fates of Liska, Prick, Hupner, Ridley and all the rest.

For him, of course, there was marriage, to the sister of a grade school chum.

"When I first met the family, it was like something out of Dickens," my Pop recalled. An old oval dining room table dominated the kitchen, high-backed chairs at either end for the parents with simple, backless benches along each side for a dozen children. The refrigerator was invariably laden with gallons of milk with loaves of Wonder Bread stacked on top.

My Pop frequently related that he was always attracted to and fascinated with families because his seemed to be so irregular, if not a bit dysfunctional. Further, the emotional dynamics of siblings were likewise unfathomable to him, an only child, something akin to Charlie Babbitt in the movie "Rain Man."

"The first time I saw your mother was at Easter Sunday mass at Holy Redeemer, still a basement church after all those years," he told us kids. "I can still envision the scene: She and her brother seated in the back because they were invariably late. Pretty with a pert nose, rubied lips, bat-wing eyebrows, she was petite but buxom. She wore a broad white holiday hat with a veil draped before her fetching pale eyes." When they married, the upper church had finally been constructed.

My two older sisters and I were born over a five year span, my mother, it was said, elated at the arrival of her only boy. My youngest sister, the so-called "surprise child" arrived seven years later. My parents divorced a few years later; in many ways, he became a better father to us and a friend to our mother afterward.

My Pop usually did not carry a grudge, but one was of long standing, dating to his Marine Corps years. While at the Whidbey Island Marine barracks, he made the acquaintance of a corporal from Milwaukee. My little sister showed me a preliminary sketch Pop wrote about the incident, burdening the NCO with numerous negative physical traits: He was a smirking martinet with a body like a small refrigerator, a square head, cratered facial skin, crowded and chaotic lower teeth and a knotted nose that Pop determined to bloody in print. Despite sharing their hometown, the corporal was responsible for my Pop´s demotion to private just a month before he was slated for a promotional exam.

As part of the small contingent at the naval air station where the Navy flew P2V submarine hunter killer Neptune bombers, Marines pulled duty at entry gates and operated a small brig for minor military miscreants. Carrying .45 pistols and 12-guage riot shotguns, guards marched prisoners to chow and work details. Those who were incarcerated were readily identified with large, white Ps painted on the backs of dungarees.

"I'd just come off of a four to eight morning watch on the main gate," my Pop explained, "and returned to the barracks to get some chow. The corporal ordered me to march the brig rats to the mess hall immediately. I complained because I hadn't eaten myself."

"That's insubordination," the corporal crabbed. "I'm writing you up for it." Thus, my Pop sustained what the Uniform Code of Military Justice described as a captain's mast, a minor offense hearing before an officer. He was demoted to private and given a month of EPD – extra police duty, sweeping and mopping floors and cleaning after normal duty hours. It was nearly a year before he regained his single stripe to private first class, and another year until he was eligible for promotion to non-commissioned officer. As a result, when he was discharged, he had not attained sergeant; he was atop the promotion list, but wanted the third stripe before he consented to ship over, re-enlist for six more years. Despite the blemish in his record, Pop was still awarded a Good Conduct medal, a proud accomplishment.

"The corporal had the balls to ask for Lana's address when he saw photos she sent me. He believed me when I told him she was my sister. I refused. If he's dead now and I find his grave, I'll piss on it!"

While my Pop enjoyed movies during the remainder of his life, they never again dominated his attention as they did prior to the Marines. He opined that something happened to them from the mid-1950s on. Of course, there were many memorable films that ranked with books and fine arts for his attention. But for the remainder of his life, the cinema never regained the dominant attention it had in his youth. Most offerings, especially Hollywood productions, left him dissatisfied, revealed inadequacies and were worth no more than a single viewing. The magic of those earlier *trompe l'oei* images that flashed on screen at 24 frames a second was never regained. To my Pop's chagrin, movies also lost something when converted into the binary code.

"There are fewer actors and more posers and caricatures, now," my Pop opined.

"Art's been overwhelmed by artifice and kitsch. We're stupefied by celebrity and mayhem now. Even music's given way to noise and performance." He grew up in an era when there was no portable music except in cars; he hated music as mere background, insisting the good tunes demanded undistracted attention.

"Listening to jazz, for instance, is like repeatedly viewing a fine painting: You see (or hear) something new each time."

He found, too, that his chosen profession had deteriorated into press release propaganda; Kirk Douglas's Jack Tatum was revivified in Matt Drudge and that ilk, transforming objective journalism into press agentry and propaganda. My Pop lasted less than two years in television news, turning his back upon a profession broadcasting only stories that were interesting and visual.

You might say in summary that my Pop was successful for a high school dropout, enjoying a Marine career, two university degrees and four decades in a public service. He finally became the writer he long wanted to be, publishing three books – minor efforts to be sure. Thing of it is, he hoped his memoir might be the fourth.

I think my Pop wanted to be self-reflexive, but it seems to me that his memoir never penetrated his own character, his own psyche. I thought he wrote some good scenes and set pieces, and created a few interesting characters, but I don't think it overcame the minutia and nostalgia or gelled into a whole. That view was reinforced when an old friend of Pop's read a chapter and pronounced that it lacked analysis.

In the end, my Pop was always proud to proclaim himself a former Marine. He regarded it just below family, career achievement and writing. November 10th, the Corps's birthday, was circled on every calendar. Honor, duty, loyalty and fidelity were important watchwords in his life. And I agreed with his regard for two latter day films that represented the Corps with distinction: "Full Metal Jacket" and "Taking Chance." You know what they say: Once a Marine, always a Marine!

So what to do with this opus now, I ask myself. I surely don't want to follow the example of John Kennedy Toole's mother who after her son's untimely death tried to peddle his manuscript of *The*

Confederacy of Dunces. For a while after publication some critics regarded it was the new generation's *Catcher in the Rye*. But it never attained that height.

Thing of it is, my Pop thought he and his time had become irrelevant anyway – and so was the narrative. He surmised that the manuscript would probably end up in the discard or rejection basket, likely unread. My little sister told me recently she might, after her boys are grown, try to assemble the voluminous assortment of additional notes that our Pop jotted about the remaining years of his Marine career. We'll see.

***